This coupon entitles you to special discounts when you book your trip through the

TRAVEL NETWORK®
RESERVATION SERVICE

Hotels ♦ Airlines ♦ Car Rentals ♦ Cruises
All Your Travel Needs

Here's what you get: *

♦ A discount of $50 on a booking of $1,000** or more for two or more people!

♦ A discount of $25 on a booking of $500** or more for one person!

♦ Free membership for three years, and 1,000 free miles on enrollment in the unique Miles-to-Go™ frequent-traveler program. Earn one mile for every dollar spent through the program. Earn free hotel stays starting at 5,000 miles. Earn free roundtrip airline tickets starting at 25,000 miles.

♦ Personal help in planning your own, customized trip.

♦ Fast, confirmed reservations at any property recommended in this guide, subject to availability.***

♦ Special discounts on bookings in the U.S. and around the world.

♦ Low-cost visa and passport service.

♦ Reduced-rate cruise packages.

Call us toll-free in the U.S. at 1-888-940-5000, or fax us at 201-567-1832. In Canada, call us toll-free at 1-800-883-9959, or fax us at 416-922-6053.

---

* To qualify for these travel discounts, at least a portion of your trip must include destinations covered in this guide. No more than one coupon discount may be used in any 12-month period, for destinations covered in this guide. Cannot be combined with any other discount or program.
**These are U.S. dollars spent on commissionable bookings.
***A $10 fee, plus fax and/or phone charges, will be added to the cost of bookings at each hotel not linked to the reservation service. Customers must approve these fees in advance.

Valid until December 31, 1997. Terms and conditions of the Miles-to-Go™ program are available on request by calling 201-567-8500, ext 55.

MAU123

Frommer's

2nd
Edition

Maui

by Lisa Legarde

*The Natural World: An Environmental Guide
to the Hawaiian Islands
and Beaches*

by Jeanette Foster

Macmillan • USA

ABOUT THE AUTHORS

Lisa Legarde was born in New Orleans and graduated from Wellesley College with a degree in English. Lisa has traveled extensively in Europe and North America and is author or coauthor of numerous Frommer's travel guides, including *Frommer's New Mexico* and *Frommer's New Orleans.*

Jeanette Foster, a resident of Hawaii, has been widely published in travel, sports, and adventure magazines. She is also a contributing writer to numerous travel guides, including *Frommer's Hawaii from $60 a Day* and *Frommer's Honolulu, Waikiki & Oahu.*

MACMILLAN TRAVEL

A Simon & Schuster Macmillan Company
1633 Broadway
New York, NY 10019

Find us online at **http://www.mgr.com/travel**
or on America Online at **Keyword: Frommer's.**

ISBN 0-02-860905-0
ISSN 1076-2817

Editor: Charlotte Allstrom
Production Editor: Michael Thomas
Design by Michele Laseau
Page Creation by Linda Quigley, Bill Levy, Bryan Towse, Heather Pope, and Toi Davis
Digital Cartography by Ortelius Design
All maps copyright © by Simon & Schuster, Inc.

SPECIAL SALES

Bulk purchases (10+ copies) of Frommer's and selected Macmillan travel guides are available to corporations, organizations, mail-order catalogs, institutions, and charities at special discounts, and can be customized to suit individual needs. For more information write to Special Sales, Macmillan General Reference, 1633 Broadway, New York, NY 10019.

Manufactured in the United States of America

Contents

List of Maps

An Invitation to the Reader

In researching this book, I discovered many wonderful places—hotels, restaurants, shops, and more. I'm sure you'll find others. Please tell me about them, so I can share the information with your fellow travelers in upcoming editions. If you were disappointed with a recommendation, I'd love to know that, too. Please write to:

Lisa Legarde
Frommer's Maui, 2nd Edition
Macmillan Travel
1633 Broadway
New York, NY 10019

An Additional Note

Please be advised that travel information is subject to change at any time—and this is especially true of prices. We therefore suggest that you write or call ahead for confirmation when making your travel plans. The authors, editors, and publisher cannot be held responsible for the experiences of readers while traveling. Your safety is important to us, however, so we encourage you to stay alert and be aware of your surroundings. Keep a close eye on cameras, purses, and wallets, all favorite targets of thieves and pickpockets.

What the Symbols Mean

✪ Frommer's Favorites

Hotels, restaurants, attractions, and entertainment you should not miss.

Ⓢ Super-Special Values

Hotels and restaurants that offer great value for your money.

The following abbreviations are used for credit cards:

AE	American Express	EU	Eurocard
CB	Carte Blanche	JCB	Japan Credit Bank
DC	Diners Club	MC	MasterCard
DISC	Discover	V	Visa
ER	enRoute		

The Best of Maui

Everyone travels differently. Some people leave home with nothing more than a suitcase, a plane ticket, and a general idea of their final destination. Others plan months in advance and do extensive research before they leave home. Most, however, decide where to go and then call on friends or utilize guidebooks to help them make good use of their time so that their trip will be both memorable and stress free. In general, this book will help you find exactly what you're looking for, and this particular section is designed to give you a start by offering suggestions on where to find the best of the best. Start with some of these places and then use the rest of the book to help you pursue other interests, and if you've got some time left at the end of it all, go adventuring.

1 The Best Beaches

Maui may be small, but altogether it has 150 miles of coastline and 32 different beaches. Most of Maui's beaches are unbeatable, but some are indeed better than others. In compiling this list I've given thought to the size, type, and locations as well as sand quality and accessibility (some are very accessible, while some are difficult to find).

- **Kapalua Beach:** Located on the west side of the island in the Kapalua resort area, this may be Maui's most spectacular beach. Calm waters, created by the rocky lava arms that flank each end of the beach lap at the edges of this pristine, curving stretch of white sand. This is a quiet beach populated mostly by tanning resort guests. The waters are calm enough for swimming and snorkeling, and there's a lovely view of the neighboring island of Molokai.
- **Kaanapali Beach:** Like Kapalua Beach, Kaanapali Beach (also on Maui's west side) is of the white-sand variety. Kaanapali is a more active resort than Kapalua, so there's a lot more beach activity as well. Families frequent this stretch of coastline, as do beginning snorkelers and windsurfers. Unlike Kapalua, this beach is not sheltered by lava reefs, and if a storm blows through, the waves here can get quite high. This is an infrequent occurrence, however; usually the waters here are rather quiet.

- **Kamaole Beach Parks I, II, and III:** Heading around to the south side of the island you'll find these three separate beach parks. Here there is a wider cross section of the population since these areas are popular with local families. Again, the beaches are white sand, and the swimming conditions are excellent (so long as there are no Kona storms brewing off on the horizon). This is a great beach to bring kids; picnic tables, barbecue grills, showers, and rest rooms are available for public use.
- **Wailea:** Another waterfront resort, Wailea is known for its impeccable series of white-sand beaches (including Keawakapu, Mokapu, Ulua, and Wailea). All are great for sunbathing and swimming. If you decide to visit any one of these beaches, you'll be treated to great views of the islands of Lanai and Kahoolawe.
- **Hamoa Beach:** Way out in the eastern part of the island, near Hana town, is this special beach, which also happened to be a favorite of Mark Twain's. Most often frequented by guests from the Hotel Hana Maui, this beach is quiet and peaceful due to high cliffs and its remote location. The surf and currents can be quite rough here, making this a favorite spot for body- and boardsurfers, but swimming is still possible on calmer days.
- **Waianapanapa State Park:** If you've never seen a black-sand beach before, this is your chance. On the way up to Hana (about $4^{1}/_{2}$ miles before Hana town), on the left-hand side you'll see signs for Waianapanapa State Park. Actually, black-sand beaches are quite rare worldwide. Unlike white-sand beaches, which are given to the land by the ocean, black-sand beaches originate on land and end in the sea. This type of beach is formed when lava flows are broken because of the erosion of wave action against the shore. Over time, the beach will disappear. Once it's gone, it's gone. Swimming is a favorite activity here, but due to unpredictable strong currents, you should not enter the water unless you are an experienced and strong swimmer. Public facilities and picnic tables are available, and camping is permitted.
- **Hookipa Beach Park:** This sandy beach in Paia is not a haven for sunbathers and swimmers; rather, it's a world-renowned windsurfing site. Mauians have been surfing here since the 1930s, and today the surf challenges the world's best windsurfers in championship events. It's worth driving out to Paia just to see the show; even if there's no competition taking place, windsurfers are always here practicing. There are public facilities and picnic tables. *Warning:* This is not the place for beginning windsurfers.
- **H. A. Baldwin Park:** Named for congressional delegate Harry A. Baldwin, this beach park is another favorite among windsurfers, but it is best for bodysurfing. Public facilities are available, as well as a soccer and a baseball field.

2 The Best Snorkeling & Scuba Diving Locations

Next to beach sitting and swimming, snorkeling and scuba diving are the most popular outdoor island activities. Many charter companies can take you off-island to explore the undersea life that surrounds Maui, but if you'd rather go out on your own, there are plenty of great places right along the Maui coastline as well. If you're inexperienced, it would be wise for you to take some lessons before setting out on your own.

- **Olowalu:** Just 5 miles south of Lahaina, you'll see a line of cars parked at the side of the road. Chances are that drivers and passengers are out snorkeling here. The water is almost always calm at Olowalu, making conditions favorable for both snorkelers and scuba divers (farther out). Marine life is abundant here because large fields of coral reef blanket the area's sandy bottom. Both divers and snorkelers should be aware that because coral formations are scattered about the ocean floor (rather than following a straight line) it's easy to lose track of where you are.

- **Black Rock:** The Sheraton Maui Resort in the Kaanapali resort (currently undergoing massive renovations) was built upon a huge lava formation known as Black Rock. The shallow depths and easy accessibility of the waters around Black Rock make this a lovely spot for snorkelers and beginning divers. Night diving here reveals an entirely different underwater world.

- **Five Graves:** Located in Makena, a scuba spot known as Five Graves can be reached from the shore. Divers enjoy exploring the many caves and lava tubes here; among the sealife, there are turtles, leaf scorpionfish, angler fish, and conger eels. Divers should stay out of this area during heavy surf conditions because a dangerous concave formation here acts like a giant "toilet bowl" when conditions are rough.

- **Molokini Crater:** You'll need to catch a ride on one of the charter boats to snorkel or dive at this islet located just off the Maui Coast, but I would certainly be remiss if I omitted it from my list because it offers some of the best snorkeling and diving on Maui. Molokini is a State Marine Life Conservation District, so there's an abundance of sealife here. Fish of all shapes and varieties, as well as eels and even giant manta rays delight and intrigue scores of divers every day.

3 The Best Travel Experiences

Since you have only a limited amount of time to explore the island, you'll need to choose your activities carefully. Below I've listed some of the best Maui has to offer.

- **Sunrise at Haleakala:** You should begin your journey to the summit of Haleakala in the wee hours in order to get there for the sunrise; it's such an unforgettable experience that you probably won't mind the exhaustion that will set in later. When the sun makes its first appearance above the horizon, you'll understand exactly why Haleakala is the "House of the Sun."

- **The Road to Hana:** You might not think that a 30-mile drive is a great travel experience, but this one is. While taking in the breathtaking scenery, drivers must negotiate 617 curves (many of which are hairpin turns) and 54 one-lane bridges. Keep your eyes peeled for waterfalls, swimming holes, the African tulip tree, and guava trees. The final destination is Oheo Gulch, a beautiful chain of swimming holes located just outside Hana town.

- **Whale-watching:** Beginning in late December and early January humpback whales make their return to Hawaii from frigid Alaskan waters so they can give birth and nurse their young until they're strong enough to make the treacherous journey back to Alaska in early May. Whale-watching excursions take place every day between January and May. Seeing the whales up close is an incredible experience.

- **A Helicopter Tour:** If you want to see Maui from the air, your best bet is a helicopter tour. **Sunshine Helicopters** (☎ 808/871-0722) offers a wide choice of tours, and they'll videotape your excursion so you can take the experience home with you. You can request touchdowns in Hana as well as a picnic lunch. If you want to add even more excitement, you can combine the helicopter tour with a horseback ride or ground tour.

- **A Trip Upcountry:** If you think Maui is all beaches and volcano, think again. There are some absolutely wonderful little towns that many people just pass right by on their way to Hana—among them the paniolo (cowboy) town of Makawao.

When you see the hitching posts, you'll think you just stepped back in time. It's great fun to browse the boutiques and specialty shops. Be sure to stop in the Rodeo General Store and Kamoda Store and Bakery.

4 The Best Outdoor Adventures

Once you've grown tired of sunbathing and sitting on the lanai at your hotel, you might want to try something a little more strenuous. Maui's terrain and location offer a host of outdoor activities suitable for everyone.

- **Hiking Haleakala:** If you're healthy enough to deal with the thin air atop Haleakala, you might want to take a walk, or hike, around in order to get a better sense of the landscape and its flora and fauna. An easy walk (about a mile in length) is the Hosmer Grove Nature Trail. It's a self-guided trail that takes about an hour to walk. A longer trail—the Halemauu Trail—will take you to the crater rim where you can enjoy great views of the north slope and Koolau Gap. Longer hikes are also possible as well.
- **Biking Down Haleakala:** If hiking doesn't turn you on, perhaps you'd enjoy signing up with a bike company such as **Maui Downhill** (☎ 808/871-2155), which specializes in trips *down* the slopes of Haleakala (they drive you to the summit). It's a 38-mile excursion, but you'll have to pedal for only about 400 yards.
- **Kayak Tours:** Yet another way to see the island is from a kayak just off the coast. There are several kayak tour companies that will provide you with equipment and lessons and will take you on a 2^1/$_2$ - to 5-hour excursion. This can be a particularly exciting experience during whale season.
- **Parasailing:** Most people have thought about going parasailing, but can't quite muster the courage to give it a try. For me, parasailing was absolutely the most memorable experience of my first trip to Maui! It seems frightening at first, but once you're up in the air you realize you're perfectly safe and then you can enjoy a unique view of the island (helicopters must fly too high to provide a view comparable to the one you'll experience while parasailing). When your ride is over, you'll just float quietly and softly toward the water.
- **Horseback Riding:** Educated, experienced tour guides, such as those who run **Ironwood Ranch** (5095 Napilihau St., Lahaina ☎ 808/669-4991) or **Pony Express Tours** (P.O. Box 535, Kula, Maui, HI 96790 ☎ 808/667-2200), will take you to some lovely remote locations where you'll be able to swim and picnic far from the crowds. Rides can take anywhere from 1 to 7 or 8 hours, depending on your experience and how much money you're willing to spend.

5 The Best of Natural Maui

Haleakala is Maui's most well-known natural spectacle, but many others are also worth seeing, including the following:

- **Iao Valley State Park:** Since ancient times, Iao Valley has been a sacred Hawaiian place. The verdant valley is absolutely breathtaking, and the "needle" (a 1,200-foot-high pillar of stone blanketed with greenery) that rises out of the valley is spectacular. The needle once served as a natural altar for Hawaiians who came here to give thanks to the "Eternal Creator." This is also a good hiking spot for those with less experience, and there are some great photo opportunities here.

- **Banyan Tree:** Right in the center of Lahaina is a remarkable sight—a banyan tree whose branches span over 1 acre of land. Planted in 1873, the banyan has served as a meeting place and shade tree for over a century. If you arrive here early in the evening, you'll be joined by a flock of boisterous mynah birds.
- **Oheo Gulch:** Mistakenly known to many as the Seven Sacred Pools, this is where Palikea Stream, which travels down the slopes of Haleakala, meets the Pacific Ocean. The area, though beautiful, was never considered sacred, and there are actually about 24 pools, not seven. Nevertheless, it is a wonderful place to visit and frolic. Its beauty is almost unsurpassed on the island; if it weren't for the throngs that visit each and every day, it probably would be.
- **Waimoku Falls:** If you want to get away from the crowd at Oheo Gulch and don't mind hiking uphill for a half-mile and then through a field and a singing bamboo forest (the total round-trip distance is 4 miles) to get to one of the most enchanting places on the island of Maui, you'll really enjoy a trip to Waimoku Falls (see Chapter 8, "What to See & Do on Maui," for more information).
- **Silversword:** Normally I wouldn't think about putting a plant in this category, but the silversword plant is so special and unique to Hawaii. It is found nowhere else in the world (and on only one other island in the Hawaiian archipelago). Evolved from the sunflower family, silversword has adapted to conditions of extreme heat and drought. *Do Not* pick silversword—it is an endangered species.

6   The Best of Maui for Kids

Believe it or not, there are lots of activities here for children. Aside from the keikis (kids) camps offered at most of the resorts, here are a few suggestions.

- **Beaches:** Maui's sandy coastline is a wonderful babysitter. Give the kids some shovels and buckets, and they'll be entertained for hours.
- **A Snorkeling Trip:** If your child can swim, he or she can snorkel. Your child might be afraid to dive with the snorkel at first, but it's not even necessary to go below the surface in order to see schools of brilliantly colored tropical fish. If you take a chartered tour with a company like **Trilogy Excursions** (180 Lahainaluna Rd., Lahaina ☎ 808/661-4743), lunch and use of underwater cameras will be included in the price of the tour (kids love having their pictures taken with the fish).
- **Hawaii Experience Domed Theater** (824 Front St., Lahaina ☎ 808/661-8314): If rain obliges you to stay indoors on one of your vacation days, never fear; there's a great place to take the kids. The Hawaii Experience Domed Theater presents a 45-minute film on a 180-degree, 60-foot-long movie screen. The film, shot from the air, land, and sea, takes you on a whirlwind tour of the island.
- **Brig *Carthaginian*** (Lahaina Wharf ☎ 808/661-8527): If you're in Lahaina, take the kids aboard an authentic replica of a 19th-century whaling vessel. Now a museum, the brig *Carthaginian* features audiovisual displays designed to educate visitors about 19th-century whaling life. The small ship is the perfect size for children.
- **Hale Kohola** (Whaler's Village, Kaanapali resort ☎ 808/661-5992): Once the kids have learned about Maui's former whaling industry, take them to Hale Kohola—the only museum of its kind in Hawaii—where they'll learn about whales and their current plight.
- **Lahaina–Kaanapali & Pacific Railroad** (Kaanapali ☎ 808/661-0089): A singing, story-telling conductor brings history to life in this reconstructed turn-of-the-century train that was once used to transport sugarcane from the plantations to

waiting ships at Lahaina Harbor. The 12-mile ride delights children of all ages. Don't forget to stop at the Depot Snack Shop where kids can taste sweet, juicy sugarcane.

- **_Atlantis_ Submarine** (665 Front St., Lahaina ☎ 808/667-2224): If you really want to give the kids a thrill, take them aboard the fully submersible _Atlantis_ submarine. The vessel dives to depths of 100 feet and glides above reef formations, making it possible to safely view sea creatures in their natural habitat. The only drawback is the lofty price.

7 The Best Places to Rediscover Historic Maui

Unfortunately, once resort hotels started popping up all over the island, interest in Hawaiian history dwindled. Over time many important historic sites were destroyed by development. These days there aren't many places where you can recapture the spirit of old Maui, but a few are working to preserve what's left.

- **Lahaina:** Still a center of island activity, Lahaina has been the pulse of Maui since it was founded centuries ago. Take a walking tour through town and visit such historic sites as the Baldwin Home (now a museum), the Hauola Stone, and the ruins of the Old Fort Wall.
- **Bailey House Museum** (2375-A Main St., Wailuku ☎ 808/244-3326): In the mid-1800s, this home—once the Wailuku Female Seminary—was purchased by Edward Bailey, a great contributor to the development of Maui. His paintings, which document 19th-century Maui life, are on display, as are "precontact" Hawaiian artifacts. In addition, visitors can see period clothing, furnishings, and an outdoor display of the original varieties of sugarcane that were brought to the island.
- **Alexander & Baldwin Sugar Museum** (3957 Hansen Rd., Kahului ☎ 808/ 871-8058): This small museum documents the history of the sugar industry on Maui. There are audiovisual displays, photographs, scale models, and artifacts dating back to the late 1870s.

8 The Best Luxury Hotels & Resorts

There are so many beautiful luxury properties on Maui, it's really difficult to decide which are the best. My choices here are purely subjective and certainly shouldn't be considered the last word. Read through the listings in the accommodations chapter before you decide—you may see something there that appeals to you more. Here are my personal favorites.

- **The Kea Lani Hotel** (4100 Wailea Alanui, Wailea ☎ 808/875-4100 or 800/ 882-4100): Kea Lani (meaning "white heaven") is an appropriate name for this luxury resort. The beautifully furnished rooms are all suites, and each has a private lanai offering exquisite views of the ocean. Oceanfront villas are equipped for large families. The staff is incredibly friendly, efficient, knowledgeable, and down-to-earth, and facilities are excellent (the pool is a main attraction).
- **The Hyatt Regency Maui** (200 Nohea Kai Dr., Lahaina ☎ 808/661-1234 or 800/882-4100): This beautifully landscaped resort has an extensive Asian and Pacific art collection. Rare pieces (like Ming dynasty wine pots and Chinese cloisonné vases) are scattered throughout the hotel. The service, restaurants, and facilities are all first-class (the pool is an attraction in and of itself).

- **The Grand Wailea Resort Hotel & Spa** (3850 Wailea Alanui, Wailea ☎ 808/ 875-1234 or 800/888-6100): Known around the island simply as "The Grand," the Grand Wailea is hands-down the grandest of them all. There's a $30 million collection of art here, and more flowers are used for landscaping this property than for any other on the island. Spa Grande is Hawaii's largest, and in it guests can treat themselves to anything from a simple facial to a shiatsu massage or aromatherapy. The dining choices here are unsurpassed, and guests can enjoy a fantastic 2,000-foot-long action pool.
- **Four Seasons Resort** (3900 Wailea Alanui, Wailea ☎ 808/874-8000 or 800/ 334-MAUI): If you want to stay in a place where personalized service (for example, someone who will spritz you with Evian water as you bake in the sun by the pool or on the beach) and attention to detail are paramount, the Four Seasons should be your top choice. The service here is world-class, and the staff is wonderful. The location is fantastic, and you couldn't ask for a greater variety of services and facilities. The Four Seasons is, without a doubt, one of the island's best properties (and it's only 7 years old).

9   The Best Moderately Priced Hotels & Resorts

- **The Kaanapali Beach Hotel** (2525 Kaanapali Pkwy., Lahaina ☎ 808/661-0011 or 800/262-8450): Like most of the moderately priced hotels and resorts on Maui, this hotel offers certain standard facilities (pool, beauty salon, water-sports equipment rental, and a variety of midpriced restaurants). However, the Kaanapali is outstanding because it has one of the best Hawaiian activities programs on the island. In addition to lei-making and quilt-making lessons (among other things), guests are offered some of the island's most authentic hula lessons.
- **Royal Lahaina Resort** (2780 Kekaa Dr., Lahaina ☎ 808/661-3611 or 800/ 44-ROYAL): One of the best buys in the Kaanapali resort, this hotel is beautifully landscaped and has simply furnished, but nicely decorated rooms. The location is beach prime, tennis facilities (10 courts and a tennis stadium that seats up to 3,500) are among the best, and there are three swimming pools.
- **Maui Coast Hotel** (2259 S. Kihei Rd., Kihei ☎ 808/874-6284 or 800/ 426-0670): This relatively new hotel in Kihei is not as well situated as some of the other properties in the area, but its rooms are large and freshly decorated. Junior suites are furnished with a pullout couch, and two-bedroom suites can accommodate up to six people. This is a great buy for families. The beach is just a short walk from the hotel.
- **Kula Lodge** (R.R. 1 Box 475, Kula ☎ 808/878-2517 or 800/233-1535): If you're looking for a change of pace from the surf and sand, Kula Lodge's châteaus are a great choice. Nestled amid eucalyptus and pine trees at an altitude of 3,200 feet, two of the châteaus are outfitted with fireplaces (perfect for taking the chill off on cooler evenings). Each of the châteaus is equipped to accommodate at least four people. This is a great choice for those who want to do as the locals do. Book well in advance if you're planning on staying at Kula Lodge.

10   The Best Alternative Accommodations

Don't be discouraged by the number of high-priced hotels and resorts on Maui (even the moderately priced accommodations might seem high for some); there are plenty of alternatives. Consider a bed and breakfast or youth hostel—even camping.

- **The Lahaina Inn** (127 Lahainaluna Rd., Lahaina ☎ 808/661-0577 or 800/ 669-3444): This beautiful 12-room inn is located right in the heart of Lahaina. Guest rooms are decorated with gorgeous antiques, floral wallcoverings, fine fabrics, and period paintings. Continental breakfast is included in the very reasonable rates. This is a great alternative to nearby high-priced resorts.
- **Olinda Country Cottage** (536 Olinda Rd., Makawao ☎ 808/572-1453): If you're enchanted with the Upcountry town of Makawao and want to stay at a nearby inn, Olinda Country Cottage should be your first choice. A renovated Tudor mansion houses two rooms. There's also a fully equipped cottage with a working fireplace on the property. Beautiful antiques, collected by owner Ellen Unterman, decorate the rooms and cottage. The views here are spectacular.
- **Waianapanapa State Park** (54 High St., Wailuku ☎ 808/243-5354): This is a favorite camping area for visitors and locals alike, but the real bargains are the two-room cabins. They're not far from the black-sand beach (mentioned earlier in this chapter), and some even permit great views of the ocean. Essentials are provided; since the cabins are usually booked six months in advance, it is important to plan ahead.
- **Maui Banana Bungalow** (310 N. Market St., Wailuku ☎ 808/244-5090 or 800/ 846-7835): As far as youth hostels go, this is a good one, and it's a particular favorite of windsurfers. Airport and beach transfer are complimentary, and rental cars can be arranged at rock-bottom rates. This is a good choice for travelers on a tight budget.

11 The Best Dining Experiences

Maui has so many excellent restaurants, it's almost impossible to single out the "best" ones, but below you'll find a sampling of my personal favorites as well as descriptions of a couple of food events worth attending.

- **Avalon Restaurant & Bar** (844 Front St., Lahaina ☎ 808/667-5559): Self-taught chef Mark Ellman (also owner of Maui Tacos, a local chain) dazzles diners every night with such signature dishes as chili-seared salmon served tiki style (a layered salad of mashed potatoes, eggplant, salmon, greens, and island salsa with a plum vinaigrette) and his fantastic dessert, the Caramel Miranda.
- **Gerard's** (174 Lahainaluna Rd., Lahaina ☎ 808/661-8939): You wouldn't necessarily expect to find a great French restaurant on Maui, but Gerard's, in the Plantation Inn in Lahaina, is just that. The elegant atmosphere is the perfect setting for such traditional favorites as foie gras and veal sweetbreads. Other dishes, including the opakapaka roasted with Hawaiian peppers and served in an orange-ginger butter, add a Pacific Rim twist to the menu. The desserts here are fantastic.
- **David Paul's Lahaina Grill** (127 Lahainaluna Rd., Lahaina ☎ 808/667-5117): Chef/co-owner David Paul Johnson is a wizard with food. Night after night he turns out beautiful, delectable, and innovative New American dishes such as Kona coffee–roasted rack of lamb, eggplant Napoléon, and tequila shrimp with fire-cracker rice. David Paul's is a must for all island visitors.
- **Roy's Kahana Bar & Grill** (4405 Honoapilani Hwy [at Kahana Gateway Shopping Center] ☎ 808/669-6909): Award-winning chef Roy Yamaguchi is another island star. He was one of the original creators of Hawaii Regional Cuisine. His lively restaurant features such specialties as island-style pot-stickers, spicy rimfire shrimp, and roasted banana pork loin.

- **Haliimaile General Store** (Haliimaile, ☎ 808/572-2666): My favorite Upcountry restaurant, for both its casual atmosphere and the superior quality of the food, is Haliimaile General Store. Specialties include a leek and goat cheese tart and Italasian shrimp and scallops. The wine list here is excellent.
- **Taste of Lahaina** (contact Lahaina Town Action Committee, P.O. Box 1271, Lahaina, Maui HI 96767 ☎ 808/667-9175): This annual food event, which takes place in September, features more than 30 island chefs. You'll have a chance to meet some of Maui's most talented chefs and sample some of the best food on the island. This event is "made-to-order" for those who can't afford and/or don't have time to sample all the island's best restaurants. There's also continuous entertainment and wine tastings.
- **Kapalua Wine & Food Symposium:** Each July brings the Kapalua Wine & Food Symposium, a weekend during which some of the world's greatest vintners and chefs gather for seminars, demonstrations, and tastings. The event culminates with the Chefs' Seafood Festival, prepared by 10 of Hawaii's top chefs, and served banquet-style by the ocean.

12 The Best of Maui After Dark

A number of bars and clubs are scattered across the island, and most of the resorts provide their own evening entertainment, but there are other things that might appeal to you in the evening hours as well.

- **Old Lahaina Luau:** Here is your chance to participate in a traditional Hawaiian luau (especially worthwhile if this is your first visit to the islands). Maui's most authentic is the Old Lahaina Luau, which takes place nightly just off Front Street in Lahaina.
- **"Tour of the Stars":** Every night a group of stargazers gathers at the Hyatt Regency Maui (200 Nohea Kai Dr., Lahaina ☎ 808/661-1234) where a computerized telescope focuses on various points in the night sky. This is a great evening activity, even if you're not a hotel guest.
- **Maui Arts & Cultural Center** (Maui Central Park [off Kahului Beach Rd.], Kahului ☎ 808/242-SHOW): While visiting Maui you might consider attending a performance at the state-of-the-art Maui Arts & Cultural Center. Events range from traditional Hawaiian hula shows to ballet and theater productions. Rock concerts by high-profile artists (for example, Blues Traveler) are held in the amphitheater.
- **A Night Sail:** Another memorable evening activity is a romantic twilight or evening sail. Many resort hotels have their own catamarans, and guests can make advance reservations through the hotel's activities desk.

2 Introducing the Valley Isle

Maui is at once multicultural, multihued, and multifaceted. A clear, crisp turquoise surrounds the island; deep, fresh greens color the landscapes of Maui's tropical rain forests; parched reds, browns, blacks, and golds are the hues of the island's beaches and "desert" flatlands; and people of almost every ethnic group complete the picture, making Maui unique among the islands of the world. These are the images that no visitor is likely to forget.

Kahului (Central Maui), where most visitors deplane and pick up their rental cars, has been the center of trade and business activity since Maui became an active participant in trade with the Europeans in the late 18th and early 19th centuries. Today, it is still the center of commerce and home to most of the island's shopping malls and fast-food restaurants. Just a few miles west of Kahului you'll find the old historic whaling town of Lahaina (its streets lined with art galleries and T-shirt shops), and the beautiful white-sand beaches of Kaanapali and Kapalua. A trip Upcountry on the slopes of Haleakala Crater (the island's dormant volcano) brings cooler temperatures, lush tropical greenery, an abundance of herb and vegetable farms, and Maui's paniolos (cowboys).

A bumpy road of switchbacks and one-lane bridges will take you along the Maui coastline and up to Hana, the island's own private paradise. Sparsely populated, Hana is a tropical rain forest where you'll find such natural wonders as Oheo Gulch (a series of waterfalls and freshwater pools), the Venus Pool (an unforgettable blue pool), and even black- and red-sand beaches. Haleakala Crater will present you with yet another geographical landscape whose cinder cones give it something of a lunar quality. Until you see them for yourself, it seems almost inconceivable that these varied landscapes exist simultaneously within only 729 square miles.

1 The Natural World: An Environmental Guide to the Hawaiian Islands

by Jeanette Foster

The Hawaii of today—with its thundering waterfalls exploding into cavernous pools, whispering palms bordering moonlit beaches, vibrant rainbows arching through the early morning mist, and fiery lava creating a blanket of destruction as it slowly pours down slopes—differs dramatically from the Hawaii that came into being at the dawn of time.

Born of violent volcanic eruptions from deep beneath the ocean's surface, the first Hawaiian Islands emerged about 70 million years ago—more than 200 million years after the major continental land masses had been formed. Two thousand miles from the nearest continent, Mother Nature's fury began to carve beauty from barren rock. Untiring volcanoes spewed forth curtains of fire that cooled into stone. Severe tropical storms, some with hurricane-force winds, battered and blasted the cooling lava rock into a series of shapes. Ferocious earthquakes flattened, shattered, and reshaped the islands into precipitous valleys, jagged cliffs, and recumbent flatlands. Monstrous surf and gigantic tidal waves rearranged and polished the lands above and below the reaches of the tide.

It took millions upon millions of years to grind lava rock into the white-sand beaches of Kauai, to chisel the familiar form of Diamond Head on Oahu, to form Maui's majestic peak of Haleakala, to create the waterfalls of Molokai's northern side, to shape the reefs of Hulopoe Bay on Lanai, and to establish the lush rain forests of the Big Island. The result is an island chain like no other on the planet—a tropical dream of a landscape, rich in unique flora and fauna, surrounded by a vibrant underwater world that will haunt your memory forever.

THE ISLAND LANDSCAPES

Hawaii is more than palm trees and white sands: Nearly every type of climate and topography in the world exists in the Hawaiian Islands, from subarctic conditions to lava-rock beaches, from verdant rain forests to arid deserts, from fertile farming areas to swamps. Each island has its own particular climate and topography.

THE BIG ISLAND   The largest island at some 4,034 square miles (and still growing), the Big Island is twice the size of all the other Hawaiian Islands combined. Measuring 93 miles long by 76 miles wide, this island is home to every type of climate zone existing in Hawaii. It's not uncommon for there to be 12 feet of snow on the two largest mountain peaks, 13,796-foot Mauna Kea and 13,680-foot Mauna Loa. These mountains are the tallest in the state; what's more, when measured from their true base on the ocean floor, they reach 32,000 feet, making them the tallest mountains in the world. At 4,077 feet, Kilauea Volcano has been continuously erupting since January 3, 1983; it has added more than 600 acres of new land to the Big Island since then. Just a few miles from the barely cooled barren lava lies a pristine rain forest, and on the southern end there's an arid desert. The rest of the island contains tropical terrain; white-, black-, even green-sand beaches; windswept grasslands; and productive farming and ranching areas producing tropical fruits, macadamia nuts, coffee, and ornamental flowers.

MAUI   When two volcanoes—Mauna Kahalawai, a 5,277-foot ancient volcano in the West Maui Mountains, and Haleakala, a 10,000-foot dormant volcano—flowed together a million or so years ago, the event gave the "Valley Isle" of Maui a range of climates from arid desert to tropical rain forest. The 728-square-mile island is the only place in the world where you can drive from sea level to 10,000 feet in just 34 miles, passing through tropical beaches, sugar and pineapple plantations, rolling grassy hills, past the timber line, up to the lunarlike surface of the top of Haleakala. In addition to 33 miles of public beaches on the southern and western shores, Maui is home to the arid dry lands of Kihei, the swampy bogs of the West Maui Mountains, the rain forest of Hana, and the desert of Kaupo.

KAHOOLAWE   Just 7 miles southwest of Maui is Kahoolawe, the smallest of the main Hawaiian Islands. This island has a unique topography: After years of over-grazing by ranchers, then a U.S. military bombing target from 1945 to 1994, the fairly flat island has lost most of its topsoil. Kahoolawe is an arid island with some beautiful white-sand beaches. Native Hawaiians, who recently reclaimed the island from the federal government, are attempting to restore, reforest, and replant the island. Access to Kahoolawe is restricted.

LANAI   This small, kidney bean–shaped island—only 13 miles wide by 17 miles long—rises out of the ocean like the shell of a turtle, with cliffs on the west side that rise to a high point of 3,370 feet. Lanai slopes down to sea level on the east and south sides. The only town on the island, Lanai City, sits in the clouds at 1,600 feet. The high point of the island is covered with Norfolk pines and is usually shrouded in clouds. The arid beaches survive on minimal rainfall. One area in particular stands out: the Garden of the Gods, just seven miles from Lanai City. Here, oddly strewn boulders lie in the amber- and ocher-colored dirt, and bizarre stone formations dot the landscape. The ancient Hawaiians formed romantic legends explaining this enigma, but modern-day scientists are still debating this mystery.

MOLOKAI   Roughly the shape of Manhattan, Molokai is 37 miles long and 10 miles wide, with a thumb protruding out of the north shore. The north shore begins on the west, with miles of white-sand beaches that fringe a desertlike landscape. At the protruding thumb—the Kalaupapa Peninsula—a fence of cliffs, some 2,000 feet tall, lines the remainder of the north side. Molokai can be divided into two areas: the dry west end, where the high point is 1,381 feet; and the rainy, tropical east and north ends, where the high point is Mt. Kamakou, at 4,970 feet.

OAHU   The island where Honolulu is located is the third largest island in Hawaii (behind the Big Island and Maui). It's also the most urban, with a population of nearly 900,000. Oahu, which is 40 miles long by 26 miles wide, is defined by two mountain ranges: the Waianae Ridge (Mt. Kaala, at 4,050 feet, is the highest point on the island) in the west and the jagged Koolaus in the east, which form a backdrop for Honolulu. The mountain ranges divide the island into three different environ-ments: The windward side of the island is lush with greenery, ferns, tropical plants, and waterfalls. On the other side, the area between the Waianae Range and the ocean is drier, with sparse vegetation, little rainfall, and an arid landscape. In between the two mountain ranges lies the central valley; it's moderate in temperature and vibrant with tropical plants, agricultural fields, and trees.

KAUAI   This compact island, 25 miles long by 33 miles wide with 137 miles of coastline, has topography ranging from the wettest spot on earth to a barren canyon. Mt. Waialeale, which stands as Kauai's high point at nearly 5,000 feet, has the dis-tinction of being Earth's wettest spot, with more than 400 inches of rain annually. Just west of Mt. Waialeale is the barren landscape of Waimea Canyon (dubbed "the Grand Canyon of the Pacific"), the result of the once 10,000-foot-tall Olokele shield volcano, which collapsed and formed a caldera (crater) some 3,600 feet deep and 14 miles across. Peaks and craters aren't Kauai's only distinctive landscape features, though; miles of white-sand beaches rim most of the island, with majestic 2,700-foot cliffs—the spectacular Na Pali Coast—completing the circle. Lush tropical jungle inhabits the north end of the island, and balmy, palm tree–lined beaches live in the south.

NIIHAU   Just 17 miles across the Kaulakahi Channel from Kauai lies the small 6- by-18-mile island of Niihau, the "forbidden island." This is a privately owned island, inhabited only by Hawaiians living a simple life (no telephones, no electrical generating plant). It's also a working cattle ranch. Niihau is very dry and barren because it sits in the lee of Kauai; moisture-bearing clouds rarely make it past Kauai's mountains. The highest point on Niihau is only 1,281 feet, but at the center of the bleak and desolate landscape lies Lake Halalii, the largest natural lake (182 acres) in Hawaii. Niihau's white-sand beaches border emerald-colored waters offshore. You can take a day trip from Kauai to Niihau if you like.

THE FLORA OF THE ISLANDS

The Hawaii of today radiates with sweet-smelling flowers, lush vegetation, and exotic plant life. Some of the more memorable plants and flowers found in the islands include:

AFRICAN TULIP TREES   Even at a long distance, you can see the flaming red flowers on these large trees, which can grow over 50 feet tall. Children in Hawaii love the trees because the buds hold water—they use them as water pistols.

ANGEL'S TRUMPET   This is a smaller tree that can grow up to 20 feet tall, with an abundance of large (up to 10 inches in diameter) pendants—white or pink flowers that resemble, well, trumpets. The Hawaiians call this *nana-honua,* which means "earth gazing." The flowers, which bloom continually from early spring to late fall, have a musky scent. However, beware: All parts of the plant are poisonous, and all parts contain a strong narcotic.

ANTHURIUM   One of Hawaii's most popular cut flowers, anthuriums originally came from the tropical Americas and the Caribbean Islands. There are more than 550 species, but the most popular in Hawaii are the heart-shaped flowers (red, orange, pink, white, even purple) with a tail-like spath (green, orange, pink, red, white, purple, and in combinations thereof). Look for the heart-shaped green leaves in shaded areas. Anthuriums are very prolific on the Big Island of Hawaii. These exotic plants have no scent, but will last several weeks as cut flowers.

BIRDS OF PARADISE   This native of Africa has become something of a trademark of Hawaii. They're easily recognizable by the orange and blue flowers nestled in gray-green bracts, looking somewhat like birds in flight.

BOUGAINVILLEA   Originally from Brazil and named for the French navigator Louis A. de Bougainville, these colorful, tissue-thin bracts (ranging in color from majestic purple to fiery orange) hide tiny white flowers. A good place to spot them is on the Big Island along the Queen Ka'ahumanu Highway stretching from the Keahole Airport to Kailua-Kona.

BROMELIADS   The pineapple plant is the best known bromeliad; native to tropical South America and the islands of the Caribbean, there are more than 1,400 species. "Bromes," as they are affectionately called, are generally spiky plants ranging in size from a few inches to several feet in diameter. They're popular not only for their unusual foliage but also for their strange and wonderful flowers, which range from colorful spikes to delicate blossoms resembling orchids. Used widely in landscaping and interior decor, especially in resort areas, bromeliads are found on every island.

COFFEE   Hawaii is the only one of the states that commercially produces coffee. Coffee is an evergreen shrub with shiny, waxy, dark-green, pointed leaves. The flower is a small, fragrant white blossom that develops into half-inch berries that turn bright red when ripe. Look for coffee at elevations above 1,500 feet on the Kona side of the

Big Island (where it has been cultivated for more than 100 years), and on large coffee plantations on Kauai, Molokai, and Maui.

FRUIT TREES **Banana** Edible bananas are among the oldest of the world's food crops. By the time Europeans arrived in the islands, the Hawaiians had more than 40 different types of bananas planted. Most banana plants have long green leaves hanging from the tree, with the flower giving way to fruit in clusters.

Breadfruit A large tree—over 60 feet tall—with broad, sculpted, dark-green leaves. The fruit is round and about six inches or more in diameter. The ripe fruit, a staple in the Hawaiian diet, is whitish-yellow.

Lychee This evergreen tree, which can grow to well over 30 feet across, originated in China. Small flowers grow into panicles about a foot long in June and July. The round, red-skinned fruit appears shortly afterward.

Macadamia nut A transplant from Australia, macadamia nuts have become a commercial crop in recent decades in Hawaii; the commercially grown trees can be seen on the Big Island of Hawaii and Maui. The large trees—up to 60 feet tall—bear a hard-shelled nut encased in a leathery husk, which splits open and dries when ripe.

Mango From the Indo-Mala area comes the delicious mango, a fruit with peachlike flesh. Mango season usually begins in the spring and lasts through the summer, depending on the variety. The trees can grow to more than 100 feet tall. The tiny reddish flowers give way to a green fruit that turns red-yellow when ripe. Some people enjoy unripe mangoes, sliced thin or in chutney as a traditional Indian preparation. The mango sap can cause a skin rash on some people.

Papaya Yellow pear-shaped fruit (when ripe) is found at the base of the large, scalloped-shaped leaves on a pedestallike, nonbranched tree. Papayas ripen year-round.

GINGERS Some of the most fragrant flowers in Hawaii are white and yellow gingers (which the Hawaiians called *'awapuhi-ke'oke'o* and *'awapuhi-melemele)*. Usually found in clumps, growing four to seven feet tall, in the areas blessed by rain, these sweet-smelling, three-inch-wide flowers are composed of three dainty petallike stamen and three long, thin petals. White and yellow gingers are so prolific that many people assume they are native to Hawaii; actually, they were introduced in the 19th century from the Indo-Malaysia area. Look for yellow and white ginger from late spring to fall. If you see them on the side of the road, stop and pick a few blossoms—your car will be filled with a divine fragrance for the rest of the day. The only downside is that, once picked, they live only briefly.

Other members of the ginger family frequently seen in Hawaii (there are some 700 species) include red, shell, and torch gingers. Red ginger consists of tall, green stalks with foot-long red "flower heads." The red "petals" are actually bracts; inch-long white flowers are protected by the bracts and can be seen if you look down into the red head. Red ginger (*'awapuhi-'ula'ula* in Hawaiian), which does not share the heavenly smell of white ginger, will last a week or longer when cut. Look for red ginger from spring through late fall. Cool, wet mountain forests are ideal conditions for shell ginger; Hawaiians called it *'awapuhi-luheluhe,* which means "drooping" ginger. Natives of India and Burma, these plants, with their pearly white, clam shell–like blossoms, bloom from spring to fall.

Perhaps the most exotic gingers are the red or pink torch gingers. Cultivated in Malaysia as seasoning (the young flower shoots are used in curries), torch ginger rises directly out of the ground; the flower stalks (which are about five to eight inches in length) resemble the fire of a lighted torch. One of the few gingers that can bloom year-round, the Hawaiians call this plant *'awapuhi-ko'oko'o,* or "walking-stick" ginger.

HELICONIAS Some 80 species of the colorful heliconia family came to Hawaii from the Caribbean and Central and South America. The brightly colored bracts (yellow, red, green, orange, etc.) overlap and appear to unfold like origami birds. The most obvious heliconia to spot is the lobster claw, which resembles a string of boiled crustacean pincers—the brilliant crimson bracts alternate on the stem. Another prolific heliconia is the parrot's beak. Growing to about hip height, the parrot's beak is composed of bright-orange flower bracts with black tips, not unlike the beak of a parrot. Look for parrot's beak in the spring and summer, when it blooms in profusion.

HIBISCUS One variety of this year-round blossom, the yellow hibiscus, is the official state flower. The four- to six-inch hibiscus flowers come in a range of colors, from lily white to lipstick red. The flowers resemble crepe paper, with stamens and pistils protruding spirelike from the center. Hibiscus hedges can grow up to 15 feet tall. Once plucked, the flowers wither quickly.

JACARANDA Beginning about March and sometimes lasting until early May, these huge, lacy-leaved trees metamorphose into large clusters of spectacular lavender-blue sprays. The bell-shaped flowers drop quickly, leaving a majestic purple carpet beneath the tree.

NIGHT-BLOOMING CEREUS Look along rock walls for this spectacular night-blooming cactus flower. Originally from Central America, this vinelike member of the cactus family has green scalloped edges and produces foot-long white flowers that open and wither at sunrise. The plant also bears an edible red fruit.

ORCHIDS In many minds, nothing says Hawaii more than orchids. The orchid family is the largest in the entire plant kingdom; orchids are found in most parts of the world. Some species are native to Hawaii, but they're inconspicuous in most places, so most people overlook them. The most widely grown orchid—and the major source of flowers for leis and garnish for tropical libations—are the vanda orchids. The vandas used in the commercial flower industry in Hawaii are generally lavender or white, but they grow in a rainbow of colors, shapes, and sizes. The orchids used for corsages are the large, delicate cattleya; the ones used in floral arrangements—you'll probably see them in your hotel lobby—are usually dendrobiums. When you're on the Big Island, don't pass up a chance to wander through the numerous orchid farms around Hilo.

PLUMERIA Also known as frangipani, this sweet-smelling, five-petal flower, found in clusters on trees, is the most popular choice of lei-makers. The Singapore plumeria has five creamy-white petals, with a touch of yellow in the center. Another popular variety, ruba—with flowers from soft pink to flaming red—is also used in making leis. When picking plumeria, be careful of the sap from the flower, as it is poisonous and can stain clothes.

PROTEA Originally from South Africa, this unusual pland comes in more than 40 different varieties. Proteas are shrubs that bloom into a range of flower types. Different species of proteas range from those resembling pincushions to a species that look like bouquets of feathers. Proteas are long-lasting cut flowers; once dried, they will last for years.

TARO   Around pools, streams, and in neatly planted fields, you'll see the green heart-shaped leaves of taro. Taro was a staple to ancient Hawaiians, who pounded the root into poi. Originally from Sri Lanka, taro is not only a food crop, but is also grown as an ornamental.

OTHER TREES & PLANTS   Banyans—among the world's largest trees—have branches that grow out and away from the trunk, forming descending roots that grow down to the ground to feed and form additional trunks, making the tree very stable during tropical storms. The banyan in the courtyard next to the old Court House in Lahaina, Maui, is an excellent example of a spreading banyan—it covers two-thirds of an acre.

Monkeypod trees are among Hawaii's most majestic trees; they grow more than 80 feet tall and 100 feet across. Seen near older homes and in parks, the leaves of the monkeypod drop in February and March. The wood from the tree is a favorite of woodworking artisans.

One very uncommon and unusual plant—in fact seen only on the Big Island and in the Haleakala Crater on Maui—is the **silversword.** Once a year, this rare relative of the sunflower family blooms between July and September. Resembling a pinecone more than a sunflower, the silversword in bloom is a fountain of red-petaled, daisylike flowers that turn silver soon after blooming.

One not so rare and unusual plant is **marijuana,** or *pakalolo*—"crazy weed" as the Hawaiians call it—which is grown (usually illegally cultivated) throughout the islands. You probably won't see it as you drive along the roads, but if you go hiking you may glimpse the feathery green leaves with tight clusters of buds. Despite years of police effort to eradicate the plant, the illegal industry continues. Don't be tempted to pick a few buds, as the purveyors of this nefarious industry don't take kindly to poaching.

THE FAUNA OF THE ISLANDS

When the first Marquesans arrived in Hawaii between A.D. 500 and 800, scientists say they found some 67 varieties of endemic Hawaiian birds, a third of which are now believed to be extinct, including the **koloa** (the Hawaiian duck). What's even more astonishing is what they didn't find—there were no reptiles, amphibians, mosquitoes, lice, fleas, not even a cockroach.

When the Polynesians from the Society Islands arrived in Hawaii, around A.D. 1000, they found only two endemic mammals: the **hoary bat** and the **monk seal.** The small bat, called *ope'ape'a,* must have accidentally blown to Hawaii earlier from either North or South America. It can still be seen during its early evening forays, especially around the Kilauea Crater on the Big Island of Hawaii. The Hawaiian monk seal, a relative of warm-water seals previously found in the Caribbean and Mediterranean, was nearly slaughtered into extinction for its skin and oil during the 19th century. Recently these seals have experienced a minor population explosion, forcing relocation of some males from their protected homes in the inlets north of the main Hawaiian Islands. Periodically, these endangered marine mammals turn up at various beaches throughout the state. They are protected under the federal Marine Mammals Protection Act. If you're fortunate enough to see a monk seal, just look; don't disturb one of Hawaii's living treasures.

The first Polynesians brought a few animals from home: dogs, pigs, and chickens (all were for eating). A stowaway on board the Polynesian sailing canoes was the rat. All four animals are still found in the Hawaiian wild today.

BIRDS

Nene Endemic to the islands, the nene is Hawaii's state bird. It is being brought back from the brink of extinction through captive breeding and by strenuous protection laws. A relative of the Canadian goose, the nene stands about 2 feet high and has a black head and yellow cheeks, a buff neck with deep furrows, a grayish-brown body, and clawed feet. It gets its name from its two-syllable, high nasal call "nay-nay." The approximately 500 nenes in existence can be seen in only three locations: at Haleakala National Park on Maui, at Mauna Kea State Park bird sanctuary, and on the slopes of Mauna Kea on the Big Island.

Pueo The Hawaiian short-eared owl, which grows to about 12 to 17 inches in size, can be seen at dawn and dusk on Kauai, Maui, and the Big Island when the black-billed, brown-and-white bird goes hunting for rodents. Pueos are highly regarded by Hawaiians; according to legend, spotting a Pueo is a good omen.

Other Birds More species of native birds have become extinct in Hawaii in the last 200 years than anywhere else on the planet. Of the 67 native species of birds in Hawaii, 23 are extinct, 29 are endangered, and one is threatened. Even the Hawaiian crow, **'alala,** is threatened.

The **a'eo,** or Hawaiian stilt, a 16-inch-long bird with a black head, black coat, white underside, and long pink legs, can be found in protected wetlands like the Kanaha Wild Life Sanctuary on Maui (where it shares its natural habitat with the Hawaiian coot), the Kealia Pond on Maui, and the Hanalei National Wildlife Refuge on Kauai, which is also home to the Hawaiian duck. Other areas to see protected birds are the Kipuku Puaulu (Bird Park) and the Olaa rain forest, both in Hawaii Volcanoes National Park on the Big Island, and at Goat Island bird refuge off Oahu, where you can see wedge-tailed shearwaters nesting.

Another great birding venue is the 4,345-acre Kokee Wilderness Forest on Kauai. Various native birds that have been spotted include some of the 22 species of the native honeycreepers whose songs fill the forest. Frequently seen are the **'apapane** (a red bird with black wings and a curved black bill), the **'i'iwi** (another red bird with black wings but with orange legs and salmon-colored bill), the **'amakihi** (a plain olive-green bird with a long straight bill), and the **'anianiau** (a tiny yellow bird with a thin, curved bill). Also seen in the forest is the **'elepaio,** a small, gray flycatcher with an orange breast and an erect tail. A curious fellow, the 'elepaio comes out to investigate any unusual whistles. The most common native bird at Kokee—and the most easily seen—is the **moa,** or red jungle fowl, a chicken that was brought to Hawaii by the Polynesians.

To get a good glimpse of the seabirds that frequent Hawaii, drive to Kilauea Point on Kauai's north shore. Here, you can easily spot **red- and white-footed boobies, wedge-tailed shearwaters, frigate birds, red-tailed tropic birds,** and the **Laysan albatross.**

OTHER FAUNA

Geckos These harmless, soft-skinned, insect-eating lizards come equipped with suction pads on their feet that enable them to climb walls and windows, so they can reach tasty insects like mosquitoes and cockroaches. You'll see them on windows outside a lighted room at night or hear their cheerful chirp.

Mongooses The mongoose is a mistake. It was brought here in the 19th century to counteract the ever-growing rat problem. But rats are nocturnal creatures, sleeping during the day and wandering out at night. Mongooses, however, are day creatures. Instead of getting rid of the rat problem, the mongooses eat bird eggs, accelerating the demise of the native bird population in Hawaii.

Snakes   Hawaii has but one tiny earthwormlike snake. Strict measures are taken to keep other snakes out of Hawaii. On the island of Guam, the brown tree snake has obliterated most of the bird population. Officials in Hawaii are well aware of this danger and are committed to preventing snakes from entering the state.

SEALIFE

Hawaii has an extraordinarily unique underwater world. Approximately 680 species of fish are known to inhabit the waters around the Hawaiian Islands. Of those, approximately 450 species stay close to the reef and inshore areas.

CORAL   The reefs surrounding Hawaii are made up of various coral and algae. The living coral grow through sunlight that feeds a specialized algae, called zooxanthellae, which in turn allows the development of the coral's calcareous skeleton. It takes thousands of years for reefs to develop. The reef attracts and supports fish and crustaceans, which use the reef for food, habitat, mating, and raising their young. Mother Nature can cause the destruction of the reef with a strong storm or large waves, but humans—through a seemingly unimportant act such as touching the coral—have proved to be even more destructive to the fragile reefs.

The coral most frequently seen in Hawaii are hard, rocklike formations named for their familiar shapes: antler, cauliflower, finger, plate, and razor coral. Wire coral looks just like its name—a randomly bent wire growing straight out of the reef. Some coral appear soft, such as tube coral; it can be found in the ceilings of caves. Black coral, which resemble winter-bare trees or shrubs, are found at depths of over 100 feet.

REEF FISH   Of the approximately 450 reef fish, about 27% are native to Hawaii and found nowhere else on the planet. This may seem surprising for a string of isolated islands, 2,000 miles from the nearest landmass. But over the millions of years of gestation of the Hawaiian Islands, as they emerged from erupting volcanoes, ocean currents—mainly from the Indo-Malay Pacific region—carried the larvae of thousands of marine animals and plants to Hawaii's reef. Of those, approximately 100 species not only adapted, but thrived. Some species are much bigger and more plentiful than their Pacific cousins; many developed unique characteristics. Some, like the lemon or milletseed butterfly fish, are not only particular to Hawaii but also unique within their larger, worldwide family in their specialized schooling and feeding behaviors. Another surprising thing about Hawaii endemics is how common some of the native fish are: You can see the saddleback wrasse, for instance, on virtually any snorkeling excursion or dive in Hawaiian waters.

Some of the reef fish you might spot while you're underwater are:

Angelfish   Often mistaken for butterfly fish, angelfish can be distinguished by the spine, located low on the gill plate. Angelfish are very shy; several species live in colonies close to coral for protection.

Blennys   Small, elongated fish, blennys range from 2 to 10 inches long, with the majority in the 3- to-4-inch range. Blennys are so small that they can live in tide pools; you might have a hard time spotting one.

Butterfly Fish   Some of the most colorful of the reef fish, butterfly fish are usually seen in pairs (scientists believe they mate for life) and appear to spend most of their day feeding. There are 22 species of butterfly fish, of which three (blue-stripe, lemon or milletseed, and multiband or pebbled butterfly fish) are endemic. Most butterfly fish have a dark band through the eye and a spot near the tail resembling an eye, meant to confuse their predators (the moray eel loves to lunch on butterfly fish).

Eels   Moray and conger eels are the common eels seen in Hawaii. Morays are usually docile unless provoked, or if there is food or an injured fish around. Unfortunately, some morays have been fed by divers and—being intelligent creatures—associate divers with food; thus, they can become aggressive. But most morays like to keep to themselves hidden in their hole or crevice. While morays may look menacing, conger eels look downright happy, with big lips and pectoral fins (situated so that they look like big ears), which give them the appearance of a perpetual smiling face. Conger eels have crushing teeth so they can feed on crustaceans; in fact, since they're sloppy eaters, they usually live with shrimp and crabs who feed off the crumbs they leave.

Parrot Fish   One of the largest and most colorful of the reef fish, parrot fish can grow as large as 40 inches long. Parrot fish are easy to spot—their front teeth are fused together, protruding like buck teeth and resembling a parrot's beak. These unique teeth allow the parrot fish to feed by scraping algae from rocks and coral. The rocks and coral pass through the parrot fish's system, resulting in fine sand. In fact, most of the sand found in Hawaii is parrot fish waste; one large parrot fish can produce a ton of sand a year. Hawaiian native parrot fish species include yellowbar, regal, and spectacled.

Scorpion Fish   This is a family of what scientists call "ambush predators." These fish hide under camouflaged exteriors and ambush their prey when they come along. Several sport a venomous dorsal spine. These fish don't have a gas bladder, so when they stop swimming, they sink—that's why you usually find them "resting" on ledges and on the bottom. Although they're not aggressive, an inattentive snorkeler or diver could feel the effects of those venomous spines—so be very careful where you put your hands and feet in the water.

Surgeon Fish   Sometimes called tang, the surgeon fish get their name from the scalpel-like spines located on each side of their bodies near the base of their tails. Some surgeon fish have a rigid spine; others have the ability to fold their spine against their body until it's needed for defense purposes. Some surgeon fish, like the brightly colored yellow tang, are boldly colored. Others are adorned in more conservative shades of gray, brown, or black. The only endemic surgeon fish—and the most abundant in Hawaiian waters—is the convict tang, (*manini* in Hawaiian), a pale white fish with vertical black stripes (like a convict's uniform).

Wrasses   This is a very diverse family of fish, ranging in size from 2 to 15 inches. Several wrasses are brilliantly colored and change their colors through aging and sexual dimorphism (sex changing). Wrasses have the unique ability to change gender from female (when young) to male with maturation. There are several wrasses that are endemic to Hawaii: the Hawaiian cleaner, shortnose, belted, and gray (or old woman).

GAME FISH   Fishing enthusiasts have a huge variety to choose from in Hawaii, from pan-sized snapper to nearly 1-ton marlin. Hawaii is known around the globe as *the* place for big game fish—marlin, swordfish, and tuna—but its waters are also great for catching other offshore fish (like mahimahi, rainbow runner, and wahoo), coastal fish (barracuda, scad), bottom fish (snappers, sea bass, and amberjack), and inshore fish (trevally, bonefish, and others), as well as freshwater fish (bass, catfish, trout, bluegill, and oscar).

Billfish are caught year-round. There are six different kinds of billfish found in the offshore waters around the islands: Pacific blue marlin, black marlin, sailfish, broadbill swordfish, striped marlin, and shortbill spearfish. Hawaii billfish range in size from the 20-pound shortbill spearfish and striped marlin to an 1,805-pound Pacific blue marlin, the largest marlin ever caught with rod and reel anywhere in the world. **Tuna** ranges in size from small (a pound or less) mackerel tuna used as bait (Hawaiians call them *oioi*), to 250-pound yellowfin ahi tuna. Other species of tuna found in Hawaii are bigeye, albacore, kawakawa, and skipjack.

Some of the best eating fish are also found in offshore waters: **mahimahi** (also known as dolphin fish or dorado) in the 20- to 70-pound range, **rainbow runner** *(kamanu)* from 15 to 30 pounds, and **wahoo** *(ono)* from 15 to 80 pounds. Shoreline fishermen are always on the lookout for **trevally** (the state record for giant trevally is 191 pounds), **bonefish, ladyfish, threadfin, leatherfish,** and **goatfish.** Bottom fishermen pursue a range of **snappers**—red, pink, gray, and others—as well as **sea bass** (the state record is a whopping 563 pounds) and **amberjack,** which weigh up to 100 pounds.

Reservoirs on Oahu and Kauai are home to Hawaii's many freshwater fish: bass (large, smallmouth, and peacock), catfish (channel and Chinese), rainbow trout, bluegill sunfish, pungee, and oscar. The state record for freshwater fish is the 43-pound, 13-ounce channel catfish caught in Lake Wilson on Oahu.

WHALES Humpback Whales The most popular visitors to Hawaii come every year in the winter, around November, and stay until the springtime (April or so) when they return to their summer home in Alaska. Humpback whales—some as big as a city bus and weighing many tons—migrate to the warm, protected Hawaiian waters in the winter to mate and calve. You can take whale-watching cruises on every island that will let you observe these magnificent leviathans close up, or you can spot their signature spouts of water from shore as they expel water in the distance. Humpbacks grow to up to 45 feet long, so when they breach (propel their entire body out of the water) or even wave a fluke, you can see it for miles.

Other whales Humpbacks are among the biggest whales found in Hawaiian waters, but other whales—like pilot, sperm, false killer, melon-headed, pygmy killer, and beaked whales—can be seen year-round, especially in the calm waters off the Big Island's Kona Coast. These whales usually travel in pods of 20 to 40 animals and are very social, interacting with each other on the surface.

SHARKS Yes, Virginia, there are sharks in Hawaii, but more than likely you won't see a shark unless you specifically go looking for one. About 40 different species of sharks inhabit the waters surrounding Hawaii; they range from the totally harmless whale shark—at 60 feet, the world's largest fish—which has no teeth and is so docile that it frequently lets divers ride on its back, to the not-so-docile, infamous—and extremely uncommon—great white shark. The ancient Hawaiians had great respect for sharks and believed that some sharks were reincarnated relatives who had returned to assist them. The most common sharks seen in Hawaii are whitetip reef sharks, gray reef sharks (about 5 feet long), and blacktip reef sharks (about 6 feet long). Since records have been kept, starting in 1779, there have been only about 100 shark attacks in Hawaii, of which 40% have been fatal. The largest number of attacks occurred after someone fell into the ocean from the shore or from a boat. In these cases, the sharks probably attacked after the person was dead.

General rules for avoiding sharks are: Don't swim at sunrise, sunset, or where the water is murky due to stream runoff—sharks may mistake you for one of their usual meals. And don't swim where there are bloody fish in the water (sharks become aggressive around blood).

The Hawaiian Islands

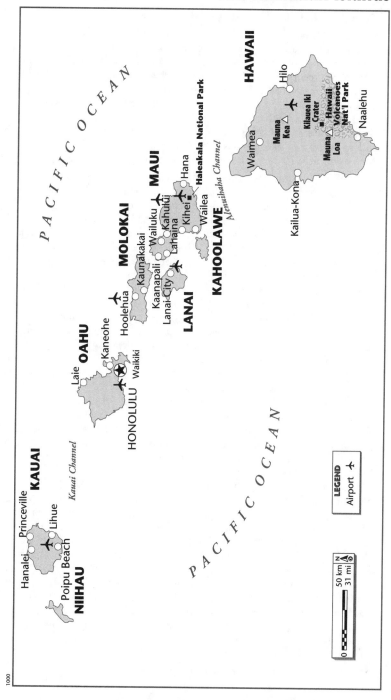

PACIFIC OCEAN

PACIFIC OCEAN

HAWAII

Hilo

Waimea

Mauna Kea △

Kilauea Iki Crater

Hawaii Volcanoes Nat'l Park

Mauna Loa △

Naalehu

Kailua-Kona

Alenuihaha Channel

MAUI

Hana

Haleakala National Park

Wailuku

Kahului

Lahaina

Kihei

Wailea

MOLOKAI

Kaunakakai

Kaanapali

Hoolehua

Lanai City

LANAI

KAHOOLAWE

OAHU

Kaneohe

Laie

Waikiki

HONOLULU

Kauai Channel

KAUAI

Princeville

Hanalei

Lihue

Poipu Beach

NIIHAU

LEGEND
Airport ✈

N

50 km
31 mi
0

HAWAII'S ECOSYSTEM PROBLEMS

Officials at Hawaii Volcanoes National Park on the Big Island saw a potential problem a few decades ago with people taking a few rocks home with them as "souvenirs." To prevent this problem from escalating, the park rangers "created" a legend that the fiery volcano goddess, Pele, did not like people taking anything (rocks, chunks of lava) from her home, and bad luck would befall anyone disobeying her wishes. There used to be a display case in the park's visitor center filled with letters from people who had taken rocks from the volcano, relating stories of all the bad luck that followed. Most of the letters begged Pele's forgiveness and instructed the rangers to please return the rock to the exact location that was its original home.

Unfortunately, Hawaii's other ecosystem problems can't be handled as easily.

MARINE LIFE   Hawaii's beautiful and abundant marine life has attracted so many visitors that they threaten to overwhelm it. A great example of this overenthusiasm is Oahu's Hanauma Bay. Thousands of people flock to this beautiful bay, a marine preserve which features calm, protected swimming and snorkeling areas loaded with tropical reef fish. It was such a perfect spot that too many people flocked here, forcing government officials to limit the number of people who can enter the bay at any one time. Commercial tour operators have been restricted entirely in an effort to balance the people-to-fish ratio.

Another marine life conservation area that suffers from overuse is Molokini, a small crater off the coast of Maui. In the 1970s, residents made the area a conservation district in order to protect the unique aquariumlike atmosphere of the waters inside the arms of the crater. Unfortunately, once it was protected, everyone wanted to go there just to see what was worth special protection. Twenty years ago, one or two small, six-passenger boats made the trip once a day to Molokini; today, it is not uncommon to sight 20 or more boats, each carrying 20 to 49 passengers, moored inside the tiny crater. One tour operator has claimed that, on some days, it's so crowded you can actually see a slick of suntan oil floating on the surface of the water.

People who fall in love with the colorful tropical fish and want to see them all the time back home are also thought to be impacting the health of Hawaii's reefs. The growth in home, office, and decor aquariums has risen dramatically in the last 20 years. As a result, more and more reef fish collectors are taking a growing number of reef fish from Hawaiian waters.

The reefs themselves have faced increasing impacts over the years. Runoff of soil and chemicals from construction, agriculture, erosion, and even heavy storms can blanket and choke a reef, which needs sunlight to survive. In addition, the intrusion of foreign elements—such as breaks in sewage lines—can cause problems for Hawaii's reef. Human contact with the reef can also upset the ecosystem. Coral, the basis of the reef system, is very fragile; snorkelers and divers grabbing on to coral can break off pieces that took decades to form. Feeding fish can also upset the balance of the ecosystem (not to mention upsetting the digestive systems of the fish). One glass-bottom boat operator reported that they fed an eel for years, considering it their "pet" eel. One day the eel decided that he wanted more than just the food being offered and bit the diver's fingers. Divers and snorkelers report that in areas where the fish are fed, the fish have become more aggressive; clouds of certain reef fish—normally shy—surround divers, demanding food.

FLORA   One of Hawaii's most fragile environments is the rain forest. Any intrusion—from hikers carrying seeds in on their shoes to the rooting of wild boars—can upset the delicate balance in these complete ecosystems. In recent years, development has moved closer and closer to the rain forest. On the Big Island of Hawaii, people have protested the invasion of bulldozers and the drilling of geothermal wells in the Wao Kele O Puna rain forest for years, claiming that the damage done is irreparable.

FAUNA   The biggest impact on the fauna in Hawaii is the decimation of native birds by feral animals, which have destroyed the bird's habitats, and by mongooses that have eaten the birds' eggs and young. Government officials are vigilant about snakes because of the potential damage tree snakes can do to the remaining birdlife.

VOG   The volcanic haze—caused by gases released by the continuous eruption of the volcano on the flank of Kilauea, on the Big Island, and the smoke from the fires set by the lava—has been dubbed "vog." The hazy air, which looks like smog from urban pollution, limits viewing from scenic vistas and plays havoc with photographers trying to get clear panoramic photographs. Some people claim that the vog has even caused bronchial ailments.

CULTURE   Virtually since the arrival of the first Europeans, there has been a controversy over balancing the preservation of history and indigenous cultures and lifestyles with economic development. The question of what should be preserved—and in what fashion—is continually being debated in Hawaii. Some factions argue that the continuously developing tourism economy will one day destroy the very thing that visitors come to Hawaii to see; another sector argues that Hawaii's cost of living is so high that new development and industries are needed so the residents can earn a living.

2 Maui Today

If you've visited Maui in the past, you'll probably be surprised at the amount of development that has occurred over the last few years. A brand new state-of-the-art arts and cultural center has just been completed, fast-food restaurants are popping up all over the place, and access to virtually every bit of prime shoreline has been "barricaded" by enormous resort hotels. Not surprisingly, the island's largest source of income is tourism, and as a result, over the years true Hawaiian culture has slowly been eradicated. People come for the sand and sun, and for the most part don't get to learn too much about native Hawaiian traditions and crafts. Fortunately, island residents have come to realize the importance of revitalizing Hawaiian culture; thus programs are being instituted in resort hotels. In addition the Maui Arts & Cultural Center is working on establishing a Hawaiian cultural program.

Though development continues on Maui's southern shore (particularly in the Makena resort), most of the rest of the island has stopped major construction projects (the biggest projects in recent years were the Arts & Cultural Center in Kahului and a new, exceedingly ugly sports center–like church, also in Kahului). The only projects scheduled for the near future are a business park in Kahului and a longer runway at the airport. The runway has sparked controversy among island residents, because if it is lengthened, then international flights can arrive directly on Maui. While this might be better for business, it might overwhelm the island with more visitors than ever before.

Ocean activities continue to be the island's most popular—from sunbathing to scuba diving; however, more and more visitors are heading for the slopes of Haleakala for hiking and horseback riding excursions.

Maui continues to be a relatively safe place to visit. The police blotter in the *Maui News* reports more petty thefts than anything else, but visitors are strongly advised to keep their rental cars locked when out exploring and to leave valuables in hotel safes whenever possible.

Almost in spite of itself, Maui remains a fairly quiet, incredibly beautiful place to visit. The pace is slow here, and visitors don't need much encouragement to trade in their loafers and heels for "slippers" (flip-flops).

3 A Look at the Past

Dateline

- **2,000,000 B.C.** The first of Maui's volcanoes breaks the ocean's surface.
- **1,000,000 B.C.** Mount Haleakala rises to the surface and molten lava flows form the island of Maui.
- **ca. A.D. 450** The first Polynesians discover the Hawaiian Islands and begin settlement.
- **A.D. 700** Colonists from Tahiti begin arriving on the islands.
- **ca. 1550** High Chief Pi'ilani rules Maui.
- **ca. 1700** Kekaulike establishes a united kingdom on Maui.
- **1778** Captain James Cook of England discovers the island chain of Hawaii. He documents sightings of the island of "Mowee," but never actually goes ashore.
- **1779** Cook meets Kalaniopu'u at Kealakekua Bay on the Big Island. The meeting is friendly, but violence later erupts, and Cook is killed.
- **1781** Kalaniopu'u dies; his son, Kiwala'o, takes control of the kingdom. Kamehameha I is appointed keeper of the war god Kukailimoku.
- **1787** French explorer Captain Jean-François de Galoup, Comte de La Pe´rouse is the first Westerner to land on Maui. He is supposed

continues

THE FIRST GREAT NAVIGATORS   Though no one is quite sure of the origins of the Polynesians, they are believed to have come from Southeast Asia and carry some of the features of several different races. It is believed that the Polynesians first migrated to the Indonesian Islands and then headed to the South Pacific where they settled on Fiji, Samoa, New Zealand, Tahiti, and the Marquesas. Having developed extraordinary navigational skills, they began exploring northward and crossed vast oceans to reach the Hawaiian Islands. The sailing vessels of the first Polynesian explorers were crude, and only a few of these adventurers survived and returned to tell their stories. Chants passed on from one generation of sailors to the next described the Hawaiian Islands and how to reach them, but for centuries migrations to the islands ceased, and Hawaii became a longed-for, far-off paradise that existed only in the imaginations of most Polynesians.

Historians are unsure about the origin of the name *Maui*, but it is known that throughout Polynesia stories of Maui abound. According to many of these tales, Maui was a mischievous demigod who, in spite of his love of practical jokes, was charming, well loved, and "blessed" with incredible powers. *Maui-tinihanga* ("Maui-of-a-thousand-tricks") is said to have, among other things, raised the sky when it was falling, snared the Sun when his mother wished for more sunlight, and fished up an island to prove himself to his brothers, all depending on which version of the story you hear.

Much of what we know about Polynesian history comes from the ancient chant (or *mele*), known as the Kumulipo—a sacred rendition of the story of Creation. The *kahuna* (Hawaiian priests of sorts) were responsible for singing the chant of the Kumulipo, which tells the story of how the islands of Hawaii, Maui, and Kahoolawe were created from the union of Papa ("earth mother") and Wakea ("sky father"). Later, Wakea joined with a second wife Kaula, and that union produced the island of Lanai. Then, apparently bored with Kaula, Wakea took Hina as his third wife, and together they created the island of Molokai. When Papa learned of Wakea's infidelities, jealous and angry, she had an affair with a young god by the name of Lua, and together they produced Oahu. Just to bring the soap opera full circle, Papa and Wakea finally reconciled and gave birth to the last islands—Kauai, Niihau, Kaula, and Nihoa.

Through the Kumulipo, some Hawaiians were able to trace their lineage all the way back to Papa and Wakea, and it was they who had the privileged status of *ali'i* (royalty). Of the ali'i there were two distinct genealogical lines: the Ulu (literally translated: "possessed by a spirit" or "inspired by a god") were the royalty of Hawaii and Maui, while the Nana'ulu were the royalty of Kauai.

Centuries passed before Polynesian migration really began in force, and the first of those who came to the islands are thought to have been from the Marquesas. They arrived in canoes up to 80 feet in length carrying entire extended families as well as foodstuffs, livestock, and provisions, and they lived a peaceful existence—giving up their traditional practice of cannibalism.

After the migration of the Marquesans, migration continued from Polynesia to Hawaii for several hundred years. However, sometime in the 1100s, war-minded Tahitians arrived in canoes that are reported to have been 100 feet or more in length and able to carry up to 80 people. Their aim was to overthrow the existing Hawaiian chiefs, and with the introduction of their gods and the system of *kapu* they succeeded. Kapu made certain practices, foods, and places either off-limits (taboo) or sacred, or both, and it changed the face of Hawaiian religious worship for many hundreds of years.

After the Tahitians settled the Hawaiian archipelago, travel between Tahiti and Hawaii continued for about a century, and then for no reason that is currently evident to historians, expeditions between the two areas stopped, and the Hawaiian Islands remained isolated from the rest of the world for about 500 years until European discovery in the 18th century.

THE MAUI DYNASTIES Though Maui's history is sketchy up until the late 16th century, we do know that each of the islands (or each district on each island) was ruled by a chief of ali'i status. Information about most of the original ruling chiefs has been lost over the years, but historians have been

to claim Maui as French territory, but never does.

- **1790** Kamehameha I unites Maui with the rest of his kingdom. The Olowalu Massacre takes place on Maui's west side.

- **1802** Kamehameha I declares Lahaina as the capital city of the islands.

- **1819** Kamehameha I dies and his son, Liholiho takes control. Before his death he appoints his widow, Ka'ahumanu, queen regent of the kingdom. The first whaling ship, the *Balena*, arrives in Lahaina from New Bedford, Massachusetts.

- **1823** The first missionaries arrive on Maui from New England; Queen Keopuolani dies and is given a Christian burial.

- **1824** Liholiho dies; Queen Ka'ahumanu assumes power because Liholiho's 11-year-old brother isn't old enough to take the throne.

- **1825** Conflicts between the whalers erupt in Lahaina; laws are passed prohibiting prostitution and the sale of alcohol.

- **1828** Operations begin at Maui's first sugar mill.

- **1832** Queen Ka'ahumanu dies; Kamehameha III takes power but refuses to accept his responsibilities; he appoints his sister to be queen regent.

- **1834** Maui's first printing press arrives from Honolulu, and the island's first printing house (Hale Pa'i) is built. The first newspaper west of the Rocky Mountains is published.

- **1835** Dr. Dwight Baldwin arrives on Maui.

- **1850** Honolulu replaces Lahaina as the capital of the Hawaiian nation.

continues

- **1873** William Lunalilo is elected by popular vote.
- **1875** The Reciprocity Act exempts Hawaiian sugar from U.S. import tariffs. Alexander and Baldwin begin building the Hamakua Ditch.
- **1891** David Kalakaua dies and his sister, Lydia Lilikuolani, the last Hawaiian monarch, takes the throne.
- **1893** The Hawaiian monarchy is overthrown by American settlers in Hawaii.
- **1898** The United States annexes Hawaii.
- **1903** The first pineapple is planted on Maui by Dwight Baldwin.
- **1941** Pearl Harbor is bombed and martial law is declared in Hawaii.
- **1946** Tourism begins on Maui with the opening of the Hotel Hana Maui, the island's first resort property.
- **1959** Hawaii becomes the 50th state of the United States.
- **1961** Hawaii's first "master-planned resort," Kaanapali , opens on Maui.
- **1976** Renewed interest in Hawaiian culture is sparked by the sailing of the *Hokule'a,* a replica of an ancient Polynesian canoe, and ancestral journeys are re-created.

able to trace royal lineage on Maui back to when the ruling chief, Pi'ilani, rose to power. Pi'ilani's rule was peaceful, but upon his death his two sons, Lono-a-Piilani and Kiha, quarreled constantly. Kiha was forced to flee to Hana, and there he fell in love with Koleamoku, daughter of the high chief of Hana. Despite Koleamoku's betrothal to Lono-a-Piilani, they secretly married, precipitating war. Kiha and his wife fled to the Big Island and the protection of his brother-in-law, Umi. Umi attacked Maui, defeating Lono-a-Piilani and thereby adding Maui to his kingdom.

One of the descendants of the Pi'ilani dynasty was a ruling chief named Kekaulike. Sometime at the beginning of the 18th century, Kekaulike and his men went to war and were able to successfully unite all of the districts of Maui. When Kekaulike passed his kingdom on to his sons, they fought over who would have more power, but after settling their differences, they ruled in relative harmony for decades.

Things on the Big Island, however, were in flux as the chiefs there and on the other islands battled for power over small kingdoms.

EUROPEAN DISCOVERY OF THE HAWAIIAN ISLANDS   In 1776, British explorer Captain James Cook set out in the HMS *Resolution* (along with another ship, the HMS *Discovery*, under the command of Charles Clerke) to explore the Pacific for the third time. After sailing around the Cape of Good Hope, past New Zealand and Tasmania, Cook came upon the islands of Oahu and Kauai in January 1778. In his diaries Cook recorded landings on the islands of Kauai and Niihau, where he replenished supplies and traded with the natives. He named the archipelago the Sandwich Islands after John Montague, the Earl of Sandwich.

With well-stocked ships and a well-rested crew, Cook continued on in his search for the Northwest Passage (his original goal). He headed toward the North American continent and then north toward the Arctic, where he searched, in vain, for the passage. When he realized that his search had proven fruitless, he decided to return to the Sandwich Islands for the winter to repair his badly damaged ships and continue his explorations. Cook and his crew returned to the Sandwich Islands in the dark of night on November 25, 1778. When the sun rose on November 26, Cook made his first sighting of the island of Maui. He was anchored approximately 3 miles offshore from the city we now know as Kahului, and that very day hundreds of Hawaiians approached his ships by canoe. Cook reported that the Hawaiians "came into the ship, without the least hesitation."

Cook and his crew traded pieces of iron for cuttlefish, potatoes, taro, fruit, and some pigs. Cook was also greeted by Kahekili, the king of Maui, who arrived dressed in full regalia, from his feather-crested helmet to his red-and-yellow-feathered cloak.

During his anchorage off Maui, Cook had other visitors, including Kalaniopu'u (ruler of the Hana district of Maui, and arch rival to Kahekili) and a young chief by the name of Kamehameha, who would later become king of the United Hawaiian Kingdom. In his journal Cook recorded the island's name phonetically: "Mowee."

On November 30, 1778, Cook recorded his first sighting of the island of "O'why'he'" (Hawaii). He spent about a month sailing around the Big Island and trading with the natives as he went; finally, on January 15, 1779, he came upon Kealakekua Bay, where he decided to anchor in order to repair his ships and gather provisions. The Hawaiians were awed by the sight of this foreigner, not only because he was very unlike themselves but because he arrived on the day and in the bay that was reserved for Lono, the great fertility god of the land. In his wooden ship Cook bore a striking resemblance to Hawaiian renditions of Lono, and since it was believed that Lono would return to Earth, the Hawaiians mistook Cook for their god. Cook was warmly but formally received and honored with a water procession, fireworks, and, several days later, the presentation of King Kalaniopu'u's own cloak, feather helmet, and kahili.

During Cook's visit to Kealakekua Bay, he and King Kalaniopu'u developed an extremely amicable friendship, but by February 4, 1779, after having clearly worn out their welcome (in part because the natives had come to understand that Cook and his men were mere mortals, and in part because they had eaten the Hawaiians out of house and home), Cook decided that they should press on.

Barely a week had passed when the *Resolution* and the *Discovery* found themselves once again at Kealakekua Bay. The weather had not been favorable, and the *Resolution* was in need of repair. While the ships were anchored in the bay, there were several incidents of thievery, and the British seamen retaliated with force. This only served to increase hostility between the Europeans and the Hawaiians. On February 14, while the ship was being repaired, Cook noticed that a small cutter had been stolen, and he decided to kidnap the king (some say he went willingly), with whom he was still friendly, and hold him until the cutter was safely returned. Unfortunately, Cook could not have predicted the hostility to which he would fall victim. After the king was taken, the natives armed themselves and threatened Cook's life. Cook fired one shot. The natives attacked, and Cook was killed.

After the death of their leader, crew members, including Captain Clerke, continued on with Cook's original plan, exploring the waters surrounding Maui, Molokai, and Lanai. On March 15, Clerke turned his ships northward and made one last attempt to find the Northwest Passage. During the search Clerke became ill and died. The four-year Cook expedition was ended, and after a brief period of trading in China, the ships returned to England.

POST-COOK EUROPEAN EXPLORATION   News of Cook's discoveries in the Pacific spread, and European trade with the Hawaiians continued, primarily in armaments. Demand for more deadly weapons had grown since Cook first traded iron daggers for provisions as power-hungry Hawaiian chiefs and ali'i sought possession of more land and additional islands. The three major players in Hawaiian rule at the time of Cook's visit were Kalaniopu'u, who ruled over the island of Hawaii and the Hana district of Maui; Kahekili, who controlled all of Maui (with the exception of the Hana district), Kahoolawe, Lanai, and Oahu; and Kaeo, the brother of Kahekili, whose domain was the island of Kauai.

The Hawaiian arms race gathered speed as Europeans, who had become involved in the fur trade, stopped in the Hawaiian Islands on their way from North America to China. Among the first European visitors to arrive after the departure of Captain

Cook was French explorer Admiral Jean-François de Galoup, Comte de La Pe'rouse, who was the first European to set foot on the island of Maui. His notes and the sketches of the ship's artist were the first written record of Maui's terrain. In La Pe'rouse's description of the Hana coast, he commented that they ". . . beheld water falling in cascades from the mountains and running in streams to the sea. . . . The trees which crowned the mountains and the verdure of the banana plants that surrounded the habitations produced inexpressible charms to our senses." Like Cook, La Pe'rouse traded pieces of iron for food and provisions. On May 30, 1786, La Pe'rouse landed in a bay (known today as La Pe'rouse Bay) just outside Lahaina. He and his crew stayed on Maui for only a short period of time, after which they set sail for the west coast of North America.

THE OLOWALU MASSACRE   By the end of the 18th century, ship captains en route to China from all over the world were dropping anchor in Hawaii to replenish supplies and repair their vessels. In 1790, the *Eleanora*, an American ship under the command of Captain Simon Metcalfe, arrived. In January, while anchored near Honuaula, off Maui, the ship's boat was stolen, and a member of the crew was killed during the night. In retaliation Metcalfe fired shots at a canoe full of Hawaiians. Many were wounded. Metcalfe pretended that the score had been evened and summoned the unsuspecting Hawaiians to his ship, giving them the impression that he was prepared to reestablish trade. Scores of canoes loaded with hundreds of Hawaiians left the shores of Olowalu. They were only a few feet from the *Eleanora* when Metcalfe gave the order for his men to open fire. The result was a bloody massacre, known to the Hawaiians as *Kalolopahu*, or "the spilled brains." About 100 natives were slain. Metcalfe and his crew set sail for the island of Hawaii.

KAHEKILI   During this period of European invasion, a young man by the name of Kamehameha was growing up and entering manhood. He had been instructed in the ways of the Hawaiian military by his uncle Kalaniopu'u (king of the Maui district of Hana and the Big Island of Hawaii), who sought to conquer the entire island of Maui. When Kalaniopu'u died in 1781, his son, Kiwala'o, succeeded his father as king; before his death, however, Kalaniopu'u granted Kamehameha a great honor and appointed him keeper of the war god Kukailimoku (often referred to simply as Ku).

Kalaniopu'u's enemy, Kahekili, was awaiting his opportunity to seize control of the Hana district, and after the death of his rival he had his chance. It took his forces about a year to conquer Hana, but a final bloody battle wiped out virtually all the defenders of Hana.

Kahekili was not satisfied with simply defeating the Hana chiefs; he also sought to gain control of the Big Island and Oahu. Initial attempts against Kamehameha and his troops on the Big Island were unsuccessful, so Kahekili focused his energies on Oahu and its ruling chief, Kahahana. In January 1783, Kahekili and his wife, Kauwahine, along with scores of warriors, stormed the beaches of Oahu and overpowered the troops of Chief Kahahana. Many died, but many others, along with Kahahana and his wife, fled. Kahahana and the chief of another district on the island of Oahu were both killed by Kahekili. He had successfully defeated the ruling chiefs of Oahu and had, with landholdings that also included Maui, Molokai, and Lanai, become the most powerful king in Hawaii.

KAMEHAMEHA TAKES MAUI   Though in 1786 Kahekili was the most powerful force in the islands, he would only hold his position for four short years. The young Kamehameha was becoming a force to be reckoned with. Keeper of the warrior god, Ku; proud owner of Thomas Metcalfe's ship, the *Fair American*, along with all its guns and its cannon; and captor of two seamen, Isaac Davis and John Young (trained in the military ways of the West), Kamehameha was preparing to become king of all the islands. He began by attempting to conquer the island of Hawaii, and for the most part succeeded, although he was unable to defeat one of the island chiefs, Keoua (cousin to Kamehameha, and son of Kamehameha's mentor, Kalaniopu'u). In 1790, frustrated by the situation on Hawaii, Kamehameha turned his attention to Maui. He, Isaac Davis, and John Young (Kamehameha's closest advisers), and all of his warriors landed on the beaches at Hana. The battle was easily won. Kahekili realized that Central Maui would be the focus of Kamehameha's next attack. He sent his son, Kalanikupule, along with all of his best warriors, to Wailuku to wait for Kamehameha and his troops. Kamehameha's troops fought hard and forced the Maui warriors to retreat into the Iao Valley. Known as the battle of Kepaniwai ("damming of the waters"), this fight proved to be the turning point for Kahekili. The battle was bloody, and bodies were said to have literally "dammed" the waterway of the Iao Valley. Many of the ali'i were able to escape through the forest and over the mountain, but Kamehameha's message was loud and clear.

Meanwhile, Kamehameha's cousin and rival, Keoua, was burning and pillaging the villages of Kamehameha's newly won districts. Kamehameha rushed back to the Big Island immediately, fought two battles with Keoua, but was still unable to defeat him.

Legend has it that Kamehameha had a dream that told him if he built a *heiau* (temple) to Ku, the war god would aid him in his struggle. He began building the war temple on a hill called Puukohola ("Hill of the Whale") overlooking Kawaihae Bay on the Big Island. Before the job was completed, Kahekili dispatched troops from the islands of Oahu, Maui, Molokai, and Kauai. They were headed for Waimea Bay off the Big Island's Hamakua coastline. Kamehameha halted operations at the war heiau so he could meet the warriors off Waimea Bay before they landed. If the battle were to take place at sea, Kamehameha would have the advantage: Both sides would be fighting with guns, but Kamehameha's sloop was fitted with two powerful cannons. Yet another bloody battle was fought, and Kamehameha again emerged victorious. Kahekili retreated and accepted Kamehameha as king of Maui, though Kahekili remained on the island and served as "chief" until his death in 1794.

With Kahekili stripped of his power, only Keoua remained. Kamehameha and Keoua continued to battle without a final outcome until Keoua and his troops, who were marching near the crater of Kilauea, were enveloped by a cloud of hot ash issued by the goddess Pele. Many of his warriors were killed. Keoua was spared, but he knew then that the gods had chosen sides.

After Keoua's retreat, Kamehameha returned to building his temple. When it was complete, a sacrifice of a high chief was required at its dedication in order to appease the war god. Kamehameha invited Keoua to the dedication. Keoua accepted the invitation, knowing his fate. When he arrived he was killed and sacrificed to Ku at the heiau's altar. Kamehameha had risen to the throne of the Big Island.

KAMEHAMEHA'S RISE TO POWER IS COMPLETE   Though Kamehameha's island power base was larger than that of any other king, he was still determined to unite all of the islands under one kingdom and made his next move to take Molokai and Maui. The battles were easily won, and the two islands were swiftly added to his kingdom. Kamehameha then turned his attention to Oahu and Kahekili's son Kalanikupule.

Landing at Waikiki, Kamehameha's army was met by defending Oahuans who fought hard, but their efforts were to no avail. Kamehameha's army was strong and drove the Oahuans to the edge of Nuuanu Pali, a great cliff, from which they were

The Sacred Wife: Chiefess Keopuolani (1778–1823)

The history of Chiefess Keopuolani, known as the "sacred" wife, is an interesting one. Keopuolani's ancestry can be traced through the genealogies of the ali'i, which go all the way back to the god and goddess Wakea and Papa.

Keopuolani was born of what Hawaiians believed to be the most sacred union possible—her mother (Queen Kalola of Maui) and father (King Kalaniopu'u of Hawaii) were brother and sister. Ancient Hawaiians thought that the union of brother and sister would intensify the ali'i bloodline. From birth, the two were closely guarded in an effort to maintain their virginity until their parents decided they were prepared to participate in the Ho Au ceremony, during which they were to conceive a child together.

On a sacred evening, King Kalaniopu'u and Queen Kalola were taken to the heiau (temple) where they remained through the night under a white kapa tent. All night the villagers stood outside the tent, under the direction of the kahunas, chanting the *mo'okua'auhau*, or genealogical succession, of the king and queen. In the morning, when the couple emerged, the king was free to go, but the queen was held under watch (to ensure the purity of the child) until the child was born. When the queen went into labor, the whole town gathered again and chanted and prayed until Keopuolani was born. King Kamehameha married Keopuolani specifically for her ali'i status. If she bore him sons, they would be guaranteed to succeed him on the throne because of their sacred status. The wise Kamehameha knew that if he were to have children with non-ali'i women (which he also did), it would not stop others from trying to usurp the throne.

Keopuolani died in 1823 and was given a Christian burial.

forced by the stronger army to jump or flee for their lives. Their chief Kalanikupule headed for the hills, but it wasn't long before he was captured, killed, and laid at Ku's altar.

After conquering Oahu, Kamehameha had only one island left to add to his kingdom—Kauai. But Kamehameha's attention was turned homeward, to the Big Island, where he was forced to return to put down a revolt.

While he was on the Big Island, Kamehameha decided to set up an interisland system of government. He realized that he needed to install loyal followers in positions of power on the other islands. The system he developed shows that he was not only a fierce warrior but also a brilliant administrative leader. He made every effort to maintain the values and customs of Old Hawaii by continuing to worship the old gods (the Europeans were already trying to convert the Hawaiians to Christianity), but he also instituted systems and policies that would revolutionize this new kingdom. All the high chiefs, even the ones who had given Kamehameha problems in the past, were appointed members of the royal court. He began a system of taxation, gathered around him a group of skilled trades- and craftspeople, and appointed a governor for each of his islands.

With his power consolidated and strengthened, Kamehameha focused on defeating Kaumuali'i, the ruler of Kauai. In 1820, with a new fleet of canoes (800 of them), a handful of newly constructed schooners, and an enormous stockpile of Western arms, Kamehameha set out to conquer Kauai, stopping first at Lahaina on Maui and then on Oahu. Unfortunately, a deadly smallpox epidemic had begun on Oahu, and by mid-1804 Kamehameha's army was devastated by the disease. The king was spared and remained on Oahu for a few more years before he decided not to fight Kaumuali'i. Instead, he asked only that the king of Kauai recognize Kamehameha as the most powerful force in the islands. It took until 1810, but finally, after much gift giving, negotiating, and the diplomatic intervention of the American Nathan Winship, Kaumuali'i relented; without further bloodshed, Kamehameha's kingdom was complete.

Almost from the moment Kamehameha united the islands of Hawaii he called for peace. There would be no more war under his rule, and the islands were to be safe for all Hawaiians. Kamehameha then moved his residence to Lahaina. He inspired his subjects with examples of hard labor, and he exercised tight control over the admittance of foreign merchants to the islands. In order to build the royal lineage, Kamehameha had taken several wives who managed to produce two sons (Liholiho and Kauikeaouli) and a daughter (Nahi'ena'ena).

By the early 19th century, all seemed well in the Hawaiian Islands. Trade was excellent, and the king was building large storehouses of money as well as goods; his heirs were strong young men; and peace reigned throughout the islands. It appeared as though Old Hawaii was approaching its golden age; however, it was to be short lived.

QUEEN KA'AHUMANU   It is believed that King Kamehameha built the royal palace at Lahaina for his favorite wife (the third of 21), Ka'ahumanu, whose father, Ke'eaumoku, had been appointed by the king to the position of governor of Maui. Born in a cave just outside Hana in 1768, Ka'ahumanu was extraordinarily beautiful by Hawaiian standards (she was very large, which is admired in Hawaiian culture) and also extremely intelligent and charismatic. Kamehameha had such faith in Ka'ahumanu's capabilities as a ruling force that when he died in 1819 (in spite of the fact that his son, Liholiho, was his successor) he granted Ka'ahumanu the title *kuhina nui* (queen regent), which gave her virtually unlimited power as a ruler of the Hawaiian Islands.

THE END OF KAPU AND THE LIBERATION OF WOMEN   At the time Liholiho ascended to the throne, some old traditions were quickly becoming outdated. The women of Hawaii had to live under certain kapu, including the one that forbade women to eat certain foods (like bananas, coconut, pork, and baked dog) and forbade them to eat in the presence of men. Other kapu forbade women from fishing in salt water and from touching (or even approaching) fishing nets. Ka'ahumanu, the woman who unapologetically donned her late husband's feather cloak and carried his spear, believed the kapu to be disgraceful and demeaning to all women, so she conspired with Liholiho's mother, Keopuolani, to abolish them. When the two most powerful women in the land joined forces, they were a power to be reckoned with.

Since Liholiho was technically the king, he had to give final approval for the abolition of the kapu. Punishment for breaking kapu was, with no exceptions, death, but the women knew that Liholiho would be unwilling to put his own mother and his father's favorite queen to death, so they felt secure in testing him. Ka'ahumanu defied tradition first by peeling and eating a banana right in front of her stepson. By the laws of kapu, he should have had her immediately executed, but legend has it that he simply ignored her, pretending that he didn't notice. Next, his mother, Keopuolani, asked him to dine with her. He refused her invitation. But the queen and Keopuolani were not discouraged by his responses—he had made it clear that he was not prepared to follow the laws of kapu if it meant that he would have to put his mother and stepmother to death. They continued eating forbidden foods in front of him, weakening him with every bite. Finally, at a banquet, all three sat down together and participated in the first *ai noa* (free eating). This was a giant step for the liberation of Hawaiian women, but the moment free eating began, the entire traditional religious structure of the islands began to fall. Not long after ai noa and the public breaking of kapu, Ka'ahumanu set forth a decree calling for the complete destruction of all temples and religious idols, making way for Western religions.

THE WHALING INDUSTRY & THE MISSIONARIES   The first whaling ships arrived in the islands in 1819, and by 1824, the year of Liholiho's death, more than 100 ships were making Hawaii a primary port of call. For the whaling men the islands were a great place to spend the winter. Of the two main whaling ports, Honolulu and Lahaina, Lahaina attracted almost three times as many ships as Honolulu. The bay at what is today's Lahaina Wharf was a natural landing spot, and captains could easily steer their ships to shore.

At Lahaina, fresh produce (bananas, melons, pumpkins, squash, and potatoes) and meat (goat, beef, turkey) were plentiful, as were women and grog shops. At anchorage, the harbormaster boarded ships and collected $10 in exchange for five barrels of Irish potatoes and "the privilege of purchasing at pleasure in the market for supplies . . . according to the rules of the place." A list of rules was also presented at that time. American sailors preferred Lahaina to Honolulu because that was where they could get Irish potatoes (grown primarily in Kula; in Honolulu, only sweet potatoes were available), and because fresh water was more plentiful.

Once ashore, the seamen had easy access to alcohol and entertainment. Life in Lahaina in the early to mid-19th century was licentious; when the missionaries arrived on Maui in 1823 there were clashes between the rowdy seamen and the puritanical New Englanders. Missionaries and government officials constantly clashed with the whaling men over what constituted "rest and relaxation." In 1825 a law was passed prohibiting women from visiting the ships. Since the time of Captain Cook's arrival in the 18th century, Hawaiian women had been offering themselves to foreign sailors; consequently, venereal disease was spreading rapidly throughout the islands. The passage of the 1825 law prompted Lahaina's first major riot. Enraged, the crew of the British whaling vessel *Daniel* prowled and rioted in the streets of Lahaina for three days. Twice they visited the home of the Reverend Richards, founder of Lahaina's first mission, and threatened his life and his home and family because they believed that he was responsible for the prohibition.

In addition to prostitution, alcohol was also the subject of dispute between the seamen and the missionaries. So, a law prohibiting the sale of alcohol was passed. The rowdy grog shops were forced to close their doors, and it wasn't until 1843 that liquor licenses were reissued.

When the missionaries first arrived on the islands, Queen Ka'ahumanu wasn't interested in adopting their religious beliefs; however, as time passed, she saw an increased need for religious direction among Hawaiians. With the abolition of kapu there were virtually no laws on the islands. Licentiousness reigned, and when Queen Ka'ahumanu came to the realization that outside forces, particularly the whaling men and their tastes for alcohol, were wreaking havoc upon her land, she determined to establish new laws. She collaborated with one of the island clergymen to frame laws based on the Ten Commandments. She outlawed murder, theft, public brawling, sex outside of marriage, and the desecration of the Sabbath. These laws became known as the *Lua-ehu* laws.

While the Lua-ehu laws helped to stem some of the violence that was occurring throughout the islands, Christianity, the driving force behind them, was a source of great angst for the Hawaiian people, especially the children who grew up torn between the new religion and ancient Hawaiian traditions. Two of the most prominent victims of these bipolar ways of life were the young King Kamehameha III (Kauikeaouli) and his sister, Princess Nahi'ena'ena. Following Hawaiian tradition, the ali'i marriage of this brother and sister was arranged at birth, and they were expected to conceive a child together. Christianity forced them to question their intended lifestyle. Kamehameha III became a hopeless alcoholic, and Princess Nahi'ena'ena was torn by internal conflict, alternating between her life of dancing, singing, and drinking, and her struggle to examine her soul.

Queen Ka'ahumanu died in 1832 (after having been baptized a Christian), leaving the throne to the 18-year-old King Kauikeaouli. Initially Kauikeaouli announced that he alone would assume power over the government and would become the primary lawmaker of the land. However, in reality, he was not interested in assuming his responsibilities and appointed his other half-sister, Kinau, *kuhina-nui* (or premier) of the land. Over the next year, Christian chiefs made a great effort to impose morality on their people, but to no avail. The Hawaiian people were still following the example of their king, who persisted in his drunken revelry.

By 1834, Princess Nahi'ena'ena could no longer resist her desire to be with her brother, and so she returned to his side in Honolulu. He begged her to take him back to Maui with her, but she refused out of fear that the missionaries would scold them; desperate, Kauikeaouli tried to kill himself. Later, the two were reunited and news of their union was formally announced. But in 1835, Nahi'ena'ena left her brother again, this time to marry Chief Leleiohoku in a ceremony performed by Reverend Richards in Lahaina. The next year, Kauikeaouli joined her in Lahaina, and Nahi'ena'ena again strayed from the ways of the church. The princess and her brother did have a child together, but he died only a few hours after birth. Nahi'ena'ena's physical condition deteriorated after the difficult birth of her son, and in December 1836, she died.

The people of Hawaii were devastated not only by the loss of their princess but because all hope of carrying on the line of ruling chiefs was lost. Christianity would prevail. Kauikeaouli stayed on Maui for eight years, proclaimed his sister's death a public holiday, and saluted her with government cannons every year. Her death affected him so greatly that he even sobered up and became one of the greatest rulers in the history of the Hawaiian Islands. He remained in power until his death in 1854.

OUT OF CHAOS COMES EDUCATION With drunken kings, brawling whaling men, prostitution, and a new religion, one might think that Hawaii, and more specifically Lahaina, was falling completely into a state of disrepair. For the most part, this was true; however, in 1823, when the kingdom's first laws against theft, brawling, murder, and sex outside marriage were being enacted, another important law was written. It decreed that anyone under the age of 26 who wanted to marry had to be able to read and write. With the enactment of that law came the opening of the first school. Queen Keopuolani was the first pupil on Monday, June 2, 1823. She wanted to learn the *palapala* (writing) and is reported to have been an excellent student who never tired of her studies.

The very next year in Lahaina, Queen Ka'ahumanu called for the establishment of schools throughout the islands so that all Hawaiians would be able to learn the palapala. Most of the original Hawaiian schools, whose pupils were restricted to the ali'i, held classes in grass huts. Seven years later the "first high school west of the Rocky Mountains," Lahainaluna School, opened in Lahaina. In 1834 the first printing house (Hale Pa'i) in the islands was built by the same missionaries who helped to build the Lahainaluna School. On February 14, 1834, the "first newspaper west of the Rockies," *Kalama Hawaii* ("Torch of Hawaii"), began publication. Today the Lahainaluna School is still operating, and you can visit the Hale Pa'i.

Eight years later schools for native children of all classes opened their doors. In Lahaina on October 10, 1840, King Kamehameha III signed the very first written Hawaiian Constitution; aside from outlining religious and political development, it included previously defined laws regarding Hawaiian education.

THE FALL OF WHALING & THE RISE OF SUGAR   In 1846 the whaling industry reached its peak. More than 600 whaling vessels arrived in Hawaiian ports, two-thirds of them dropping anchor off Maui. Between 1845 and 1860, whaling remained profitable, both for the sailors and for the people of Hawaii, but in the late 1850s, with the discovery of oil, the industry's decline was inevitable. Lahaina's economy suffered, and the town ceased to be a bustling center of activity. Honolulu became the capital city of the island chain.

With the whaling industry in decline, Hawaiians were forced to look for other economic opportunities. What they discovered had been there all along—sugar. The Polynesians introduced sugarcane to the islands when they first began settling Hawaii, and since then it had been growing wild on the islands. Hawaii's first sugar plantation was started in Hana in 1849, by a whaler named George Wilfong. He planted about 60 acres of sugarcane and set up a crude sugar refinery. He used whale blubber to heat sugarcane juice until high-quality sugar crystals formed.

Prior to speculation in sugar, Hawaiian land was being sold off systematically by Kamehameha III. Unfortunately, the Hawaiians did not understand the concept of owning parcels of land. They believed that the land belonged to the gods or Mother Earth and could not be possessed. They lived off the land and took from it only what they needed. As a consequence, most of the land being sold was bought up by foreigners, and the Hawaiians were finding themselves without homes and without work. Their only alternative was to work for the men who purchased the land. Those who did work on the sugar plantations were nothing more than indentured servants.

In 1850, the Masters and Servants Act allowed the plantation owners to import cheap labor under contract from abroad to work their lands. Soon thereafter, the Chinese were among the first to be "imported," followed by the Japanese. Working conditions were so horrendous that few survived the hardships of plantation life, and battles for workers' rights ensued. Eventually, plantation workers were able to secure privileges which, among other things, included access to better living conditions.

In 1846, six of the eleven Hawaiian sugar mills were located on Maui. In 1853 steam power was introduced to Maui, which reduced the need for water and animal power. The next year, Captain Edwards arrived at Lahaina anchorage with a hardier variety of sugarcane, which became known as "lahaina cane." For $14,000 Captain James Makee and C. Brewer II purchased Maui's Hailiimaile plantation, and in 1862, C. Brewer and Company (along with one Mr. Edward Bailey) organized the Wailuku Sugar Company, also on Maui. The 1860s marked a distinct period of growth in the number of sugar plantations on Maui.

Demand for Hawaiian sugar increased during the California Gold Rush, but it soared during the Civil War, since sugar production in the Southern states fell. Since the United States provided the market, and most plantations were owned by Americans, it became clear that it was in the best interest of the United States and Hawaii for the U.S. government to allow tariff-free sugar imports to the United States. In 1875, the Reciprocity Act exempted sugar from import duties so long as the United States had, among other things, access to Pearl Harbor.

CLAUS SPRECKELS   Just as the Reciprocity Act of 1875 was being enacted, an enterprising young Californian was arriving in the islands aboard the steamer, *City of San Francisco*. His name was Claus Spreckels. During his visit to Hawaii, he became interested in purchasing land on Maui. He took time to learn about the sugar business from Henry Baldwin and Sam T. Alexander, who were in the process of setting up their own sugar refinery and were puzzling over an irrigation ditch at the time of Spreckels's visit. The brothers-in-law are credited with having pulled off what was probably the single most difficult undertaking in the Hawaiian sugar industry—the building of the Hamakua Ditch. The men wanted to divert water across the 300-foot-deep, 800-foot-wide Maliko Gulch with 1,100 feet of pipe. The project was arduous, and the men encountered several stumbling blocks along the way, including the fact that workers refused to work under such hazardous conditions. Henry Baldwin had lost one of his arms in an unfortunate accident in the sugar mill. Legend has it that the one-armed Baldwin went so far as to lower himself into the 300-foot-deep Maliko Gulch just to prove to his workers that it could be done.

While on Maui in 1876, Spreckels purchased part of the Waihee Plantation, and after seeing what Alexander and Baldwin had gone through to bring water to their cane fields, was concerned about securing water rights to irrigate his own land. He left Maui to puzzle over his purchase and returned two years later with his engineer, Hermann Schussler, who would help him begin the project. On that visit he also became friendly with King Kalakaua, and through him was able to purchase approximately 40,000 acres of land plus the water rights for the north side of Haleakala. With Schussler's help, Spreckels built a 30-mile ditch made up of thousands of feet of pipe and almost 30 tunnels that would carry approximately 60 million gallons of water a day. In spite of the incredible amount of water carried to Spreckels's Hawaiian Commercial and Sugar Company, he found that he needed more; at an annual cost of $10,000, he rented part of the water supply controlled by another of Maui's sugar companies.

Many resented the way Spreckels made his fortune in the islands. He took advantage of his knowledge of the Reciprocity Act and bought large tracts of land for sugar farming before anyone else knew about it, and he paid off Hawaiian royalty to reduce the "red tape." However, the positive contributions he made far outweighed the negatives, especially for the island of Maui, its economy, and its people. By the 1880s Spreckels had invested more than $4 million in the Hawaiian economy. Kahului became the economic center of the island, since it served as the port for his steamships as they carried sugar and other products to and from the mainland. He also introduced "controlled irrigation," use of the steam plow, and utilization of trains to haul the fruits of his labor. With the construction of Spreckelsville and the 30-mile ditch to carry water for the sugarcane, Spreckels also shifted the focus of Maui's economy from Lahaina to Upcountry towns.

The sugar industry proved quite profitable for Spreckels, but in 1898 (at the age of 70), he lost control of his sugar plantation when he was bought out by the famed Alexander and Baldwin, who became incorporated in 1900. Since then, Alexander & Baldwin, Inc., expanded, adding to its holdings—among other things—more land, mills, and a shipping company. The interests of Alexander & Baldwin are worldwide, and by the late 1970s, the company owned almost 100,000 acres, most of which were on Maui.

THE DECLINE OF THE HAWAIIAN POPULATION & A REVO-
LUTION   During the sugar boom, Chinese and Japanese were arriving by the boat-load, as were Portuguese, Filipinos, Koreans, Puerto Ricans, and Germans— all looking for work in the Hawaiian paradise. They brought their religions, cultures, and languages with them, creating an international melting pot. They also brought a variety of diseases to which Hawaiians had no natural resistance; consequently, there was a precipitous decline in the native population. In 1876 89% of the population was either all or part Hawaiian; by 1900 the percentage had fallen to 26%. The initial decline in the native population that occurred during the early years of the sugar industry is actually one reason why sugar plantation operators looked abroad for their labor force.

The Kamehameha monarchy survived during the early days of the sugar industry. In 1872, however, Lot Kamehameha (Kamehameha V) died, leaving no successor. In 1873, William Lunalilo was elected by popular vote, but he died childless a year later. David Kalakaua (who was responsible for negotiating the agreement that led to the Reciprocity Act) took his place. After Kalakaua's death in 1891, his sister, Lydia Liliuokalani, ascended the throne. She is remembered as the last Hawaiian monarch.

When the 52-year-old Queen Lilioukalani took office, the native population was at an all-time low. The Constitution of 1887, instituted under King Kalakaua, had given Hawaiians and foreigners alike the right to vote if they met certain property and income restrictions. With the influx of American businessmen and plantation owners, and the declining native population, it became obvious that Americans had more control over Hawaii than did its native citizens. Lilioukalani sought to rectify the situation by assuming more political power. At the same time, the McKinley Act went into effect, allowing raw sugar from foreign countries to enter the United States duty-free, effectively reversing the provisions of the 1875 Reciprocity Act and devastating the Hawaiian sugar industry. Queen Lilioukalani did not intervene on behalf of the plantation owners, thereby alienating them. A small group of about 30 men, headed by Honolulu publishing giant Lorrin Thurston, set out to overthrow the queen. The queen had little military support on her side, but the revolution aries had the full backing of the U.S. government (which wanted to annex the islands); therefore, Queen Lilioukalani was easily ousted. January 17, 1893 marked the end of the Hawaiian monarchy and the beginning of American control.

Lilioukalani surrendered to John Stevens, the American ambassador, hoping that the U.S. government would be sympathetic to her predicament and would help to reinstate her as monarch. Unknown to her, the United States actually supported the coup, and when she attempted to orchestrate a counterattack against her enemies in 1895, she was again defeated. Humiliated, Lilioukalani was held prisoner under house arrest and was forced to sign an agreement stating that she would never again attempt to gain control of the Hawaiian throne. She was also required to pledge allegiance to the new republic. Later she was obliged to stand trial in front of a military commission that sentenced her to five years of hard labor and fined her $5,000 for plotting to establish a new cabinet during the counterrevolution.

Although most native Hawaiians remained loyal to the monarchy, they were powerless against the new republic, primarily because they did not meet the income and property requirements necessary to vote. Annexation was inevitable, despite opposition from the Japanese; on July 17, 1898, the annexation agreement was signed by President McKinley.

Lilioukalani remained in Hawaii until her death in 1917. During her time in seclusion she wrote *Hawaii's Story* and the famous, familiar hula song, "Aloha O'e."

EARLY 20TH-CENTURY HAWAII For a long time, Maui remained the sleepy island it had been prior to the overthrow of Queen Lilioukalani, but early in the 20th century, increasing Western influence became evident. Throughout the islands Hawaiian culture was almost completely eradicated. The native religion and traditions were gone, and the Hawaiian language, which had previously served as the historical record for Hawaiians, had virtually disappeared while the number of missionary-educated Hawaiians increased. Also, the number of interracial marriages was increasing.

Foreign military leaders began to develop more than a passing interest in the Hawaiian Islands. The United States, in particular, recognized their strategic importance and proceeded to install troops at Camp McKinley on Oahu. Two years later another base, the Schofield Barracks (named in honor of General Schofield—the first to survey Pearl Harbor in 1872), was established, and Pearl Harbor was officially opened in 1911.

WAR AND STATEHOOD Except for shortages of commodities, World War I had little effect on the Hawaiian Islands. The dramatic bombing of Pearl Harbor on December 7, 1941, however, brought Hawaii and the United States into World War II.

Mauians were stunned by the Japanese attack on Pearl Harbor, and they immediately set about protecting their beaches with whatever military equipment they had. Islanders awaited the expected Japanese invasion, but it never happened. Kahului Harbor was bombed by a submarine, and one ship was sunk off Maui's coastline; otherwise, Maui saw very little military action. A military outpost, known as Camp Maui, was established at Kokomo, and for several years it served as a training ground and recreational center for the Fourth Marine Division. Some native Mauians also served in World War II. Commanded by Americans of Japanese ancestry known as *Nisei*, Hawaiian military units won a total of 18,143 decorations during World War II—the most decorated battalion of all.

World War II served to solidify Hawaii's alignment with the United States. In fact, after the war, most Hawaiians (especially the Japanese) considered themselves to be Americans. From the time Lilioukalani was removed from the throne, American government officials had been talking about making Hawaii the nation's 50th state; but it wasn't until March 12, 1959, that Congress passed the Hawaii State Bill.

MAUI: POSTSTATEHOOD DEVELOPMENT After Hawaii was admitted to the Union as America's 50th state, the islands remained relatively quiet for a period of time. The violence of the Korean and Vietnam Wars had little effect on the Hawaiian way of life. However, Maui did see its share of hippies (known as *das hipas*, or "lost sheep," to Hawaiians) who migrated there en masse. They settled in the Upcountry towns of Paia and Haiku, opening craft shops and health-food stores. Today, Paia still reflects the hippie influence with offbeat shops and health-food restaurants. Artists were drawn to the island because of its next-to-perfect climate, its brilliant colors, and its clarity of light.

It wasn't long before a wealthier class of people discovered Maui and began visiting the island and building vacation homes. The price of real estate soared, and it soon became clear that Maui's economic future would depend on developing tourism. A company known as Amfac (American Factors) owned land in Kaanapali , just 4 miles west of Lahaina, and they quickly realized the economic potential of their near-perfect, beachfront location. They built one of the most successful resort properties on the island. Restoration of the town of Lahaina was also beginning, and with it came a colony of artists who showed their work every Saturday under the banyan tree in the center of town. The Lahaina that had become a virtual ghost town after the whaling fleet abandoned its shores once again became a bustling center of activity.

Though the tourist industry was rapidly developing, much of Maui remained pristine and untouched as late as 1970. But, alas, it wasn't long before private developers began constructing high-rise condominiums along the shore from Maalaea to Kihei. Farther inland, along the Kihei hills, wealthy Americans began building million-dollar homes, and the once unsupportive scrubland was transformed as homeowners cultivated a tropical landscape. Because tracts of land in the Kihei area were independently owned, there was no general plan for the types of businesses and restaurants that would open their doors to island visitors. Thus, many fast-food restaurants and shopping centers were built. The whole of Wailea (the area from Kihei to Makena), on the other hand, was owned by Alexander & Baldwin and the Matson Navigation Company. Its 1,500 acres of lava fields, dotted with kiawe, and laced with yet another coastline of white-sand beaches, were another perfect location for the development of a full-service resort. Architects planned and designed the Wailea landscape with a new understanding of the necessity of preserving the area's historic sites. They unearthed the remains of an old Hawaiian village, a heiau, and the foundations of a chief's house, all of which were restored and can be visited today.

On Maui's west side, beyond Kaanapali, was a parcel of land that since 1911 had been used by the Maui Pineapple Company (started by Henry P. Baldwin) as a pineapple plantation. Under the direction of company president Colin Cameron, the company's name was changed to Maui Land & Pineapple Company, and development of another major resort, Kapalua, began. By the late 1970s, the Kapalua resort began selling its yet-unbuilt condominiums for more than $100,000. (Much of the Kapalua resort area is still a working pineapple plantation.)

Today, although sugarcane and pineapple are still grown on Maui, and smaller interests are devoted to raising cattle and diversified agriculture, the island's major economic interest is tourism.

4 Art & Architecture

ART

Art has always been integral to Hawaiian life. The art of early Hawaii often took forms that were useful in everyday life. Kapa cloth was used as bedding and clothing. Beautiful featherwork capes, cloaks, helmets, and leis were worn by the Hawaiian ali'i to indicate rank; and beautifully carved wooden bowls were designed specifically to hold poi, a staple of daily Hawaiian life. Ancient Hawaiians took great pride in their work and elevated its execution to an art form. Unfortunately, some of the traditional arts and crafts of Hawaii have died out, due in part to the commercialization of the islands and in part to the diminished natural supply of craft materials.

Today, native Hawaiian art is highly prized, and efforts are being made to revitalize traditional arts and crafts. Most hotels on Maui sponsor lei-making classes, and some even hold quilt-making lectures and demonstrations. Arts and crafts shows are held every year to celebrate local artisans.

The following is a description of various traditional Hawaiian arts and crafts, which will, I hope, lead you to a greater understanding and appreciation of Hawaiian culture.

KAPA (TAPA) CLOTH   Before woven fabrics made their way from Europe and the U.S. mainland to Hawaii, Hawaiian women made cloth from the bark of various trees and plants. The kapa-making process was long and somewhat tedious, but yet so much a part of daily life that many households maintained a separate hut specifically for that purpose. Each day, village men would go out searching for wauke, mamake, ma'aloa, or poulu plants, whose branches they would cut and take back to their wives. The women would peel the bark from the branches (not in strips, but whole), and then set the inner bark in a stream to soak until it reached the desired softness. After the bark had soaked long enough, the women would beat it on a log *(kua)* with a round club *(hohoa)* until it was flat and paper-thin. The soaking and flattening process might take up to four days. The last step was to set the kapa in the sun to dry. Mamake bark was preferred above all others because its cloth was the most durable; mamake, however, was not soaked first, but rather steamed in an oven with a *pala'a* (a fern that gave out a dark red dye in the cooking process). After the steaming process was finished, mamake would be soaked and beaten just like the other types of bark.

Most Hawaiian women dyed their kapa using the color of a variety of different plants. The mao plant would stain the cloth green, while the hoolei gave it a yellow tint. It was also customary for women to print patterns on the cloth. Almost every design was different and as individual as the artists who created them.

So old is the art of making kapa that it is even mentioned in the mythology of the demigod Maui. It is said that his mother complained that the sun moved too quickly across the sky and her kapa didn't have enough time to dry in the afternoon. Maui, sensitive to the needs of his mother, snared the sun by lassoing his legs (all 16 of them) and threatened to hold him there forever if he didn't slow his pace through the sky. The sun, like the rest of us, enjoyed a good night's sleep, so he agreed to slow down.

HAWAIIAN QUILTS   Not so ancient as the art of kapa, but equally as beautiful, quilting has been practiced in Hawaii since the mid-19th century. In fact, Hawaii's first quilting bee took place on April 3, 1820. Basic quilting techniques were introduced to Hawaiian women by missionary women from New England; however, the appliqués and stitch patterns you'll see on original Hawaiian quilts are authentically Hawaiian. Early quilt patterns were similar to designs found on kapa cloth, and quite often women were inspired to create original designs by dreams or major events in their lives.

Usually the quilt consisted of a single-colored appliqué on a white background. The material to be used for the appliqué could be cut freehand, or with a paper pattern. Interestingly, the "paper" pattern was often made of kapa. Usually the appliqué material would be folded four or eight times before it was cut so the pattern would be uniform in all sections of the quilt. Typically, the designs were inspired by the leaves of various trees and plants, such as the fig or breadfruit trees and ferns. Outlines of pineapples, the octopus, and the sea turtle were also popular design elements.

Many of the patterns were unique to a particular artist, and most of the women knew the designs of their fellow quilters. If a woman created a particular design, it would forever be associated with her. Other women were not allowed to copy her design without crediting her. However, if a pattern was not carefully guarded before a quilt was completed, it could be (and often was) stolen by someone else who might try to claim it as her own.

While the patterns and design elements of the appliqué were important, so were the stitches around the appliqué, because the stitching is actually what makes a quilt a quilt. Traditional New England–style stitch patterns used parallel lines and diagonals; Hawaiian women incorporated these patterns into their early work, but later they began inventing their own freehand stitch patterns which are much more elaborate and, in many ways, more beautiful than what we recognize as traditional stitching. This technique is referred to as "quilting following the pattern." The stitches flowed in free-form lines around the appliqué, in most cases following the pattern of the appliqué, but I've seen quilts with free-form stitching around the appliqué, and cross-hatching superimposed on the appliqué. You can view antique quilts of the type described above at some of the island's hotels.

FEATHERWORK   Unfortunately, little is known about the origins of Hawaiian featherwork because over the years its history has been lost. But David Malo wrote that "the feathers of birds were the most valued possessions of the ancient Hawaiians," and around 1778 Captain Cook and members of his crew marveled at Hawaiian featherwork in their writings. Some of the ali'i of Kauai who greeted Cook and his shipmates went aboard the ship wearing feather cloaks, leis, and helmets and presented Cook with half a dozen feather cloaks. He was awed by the brilliant colors and the intricacy of the work.

Because feathers were so sacred, a guild of professional bird catchers was established on the islands. They caught the birds by enticing them onto a branch or stick covered with a sticky substance, trapping them, or throwing stones at them until they fell to the ground. The most valued feathers were yellow, particularly those found under the tail and wings of the mamo. Red feathers, especially those of the i'iwi, were next in order of desirability, and black feathers were considered the least valuable. Today many of the birds with the most prized plumage have become extinct.

LEI HULU   Hawaiian women wore adornments known as *lei hulu* on their heads and around their necks. They were constructed in several ways: Some were completely cylindrical (or *pauku*), such as the more common flower leis you'll see today. Some pauku might have been made from the light yellow feathers of the o'o, while others were made of green, red, black, and yellow feathers (some in a spiral pattern, others in blocks of color). Another style of lei was known as *kamoe*. Here the feathers were laid flat and attached directly to the lei backing. Leis made entirely of yellow feathers were the most highly prized; next came leis made of any other single color; least valuable were those made of two or more colors. The lei hulu *manu* was worn by women of the ali'i class to distinguish them from Hawaiian commoners, and later, men wore the leis as hatbands.

KAHILI   These plumed staffs of state resembled giant bottle brushes. Everywhere the king went the kahili (and kahili bearer) followed. In the evenings when the king slept, the kahili were used to keep flies from settling on his highness's face. One report insists that rather than flies, the kahili were used to chase off bad *mana* (the Hawaiian equivalent of karma). No Hawaiians except the ali'i could carry kahili. Because of their association with Hawaiian royalty, kahili were made with great care and came in an endless variety of shapes and sizes. The feathers used for kahili usually came from the tails and wings of larger birds, such as the nene, the frigate bird, and even ducks and chickens. The handles were frequently made of tortoiseshell or whalebone, and the staffs might reach 10 to 25 feet in height.

HEADGEAR   *Manihole*, or feathered headgear, were also mentioned in the journals of Captain Cook, who described these ornate head coverings as "caps . . . made so as to fit very close to the head with a semicircular protuberance on the crown exactly like the helmets of old." He also commented that "the Ground-work of the Cap is Basket Work, made in a form to fit the Head, to which the Feathers are secured." Since Hawaiians believed the head was the most important part of the body, they believed feathers had the power to ward off evil; thus, the helmet was as much a physical adornment as a form of protection for the wearer.

There were several different types of manihole, including the crescent-crested, low-crested, wide-crested, hair helmets, and ornamented helmets. No one really knows the significance of each style because these things were never documented, but it is safe to assume that all who wore them had some connection to Hawaiian royalty. Generally the helmets that survive today have lost most of their feathers, and so what you'll see is the "basket work" described by Captain Cook. A few, however, have been well preserved over the years—for example, the helmet of Kaumuali'i, the last king of Kauai, covered with red feathers and trimmed (on the crest) with feathers of an exquisite gold, which can be seen at the Bishop Museum on Oahu.

If you have the good fortune to see a manihole helmet, you'll no doubt be struck by the number of feathers used in its creation. It is unfortunate that there is no written record about the people who created these wonderful head coverings. I, for one, wonder about the people who had the patience to sit for endless hours, painstakingly weaving each feather into the underlying basketwork.

CAPES   Perhaps the most spectacular and beautiful pieces of Hawaiian featherwork are the capes and cloaks once worn by Hawaiian royalty. It is believed that they were worn as a means of identification in battle. Each high chief or king had his own design. From Cook's writings, however, it is clear that these capes were worn on other occasions as well.

Most of the capes (which reached to the feet of the wearer) had a background color of red or yellow; the design elements (such as circles, triangles, or crescent shapes) were typically made of the opposite color (yellow on red or vice versa). Sometimes black feathers would be introduced into the pattern as well. Some people believe that the geometric designs represented gods or birds, but in truth, not much is known about the patterns. Unless you visit the Bishop Museum on Oahu, you probably won't be able to see a feather cape, but many bookstores carry books about Hawaiian featherwork.

LEIS   Of all the ancient Hawaiian art forms, traditional lei-making is the only one that has survived intact throughout the ages and is still being practiced island-wide today. Past and present, each type of lei has its own special significance. Leis are presented at all kinds of comings and goings—births, deaths, weddings, graduations, departures to another land, homecomings—and they encompass the true spirit of aloha. During your trip you'll have no trouble finding flower and ti leaf leis; if you're lucky, you'll come across an even rarer lei to take home and share with your friends.

Perishable Leis   All sorts of perishable leis are being made in the islands today, especially the flower lei. Leis made with fragrant plumeria blossoms are particularly popular with tourists. These flowers grow almost everywhere on the island and are easily strung. My personal favorite flower lei is made with white ginger, which has a light but distinctive fragrance. The white ginger blossoms are typically gathered in the evening when they are about to open, which ensures that they'll last longer; if someone presents you with a white ginger lei, you should be deeply flattered, for it is one of Hawaii's special leis. Gardenia leis are also quite fragrant, but are less common. Experienced Hawaiian lei-makers can construct one with virtually any flower of any shape or size. I've even heard that some people have made leis of the very delicate bougainvillea blossom. The manner in which the flowers are strung depends entirely on the shape and size of the flowers being used.

Leis can also be made of almost any variety of fern. Primitive-looking ti leaf leis can be extraordinarily beautiful because the ti leaf is pliable and easily manipulated. Primitive Hawaiians believed that the ti plant had special healing powers, and the kahuna of ancient Hawaii often used it to ward off evil spirits. If you buy a ti leaf lei to wear home, don't throw it out or hang it up to dry when you get home. Put it in the freezer; it will keep its shape and color until you feel like wearing it again.

Nonperishable Leis   While flower and ti leaf leis are most often purchased by visitors to the islands, there are several types of nonperishable leis that you can take home and keep forever. Some of the most popular are *lei pupu* (shell leis) and *lei hua* (seed leis).

Shell leis can be either simple or extremely intricate. Early Hawaiians gathered shells from the beaches of Kauai and Niihau and either filed them down to make holes for stringing or strung them using the shells' natural holes. The first lei pupu were typically made up of several separate strands, each holding up to 200 shells. Other lei pupu were fashioned out of shells that are flat, like buttons, after having been worn down by the constant wave action of the ocean. Ancient Hawaiians collected the shell fragments that had washed ashore, punched holes in them, and strung them together. Many of today's shell leis are made much as they were in ancient Hawaii. Lei pupu might be sold for a few dollars or a few hundred dollars, depending on the quality and rarity of the shells. If you'd like to purchase a really fine shell lei, try to find one that was made on Kauai.

The most common seed lei is the kukui nut lei. I say common, but even as I write, these leis are becoming rarer. This is largely because the process of polishing the kukui nuts is so difficult and time-consuming that it is simply not cost-effective. The fruit of the candlenut tree, the kukui nut, might be blond, brown, or black. In Old Hawaii, the leis made of black kukui nuts were the most coveted. The nuts would be gathered by lei-makers after they'd fallen from the tree, and then sorted according to shape and size. The difficulty comes in polishing the nuts. In Old Hawaii, all the polishing was done by hand. The outer layer of the shells in their raw form has a cloudy, whitish coating that must be removed. Then the grooves, which give the nut a walnutlike quality, have to be filed down, and finally, the shell is polished to a high shine. Ancient Hawaiians utilized natural files, such as sea urchin spines, and natural sandpaper, such as shark skin. The final polishing was done with a pumice stone. Old-time kukui nut lei-makers had an interesting way of extracting the nutmeat from the shell—they would make a hole in the top and bottom of the nut, and then they would bury it until the nutmeat had been eaten out by insects. Today there are polishing machines available, but most kukui nut lei-makers believe it's best to polish the shells by hand. Kukui leis are moderately expensive, depending on where you buy them, but they are uniquely Hawaiian, and they're quite beautiful.

Currently, other seeds in a variety of shapes and sizes are being used in lei-making, but they're more difficult to find. On my last trip to Maui I also visited Molokai, where I found a rare kukui nut and ekoa seed lei.

WOOD CARVING   For ancient Hawaiians wood carving was a way of life. Primitive wood sculptures have been found all over the islands, and it seems that they were used for religious as well as practical purposes. Many religious figures were sculpted for the dedication of a heiau, or for a religious ceremony, and are thought to have represented particular Hawaiian gods. Ancient Hawaiians also carved food vessels (such as poi bowls), canoes, and furnishings out of wood. Some of the woods used by ancient woodcraftsmen included koa and ohi'a, both of which can be found on Maui today.

Koa wood is especially favored by present-day artists, but due to its extensive use in Hawaiian culture (both past and present), it is becoming increasingly difficult to find. As a result, koa pieces you find in gift shops, from bracelets to bowls, are fairly costly. You'll probably end up buying a koa piece anyway—the wood is so rich and light that you'll have a difficult time passing it by. *A word of advice:* Be wary of carved figurines. Though they might appear to be Hawaiian, chances are they aren't even made in Hawaii.

SCRIMSHAW   This art form deserves mention particularly in regard to the island of Maui because of its history as the whaling capital of the islands. You'll find a number of shops that specialize in scrimshaw on Lahaina's Front Street. The primary sources for scrimshaw ivory used to be whalebone and elephant tusk; however, gathering ivory from those sources is strictly forbidden today, so most of the new scrimshaw is done on walrus tusk, which can be legally hunted by Eskimos. Typically, scrimshaw is used in making jewelry, including earrings, rings, bracelets, belt buckles, and brooches, and the etchings are usually of seascapes, whales, and ships. Prices on fine pieces of scrimshaw might run into thousands of dollars.

ARCHITECTURE

When the Polynesians arrived in Hawaii, they knew how to build shelters with walls and thatched roofs, but it is generally believed that the first Hawaiians, like Papa and Wakea of Hawaiian mythology, lived in caves. The first man-made freestanding structures are thought to have been built of wood and tree bark. It wasn't until much later that the Polynesians introduced their "thatching" architecture to the islands.

Historical accounts tell us that houses of varying sizes and construction materials were built according to class standards. The homes of chiefs, or the ali'i, were large and might consist of a number of buildings, each serving a different purpose in the life of the chief. The homes of commoners (or the *maka'ainana*) were much smaller. Some maka'ainana didn't even have homes and were said to have sponged off their generous friends for shelter during inclement weather. Most of the early Hawaiian homes took the shape of a thatched tent. Some of the thatched gabled roofs were supported by four wood or stone walls, while others had only two or three walls.

Ancient Hawaiians typically slept on woven mats under kapa cloth sheets. Homes were usually lighted by the oil produced from the kukui nut. In order to remove the shells, the nuts were baked until the shells cracked. The oil-laden kernels were strung together on the hard, central rib of a palm leaf, creating a sort of jointed candle. A typical kukui-nut candle was about 12 kernels in length, and each kernel burned for approximately 3 minutes. Since the life of each candle was short, scores of them could be found hanging in Hawaiian homes at any one time. Kukui oil was also used in stone lamps with wicks made of kapa cloth strips.

When the missionaries began settling on the islands, they brought other architectural styles with them. After living in a grass hut in Lahaina for 4 years, Reverend William Richards, a New England missionary, built the first coral-stone house in Hawaii in 1823. Next door to the Richards's home, a man by the name of Ephriam Spaulding built another coral-stone house. It was later occupied by Dr. Dwight Baldwin. Known today as the Baldwin Home, it has been fully restored by the Lahaina Restoration Foundation.

Today you won't find any grass huts on the island, but you'll see just about everything else—from ramshackle ranch-style homes to stately, two-story New England–style buildings.

5 Religion & Folklore

Before the missionaries arrived in the 19th century, the Hawaiians had their own mythology and religion. It grew out of a deep respect for nature—plants and animals that provided food, earth that supplied the materials to build shelters, the sun that gave warmth and light, and rain that quenched their thirst and watered their taro patches. Ancient Hawaiians believed that all human life evolved from animal life, and therefore, everything in nature was sacred. The religion, Huna, taught that everything in the world had a partner, or an opposite—a polarity similar to the principle of yin and yang.

Huna literally means "secret," and the kahuna, or priests, were the "keepers of the secrets." The kahuna were drawn from members of the ruling class (the ali'i) as children. To be chosen as kahuna, the ali'i children had to demonstrate an interest in learning and a high level of intelligence, for they were being trained not only as priests who could recite the mele of ancient Hawaiians, but also as doctors, lawyers, teachers, astronomers/navigators, agriculturalists, artists, and sorcerers. In addition to worshiping the highest gods—Kane, Ku, Lono, Kanaloa, and Hina—the kahuna could transfer mana (a force similar to karma) to a subgroup of gods. Many times, this transference of mana (known as *ho'omanana*) was done on the bones of dead chiefs so their remaining family members and their descendants would be protected.

Ancient Hawaiians believed that when a person died, his or her soul would go to *po* ("place of night") to be eaten by the gods, but they didn't believe this was the end for the human soul. They believed that all human souls would be reincarnated (*hou-ola*, "new life") so that eventually the souls might also become gods.

In Old Hawaii, organized worship generally took place in the heiau (temple), where the kahuna presided over the ceremonies. Most heiaus were constructed with stone foundations (many of which can be seen throughout the islands today), but the actual shelters were built of straw or wood and have long since disappeared. Though human sacrifices were known to have been made at certain temples, most were simply places of idol worship. When Queen Ka'ahumanu abolished the taboo that had previously restricted women (who were considered less well developed than men) from eating certain foods or participating in ceremonies or events, she also ordered the destruction of the heiau and all religious idols, which left the Hawaiian people receptive to the Christian missionaries who were already settling in Hawaii.

Although Christianity all but eradicated the Huna, it filled a spiritual void in the lives of Hawaiians; it also brought education to the islands. Today you'll find churches and temples of all faiths throughout the islands, including a smattering of Buddhist temples and one synagogue (on Oahu).

6 Peoples & Language

Maui's population of 92,000 reflects a multiculturalism found virtually nowhere else in the world. Its people represent a unique ethnic mix of Hawaiian, Filipino, Portuguese, Japanese, Korean, Irish, German, Chinese, and *haole* (Caucasian) people, most of whom immigrated to Hawaii in search of a better life. They brought with them their languages, cuisines, modes of dress, art forms, and cultural entertainments, all of which have impacted Maui's social structure. Cultural influences can be experienced today on Maui simply by taking a walk along the beach, where you might hear a surprising variety of languages. A walk down Front Street will dazzle you with art galleries that hold the works of Asians, Hawaiians, and haoles alike. Island restaurants represent a cross section of cultural tastes and the blending of the spices of East and West.

PEOPLES

HAWAIIANS   The story of the native Hawaiian people is one of disaster. Today, the number of full-blooded Hawaiians is a mere fraction of the 300,000 who were living on the islands when Captain Cook arrived in 1778. The early introduction of venereal diseases by Cook's shipmates proved devastating for the Hawaiians, whose women displayed little or no inhibition when it came to sexual contact with European sailors. By 1820, the Hawaiian population was estimated at less than half of what it was in 1778. The influx of foreign visitors also brought other diseases, both major and minor, against which Hawaiians had no natural resistance; wars between ruling chiefs also contributed to the decline of the Hawaiian population. It is also believed that one-quarter of all Hawaiian men simply shipped out, never to return, as they pursued careers in the whaling industry and found their livelihoods elsewhere. The final blow to the Hawaiian race came, simply, with the increase in interracial marriages. Today, most of those who claim Hawaiian heritage are not full-blooded Hawaiian; in fact, there are probably only about 1,500 people today who are 100% Hawaiian.

CHINESE   It is believed that the first Chinese to arrive on the Hawaiian archipelago came aboard an American ship skippered by Captain John Meares. They were a group of carpenters who built Meares a ship he called the *North West American*. None of the Chinese carpenters remained on the islands after their trip with Meares; however, in 1789 when Captain Simon Metcalfe visited Hawaii, it is believed that several Chinese went ashore with John Young during the Olowalu Massacre. No one is sure if any of them survived.

The first real migration of Chinese to the Hawaiian Islands began in 1852 when the first contract field laborers arrived from Hong Kong. Their passage was paid, and their 5-year contracts granted them a salary of $3 a month plus room and board. They worked long, hard days on the sugar plantations and looked forward to the end of their contracts when they could begin to set themselves up in business, leaving plantation work to the next wave of immigrants. Some of the first interracial marriages in Hawaii were between the Chinese and the native Hawaiians. Today the Chinese population on Maui remains strong, although it comprises only a small percentage of the general population.

JAPANESE   Some historians believe that the Japanese arrived in Hawaii long before Captain Cook dropped anchor; however, the first documented arrivals of Japanese (who intended to stay) took place in 1868. Originally, more than 300 Japanese planned to migrate to Hawaii in search of plantation work, but only about one-third of that group actually left Japan because their government disapproved. Japanese immigration then ceased until 1885, when huge numbers of Japanese workers once more began immigrating to Hawaii. Only 15 years later, the Japanese population in Hawaii was estimated to be just over 60,000. Japanese workers were as industrious as the Chinese, but they found themselves victims of cruel discrimination and were not given the same opportunities as their Chinese and Hawaiian coworkers.

Eventually, in spite of the discrimination, the Japanese were able to advance through the ranks from plantation workers to the status of professionals. The children and grandchildren of the first large group of immigrants were educated in American schools and developed a strong allegiance to the United States—so much so that many of them fought valiantly for the United States in World War II. After the war, these men of Japanese ancestry who emerged as heroes were able to take advantage of the G.I. Bill, which allowed them to pursue a college education. Many of them became doctors, dentists, lawyers, teachers, and businessmen. The first Japanese-American governor of Hawaii, George Ariyoshi, was elected in 1974. Currently, those of Japanese ancestry make up about 25% of Hawaii's total population (23% of Maui's population).

HAOLES   Today the word *haole* refers to any person of Caucasian descent. Basically, to Hawaiians, it really doesn't matter where you're from—if your skin is white, you're a haole.

The haole history of Hawaii goes all the way back to John Young and Isaac Davis, members of Captain Simon Metcalfe's crew who were held as prisoners by King Kamehameha during the Olowalu Massacre in 1790. More significant, though, were the numbers of haole immigrants who came as missionaries from New England. They established themselves permanently on the islands long before the Chinese and Japanese and have since been the most powerful economic force ever to settle in Hawaii, adopting a "colonist" attitude toward the natives, whom they looked down upon and whose customs and cultural activities they considered primitive and, oftentimes, disgusting. Most of the New England missionaries did not mingle with the Hawaiians, and so dilution of pure haole bloodlines among the missionaries was rare.

Another group of haoles living on the islands is the Portuguese. Between 1878 and 1887 approximately 12,000 Portuguese immigrants arrived in Hawaii, and another 6,000 came in the early 1900s. The olive-skinned Portuguese immigrants were welcomed with traditional Hawaiian aloha, mainly because they were dark enough not to be considered haole. Many Portuguese men and women worked on sugar plantations and rose into the top ranks of plantation laborers. They weren't too well educated, which is probably why some Hawaiians constantly crack jokes about the Portuguese. Here again, as with the other ethnic groups, there was some interracial marriage between the Portuguese and the Hawaiians. When members of the white population marry Hawaiians, their offspring are referred to as *hapa-haole*, or "half-white, half-Hawaiian."

Much later, with the development of resort properties, more haoles arrived; this time they came primarily from the U.S. mainland, and they have upheld the haole tradition of taking a controlling interest in Hawaii's economy, sometimes at the expense of Hawaii's native people. Today, haoles make up approximately 33% of Hawaii's general population (they number close to 36% on Maui).

FILIPINOS   American nationals since the Spanish-American War in 1898, Filipinos did not have as much difficulty immigrating to Hawaii as the Chinese or Japanese did, mainly because they were not restricted by the same kinds of immigration laws that stopped many Asians. Hailing from the northern Philippines, 120,000 Filipinos were brought to Hawaii as plantation laborers between 1907 and 1931. Since Japanese workers in Hawaii had gone on strike in 1909, the plantation owners looked elsewhere for workers. They couldn't believe their luck when they discovered that Filipinos would take the lowest-paying jobs and work under conditions that other groups found unacceptable.

Like the Chinese, most of the Filipinos who immigrated to Hawaii were men (between 1924 and 1930 the ratio of Filipino men to Filipino women in Hawaii was approximately 19 to 1) who planned to return to their families and homeland after they had saved some money. By 1950 the Filipino population was about one-eighth of Hawaii's general population. Today the Filipino population is 14% of Hawaii's general population, but the percentage of Filipinos living on Maui is considerably less.

OTHER PEOPLES   The rest of the Hawaiian population is made up of Koreans (who immigrated between 1903 and 1905), Puerto Ricans (who arrived at approximately the same time as the Koreans), African Americans, Vietnamese, and a small but fast-growing group of Samoans.

LANGUAGE

With such a diverse population, it should come as no surprise that Maui is a multi-tongued island. Of course, English is the dominant language spoken here, so you won't have any trouble communicating. Occasionally you'll hear some Chinese, Japanese, Portuguese, and Spanish, but there are two Hawaiian languages that are the key to understanding Hawaii's spirit and culture.

PIDGIN   During the period when migrant plantation workers were coming to the islands from all over the world, all speaking different languages, communication was difficult. Over time they all learned to communicate with each other in a language now known as pidgin. Pidgin is a true reflection of Hawaii's ethnic mix since it is quite literally a combination of several languages. Its base is Hawaiian, but it contains English, Japanese, Filipino, Chinese, and Samoan elements. The Portuguese also made their own unique contribution to pidgin in terms of intonation and musicality.

Some people consider pidgin low-class, nonsensical, and illiterate, and many have even tried to wipe it out, but to no avail. *Brah* (brother), *cockaroach* (steal), *geev um* (sock it to them), *hele on* ("right on" or "hip"), *lesgo* (let's go), and *tita* (short for "sister," but used only with friendly, earthy types) are just a few of the words you might pick up during your trip. Today, pidgin is such a part of daily Hawaiian life that the Hawaiian House of Representatives has declared it one of Hawaii's official languages. If you'd like to learn more, try reading the very funny *Pidgin to Da Max* and *Fax to Da Max* (Bess Press, Honolulu), both of which are humorous "studies" of the language.

HAWAIIAN   The Hawaiian language has its roots in the languages of the Polynesians; however, the Hawaiian spoken today is probably very different from the Hawaiian of old. Over the years, as the oral tradition changed to a written one, translations and transcriptions inadvertently changed the spellings and meanings of certain words and phrases. For a long while, after the introduction of English and pidgin, Hawaiian was a dying language. Fortunately, today it is experiencing a rebirth through courses of study and the Hawaiian people's general interest in their roots.

Two of the most commonly used Hawaiian words are *aloha* ("hello" or "goodbye"; an expression of love) and *mahalo* ("thank you"). I've put together a short list of words and phrases for you in the appendix of this book. If you're interested in learning more, virtually every bookstore stocks a Hawaiian dictionary or two.

7 Outdoor Activities

The outdoor sports enthusiast will not be disappointed on a trip to Maui. A wide array of water sports (usually including lessons from an instructor and any equipment you might need) is available to people at all levels of experience. Perhaps you'd like to head out on a deep-sea fishing expedition, or stay closer to shore while snorkeling near a coral reef. Boating, windsurfing, surfing, and scuba diving are also offered island-wide. If, after a while, you're beginning to feel like one of the sea creatures you've been studying through your snorkel mask, you can also take advantage of your hotel's freshwater pool.

If you start to become waterlogged, there are plenty of activities that will get you out of the water and onto dry land. Tennis facilities abound all over the island, as do golf courses. Every major resort area, such as Kaanapali, Kapalua, and Wailea, have challenging courses of their own, and in most cases the views are spectacular. If golf and tennis aren't your cup of tea, island hiking is unsurpassed. You can head out on your own, or sign up with one of the agencies that put together organized hikes. Biking is also fairly popular. If you get tired of exercising, try one of the downhill biking tours that takes you to the summit of Haleakala and requires only about 40 yards of actual pedaling; or, see the island on horseback.

For more information on the various sports activities offered on Maui, see Chapter 9, "Maui Sports & Recreation."

8 Cuisine

FOOD

Maui's diversity in cuisine reflects its multicultural roots. You'll find everything from local Hawaiian cuisine to the fine Eastern cuisines of Japan and Thailand.

Consult the Appendix of this book for a "Glossary of Island Foods."

LUAUS   You'll no doubt treat yourself to a luau sometime during your visit to Maui, and it might be your only taste of traditional Hawaiian cuisine. No luau is complete without *poi* and *kalua* pig (pig baked in an underground oven called an *imu*), but you'll probably also find chicken luau, *pipikaula*, and *laulau* (see definitions in Appendix) on the main menu. Sweet potatoes and macaroni salad are typical accompaniments. Dessert will probably include *haupia* (coconut pudding) and fresh fruit. For information about choosing a luau, see Chapter 8, "What to See and Do on Maui."

LOCAL FOOD   Not really traditional Hawaiian cuisine, "local food" acquired the name because of its popularity with the locals. It's basically of the plate-lunch variety, consisting of deep-fried foods; teriyaki beef, chicken, or pork; and a side dish of the ever-present macaroni salad.

HAWAIIAN REGIONAL CUISINE   In a word: spectacular. You simply can't visit Maui without sampling the island's best cuisine. A delightful combination of local produce and fish plus Eastern and Western spices, Hawaiian regional cuisine is also known as Pacific Rim cuisine. You'll find it prepared in the island's best restaurants, including the Plantation House Restaurant, Avalon Restaurant & Bar, and Roy's Kahana Bar & Grill, to name a few.

ASIAN CUISINES   Japanese restaurants can be found all over the island, and most have excellent sushi bars. You'll also find a scattering of Thai and Chinese restaurants. Noodle shops are also popular among the locals.

DRINK

Soft drinks in Hawaii are much the same as those you'll find on the mainland; however, there are also some unusual juices, including orange/guava/passion fruit juice, which is absolutely delicious.

Tropical fruit drinks are the most popular alcoholic beverages for island visitors— try a mai tai or a lava flow. Another interesting drink is Maui blanc; it's a pineapple wine that is made at the island's Tedeschi Vineyards. Early versions of the wine were almost sickeningly sweet, but recent years have seen a surprisingly light wine that leaves only a slight pineapple taste on your palate afterward. Hawaiians also make an interesting passion-fruit wine and a couple of champagnes—a blush and a red. Give them all a try, and as they say in Hawaiian, *okole maluna* (oh-ko-lay mah-loo-nah), or "Bottoms up!" (For more information on Tedeschi Vineyards, see Chapter 8, "What to See & Do on Maui.")

9 Dance

If you know anything about Hawaii, you know that the *hula* is the dance of the Hawaiian people. No other people in the world perform this unique dance, which is as beautiful to watch as it is difficult to perform.

Earliest accounts of Hawaiian dancing reported that two forms were practiced in the islands. The *ha'a* was performed only in the heiau (temple), and the hula was performed as a public entertainment. As a sacred dance, the ha'a was performed only by men and taught, choreographed, and directed by the kahuna. The audience was primarily Hawaiian royalty or high-ranking chiefs. The ha'a often had religious overtones (it was frequently performed in conjunction with certain religious ceremonies, rituals, and chants) and was often shadowed in secrecy. The dances are also reported to have been extremely masculine and sexual. Men who wanted to become ha'a dancers had to go through a rigorous selection process. Some even believe that the dances were used as a sort of training program for the military because it was from groups of ha'a dancers that members of the Hawaiian *'olohe* (secret military society) were chosen.

Just before the missionaries arrived on Maui, much of Hawaiian culture was changing due to political and religious unrest. Queen Ka'ahumanu ordered the destruction of all temples and religious idols, which effectively destroyed Hawaiian religion, and with it, the ha'a. The arrival of the missionaries in 1823 accelerated its end.

However, the hula, which had previously served as a form of entertainment for the Hawaiian maka'ainana (common people), managed to survive. This form of dance was less sexual, less religious in overtone, and more likely to be performed by women dancers. The hula required that the dancer (who often developed large hip and thigh muscles—called *hula ku*—as a result of the hip-rotating action of the hula) have poise, grace, strength, and balance. What makes the hula unique is its costumery and its obvious representations of environmental events. Hula requires the dancer to have complete control over every part of his or her body; performed well, the hula should appear to be completely fluid and effortless. Every movement has a specific meaning, and every expression of the dancer's hands carries significance. The movements of the dancer's body might represent certain plants, animals, or even war. Chants accompany the movements and aid in telling the dancer's story.

Between 1832 and 1873 hula dancers adopted certain European dance steps; as Hawaiians became increasingly sterile due to the introduction of venereal diseases by the Europeans, fertility dances *(mele ma'i)* in a public forum became much more popular. In many ways, Hawaiian dance wasn't dying out—it was gaining popularity among the islanders. At this time there were hula schools, or *halau*, throughout the islands, but it wasn't until the mid-1870s that the hula experienced a real growth spurt.

Those most responsible for the resurgence in the popularity of the hula were King Kalakaua and his family, who ascended to the Hawaiian throne in 1873. They became ardent supporters of traditional Hawaiian customs and culture and documented in writing the history of the hula by studying oral chants and traditions associated with early Hawaiian dance. They declared the hula a traditional symbol and expression of Hawaiian identity, promoted the use of grass skirts as costumes, and encouraged women to take major roles in dance performances. Not only did they preserve the past and promote the hula, but they assured it a future by organizing more halau throughout the islands and by introducing stringed instruments (including the violin, guitar, and ukulele) as musical accompaniment.

With the advent of the 20th century, Hawaiian dance became well known around the world. In fact, during both world wars hula troupes were transported from Hawaii to the mainland and around the islands for the entertainment of the U.S. servicemen. As the radio introduced Hawaiian music to the world, people began to fantasize about the dance of the Pacific island paradise. It wasn't long before civilians around the world got their first glimpse of the hula at the movie theater.

Not long after hula's celluloid introduction to the world, certain elements of the dance began to change. It became a more commercial enterprise with the addition of hapa-haole (half-Anglo) dances and dancers. Hula was cheapened with the addition of plastic "grass skirts" and plastic flower leis. The instrumental accompaniment, rather than the dance itself, became the primary focus of a performance. The dancers, almost always women, took an ornamental role. Less experienced dancers were accepted into hula troupes as the demand for performers increased. Traditions of the ancient hula were being forgotten, and hula chanting even began to disappear.

After World War II, the popularity of hula took a downward turn. Demand for live performances declined—often confined primarily to tourist luaus. As the continuing influx of Asians and Europeans brought new music and dance to the islands, Hawaiians lost interest in their native dance and began to show a preference for rock and roll. Due to the growth of the tourist industry, the government no longer saw a need to promote Hawaiian culture. With all of these factors working against the hula, one might think the dance would have died out completely, but the general public's declining interest actually led to efforts to preserve the hula. Those involved in the preservation of Hawaiian culture were free to revitalize the old traditions without interference by non-Hawaiian interests. During the postwar period, the University of Hawaii maintained an interest in the dance, and an all-male dance group was formed at the Church College of Hawaii in 1958.

After 1960 there was a resurgence of interest in Hawaiian culture. The Hawaiian school system was restructured, and the hula was given a more prominent role in students' lives; the government took a renewed interest in the dance by sponsoring special festivals and events to celebrate the dance and by granting honors to individuals who made lifetime contributions to the hula.

Today there is a return to the hula of old. Plastic grass skirts and flowers have thankfully been replaced by ti leaf skirts and fresh flower leis. Children all over the state compete for the few highly coveted spots in hula troupes just as they did in Old Hawaii. The number of men and boys involved has increased dramatically, and competition among the troupes is fierce. Today's best hula troupes often travel worldwide demonstrating their skills and spreading interest in traditional Hawaiian culture.

10 Recommended Books & Recordings

BOOKS
HISTORY, POLITICS & SOCIOLOGY

A number of books have been written about how Hawaii came to be what it is today. For a look back to the origins of the Hawaiian people, Abraham Fornander's *An Account of the Polynesian Race: Its Origins and Migrations and the Ancient History of the Hawaiian People to the Times of Kamehameha I* (Charles E. Tuttle Company, 1969) is a great source of information. If you're interested in doing some further reading, try John Dominis Holt's *Monarchy in Hawaii*, 2nd ed. (Topgallant Publishing Co., 1971). J.C. Beaglehole's *The Life of Captain James Cook* (Stanford University

Press, 1974) gives insight into the great navigator's life, and H. Bradley's *American Frontier in Hawaii: The Pioneers, 1789–1843* (Stanford University Press, 1942) tells of American expansion to the Hawaiian Islands.

Perhaps you'd like to learn a bit more about the Baldwins (their home is now a museum)—try Irma Gerner Burns's *Maui's Mitee and the General: A Glimpse into the Lives of Mr. and Mrs. Frank Fowler Baldwin* (Ku Paa Inc., 1991). For some insight into how the Old Hawaiian monarchy clashed with modern society, read Helena G. Allen's *The Betrayal of Liliuokalani: Last Queen of Hawaii 1838–1917* (Mutual Publishing, 1982). Over the years I've enjoyed reading about ancient Hawaiian traditions and beliefs. Some great books to begin with are M. Beckwith (ed.), *The Kumulipo* (University of Hawaii Press, 1981) and David Malo, *Hawaiian Antiquities* (Bishop Museum Press, 1951, translated by Dr. Nathaniel B. Emerson). The Malo book is particularly fascinating. Excellent historical accounts include Gavan Daws, *Shoal of Time: A History of the Hawaiian Islands* (University of Hawaii Press, 1968) and Edward Joesting, *Hawaii: An Uncommon History* (W. W. Norton & Company, Inc., 1972)—both are comprehensive histories of all the Hawaiian Islands. A book whose main focus is on the history of Maui is Cummins E. Speakman Jr., *Mowee: An Informal History of the Hawaiian Islands* (Pueo Press, 1978)—it's an excellent, excellent book. If Lahaina's history has piqued your interest, I'd recommend reading Maui Historical Society's *Lahaina Historical Guide* (Charles E. Tuttle Company, 1961), and Roy Nickerson, *Lahaina: Royal Capital of Hawaii* (Hawaiian Service, 1978).

NATURE

There are innumerable books about Maui's natural environment. To learn more about tropical flora I'd recommend Dorothy and Bob Hargreaves's *Hawaii Blossoms* (Ross-Hargreaves, 1958) and *Tropical Trees of Hawaii* (Ross-Hargreaves, 1964). Angela K. Kepler's book, *Exotic Tropicals of Hawaii: Heliconias, Gingers, Anthuriums & Decorative Foliage* (Mutual Publishing, 1989) and Angela and Cameron B. Kepler's *Haleakala: A Guide to the Mountain* (Mutual Publishing, 1988) are both quite good.

If you'd like to do some further reading about Hawaii's underwater life and where to see it, Rod Canham's *Hawaii Below: Favorites, Tips, and Secrets of the Diving Pros* (Watersport Publishing Inc., 1991) is a great source. And, naturally, the Hawaii Audubon Society publishes the best book on the birds of Hawaii—look for *Hawaii's Birds* (Hawaii Audubon Society, 1989).

ART, MUSIC & DANCE

The arts and crafts of Hawaii are interesting and unusual, but unfortunately it's difficult to find areas where they're being actively pursued. Peter H. Buck's (Te Rangi Hiroa), *Arts and Crafts of Hawaii*, vols. 1–14 (Bishop Museum Press, 1957) are wonderful books that tell you everything you ever wanted to know about ancient Hawaiian art and how it applied to daily life in the Old Hawaiian society. J. Halley Cox and William H. Davenport have put together a lovely book on Hawaiian wood carving, *Hawaiian Sculpture* rev. ed., (University of Hawaii Press, 1988) that's worth looking for if you have an interest in sculpture. Featherwork was such an important part of Hawaiian life that I would be remiss if I failed to mention John Holt Dominis's *The Art of Featherwork in Old Hawaii* (Topgallant Publishing Co., 1985). Of course, the making of leis and quilts are a large part of Hawaiian culture, even today, but if you want to know more about the origins of these arts, try reading Marie A. McDonald's *Ka Lei: The Leis of Hawaii* (Ku Pa'a Inc. and Press Pacifica, 1989) and Stella M. Jones's *Hawaiian Quilts* (Daughters of Hawaii and the Honolulu Academy of Arts and Mission Houses Museum, 1973).

The best reference book on Hawaiian music is George S. Kanahele (ed.), *Hawaiian Music and Musicians: An Illustrated History* (University Press of Hawaii, 1979). Hawaiian music and the hula go hand in hand, so you'll need to do some reading about traditional Hawaiian dance as well. Try Ishmael Stagner, *Hula* (Institute for Polynesian Studies, Brigham Young University, 1985).

RECORDINGS

Through the centuries, Hawaiian music, which originally took the form of chanting to the accompaniment of a sharkskin drum, has gone through many changes. European classical composers were the first to leave their mark, next came jazz musicians, and finally, rock and roll artists. Each musical genre contributed to a change in Hawaiian music, from intonation to instrumentation. This is why today there is no such thing as true Hawaiian music.

If you're interested in a more traditional sound, something you're not likely to hear much of today, try a recording from Emma Veary or Palani Vaughan. Aunty Edith Kanakaole is well known for her emotional renditions of classic Hawaiian chants. The Brothers Cazimero, the Sons of Niihau, and Aunty Genoa Keawe are also popular traditionalists.

Well-known modern male musicians include Frank Hewett, Jerry Santos, and Alfred Apaka; female artists include Karen Keawe Hawaii, Nohelani Cypriano, and Melveen Leed. "Gabby" Charles Philip Pahinui is a wonderful slack key guitarist who, in his younger days, was heavily influenced by jazz. Pahinui has three musician sons, Cyril, Martin, and Bla. In addition to performing on their own, Cyril and Martin recorded with the Peter Moon Band. Current artists to look for include Keali'i Reichel, HAPA, and Henry Allen.

Planning a Trip to Maui

This chapter is devoted to the when, where, and how of your trip—the advance-planning issues required to get it together and take it on the road.

After deciding where to go, most people have two fundamental questions: "What will it cost?" and "How do I get there?" This chapter will answer both questions and provide other essential information.

1 Visitor Information & Entry Requirements

SOURCES OF INFORMATION No matter what your point of origin, you should contact the **Maui Visitors Bureau** (1727 Wili Pa Loop, P.O. Box 580, Wailuku, HI 96793; ☎ 808/244-3530 or 800/525-MAUI), a branch of the Hawaii Visitors Bureau either before you go or once you get to Maui. They will supply you with all kinds of information, ranging from activities to accommodations.

The state agency responsible for tourism is the **Hawaii Visitors Bureau.** For those who live in the United States, there is one office in New York City. It is located at 350 Fifth Ave., Suite 808, New York, NY 10118 (☎ 212/947-0717). In Canada call 604/669-6691.

If you're coming from Australia, you can contact the Hawaii Visitors Bureau, c/o Walshes World, 92 Pitt St., 8th Floor, Sydney, NSW 2000, or G.P.O. Box 51, Sydney, NSW 2001 (☎ 61-2-235-0194).

From New Zealand, write c/o Walshes World, 87 Queen St., 2nd Floor, Dingwall Bldg., Auckland, or Private Bag 92136, Auckland 1, New Zealand (☎ 64-9-379-3708).

The address of the United Kingdom office is P.O. Box 208, Sunbury on Thames, Middlesex, TW16 5RJ, England (☎ 44-181-941-4009; fax 44-181-941-4011).

If you have accesss to the Internet, you might start at http://www.maui.net or http://maui.net/%7Emol/molhome.html. From there you'll find all sorts of up-to-the-minute information on Maui activities, accommodations, restaurants, and current events.

ENTRY REQUIREMENTS **Documents** Canadians only need proof of Canadian residence to enter the United States. Those from

What Things Cost on Maui	U.S. $
Taxi from Kahului Airport to West Maui	42.00–45.00
Local telephone call	.25
Double room at the Grand Wailea (deluxe ocean view)	445.00
Double room at the Royal Lahaina (moderate garden view)	175.00–195.00
Double room at the Maui Sunset (inexpensive one-bedroom condo unit)	115.00–135.00
Lunch for one at Avalon (expensive)	25.00
Lunch for one at Scaroles Ristorante (moderate)	18.00
Dinner for one without wine at Roy's Kahana Bar & Grill (expensive)	38.00
Dinner for one without wine at Ming Yuen (moderate)	18.00–20.00
Bottle of beer	3.00–5.00
Cup of coffee	1.00
Coca-cola	1.50
Roll of ASA 100 Kodacolor film, 36 exposures	6.50
Movie ticket	5.00–7.00

the United Kingdom need only a valid passport. Australians and New Zealanders must have both a passport and a tourist visa to enter the country. (See Chapter 4, "For Foreign Visitors," for further details.)

Customs/Agricultural Regulations   In addition to the regulations detailed below, there are regular U.S. Customs requirements for foreign visitors (see Chapter 4, "For Foreign Visitors").

No one traveling to Maui is allowed to carry foodstuffs, plants, or seeds onto the island without prior permission. Any of these items you carry off the plane (even if it's just a banana) must be declared and inspected by the U.S. agricultural officers at the airport. Fido won't have any fun on this trip because pets entering Hawaii must be quarantined for three months on Oahu to ensure that they don't have rabies.

Please respect the regulations placed on the import of foods, plants, and animals because not doing so could have a devastating effect on the island's plant and animal life; harmful tiny insects and bacteria could be hitching a ride with you. The rules are strict because Hawaii has already lost an enormous number of indigenous species, and the state is trying to protect those that still remain.

2 When to Go

CLIMATE   Maui's climate is tropical; however, its intensity varies depending on where you are on the island. If you stay in the Kapalua area of West Maui, you will be treated to warm sunny weather during the day with infrequent rain showers and refreshing trade winds in the evening. Only a few miles up the road in Lahaina (meaning "Merciless Sun"), rain showers are less frequent, and the sun is much more intense. Still hotter and much more arid are the towns of Kihei, Maalea, Wailea, and Makena. If you go Upcountry to Kula, Paia, and Makawao, you'll feel a drop in temperature and an increase in humidity—especially in the evening. Finally, at the

Maui's Average Island-Wide Temperatures

	Jan	Mar	May	June	Sept	Nov
Low °F	62	62	64	62	64	60
High °F	80	83	86	85	90	82

top of Haleakala Crater you will find the most extreme variations in temperature. In the evening and early hours of the morning it's usually cold, and during the day the temperature is about 20 degrees lower than elsewhere on the island.

Island temperatures average between 70 and 77 degrees Fahrenheit, but I've seen the mercury rise above 90 degrees in places like Kihei and Lahaina. September and October are typically Maui's hottest months, but this is the low season, so hotel rates are less expensive.

Annual rainfall averages between zero and 10 inches; thus, if you get caught in a shower, it won't last long, and it certainly would not be enough to drive most sunbathers off the beach. You may also discover that while it may be raining in Kapalua, it could be sunny in Lahaina.

MAUI CALENDAR OF EVENTS

In addition to the annual events listed here, many other small or one-time events are held throughout the year. Contact the Maui Visitors Bureau, 1727 Wili Pa Loop, Wailuku, Maui, HI (☎ 808/244-3530) for a full calendar of events. Events are also listed on the Internet (see above).

January
- **Celebration of Whales.** Three days of discussions, whale-watching excursions, entertainment, and an art exhibition at the end of January. Contact the Four Seasons Resort, 3900 Wailea Alanui, Wailea, Maui, HI 96753 (☎ 808/874-8000) for details.
- **Lahaina Whale Festival.** The town of Lahaina celebrates the coming of the whales. During the second week of January a series of ongoing special events is held throughout Lahaina. Contact the Lahaina Town Action Committee, P.O. Box 1271, Lahaina, Maui, HI 96767 (☎ 808/667-9175) for more information.

February
- **Art Maui.** This annual juried show of works by Maui artists is held from mid-February to mid-March at the Maui Arts & Cultural Center in Kahului. Admission is free and all are welcome. Call 808/242-SHOW for details.

March
- **27th Annual Maui Marathon.** Runners from all over the world come to Maui to compete in this event, which takes place in mid-March. The course runs from Kahului to Kaanapali. For more information call 808/871-6441.

April
- **Annual Maui O'Neill Pro Board Association Competition.** Professional windsurfers come to Maui each year to compete in this competition, which is held during the first two weeks of April. The first event of the pro tour, it takes place at Hookipa Beach Park. For more information call 808/575-9264.
- **5th Annual Ritz-Carlton Kapalua Celebration of the Arts.** This three-day event celebrates the arts, culture, and people of Hawaii. A variety of entertainment, workshops and demonstrations are scheduled. Call 808/669-6200 for exact dates.

May

- **Lei Day.** An island-wide celebration with lei-making competitions, and Lei Day Pageants in the local schools. Contact the Maui Visitors Bureau, P.O. Box 580, Wailuku, Maui, HI 96793 (☎ 808/244-3530) for details on the locations of specific events.
- **9th Annual Bankoh Hoomanao Challenge.** Each year around the end of May, this outrigger canoe race runs from Maui to Oahu. Call 808/537-8660 for further details.

June

- **Kamehameha Day Celebration.** Lahaina sponsors this annual parade to celebrate Hawaii's great king, Kamehameha. Contact the Lahaina Town Action Committee at 648 Wharf St., Lahaina, Maui, HI 96767 (☎ 808/667-9175) for more information.
- **Annual Upcountry Fair.** Held at the Eddie Tam Center in Makawao, the Annual Upcountry Fair is an old-fashioned farm fair that features 4-H products, food, and live entertainment. Admission is free; call 808/572-8883 for additional details.

July

- **Makawao Parade & Rodeo.** A grand-scale Fourth of July celebration, complete with paniolo. Admission is free. Call 808/573-0099 for more information.
- **Fourth of July Celebrations.** Fireworks displays take place at the Aston Wailea Resort (☎ 808/879-1922) and at the Kaanapali Resort (☎ 808/661-3271).
- **Kapalua Wine & Food Symposium.** For one weekend in July, an international delegation of experts come together for gourmet meals, wine tastings, and panel discussions. For more information, contact the Kapalua Wine Society, 500 Bay Dr., Lahaina, Maui, HI 96761 (☎ 808/669-0244 or 800/KAPALUA).
- **Lantern Boat Ceremony/Bon Dance.** An interesting Buddhist ceremony to honor the souls of the dead. Call the Lahaina Jodo Mission at 808/661-4304 for details.

August

- **Maui Onion Festival.** This annual festival, which takes place in the Kaanapali resort area, features food, live entertainment, and the Maui Onion cook-off. Contact the Kaanapali Beach Resort Association, 45 Kai Ala Drive, Suite 118A, Kaanapali, Maui, HI 96761 (☎ 808/661-3271 or 800/245-9229), for more information.

September

- **Taste of Lahaina.** Scores of Maui chefs participate in this fund-raising food tasting. There are live entertainment, wine tastings, and cooking demonstrations. You buy scrip tickets when you arrive and use them to sample the specialties offered by various Maui restaurants. Contact the Lahaina Town Action Committee, P.O. Box 1271, Lahaina, Maui, HI 96767 (☎ 808/667-9175), for more information.
- ✪ **Maui Triathlon.** Triathletes compete in a combination 1,500-meter swim, 40-kilometer bike ride, and 10-kilometer run. Call 808/572-5071 for details.
- **Hana Relays.** This famous race takes place along the grueling course known as the Hana Highway. Teams of runners look forward to competing in this event each year. Call 808/871-6441.

October

- **Maui County Fair.** Located at the War Memorial Complex in Wailuku, the Maui County Fair features a parade, arts and crafts, ethnic foods, amusements, and a grand orchid festival. Call 808/242-0909 for details.

- **Hula O Na Keiki.** Kaanapali Beach Hotel sponsors a children's hula competition. *Keikis* compete solo in ancient and contemporary dance. There is an admission fee. Contact the Kaanapali Beach Hotel, Kaanapali Beach, Kaanapali, Maui, HI 96761 (☎ 808/661-0011) for further details.
- **Aloha Classic.** This is the final event in the Pro Boardsailing Association's World Tour. Participants from all over the world compete. The Aloha Classic is held in late October or early November at Hookipa Beach Park near Paia, and the admission is free. Call 808/575-9151 for more information.
- **Halloween in Lahaina.** Halloween in Lahaina is indeed a special event. People come from all over the world to take part in the parade on Front Street. Contact the Lahaina Town Action Committee at P.O. Box 1271, Lahaina, Maui, HI 96767 (☎ 808/667-9175), for more information.

November

- **Hawaii International Film Festival.** Films from Asia, the Pacific, and North America are screened at the Maui Arts & Cultural Center in Kahului. Seminars and workshops are available. Call 800/752-8193 for information.

December

- **Na Mele O Maui.** Festival celebrating island arts, crafts, dances, and music. Contact the Kaanapali Beach Resort Association, 45 Kai Ala Drive, Suite 118A, Kaanapali, Maui, HI 96761 (☎ 808/661-3271 or 800/245-9229).
- **Gala Tree-Lighting Ceremony.** A month-long holiday celebration is sponsored annually by the Ritz-Carlton, Kapalua. It includes brunches, dinners, a life-size gingerbread house, and keiki hula. For more information, contact the Ritz-Carlton Kapalua, 1 Ritz-Carlton Dr., Kapalua, Maui, HI 96761(☎ 808/669-6200).
- **Santa Comes to Wailea.** On Maui Santa arrives not in a sleigh with reindeer but in an outrigger canoe. He lands at Wailea Beach near the Aston Wailea Resort. Contact the Aston Wailea Resort, 3700 Wailea Alanui, Wailea, Maui, HI 96753 (☎ 808/879-1922) for information.
- **Christmas House.** Every year at the Hui Noeau Visual Arts Center in Makawao there's a Christmas craft show featuring handcrafted items. There's a nominal admission fee. For information, contact the Hui Noeau Visual Arts Center, 2841 Baldwin Ave., Makawao, Maui, HI 96790 (☎ 808/572-6560).
- **Maui Invitational Basketball Tournament.** Each December, top college teams participate in this tournament at the Lahaina Civic Center. Call 312/755-3577 for more information.

3 Health & Insurance

STAYING HEALTHY   Fortunately for travelers to Maui, there are few health concerns. You'll need no vaccinations; in fact, those who live in this island paradise live an average of 5.5 years longer than those who live on the mainland. Tap water on the island is clean, so you needn't worry about picking up water-borne bacteria in a restaurant or hotel room. However, some of Maui's streams and waterways are polluted, so don't drink the water while you're out hiking. It's a good idea always to carry fresh water when you hike. One liter per person should be adequate; even though you may not feel thirsty, it's a good idea to drink steadily as you hike because you can easily become dehydrated.

Sun Safety   Many people who travel to Maui are interested in one thing—a deep, dark, tropical tan. If you're careful, you can certainly leave with the darkest tan you've ever had. However, the Maui sun is strong, and you can burn in less than

10 minutes if you're fair-skinned. At the beginning of your trip, stay in the sun for short periods of time and use a sunscreen with a high SPF. As you tan you'll be able to spend more and more time in the sun (with a lower SPF) without fear of getting burned to a crisp.

Some people complain that they develop white dots, bumps, or spots on their skin that won't tan no matter how long they spend in the sun. I've been told that the spots are harmless and you shouldn't worry if you get them so long as you're not experiencing discomfort. If for some reason they become painful or itchy, it would be advisable for you to see a doctor.

Ocean Safety   Maui's beautiful beaches and clear waters are enticing, but you should approach the water with caution, regardless of what it looks like on the surface. Most beaches don't have lifeguards, so it's up to you to protect yourself and your family. Don't ever swim alone, and always locate rocks, strange currents, and coral reefs before you enter the water. Wherever you decide to swim, don't just dive right in—you could be in for a nasty shock. Sometimes the water looks deeper than it actually is, and if you dive headfirst, you may get pulled out feet first.

If you see warning signs posted on the beach, take them seriously. Respect the ocean. If you ever get caught in a riptide (a scary but temporary event), don't panic, and don't try to swim directly against it. Don't waste your energy flailing about and yelling for help; just swim on a diagonal across the riptide and you'll be back in safer waters in no time. If you get tired and need to rest, float on your back.

When surfing or body surfing, never ride the waves straight into the beach—surf to shore at an angle. If you're an inexperienced surfer, stay out of the water when the surf is very high because it's probably stronger than it looks, and you're probably weaker than you think you are.

Finally, never, ever, turn your back on the ocean.

Sea Creatures   For the most part, you're not in danger of being attacked by much in Maui waters. If you're swimming, the most you'll probably encounter is a jellyfish or man-of-war. If you run into one, give it a wide berth and swim carefully around it. They have a nasty sting, and if you are stung, you should seek medical attention. If you go farther out in the water (surfing or windsurfing), there's always a chance that you'll encounter a shark. If you do, I've been told that you should try to stay calm (I'm not sure how) and yell for help. Swimming frantically will only attract the animal's attention.

Look out for sea urchins if you're walking on the ocean floor—they have spines, and if you get one in your foot, it will be extremely painful. Another thing you should be careful of before you put your feet down is coral. If you step on coral, not only are you going to scratch your feet (which is much more painful than it sounds), but you'll also be destroying some very fragile marine life.

INSURANCE   Before leaving home, check your medical insurance policy to be sure it will cover you on your trip. If it doesn't, it's wise to purchase a relatively inexpensive traveler's policy, widely available at banks, travel agencies, and automobile clubs. In addition to medical assistance, including hospitalization and surgery, it should include the cost of an accident or death, loss or theft of baggage, costs of trip cancellation, and guaranteed bail in the event of an arrest or other legal difficulties.

4 Tips for Travelers with Special Needs

FOR TRAVELERS WITH DISABILITIES   There are a couple of agencies you might want to contact for information before you leave home. **Over the Rainbow**

Disabled Travel Services, at 186 Mehani Circle, Kihei, Maui, HI 96753 (☎ 808/ 879-5521), specializes in assisting disabled travelers to Maui. **The Commission on Persons with Disabilities,** State Office Building, 54 High St., Wailuku, HI 96793 ☎ 808/243-5441), will send you an *Aloha Guide to Accessibility* order form if you call ahead. There are six different guides available, including the following: general information, beaches and parks, attractions, and shopping. Each one costs $3 to $5, but you can order the entire bunch for $15.

When making hotel reservations, let the hotel know in advance if you have any special needs—that way they and your room will be ready for you when you arrive.

Several car-rental companies on the island offer cars with hand controls, including Avis, Budget, and National. All of them require confirmation of the hand controls 48 hours in advance of pickup and a deposit of $50 for the use of the hand controls. The deposit will be refunded when you return the car.

FOR SENIORS   Travelers over the age of 65—and in some cases even 55—might qualify for a variety of discounts that aren't available to the average adult traveler. When you make your reservations, ask about senior-citizen discounts—some hotels offer 10% to 20% off. Some attractions offer up to 50% discounts off the regular adult admission price. In most cases the discounts are listed in this book, but it's a good idea to get into the habit of asking, just in case they don't advertise senior discounts.

If you are retired and are not already a member of the **American Association of Retired Persons (AARP),** consider joining. The AARP card is valuable throughout the United States in your search for travel bargains.

FOR FAMILIES   Discounts for children abound. For instance, most hotels will allow children to stay free in their parents' room. Children are also eligible for steeply discounted admission prices at most attractions—children ages 5 to 12 (sometimes even as high as 18) might pay only half of the adult admission price; in many cases children 5 and under are admitted free.

Although Maui is a wonderful place to travel with children (mainly because of its abundance of outdoor activities), sometimes Mom and Dad need a break, and the best way to make sure that you're going to have time alone is to stay in a hotel that provides a good children's day-care program (see individual resort and hotel listings in Chapter 6, "Maui Accommodations"). Many of the hotels have day-long outdoor and indoor activity programs for children, including lunch. If you're hoping for a romantic dinner for two, most of the hotels either have babysitting services or can refer you to the island's most reliable services.

FOR STUDENTS   It's a good idea to carry your student identification with you at all times because you never know when you might be able to use it to get a discount.

5 Getting There

Unless you're on a cruise, your only travel option is to arrive by plane, which can be quite an adventure, depending on your point of origin. In most cases you'll have to fly to Honolulu first and then switch to a smaller plane for the short hop to Maui.

FLIGHTS FROM THE U.S. MAINLAND TO MAUI   There are only three airlines that fly direct from the U. S. mainland to Maui. If you're traveling to Maui from the East Coast, these direct flights might make a big difference in your schedule. You will have to change planes only once, and you won't have a layover in Honolulu, which could save you a significant amount of time (thereby enabling you to get to bed sooner). All three airlines fly into Maui's Kahului Airport.

United Airlines (☎ 808/242-7911 or 800/241-6522) offers one nonstop flight daily from Los Angeles to Maui and one from San Francisco to Maui. Each flight departs mid- to late morning, so if your point of origin is on the East Coast you'll have to get a very early flight out to make the connection. United Airline flights originating in other major cities stop in San Francisco or Los Angeles.

Hawaiian Airlines (☎ 808/871-6132 or 800/367-5320) has several daily nonstop flights from San Francisco or Los Angeles to Maui.

Delta Airlines (☎ 800/221-1212) also offers a nonstop flight from the mainland to Maui.

Other airlines fly from the mainland to Honolulu, where you can hop one of the interisland carriers. They include **Continental Airlines** (☎ 808/523-0000 or 800/525-0280); **American Airlines** (☎ 244-5522 or 800/223-5436); **Canadian Airlines International** (☎ 800/426-7000); **China Airlines** (☎ 808/955-0088); **Japan Airlines** (☎ 800/525-3663); **Lufthansa** (☎ 800/645-3880); **Northwest Airlines** (☎ 800/225-2525); and **TWA** (☎ 800/221-2000).

FLIGHTS FROM HONOLULU TO MAUI   There are only a few interisland carriers, the largest of which are **Hawaiian Airlines** (☎ 808/871-6132 or 800/367-5320) and **Aloha Airlines, Inc.** (☎ 808/244-9071). Both airlines fly regularly from Honolulu to Maui. Hawaiian Airlines offers the Hawaiian Airpass, which allows you to make unlimited interisland flights in a given period of time for a flat rate. At press time, a 5-day pass costs $162.73; an 8-day pass goes for $180.91; a 10-day pass will run you $217.27; and a 15-day pass costs $253.64. The newest airline, **Mahalo Airlines** (☎ 800/277-8333), is giving both Hawaiian and Aloha Airlines a run for their money.

Air Molokai (☎ 808/877-0026) and **Aloha Island Air, Inc.** (☎ 808/244-9071 or 800/323-3345) are smaller companies, but they're just as reliable, and you'll probably be able to get cheaper fares. Both airlines offer regular flights from around 6am to 7pm. If you're afraid of small planes, you're better off going on Hawaiian or Aloha Airlines.

FINDING THE BEST AIRFARE   Advance Purchase Excursion (APEX) fares vary depending on how many days in advance you make your booking. A reservation must be made 14 or 21 days in advance, and you must stay at your travel destination for a certain number of days to qualify for the reduced fare. If you're flying from New York to Los Angeles or San Francisco, and then on to Honolulu, you'll probably spend anywhere from $650 to $1,300 round-trip, depending on when you plan to travel. First-class tickets are considerably more—well in excess of $2,000 round-trip in most cases.

There are always cheaper alternatives, however. Be on the lookout for special promotional fares. In many cases you'll find them advertised in the newspaper or even on television. There will probably be restrictions placed on your dates of travel, but it can't hurt to try.

Finally, call a discount travel agency that has booked blocks of tickets and sells them at a steeply discounted rate. You may get up to 40% off a regular economy (or first-class) fare, but once you've paid for your tickets, you won't be able to make any changes at all, so make sure about your departure and return dates before you hand over any money.

MAUI'S AIRPORTS

AIRPORTS   Maui has three airports, but most likely you'll arrive at **Kahului Airport** (☎ 808/872-3893), which was recently renovated and has plans to build a longer runway. That means more long-distance flights will eventually be landing directly on Maui. The project is scheduled to take several years, though. It is easy to find your way around the airport; all the car-rental booths are located directly outside the baggage claim area.

If you're not renting a car at the airport, most hotels have shuttles that will pick you up at the airport and take you to your hotel, but you should check in advance to see if you need reservations or if they have a regular shuttle schedule.

Kapalua—West Maui Airport (☎ 808/872-3830) is Maui's newest airport, and it's quite convenient if you're planning to stay at any of the hotels in Kapalua or the Kaanapali resorts. You can rent a car and drive to your hotel from the airport, or check with your hotel before you arrive to see if it offers a shuttle service. If you're staying in Kapalua, the drive will only be about 10 or 15 minutes, and if your hotel is in Kaanapali it will take you about 20 or 25 minutes (from Kahului Airport, it would take you 35 or 40 minutes).

Hana Airport (☎ 808/248-8208) is a tiny airport that services Aloha Island Air commuter flights from Kahului airport several times daily.

4 For Foreign Visitors

Although American fads and fashions have spread across Europe and other parts of the world so much that America may seem like familiar territory before your arrival, there are still many peculiarities and uniquely American situations that any foreign visitor will encounter.

1 Preparing for Your Trip

ENTRY REQUIREMENTS

DOCUMENT REGULATIONS Canadian citizens may enter the United States without passports or visas; they need only proof of Canadian residence.

Citizens of the United Kingdom, New Zealand, Japan, and most western European countries traveling with valid passports may not need a visa for fewer than 90 days of leisure or business travel to the United States, providing that they hold a round-trip or return ticket and enter the United States on an airline or cruise line participating in the visa waiver program. (Note that citizens of these visa-exempt countries who first enter the United States may later visit Mexico, Canada, Bermuda, and/or the Caribbean Islands, and then reenter the United States, by any mode of transportation, without needing a visa. Further information is available from any U.S. embassy or consulate.)

Citizens of countries other than those stipulated above, including citizens of Australia, must have two documents: a valid **passport** with an expiration date at least six months later than the scheduled end of the visit to the United States and a **tourist visa,** available without charge from the nearest U.S. consulate. To obtain a visa, the traveler must submit a completed application form (either in person or by mail) with a $1^1/_2$-inch-square photo and demonstrate binding ties to the residence abroad.

Usually you can obtain a visa at once or within 24 hours, but it may take longer during the summer rush from June to August. If you cannot go in person, contact the nearest U.S. embassy or consulate for directions on applying by mail. Your travel agent or airline office may also be able to provide you with visa applications and instructions. The U.S. embassy or consulate that issues your visa will determine whether you will be given a multiple- or single-entry visa and any restrictions regarding the length of your stay.

MEDICAL REQUIREMENTS   No inoculations are needed to enter the United States unless you are coming from, or have stopped over in, areas known to be suffering from epidemics, particularly cholera or yellow fever.

If you have a disease necessitating treatment with medications containing narcotics or drugs that require a syringe, carry a valid signed prescription from your physician to allay any suspicions that you might be smuggling drugs.

CUSTOMS REQUIREMENTS   Every adult visitor may bring in, free of duty: 1 liter of wine or hard liquor; 200 cigarettes or 100 cigars (but no cigars from Cuba) or 3 pounds of smoking tobacco; and $100 worth of gifts. These exemptions are offered to travelers who spend at least 72 hours in the United States and who have not claimed them within the preceding six months. It is altogether forbidden to bring into the country foodstuffs (particularly cheese, fruit, cooked meats, and canned goods) and plants (vegetables, seeds, tropical plants, and so on). Foreign tourists may bring in or take out up to $10,000 in U.S. or foreign currency with no formalities; larger sums must be declared to Customs on entering or leaving.

INSURANCE

There is no national health-care system in the United States. Because the cost of medical care is extremely high, I strongly advise every traveler to secure health insurance coverage before setting out.

You may want to take out a comprehensive travel policy that covers (for a relatively low premium) sickness or injury costs (medical, surgical, and hospital); loss or theft of your baggage; trip-cancellation costs; guarantee of bail in case you are arrested; costs of an accident, repatriation, or death. Such packages (for example, "Europe Assistance" in Europe) are sold by automobile clubs at attractive rates, as well as by insurance companies and travel agencies.

MONEY

CURRENCY & EXCHANGE   The U.S. monetary system has a decimal base: one American **dollar** ($1) = 100 **cents** (100¢).

Dollar bills commonly come in $1 (a "buck"), $5, $10, $20, $50, and $100 denominations (the last two are not welcome when paying for small purchases and are not accepted in taxis or at subway ticket booths). There are also $2 bills (seldom encountered).

There are six denominations of coins: 1¢ (one cent or "penny"), 5¢ (five cents or "nickel"), 10¢ (ten cents or "dime"), 25¢ (twenty-five cents or "quarter"), 50¢ (fifty cents or "half dollar"), and the rare $1 piece.

Note: The "foreign-exchange bureaus" so common in Europe are rare even at airports in the United States, and nonexistent outside major cities. Try to avoid having to change foreign money (or traveler's checks denominated in a currency other than U.S. dollars) at a small-town bank or even a branch bank in a big city. In fact, leave any currency other than U.S. dollars at home—it may prove a greater nuisance to you than it's worth.

TRAVELER'S CHECKS   Traveler's checks denominated in U.S. dollars are readily accepted at most hotels, motels, restaurants, and large stores. But the best place to change traveler's checks is at a bank. Do not bring traveler's checks denominated in other currencies.

CREDIT CARDS   The method of payment most widely used is the credit card: Visa (BarclayCard in Britain), MasterCard (EuroCard in Europe, Access in Britain,

Chargex in Canada), American Express, Diners Club, Discover, and Carte Blanche. You can save yourself trouble by using "plastic money" rather than cash or traveler's checks at most hotels, motels, restaurants, and retail stores (a growing number of food and liquor stores now accept credit/charge cards). You must have a credit card to rent a car. It can also be used as proof of identity (often carrying more weight than a passport) or as a "cash card," enabling you to withdraw money from banks and automated-teller machines (ATMs) that accept it.

SAFETY

GENERAL While tourist areas are generally safe, crime is on the increase everywhere, especially in large U.S. cities. You may wish to contact the Maui Visitors Bureau before you arrive. They can provide you with safety information.

Remember that hotels are open to the public, and in a large hotel, security may not be able to screen everyone who enters. Always lock your room door; don't assume that once inside your hotel you are automatically safe and no longer need to be aware of your surroundings.

DRIVING Question your rental agency about personal safety, or ask for a brochure on traveler safety tips when you pick up your car. Obtain written directions (or a map with the route clearly marked) from the agency showing how to get to your destination. And, if possible, arrive and depart during daylight hours.

In recent years, more and more crime in all U.S. cities has involved cars and drivers, most notably what is called "carjacking." If you drive off a highway into a doubtful neighborhood, leave the area as quickly as possible. If you have an accident, even on the highway, stay in your car with the doors locked until you assess the situation or until the police arrive. If you are bumped from behind on the road or are involved in a minor accident with no injuries and the situation appears to be suspicious, motion to the other driver to follow you to the nearest police precinct, well-lighted service station, or all-night store. *Never* get out of your car in such situations.

If you see someone on the road who indicates a need for help, do *not* stop. Take note of the location, drive on to a well-lighted area, and telephone the police by dialing **911.**

Park in well-lighted, well-traveled areas if possible. Always keep your car doors locked, whether the car is attended or unattended. Look around you before you get out of your car, and never leave any packages or valuables in sight. If someone attempts to rob you or steal your car, do *not* try to resist the thief/carjacker—report the incident to the police department immediately.

Also, make sure that you have enough gasoline in your tank to reach your intended destination, so that you're not forced to look for a service station in an unfamiliar and possibly unsafe neighborhood—especially at night.

2 Getting to & Around the U.S.

GETTING TO THE U.S. Travelers from overseas can take advantage of the **APEX (Advance Purchase Excursion) fares** offered by all the major international carriers. Aside from these, attractive values are offered by **Icelandair** on flights from Luxembourg to New York and by **Virgin Atlantic Airways** (☎ **02/937-47747** in the U.K. or 800/862-8621 in the U.S.) from London to New York/Newark and to Los Angeles.

Another option for British travelers is **British Airways** (☎ **081/897-4000** in the U.K. or 800/247-9297 in the U.S.), which offers direct flights from London to New York and to Los Angeles. Canadian readers might book flights on **Air Canada**

(☎ **800/776-3000**), which offers service from Toronto, Montréal, and Calgary to New York and to Los Angeles. Among many other international carriers serving both New York and Los Angeles airports is **SAS** (☎ **800/221-2350** in the U.S.).

The visitor arriving by air should make a very generous allowance for delays in planning connections between international and domestic flights—an average of two to three hours at least.

In contrast, travelers arriving by car or by rail from Canada will find that the border-crossing formalities have been streamlined practically to the vanishing point. And air travelers from Canada, Bermuda, and some places in the Caribbean can frequently go through Customs and Immigration at the point of departure, which is much quicker and less painful.

For further information about travel to and arriving in Hawaii, see "Getting There" in Chapter 3, "Planning a Trip to Maui."

GETTING AROUND THE U.S.   Some large American airlines (for example, TWA, American Airlines, Northwest, United, and Delta) offer travelers on their transatlantic or transpacific flights special discount tickets under the name **Visit USA,** allowing travel between any U.S. destinations at minimum rates. They are not on sale in the United States, and must, therefore, be purchased before you leave your foreign point of departure. This system is the best, easiest, and fastest way to see the United States at low cost. You should obtain information well in advance from your travel agent or the office of the airline concerned, since the conditions attached to these discount tickets can change without advance notice.

FAST FACTS: For the Foreign Traveler

Automobile Organizations   Auto clubs will supply maps, suggested routes, guidebooks, accident and bail-bond insurance, and emergency road service. The major auto club in the United States, with 955 offices nationwide, is the **American Automobile Association (AAA).** Members of some foreign auto clubs have reciprocal arrangements with the AAA and enjoy its services at no charge. If you belong to an auto club, inquire about AAA reciprocity before you leave. The AAA can provide you with an **International Driving Permit** validating your foreign license. You may be able to join the AAA even if you are not a member of a reciprocal club. To inquire, call the AAA (☎ **800/222-4357**). Since some automobile-rental agencies now provide these services, inquire about their availability when you rent your car.

Business Hours   See "Fast Facts: Maui" in Chapter 5, "Getting to Know Maui."

Climate   See "When to Go" in Chapter 3, "Planning a Trip to Maui."

Currency Exchange   You will find currency-exchange services at major airports with international service. Elsewhere, such services may be quite difficult to come by. On Maui you can exchange currency at most hotels.

Drinking Laws   The legal drinking age in Hawaii is 21.

Electric Current   The United States uses 110–120 volts, 60 cycles, compared to 220–240 volts, 50 cycles, in most of Europe. Besides a 100-volt converter, small appliances of non-American manufacture (such as hair dryers or shavers) will require a plug adapter, with two flat, parallel pins.

Embassies/Consulates   All embassies are located in the national capital, Washington, D.C.; some consulates are located in major cities, and most countries maintain a mission to the United Nations in New York City. The embassies and some consulates of the major English-speaking countries and Japan are listed below. If you are from another country, you can get the phone number of your embassy by calling "Information" in Washington, D.C. (☎ **202/555-1212**).

The embassy of **Australia** is at 1601 Massachusetts Ave. NW, Washington, DC 20036 (☎ **202/797-3000**). In Hawaii the consulate is at 1000 Bishop St., Penthouse, Honolulu, HI 96813 (☎ **808/524-5050**). In Los Angeles, the consulate is at 611 N. Larchmont Blvd., Los Angeles, CA 90004 (☎ **213/469-4300**).

The embassy of **Canada** is at 501 Pennsylvania Ave. NW, Washington, DC 20001 (☎ **202/682-1740**). There's a Canadian consulate in Los Angeles at 300 S. Grand Ave., Suite 1000, Los Angeles, CA 90071 (☎ **213/346-2700**).

The embassy of the **Republic of Ireland** is at 2234 Massachusetts Ave. NW, Washington, DC 20008 (☎ **202/462-3939**). The consulate in San Francisco is at 655 Montgomery St., Suite 930, San Francisco, CA 94111 (☎ **415/392-4214**).

The embassy of **New Zealand** is at 37 Observatory Circle NW, Washington, DC 20008 (☎ **202/328-4800**). The consulate in Los Angeles is located at 12400 Wilshire Blvd., Suite 1150, Los Angeles, CA 90025 (☎ **310/207-1605**).

The embassy of the **United Kingdom** is at 3100 Massachusetts Ave. NW, Washington, DC 20008 (☎ **202/462-1340**). The consulate in Los Angeles is located at 11766 Wilshire Blvd., Suite 400, Los Angeles, CA 90025 (☎ **310/477-3322**).

The embassy of Japan is at 2520 Massachusetts Ave. NW, Washington, DC 20008 (☎ **202/939-6700**). The consulate in Hawaii is located at 1742 Nuuanu Ave., Honolulu, HI 96817 (☎ **808/536-2226**).

Emergencies   Call **911** to report a fire, call the police, or get an ambulance. This is a toll-free call (no coins are required at a public telephone).

If you encounter traveler's problems, check the local directory to find an office of the **Traveler's Aid Society,** a nationwide, nonprofit, social-service organization geared to helping travelers in difficult straits. Their services might include reuniting families separated while traveling, providing food and/or shelter to people stranded without cash, or even emotional counseling. If you're in trouble, seek them out.

Gasoline (Petrol)   One U.S. gallon equals 3.8 liters, while 1.2 U.S. gallons equal 1 Imperial gallon. You'll notice there are several grades (and price levels) of gasoline available at most gas stations.. Unleaded gas with the highest octane is the most expensive. Although each gas company has a different name for each octane level, most fall into the "regular," "super," and "plus" categories (rental cars usually take the least expensive— "regular" unleaded).

Holidays   On the following legal national holidays, banks, government offices, post offices, and many stores, restaurants, and museums are closed: January 1 (New Year's Day), third Monday in January (Martin Luther King Jr. Day), third Monday in February (Presidents' Day, Washington's Birthday), last Monday in May (Memorial Day), July 4 (Independence Day), first Monday in September (Labor Day), second Monday in October (Columbus Day), November 11 (Veterans' Day/Armistice Day), fourth Thursday in November (Thanksgiving Day), and December 25 (Christmas Day).

Finally, the Tuesday following the first Monday in November is Election Day, and this is a legal holiday in presidential-election years.

Legal Aid   The well-meaning foreign tourist will probably never become involved with the American legal system. However, there are a few things you should know— just in case. If you are stopped for a minor infraction, such as speeding or some other traffic violation, never attempt to pay the fine directly to a police officer; you could be arrested on the much more serious charge of attempted bribery. Pay fines by mail or directly to the clerk of the court. If you are accused of a more serious offense, it's wise to say and do nothing before consulting a lawyer. Under U.S. law, an arrested person is allowed one telephone call to a party of his or her choice. Call your embassy or consulate.

Mail If you want your mail to follow you on your vacation but you aren't sure of your address, your mail can be sent to you, in your name, **c/o General Delivery** at the main post office of the city or region where you expect to be. The addressee must pick it up in person and produce proof of identity (driver's license, credit card, passport, etc.).

Generally found at intersections, mailboxes are blue with a red-and-white stripe and carry the inscription U.S. MAIL. If your mail is addressed to a U.S. destination, don't forget to add the five-figure postal code, or ZIP (Zone Improvement Plan) Code, after the two-letter abbreviation of the state to which the mail is addressed (HI for Hawaii, CA for California, NY for New York, and so on).

Newspapers/Magazines National newspapers include the *New York Times, USA Today,* and the *Wall Street Journal.* National news weeklies include *Newsweek, Time,* and *U.S. News & World Report.* European newspapers and magazines are difficult to come by in Hawaii.

Radio/Television Audiovisual media, with four coast-to-coast networks—ABC, CBS, NBC, and Fox—joined in recent years by the Public Broadcasting System (PBS) and the cable network CNN—play a major part in American life. In big cities, televiewers have a choice of a few dozen channels (including basic cable); most of them transmit 24 hours a day. There are also pay-TV channels that show recent movies or sports events. All options are usually indicated on your hotel TV set. You'll also find a wide choice of local radio stations, each broadcasting particular kinds of talk shows and/or music—classical, country, jazz, pop, gospel—punctuated by news broadcasts and frequent commercials.

Restrooms Visitors can usually find a restroom in a bar, restaurant, hotel, museum, department store, or service station.

Safety See "Safety" in "Preparing for Your Trip," above.

Taxes In the United States, there is no VAT (Value-Added Tax) or other indirect tax at a national level. Every state, and each city in it, has the right to levy its own local tax on purchases, including hotel and restaurant bills, airline tickets, and so on. In Hawaii, the state sales tax is 4.17%, and the lodging tax is 9.17%.

Telephone/Fax The telephone system in the United States is run by private corporations, so rates, especially for long-distance service, can vary widely—even on calls made from public telephones. Local calls in the United States usually cost 25¢.

Generally, hotel surcharges on long-distance and local calls are astronomical. You can save money by calling collect, charging your call to a credit card, or using a public pay telephone, which you will find clearly marked in most public buildings and private establishments, as well as on the street. Outside metropolitan areas, public telephones are more difficult to find; stores and gas stations are your best bet.

Most **long-distance** and **international** calls can be dialed directly from any phone. For calls to Canada and other parts of the United States, dial 1 followed by the area code and the seven-digit number. For international calls, dial 011 followed by the country code, city code, and the telephone number of the person you wish to call.

For **reversed-charge** or **collect calls** and for **person-to-person calls,** dial "0" (zero, not the letter "O") followed by the area code and number you want; an operator will then come on the line, and you should specify that you are calling collect, or person-to-person, or both. If your operator-assisted call is international, ask for the overseas operator.

For local **directory assistance** ("Information"), dial 411; for **long-distance information,** dial 1, then the appropriate area code and 555-1212.

Most hotels have **fax** machines available for guest use (be sure to ask about the charge to use it), and many hotel rooms are even wired for guests' fax machines. You'll probably also see signs for public faxes in the windows of local shops.

Telephone Directory There are two kinds of telephone directories available to you. The general directory is the so-called White Pages, where private and business subscribers are listed in alphabetical order. The inside front cover lists emergency numbers—for police, fire, and ambulance, as well as other vital numbers (the Coast Guard, poison-control center, crime-victims hotline, and so on).

The second directory, printed on yellow paper (hence its name, **Yellow Pages**), lists all local services, businesses, and industries by type of activity, with an index at the back. The listings cover a wide variety of fields, including automobile repairs (by make of car), drugstores (pharmacies), and restaurants (by type of cuisine and geographical location).

Time The United States is divided into four time zones (six, if Alaska and Hawaii are included). From east to west, these are: Eastern Standard Time (EST), Central Standard Time (CST), Mountain Standard Time (MST), Pacific Standard Time (PST), Alaska Standard Time (AST), and Hawaii Standard Time (HST). Always keep changing time zones in mind if you are traveling (or even telephoning) long distances in the United States. For example, noon in New York City (EST) is 11am in Chicago (CST), 10am in Denver (MST), 9am in Los Angeles (PST), 8am in Anchorage (AST), and 7am in Honolulu (HST). Hawaii does not observe Daylight Saving Time.

Tipping This is part of the American way of life, based on the principle that one should pay for any special service received. (Often service personnel receive little direct salary and must depend on tips for their income.) Here are some rules of thumb:

In **hotels**, tip bellhops $1 per piece of luggage carried, and tip the chamber staff $1 per day. Tip the doorman or concierge only if he or she has provided some specific service (for example, calling a cab for you or obtaining difficult-to-get theater tickets).

In **restaurants, bars, and nightclubs**, tip the service staff 15% of the check, tip bartenders 10% to 15%, tip checkroom attendants $1 per garment, and tip valet-parking attendants $1 per vehicle. Tip the doorman only if he has provided some specific service (such as calling a cab for you). Tipping is not expected in cafeterias and fast-food restaurants.

Tip **cab drivers** 15% of the fare.

As for **other service personnel**, tip redcaps at airports or railroad stations $1 per piece of luggage, and tip hairdressers and barbers 15% to 20%.

Tipping cinema and theater ushers and gas-station attendants is not expected.

THE AMERICAN SYSTEM OF MEASUREMENTS

Length

1 inch (in.)			=	2.54cm			
1 foot (ft.)	=	12 in.	=	30.48cm	=	.305m	
1 yard (yd.)	=	3 ft.			=	.915m	
1 mile	=	5,280 ft.				=	1.609km

To convert miles to kilometers, multiply the number of miles by 1.61 (for example, 50 mi. × 1.61 = 80.5km). Note that this conversion can be used to convert speeds from miles per hour (m.p.h.) to kilometers per hour (kmph).

To convert kilometers to miles, multiply the number of kilometers by .62 (example, 25 km × .62 = 15.5 mi.). Note that this same conversion can be used to convert speeds from kilometers per hour to miles per hour.

Capacity

1 fluid ounce (fl. oz.)			=	.03 liter		
1 pint (pt.)	=	16 fl. oz.	=	.47 liter		
1 quart (qt.)	=	2 pints	=	.94 liter		
1 gallon (gal.)	=	4 quarts	=	3.79 liters	=	.83 Imperial gal.

To convert U.S. gallons to liters, multiply the number of gallons by 3.79 (example, 12 gal. × 3.79 = 45.48 liters).

To convert liters to U.S. gallons, multiply the number of liters by .26 (example, 50 liters × .26 = 13 U.S. gal.).

To convert U.S. gallons to Imperial gallons, multiply the number of U.S. gallons by .83 (example, 12 U.S. gal. × .83 = 9.95 Imperial gal.).

To convert Imperial gallons to U.S. gallons, multiply the number of Imperial gallons by 1.2 (example, 8 Imperial gal. × 1.2 = 9.6 U.S. gal.).

Weight

1 ounce (oz.)			=	28.35g			
1 pound (lb.)	=	16 oz.	=	453.6g	=	.45kg	
1 ton	=	2,000 lb.	=		907kg	=	.91 metric ton

To convert pounds to kilograms, multiply the number of pounds by .45 (example, 90 lb. × .45 = 40.5kg).

To convert kilograms to pounds, multiply the number of kilos by 2.2 (example, 75kg × 2.2 = 165 lb.).

Area

1 acre			=	.41ha	
1 square mile	=	640 acres	=	2.59ha	=	2.6km

To convert acres to hectares, multiply the number of acres by .41 (example, 40 acres × .41 = 16.4ha).

To convert hectares to acres, multiply the number of hectares by 2.47 (example, 20ha × 2.47 = 49.4 acres).

To convert square miles to square kilometers, multiply the number of square miles by 2.6 (example, 80 sq. mi × 2.6 = 208km).

To convert square kilometers to square miles, multiply the number of square kilometers by .39 (example, 150km × .39 = 58.5 sq. mi.).

Temperature

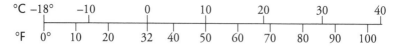

To convert degrees Fahrenheit to degrees Celsius, subtract 32 from °F, multiply by 5, then divide by 9 (example, 85°F–32 × $^5/_9$ = 29.4°C).

To convert degrees Celsius to degrees Fahrenheit, multiply °C by 9, divide by 5, and add 32 (example, 20°C × $^9/_5$ + 32 = 68°F).

Getting to Know Maui 5

If you look at a map of the island of Maui, you'll notice that its shape resembles the head and torso of a man. The island is 25 miles wide and 40 miles long, and though driving can be rough and time-consuming, you'll have no trouble finding your way around. If you're even the slightest bit adventurous, you'll come to know Maui quite well by the time you leave, even if you spend only a week on the island. The people of Maui are generally friendly and helpful, but if you need extra assistance, you'll find just about everything you'll need to know listed in this chapter.

1 Orientation

VISITOR INFORMATION

The **Maui Visitors Bureau** is located at 1727 Wili Pa Loop (P.O. Box 580), Wailuku, HI 96793 (☎ 808/244-3530) in the industrial area of Wailuku in Central Maui. To get there from the airport, follow the sign to the airport exit, go right on Route 36 (the Hana Highway) to Kaahumanu Avenue. Go left on Kaahumanu Avenue (Route 32). Follow it past Maui Community College (on the right) and the Wailuku War Memorial Park (also on the right) onto East Main Street in Wailuku. Go right when you get to North Market Street and right again onto Mill Street. Go left on Kala Street and then left again onto Wili Pa Loop.

ISLAND LAYOUT
MAIN STREETS & ARTERIES

There are main highways, or *pi'ilani,* that will take you to each town, community, or resort area. The highway you'll take from Kahului to Lahaina, Kaanapali, Kahana, Napili, and Kapalua is the Honoapilani Highway, or Route 30. To get to most of the condos in Kahana and Napili, you'll want to take the Lower Honoapilani Highway, which can be reached by means of almost any street that heads off *makai* (toward the water) of the Honoapilani Highway.

Lahaina's main street is Front Street, where (or close to) you'll find all major establishments and places of business.

To go from Kahului Airport to Kihei, Wailea, or Makena (the south side), take the Mokulele Highway (Route 350) to the Pilani Highway (Route 31), which runs from Maalaea (pronounced "Ma-lye-ya") all the way to Makena (presently the end of the line on this side of the island). All the hotel and condominium properties are located makai (toward the water), off the Pilani Highway. The main road through Kihei is Kihei Road, which runs north–south along the coastline through Kihei and right up to Wailea. The main road through Wailea is Wailea Alanui Drive, which extends all the way through the resort area and connects to Makena Road.

Be aware that you can go from Lahaina to the south coast via the Honoapilani Highway and the Pilani Highway, which connect near Maalaea.

The main road from Kahului to Wailuku is Kaahumanu Avenue (Route 32), which will take you right onto Wailuku's Main Street. The other main artery in Wailuku, where you'll find restaurants and shops, is North Market Street.

To go Upcountry to Paia, take the Hana Highway (Route 36) from Kahului. This portion of the Hana Highway is not the one of "switchback" fame. That comes later as you continue along past Haiku, and it will take you all the way up to Hana on the island's east coast.

Further Upcountry from Paia is Makawao, which can be reached in one of two ways. You can drive to Paia as described above and then take a right on Baldwin Avenue (Paia's main drag) and follow it to Makawao; or you can take the Haleakala Highway (Route 37) to Makawao Highway (Route 400), where you'll take a left. It will take you right into Makawao. The first route will get you there a little more quickly.

Instead of going left off Haleakala Highway, continue along, and Haleakala Highway will turn into Kula Highway, which will lead you directly into the town of Kula.

If you go left off the Kula Highway, another Haleakala Highway will take you up to the summit of Haleakala Crater and Haleakala National Park.

FINDING AN ADDRESS

Finding an address on Maui is fairly simple, especially if you're looking for a shop, restaurant, or hotel. Generally, commercial establishments are located off one of the main roads mentioned above.

The notable exception to this rule is Kahului. Note that Papa Street runs in a half circle around the city of Kahului, and just about every street you'll need to find intersects with Papa Street at one time or another. Block numbers are posted on the street signs, so you can tell if you are in the general area of the address you're looking for without having to squint at building numbers. If you still can't find what you're looking for, stop and ask someone—most people are more than happy to help.

Islanders often use the Hawaiian words *mauka,* meaning "inland," and *makai,* meaning "toward the water," when giving directions.

STREET & ROAD MAPS

Street maps of the various towns of Maui are difficult to come by. There are some decent maps in the front of the local phone book, and I found a book titled *Maui Road Maps* in several of the island's bookstores that proved to be quite helpful. A local publication, it shows most of the streets in the major towns on Maui.

Good road maps for Maui are also difficult to find; however, several are available from the Maui Visitors Bureau (see "Visitor Information," above). You might also ask your rental-car agency if they have the map published by the University of Hawaii Press—it's a full-color topographic map with details of Lahaina, Wailuku, and Kahului; otherwise, check at one of the Waldenbooks stores around the island. There's a Waldenbooks in Whalers Village and Lahaina Cannery Mall, both in Lahaina; Kaahumanu Center and Maui Mall Shopping Center in Kahului; and in the Kukui Mall in Kihei.

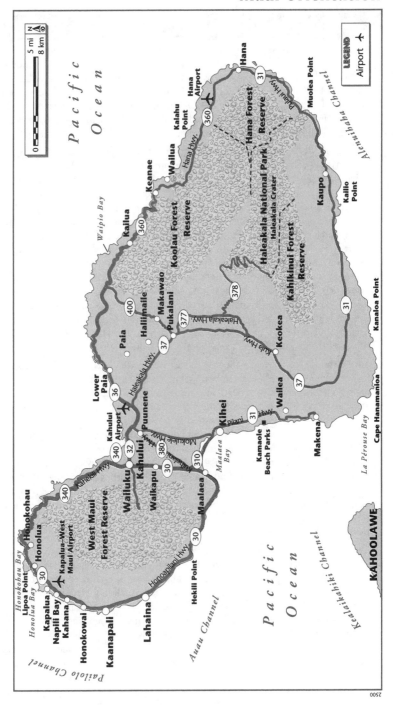

2 Neighborhoods in Brief

Central Maui   The small strip of land that connects the head and shoulders of Maui is known as Central Maui. Major roads that connect the east side to the west side go through this area. The two major towns here are Kahului and Wailuku. Kahului is home to Maui's airport as well as many of Maui's malls and department stores. There are only a few accommodations in the Kahului area, and they're not the nicest places on the island. Only a couple of miles from Kahului is Wailuku, which has an eclectic mix of shops, restaurants, and accommodations. You'll find art galleries and antique shops on Main Street in Wailuku, as well as a less attractive industrial area.

West Maui   The resort areas of Kaanapali and Kapalua, as well as the towns of Lahaina, Napili, and Kahana, lie in West Maui. Lahaina is where most of the action takes place. Tourists and locals alike mingle in historic Lahaina because it's where you can find some of the island's finest restaurants, as well as the Baldwin House Museum, the famous banyan tree, art galleries, jewelry stores, antique shops, T-shirt shops, and a couple of bars. Farther along the island's west coast you'll come to the resort area of Kaanapali, which includes the Marriott Hotel, the Westin, the Hyatt, the Royal Lahaina, the Sheraton, and several others. The Kaanapali resort is the largest and most active (especially in terms of nightlife) of all the island's resorts. It also has some incredible white-sand beaches. As you continue along the coast, you'll pass Napili and Kahana, much more subdued areas where you'll find most of the area's condominiums. Beyond Napili is the Kapalua resort, site of some of the island's most beautiful golf courses. Kapalua is home to the Kapalua Bay Hotel, several condominiums, and the newest addition to the hotel scene—the Ritz-Carlton Hotel.

South Maui   South Maui is the area of coastline between Maalaea and Makena. The quaint fishing town of Maalaea is worth taking a quick drive through, although there are no tourist-oriented shops and only one restaurant worth noting. The next town along the coast is Kihei, which is filled with condominiums, fast-food restaurants, strip malls, and—in spite of it all—some of the island's best beaches. Kihei is where you'll find some less-expensive lodging and dining options, and it's very popular with the locals who gather to picnic on the beaches or do a little windsurfing. Since it's a resort area, Wailea is much quieter than Kihei. There are many major hotels in the Wailea resort, including the Grand Wailea (which is worth a sightseeing trip in and of itself) and a couple of golf courses. Like Kaanapali, Wailea has some beautiful beaches, and only a few of them are heavily populated. Just beyond the Wailea resort is Makena. With a handful of historic sites and only a couple of hotels, Makena's main attraction is its beaches. Makena has Little Beach, Maui's only nude beach.

Upcountry   Upcountry Maui is a completely different experience than any other you'll have on the island. First of all, there are no beaches. Second, the temperature is often 10 to 20 degrees cooler, and at night you might even need a jacket. Technically, the Upcountry region begins in Paia, where you'll find Hookipa Beach Park and some of the best windsurfing on the island. As you continue Upcountry to Makawao, you'll leave the beaches behind, and see instead farmland and even a log cabin or two. In Kula, look for Tedeschi Vineyards, one of two island wineries. In the same area you'll find the farms that produce the famous sweet Maui onions and herbs for many of the area's restaurants. If you're there on July 4th you'll be treated to a unique rodeo.

East Maui   Basically what you'll find in East Maui is Hana, the tropical forest where waterfalls dot the countryside amid guava and African tulip trees. The road to Hana

Central Maui

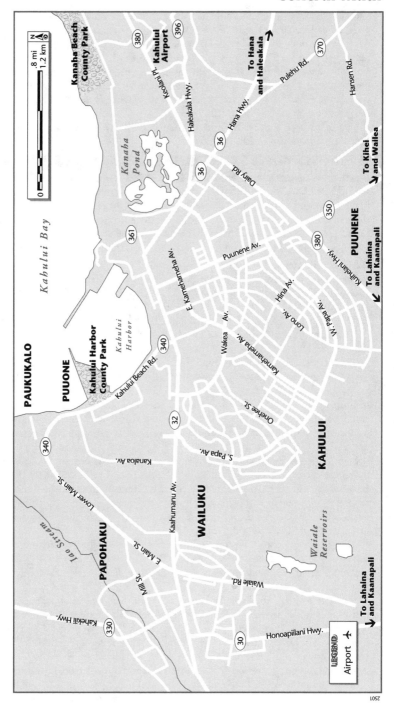

takes a series of switchbacks and is narrow and bumpy—a challenge to the skill, patience, and stomach of even the best driver and least queasy passenger. There is a small airport for those who don't wish to make the 3-hour drive, and there are a few hotels, and even fewer restaurants. Before you get to Hana you can stop at the Hana Gardenland Cafe where Hillary Clinton breakfasted three mornings in a row during her trip to the island. If you follow the Hana Highway through the town of Hana, you'll arrive at Mark Twain's favorite beach, Hamoa Beach. There's also a black-sand beach and a red-sand beach, as well as several blue pools that can be found by only the most intrepid tourist. Beyond all that, you'll come to the famous Seven Sacred Pools, or Oheo Gulch.

3 Getting Around

BY PUBLIC TRANSPORTATION   Basically, there is no public transportation on Maui. Consequently, several of the resorts have started their own shuttle services to transport visitors all over the resort, and in the case of the Kaanapali Trolley, into Lahaina several times a day. The Wailea Shuttle runs all around the resort as well, taking people from hotels to condos to golf courses to tennis courts all day long.

BY CAR   Rentals   The only way to get around Maui is by car. All the major car-rental agencies have offices on Maui, including **Dollar Rent-A-Car,** which has branches at Kahului Airport (☎ 808/877-2731), Kaanapali (☎ 808/667-2651), and Hana (☎ 808/248-8237); **Alamo** at Kahului (☎ 808/871-6235) and Kaanapali (☎ 808/661-7181); **Avis** at Kahului (☎ 808/871-7575), Kihei (☎ 808/874-4077), and Kaanapali (☎ 808/661-4588, or 800/831-8000); **Budget Rent-A-Car** at Kahului (☎ 800/527-0700).

Each of these agencies offers unlimited mileage and most have convertibles for rent. The one drawback to these rental companies is that their prices are fairly high. Cars can range from $50 to $90 a day—without coverage, and without the recently instituted mandatory $2-a-day Hawaiian surcharge. Check with your credit-card companies before you leave home to make sure that they do in fact guarantee insurance coverage on a rental car, so you can decline that extra cost when you pick up your car.

Some other, less well-known rental agencies offer lower rates because their cars are not in the greatest shape. **Word of Mouth Rent-A-Used-Car** located at 150 Hana Hwy. (☎ 808/877-2436 or 800/533-5929) is a good bet. With them, you'll also get unlimited miles and airport pickup. You won't feel out of place driving around in one of their used cars—that's what most of the locals drive. You'll probably escape the attention of Maui's petty thieves as well.

Most of the car companies rent some kind of four-wheel-drive car, but only **Adventures Rent-A-Jeep** at 190 Papa Pl. (☎ 808/877-6626 or 800/701-JEEP) specializes in off-road vehicles. They have more than 30 Wrangler and Cherokee four-wheel drives in their fleet.

Note: Most of the rental companies will ask you to sign a piece of paper stating that you'll downshift your car when descending Haleakala Crater. This is to protect the brakes on the car as much as it is to protect you. If you don't downshift, you'll have to use the brake all the way down, and then you'll suddenly find yourself the center of attention as you coast down the crater with clouds of smoke billowing behind you. If that goes on long enough, your brakes might fail. Also, if your rental car is not meant to be used off-road, don't use it off-road. If anything should happen to the car while you are driving it off-road, the rental company will make you pay for any damage and towing charges. They won't go easy on you either.

Some money-saving advice: Before you make a reservation directly with the rental agency, check to see if your hotel offers a room/car package (most do)—it could save you a bundle.

Parking   Parking places on Maui are fairly easy to come by. In most towns you can park on the street; if there are time limitations, usually a parking lot is available that allows you unlimited time. The only town where parking might be difficult is Lahaina. You probably won't be able to find a space on the street, but if you're lucky you'll get a place to park in one of the free lots. However, if you should have to pay to park, it probably won't cost more than $10 for a whole day.

Driving Rules   For the most part, driving rules are the same on Maui as the rest of the United States. Pay attention to the speed limit, observe all traffic signals and signs, and make a right turn on a red light only after coming to a complete stop. Hawaii has a mandatory seat-belt law, so don't forget to buckle up. Since the speed limit may change three or four times on the same stretch of road, pay careful attention to road signs.

Gas stations on Maui can be scarce, and driving is often rough, obliging you to use more gas than you might anticipate, so it's a good idea to keep your tank fairly full at all times. If you are coming to Maui from the U.S. mainland, you may be in for a shock over gas prices—at press time, regular unleaded gas was approximately $1.65 a gallon.

BY TAXI   There are many taxi companies on Maui, including **Yellow Cab of Maui** (☎ 808/877-7000). However, I wouldn't recommend trying to get around the island by cab. A ride from the airport to Lahaina will cost you between $42 and $45, and it's only about 20 miles.

BY FERRY   If you want to go to Molokai or Lanai and you don't feel like flying, you can go by ferry. **Expeditions** (☎ 808/661-3756) will take you to Lanai from the public dock adjacent to the brig *Carthaginian* at the Lahaina Wharf. You should make reservations in advance because the boat is fairly small. The ride to Lanai will take about an hour and is very pleasant, especially if you can get a seat on the upper deck. There are four or five departures daily, and round-trip fare is $50. Plan to get there 15 minutes in advance of the scheduled departure.

The *Maui Princess* (☎ 808/667-6165), operated by Island Marine Activities ferries passengers to Molokai twice a day. You should arrive at *Maui Princess's* slip at the Lahaina Wharf 15 minutes prior to your departure time, and you can purchase your tickets there. The round-trip fare is $70 plus tax. At press time passengers didn't have to make a reservation in advance, but call ahead to be sure. **Island Marine Activities** offers several package trips to Molokai, which may save you some money, so you might want to inquire when you call to confirm departure times.

BY MOPED   If you don't feel like spending a bundle on a rental car and don't have the energy to ride a bicycle all over the island, your best alternative might be to rent a moped. Try **A & B Moped Rental** at 3481 Lower Honoapilani Road (☎ 808/ 669-0027) or the **Kukui Activity Center** at 1819 S. Kihei Rd., Bldg. E (☎ 808/ 875-1151).

BY BICYCLE   It is possible to get around Maui on bicycle (although you'll have to be in excellent shape), and there are even designated bike lanes in some areas. Many people rent bikes so they can do some off-road exploration—places where a car won't go (or the rental agency won't allow the car to go). **West Maui Cycles** at Honokowai (☎ 808/669-1169) and **South Maui Bicycles** at 1913C S. Kihei Road (☎ 808/ 874-0068) are reputable bicycle-rental agencies.

HITCHHIKING   Though hitchhiking is never recommended, many local people get around by hitchhiking (which is understandable, given the absence of public transportation). As in most states, hitchhiking on Maui is illegal, and if you've got your thumb in the wind, you could be arrested. Locals don't solicit rides—they just hang around on the side of the road hoping someone will take pity on them and ask them if they'd like a ride. So, if you do decide to hitchhike, which, for the record, I don't recommend (especially for women traveling alone), try not to be obvious about it.

FAST FACTS: Maui

Airports   See "Getting There" in Chapter 3, "Planning a Trip to Maui."

American Express   There are three travel desk offices on the island. You'll find them at the Grand Wailea (☎ 808/875-4526), the Ritz-Carlton Kapalua (☎ 808/669-6016), and the Westin Maui (☎ 808/661-7155). If you need to report lost or stolen traveler's checks call 800/221-7282.

Area Code   The area code for all the Hawaiian islands is 808.

Babysitters   Most hotels will help you make arrangements with a babysitting service if they don't offer their own, but if you're staying in a condominium, try calling the Nanny Connection (☎ 808/875-4777). They provide babysitters to hotels or condos. Before you leave your child with any babysitter, even one sent by an agency, check to make sure that the person is reliable.

Business Hours   Everything in Maui will be open by 9am—in fact, most places open their doors sometime between 8 and 8:30am because Mauians like to get an early start so they can quit early and get to the beach before the sun goes down. They also start early because of the time difference between the islands and the mainland. *Pau hana* (or "end work") is between 4 and 5pm. Most banks open at 8:30am and close at 3pm daily except Friday (when they close at 5 or 6pm). Malls and department stores stay open until about 9pm during the week.

Camera & Film   Many of the hotels have photo-processing centers where you can buy film and inexpensive cameras, and get film developed in an hour. You can also have film processed for a reasonable price at any of the Longs Drug Stores on the island, as well as in ABC Discount Stores. If your photographic needs are more extensive, try Roy's Photo Video Center in the Maui Mall (☎ 808/871-4311) or the Kahului Camera Image Center at 180 Wakea Ave. Bay G (☎ 808/871-6848).

Car Rentals   See "Getting Around," above.

Climate   See "When to Go" in Chapter 3, "Planning a Trip to Maui."

Dentists   There are many dentists on Maui; if you need to find a good one in an emergency, call the Dental Referral Service (☎ 800/917-6453).

Doctors   If you're staying in Lahaina, Kaanapali, or Kapalua and become ill (but it's not an emergency), call Doctors on Call (☎ 808/667-7676). They'll send a doctor to your hotel at almost any time. The Kihei Clinic at 1993 S. Kihei Rd., Suite 19 (☎ 808/879-1440), welcomes visitors, and they also make "hotel" calls. Upcountry Medical Center at 81 Makawao Ave. (☎ 808/572-9888) is open daily.

Driving Rules   See "Getting Around," above.

Drugstores   See "Pharmacies," below.

Embassies/Consulates   See "Fast Facts: For the Foreign Traveler" in Chapter 4.

Emergencies For police, fire, or ambulance, dial ☎ **911**.

Eyeglass Repair If you need your glasses repaired or need an entirely new pair, the Eye Gallery at 1325 S. Kihei Road in Kihei Professional Plaza (☎ 808/ 879-8544) specializes in same-day service for most jobs. The Aloha Eye Clinic Ltd. Optical Department at 239 Wakea Ave. in Kahului (☎ 808/871-7485) also offers same-day service for most prescriptions.

Hospitals The island's major hospitals are: Maui Memorial Hospital at 221 Mahalani in Wailuku (☎ 808/244-9056 or 242-2343 for emergencies); Kula Hospital at 204 Kula Hwy. (☎ 808/878-1221); and Hana Medical Center in Hana (☎ 808/248-8294).

Hotlines HELPLINE, crisis counseling (☎ 808/244-7407); Women Helping Women, abuse counseling (☎ 808/579-9581); Maui AIDS Foundation (☎ 808/ 242-4900); Sexual Assault Crisis Center (☎ 808/242-4357).

Libraries There are branches of the Hawaii State Public Library System in Wailuku (☎ 808/243-5566), Hana (☎ 808/248-7714), Kahului (☎ 808/ 873-3097), Kihei (☎ 808/875-6833), Lahaina (☎ 808/662-3066), and Makawao (☎ 808/572-8094).

Liquor Laws The legal drinking age in Hawaii is 21. There are heavy penalties for anyone caught driving under the influence of alcohol.

Newspapers/Magazines The principal daily newspaper is the *Maui News,* but many towns put out their own papers as well. The island's magazine, *Maui Inc.,* is a bimonthly business publication.

Pharmacies Your best bet for a drugstore or pharmacy is Longs Drug Store. There are several located all over the island. In Kahului there's one in the Maui Mall (☎ 808/877-0041, or 808/877-0068 for prescriptions). In Kihei there's one at 1215 S. Kihei Rd. (☎ 808/879-2259 or 808/879-2033 for prescriptions). In Lahaina you'll find one in the Lahaina Cannery Mall (☎ 808/667-4384 or 808/ 667-4390). If you're Upcountry, try Paradise Pharmacy, 81–21 Makawao Avenue (☎ 808/572-1266).

Post Offices Many people wonder if it costs more to send a letter or postcard from Maui to the mainland than it does within the 48 contiguous states. It doesn't. Postage for a regular letter is 32¢. There are **post offices** in Haiku (☎ 808/575-2773), Hana (☎ 808/248-8258), Kahului (☎ 808/871-4710), Kihei (☎ 808/879-2403), Kula (☎ 808/878-1765), Lahaina (☎ 808/661-0550 or 808/ 667-6611), Makawao (☎ 808/572-8895), Paia (☎ 808/579-9205), Pukalani (☎ 808/572-8235), Puunene (☎ 808/871-4744), and Wailuku (☎ 808/ 244-4815). The main post office is on Oahu, so most of the mail that originates on Maui is sent to Oahu to be postmarked.

If you want to send something novel home to your friends and family, write them a coconut postcard—you literally write on a coconut, and the post office will mail it for you.

Police For police, in an emergency only, dial **911.**

Safety All in all, Maui is a safe place to visit, but when traveling, you should always exercise caution. No matter what you do, as a tourist you'll probably stand out. One of the biggest problems in Maui is car theft. Tourists' cars are easy to spot because they're generally in much better shape than the cars driven by locals. Don't leave money or valuables in the car, and always keep the doors and windows locked when you're parked at the beach or at a major tourist destination.

Television   Most hotels have full cable television service, and many of them now offer a channel specifically for tourists. Check your hotel television directory for details.

Time Zone   Maui is 5 hours behind Eastern Standard Time, 4 hours behind Central, and 2 hours behind Pacific. Remember, however, that Maui does not observe Daylight Saving Time, so add an hour when this is in effect on the mainland.

Weather   Call 808/244-8934, ext. 1520.

Maui Accommodations   6

Maui has always welcomed visitors with the warmest aloha, and to-day, islanders carry on the tradition by providing visitors with a wide variety of accommodations in many price categories. There are high-rise hotels, condominiums, and bed-and-breakfast inns from which to choose.

Deciding where you want to stay on Maui will depend largely on how much you want to spend and what kind of atmosphere best suits your personality. If you're looking to be at the center of the action, enjoy a good round of tennis or golf, and can afford to spend a fair amount on accommodations, Kaanapali is probably your best bet. It's near Lahaina, and there's always something happening in Kaanapali. If you want to spend less but still want to be in a lively location, try Kihei; here you can rent a condominium on or off the beach for slightly more reasonable rates. You can do the same in Napili or Kahana, but it's a bit of a drive to get to Kaanapali or Lahaina. If you're looking for peace and quiet in addition to good golf and tennis, try to stay in either Kapalua or Wailea resorts. Kapalua, which is smaller than Wailea, has only a couple of hotels and condominiums. Wailea has several hotels and condos, isn't as large as Kaanapali, but might be a bit more expensive than Kaanapali, depending on the hotel you choose. You can really save a bundle if you opt to stay Upcountry in a bed-and-breakfast inn, but it will probably take you an hour or more (unless you're in Hana) to get to the beach. Upcountry accommodations attract lo-cals who want to get away from tourists and cool off a little.

Hotel rates will usually include full resort privileges. Unless you have a golf package, you will have to pay extra for golf, and you'll probably have to pay extra for tennis. Water-sports equipment (such as snorkels and boogie boards) can be rented through the hotel for a nominal fee, and beach towels are typically provided free of charge to hotel guests.

Condominiums within a resort usually offer access to golf and tennis; however, your general expenses are likely to be lower because you'll have a kitchen where you can prepare breakfast and pack a lunch for the beach, and you won't be at the mercy of the hotel for all your meals. A few condos provide a grocery start-up package of milk, juice, and coffee (some provide other items as well), but don't assume that you'll have milk for your morning coffee—ask before you arrive. Many will also offer to do your grocery shopping for you, but the service is costly.

The accommodations listed in this chapter have been carefully chosen to reflect a range of prices, and I have attempted to supply you with rates that will be accurate for the life of this book, but you might find slight discrepancies when you call to make reservations. Hotels listed under the category **Expensive** are $200 and up; **Moderate** hotels range from $100 to $200; the **Inexpensive** category covers everything under $100. All accommodations are subject to 4.17% Hawaii state sales tax and a 9.17% hotel tax, so before you make a reservation be sure to figure in the tax.

1   West Maui

West Maui includes the Kaanapali and Kapalua resort areas, Lahaina, and the area between Kaanapali and Kapalua. A youngish crowd tends to be attracted to Kaanapali, where there's always something going on. For those on a budget who can't afford to stay in Kaanapali, but still want to be at the center of activity, some of the hotels in Lahaina, or just off the highway between Kaanapali and Kapalua, would be a better option. Kapalua, on the other hand, is a good choice for those looking for a quiet, relaxing golf or tennis vacation.

KAANAPALI
EXPENSIVE

✪ Hyatt Regency Maui
200 Nohea Kai Dr., Lahaina, Maui, HI 96761. ☎ **808/661-1234** or 800/233-1234. Fax 808/ 667-4498. 815 rms, 32 suites. A/C MINIBAR TV TEL. $240–$260 terrace view; $295–$320 golf/ mountain view; $325–$350 ocean view; $355–$380 deluxe ocean view; $390–$420 Regency Club mountain view; $430–$450 Regency Club ocean view. Extra person on standard floors $25, on Regency Club floors $45. Children 18 and under stay free in parents' room. Special packages are available. AE, DC, JCB, MC, V. Complimentary parking validation for hotel guests.

When the Hyatt opened in 1980 it was among the few hotel properties in the Kaanapali resort area, and at that time was one of the island's most opulent. Today it is still a first-class establishment surpassed perhaps by only one of the newer properties on the island. Enter through the beautifully landscaped, open-air atrium dotted with palm trees, tropical birds, and pieces from the hotel's extensive Asian and Pacific art collection. In the lobby garden alone you'll find a large pair of Chinese cloisonné vases, some Japanese dragon pots, and Thai elephant bells. This is only the beginning—the hotel holds a veritable treasure trove of art. All public spaces are decorated with original pieces of artwork, including specially commissioned Hawaiian quilts, Burmese and Cambodian buddhas, Ming dynasty wine pots, Chinese stone animals, and a breathtaking 17-foot-high cast-bronze sculpture titled "The Acrobats." Even the elevators here are spectacular: Teak-paneled interiors are accented with brass fixtures, and luxurious Chinese carpets cover the floors.

The hotel consists of three connected wings, the tallest of which is nine stories. The only things standing between the beach and the hotel are the pool, a row of palm trees, and a small strip of grass. All guest rooms, which were renovated in 1995, offer views of the ocean, the West Maui mountains, Kaanapali golf courses, or the hotel's gardens; the rooms are pleasantly decorated with rich floral bedspreads, teal and peach color schemes, wood furnishings, and Asian lamps—a welcome change from the typical beige or sandy-colored interiors of many Maui hotels. Accommodations here are furnished with either king or double beds, separate sitting areas, and private lanais. Amenities include in-room safes, hair dryers,

Kaanapali Coast Accommodations

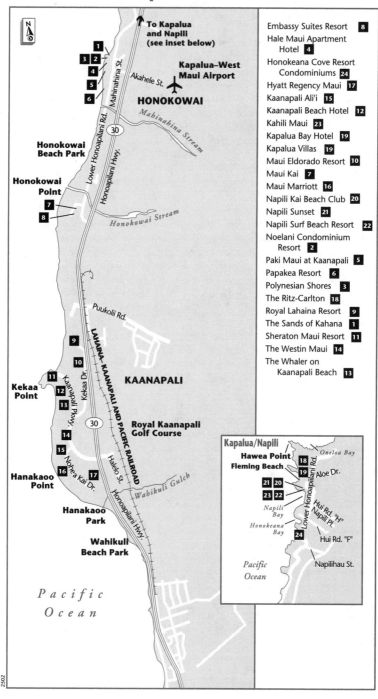

Embassy Suites Resort **8**

Hale Maui Apartment Hotel **4**

Honokeana Cove Resort Condominiums **24**

Hyatt Regency Maui **17**

Kaanapali Ali'i **15**

Kaanapali Beach Hotel **12**

Kahili Maui **23**

Kapalua Bay Hotel **19**

Kapalua Villas **19**

Maui Eldorado Resort **10**

Maui Kai **7**

Maui Marriott **16**

Napili Kai Beach Club **20**

Napili Sunset **21**

Napili Surf Beach Resort **22**

Noelani Condominium Resort **2**

Paki Maui at Kaanapali **5**

Papakea Resort **6**

Polynesian Shores **3**

The Ritz-Carlton **18**

Royal Lahaina Resort **9**

The Sands of Kahana **1**

Sheraton Maui Resort **11**

The Westin Maui **14**

The Whaler on Kaanapali Beach **13**

2502

coffeemakers, and irons and ironing boards. In addition to the standard rooms, there are private-access Regency Club rooms located on the top two floors in the Atrium Tower. Each of the Regency Club floors has a private concierge who handles all special requests, the complimentary breakfast service, and sunset cocktails and hors d'oeuvres. The hotel's suites range from the Ocean Suite, a one-bedroom unit with two lanais and two TV sets, to the Deluxe Suite with a living room, dining area, three lanais, two TV sets, and a wet bar. If you've got money to burn, consider the Presidential Suite, which has seven lanais, a full dining room, library, dressing room, sauna, Jacuzzi, and two full baths.

The Hyatt offers some special programs, including the rooftop astronomy program—Tour of the Stars. In January 1991, the Hyatt announced that a "revolutionary new telescope system" for "public, educational, and recreational astronomy" had been developed, and the prototype had been installed on the hotel's rooftop. Developed by Bill Leighty of Juneau, Alaska, this incredible telescope is outfitted with a computer that has the capacity to identify and locate 1,000 different stars, planets, clusters, nebulae, and galaxies. While the viewer observes various star formations, he or she can listen to a prerecorded message about the stars being viewed. Reservations for this program are a must, and there is an admission fee. Garden, art, and wildlife tours are also available, as are hula and Hawaiian arts and crafts lessons.

Dining/Entertainment: One of the hotel's fine dining establishments, **Swan Court,** serves a buffet breakfast and a continental dinner daily (see Chapter 7, "Maui Dining," for details). **Spats Trattoria,** an Italian restaurant featuring northern Italian cuisine, is the hotel's other fine dining venue (see Chapter 7 for details). A more casual approach would take you to the **Lahaina Provision Company,** an open-air surf-and-turf garden restaurant. The Provision Company offers two unique specialties—the Tropical Salad Bar at lunch and the Chocoholic Bar at dinner. The **Pavillion** is the hotel's other poolside dining spot, where diners enjoy breakfast (indoors or out) from 6 to 11:30am and lunch and snacks from 11:30am to 6pm. The Pavillion serves everything from fruit plates to pancakes to bagels for breakfast, and burgers, pizza, sandwiches, and salads at lunch. The Hyatt offers its own luau on the **Sunset Terrace** every night except Sunday (see Chapter 8, "What to See & Do on Maui," for details). For tropical drinks and smoothies, try the **Grotto Bar,** which is tucked away under the dual waterfalls. The Lahaina Provision Company's lounge is open daily, and the **Weeping Banyan** (in the lobby, floating on the koi pond) offers contemporary Hawaiian music nightly.

Services: Concierge service offers all sorts of information about the resort and the island. Room service and babysitting services are available on request. The Aloha Service activity desk is available to help guests plan island sightseeing, as well as arrange cruises and airline reservations.

Camp Hyatt is the hotel's children's program that offers daytime and evening supervised activities for 3- to 12-year-olds. Nondenominational church services are offered every Sunday.

Facilities: The hotel's Great Pool is one of the main attractions. It holds 750,000 gallons of water and spans a half-acre. In the pool there's a swim-up cocktail bar, a 150-foot water slide, and a swinging rope bridge for guests to enjoy. The Regency Health Club has a weight and exercise room, Jacuzzi, sauna, and massage studio (both Eastern and Western techniques are practiced by the masseurs). Aerobics classes are offered daily. Six hard-surface tennis courts are available for guest use. The Kaanapali golf courses are available for guest use (see Chapter 9, "Maui Sports & Recreation," for detailed golf course listings). There is a game room on the premises, as well as a small lending library. Rental equipment for snorkeling is available through the hotel, and *Kiele V*, the Hyatt's 55-foot catamaran, sponsors snorkeling trips as well as whale-watching excursions and evening cruises. In addition, hotel guests may rent bicycles, kayaks, boogie boards, video cameras, and underwater cameras. Several floors have been set aside for nonsmokers.

Kaanapali Ali'i

50 Nohea Kai Dr., Lahaina, Maui, HI 96761. ☎ **808/667-1400** or 800/642-MAUI. Fax 808/661-1025. 264 units. A/C TV TEL. High season (Jan 5–Apr 15 and July 1–Aug 31) 1-bedroom $245 garden view, $260 deluxe garden view, $305 ocean view; 2-bedroom $310 garden view, $335 deluxe garden view, $400 ocean view, $490 oceanfront; $650 Club Ali'i Suite. Low season (Apr 16–June 30 and Sept 1–Dec 15) 1-bedroom $215 garden view, $225 deluxe garden view, $260 ocean view; 2-bedroom $270 garden view, $280 deluxe garden view, $335 ocean view, $425 oceanfront; $650 Club Ali'i Suite. AE, MC, V. Free parking.

All the condominium units at the Kaanapali Ali'i are spacious—the oceanfront accommodations range in size from 1,500 to 1,900 square feet, and each is developer or individually owned and decorated. One-bedroom units can accommodate up to four, and two-bedroom units are large enough for six. There is no charge for an extra person if existing bedding is used. Each unit comes equipped with a washer and dryer, dishwasher, whirlpool bathtub, and private lanai. Guests can use the on-site exercise room, pool, wading pool, Jacuzzi, saunas, barbecue grills, and beach activities desk. Three tennis courts are available for guest use. No fee is charged for court time; however, if you would like lessons there is a nominal charge. There are no restaurants on the property, but guests of the Kaanapali Ali'i have charge-back privileges at the Westin and Maui Marriott and may order room service from the Maui Marriott (located next door).

If you choose to have Club Ali'i Service, additional amenities include a full-size rental car, fully stocked bar, plush terrycloth robes, and the "Maui Morning" grocery package (including champagne). Daily maid service is included in the rates for all guests.

✪ Maui Marriott

100 Nohea Kai Dr., Lahaina, Maui, HI 96761. ☎ **808/667-1200** or 800/763-1333. Fax 808/667-8300. 720 rms, 19 suites. A/C TV TEL. $195 mountain golf; $260 mountain ocean; $280 ocean view; $310 deluxe ocean; $400–$1,000 suite. Room & car, honeymoon, and golf packages are available. AE, DC, JCB, MC, V. Parking $7 per day valet- or self-parking in covered garage.

One of my favorite resort hotels on the island, the Maui Marriott offers its guests a casual, comfortable atmosphere, a well-trained and friendly staff, and all the amenities you'd find in any luxury hotel in the area. The most significant difference between the Marriott and some of the other hotels in this category is the way you feel when you enter the hotel. Instead of worrying about your appearance, you'll want to let your hair down, change into your favorite T-shirt and a pair of shorts, and head for the beach. The staff is efficient and extremely friendly—not stuffy or overtrained as is the staff at other island properties.

The open-air lobby is tastefully furnished and landscaped with waterfalls, palm trees, and scores of varieties of tropical plants. The hotel's two nine-story wings are named for the island each one faces (Molokai and Lanai), and they flank the lobby area. Each room in the hotel is entered via the open-air, bougainvillea-lined promenades that look down into the superbly landscaped lower lobby.

All the hotel's spacious rooms have been recently refurbished with light-wood furnishings, and a bright, airy color scheme. Each is equipped with a king-size or two double beds as well as a queen-size sofa sleeper, and features such amenities as a minirefrigerator, in-room safe ($3 a day charge), ironing board and iron, hair dryer, daily newspaper, daily complimentary Kona coffee, and direct-dial telephones with voice mail. It's difficult to imagine that anyone could want for anything in one of the Marriott's rooms. Each of the rooms also has a private lanai; although about 10% of the rooms do not have ocean views, those facing *mauka* ("inland") provide beautiful mountain views.

The hotel has a full guest services desk and complimentary activities program where you can arrange to attend exercise classes, snorkeling and marine life lessons, island food demonstrations, and classes in Hawaiiana (including lei-making, hula dance and ukelele lessons, and Hawaiian quilt-making and language lessons). They will also arrange helicopter and boat rides, scuba diving, parasailing, horseback riding, deep-sea fishing, whale-watching tours, and golf at your request.

Dining/Entertainment: Three bars are available to guests on the property. The **Lobby Bar,** which is located directly across from the check-in desk, features karaoke as well as live stand-up comedy. The **Makai Bar** is a popular spot with hotel guests and locals alike. If you arrive early enough, you'll be able to watch the sun set while enjoying tropical drinks, pupus, and live local entertainment. The **Kau Kau Grill & Bar** serves poolside cocktails as well as breakfast and salads, burgers, and sandwiches throughout the day. There is also a poolside **Pizza Hut** kiosk. The **Moana Terrace** restaurant serves a buffet breakfast as well as a dinner buffet or à la carte menu. **Lokelani** (see Chapter 7, "Maui Dining," for details), a more formal restaurant (although the dress code is fairly casual—resort wear is acceptable), serves dinner only and specializes in fresh fish and regional cuisine. **Nikko** (see Chapter 7 for details), the hotel's Japanese restaurant, features the ancient technique of teppan-yaki cooking for dinner only. The Marriott also offers a sunset luau on Kaanapali Beach that features Hawaiian/Polynesian music and a show (see Chapter 8, "What to See & Do on Maui," for information).

Services: Room service from 6am to 10pm daily; 24-hour babysitting and interpreter services; tour and car-rental desks; notary, facsimile, and express mail.

Facilities: Two swimming pools, two whirlpools, separate children's pool, tennis courts (three lighted for night play), pro shop, massage therapy, two exercise areas with Nautilus and Universal weights and cardiovascular machines, a video game room and 9-hole putting green. Full service beauty salon, photo shop, and florist, along with 18 retail shops in the lobby gallery (offering everything from sundries, souvenirs, and logo wear to fine family apparel, jewelry, art, and sculpture).

Sheraton Maui Resort

2605 Kaanapali Pkwy., Lahaina, Maui, HI 96761-1991. ☎ **808/661-0031** or 800/325-3535. 494 rms. A/C TV TEL. 139 Molokai wing; $159 standard room; $180 mountain cottage; $215 garden view; $250 partial ocean view; $270 ocean view; $320 oceanfront cottage or Molokai wing suite; $570 garden suite; $630 cliff suites. Extra person $25. Children 17 and under stay free in parents' room with existing bedding. Special packages are available. AE, CB, DC, DISC, ER, JCB, MC, V. Parking $3.50 per day.

Built atop Black Rock Promontory in 1963, the Sheraton Maui was the first in a long line of resort hotels to line the beautiful stretch of white sand known today as Kaanapali Beach. Because it was the first, it is also one of the most spread out. Covering 23 acres, the buildings that make up the Sheraton Maui are low-rise and have been constructed in a melange of architectural styles. There is one large eight-story building, but the rest of the rooms are housed in the 26 separate cottages, each of which has four units on the first floor and two on the second. The rates for all rooms, whether in the main building or the cottages, vary only according to view.

Currently the Sheraton is undergoing a massive renovation; thus, I do not know what the rooms and new buildings will look like or what the new amenities will be.

If you're interested in staying at the Sheraton, I would recommend that you call to make sure they are open (they were planning to close the hotel down during renovations) and to find out what their rates are (they expected no major price increase).

One of the Sheraton's major attractions is the cliff-diving and torchlighting ceremony every evening at sunset. In ancient times, Mauians designated Black Rock as one of three *uhane-lele* (or "soul leaping") spots in all of the Hawaiian Islands. It was believed that the souls of the dead would leap into the ocean from Black Rock just as the sun was setting and would follow the sun to the sea of Kailalo (Eternal Paradise). Much later, Kahekili, the last king of Maui, was trying to keep his title (and rouse a weary army) as he fought against Kalaniopu'u, the high chief of the island of Hawaii; in a show of inspiration to his warriors he leapt from Black Rock into the ocean. Today the tradition continues as a scantily clad young man lights the evening torches as he runs to make his leap from Black Rock.

The beach in front of the Sheraton also attracts a large green sea turtle in the early mornings, and guests who rise early enough and are quiet enough might be able to catch a glimpse of this wonderful creature.

Dining/Entertainment: The Sheraton's **Discovery Room** restaurant offers guests a panoramic view of Black Rock Promontory, Kaanapali Beach, and the islands of Molokai and Lanai. The Discovery Room features breakfast and dinner buffets, as well as à la carte dining. **On the Rocks Bar** serves lunch daily and cocktails every evening. The **Snack Shop** is open for continental breakfast and quick lunches. The **Sundowner Bar** is open from 10am to 8pm daily, and there is a karaoke bar on the eighth floor that is open nightly from 9pm to midnight. The Sheraton Maui also has an evening luau (except on Sunday).

Services: Valet laundry service; babysitting service; room service; Avis Rent-A-Car direct line; nondenominational poolside religious services on Sunday.

Facilities: 24-hour coin-op laundry facilities; two outdoor pools; three outdoor tennis courts; activities desk to help arrange sightseeing tours, boat cruises, fishing excursions, and more; access to nearby Kaanapali golf courses.

✪ The Westin Maui

2365 Kaanapali Pkwy., Lahaina, Maui, HI 96761. ☎ **808/667-2525** or 800/228-3000. Fax 808/661-5764. 761 rms, 28 suites. A/C MINIBAR TV TEL. $245 terrace; $285 garden view; $310 golf/mountain view; $350 ocean view; $380 deluxe ocean view; $410 oceanfront; $450 Royal Beach Club. Additional person in standard rooms $25, Royal Beach Club Room $45. Children 17 and under stay free in parents' room. 25% discount on additional rooms occupied by children. Complimentary valet- and self-parking available.

Located on some of Kaanapali's prime oceanfront property, next door to the Whalers Village Shopping Complex, the Westin Maui is something of a beachfront fantasy land. The moment you enter the spacious open-air lobby you will feel relaxed. At check-in you're greeted with warm hospitality and an equally warm hand towel with which to refresh yourself while waiting for your room key. The resort's five swimming pools, located just outside the lobby area, are surrounded by lush gardens and a variety of tropical birds sitting atop their own personal perches or swimming in the small outdoor ponds. In addition, the hotel has a $2 million art collection scattered throughout many of the public spaces.

Guest rooms, all of which were renovated in 1995, are located in the Ocean Tower or Beach Tower; they offer views either of the ocean or of the Kaanapali golf courses and the West Maui Mountains. Each room is freshly decorated with an "elegant floral look" and is furnished with either a king-size or double beds. In addition to the standard amenities, you'll find in-room safes, an iron and ironing board, coffeemakers, and private lanais.

The Royal Beach Club, located on the top two floors of the Beach Tower, is comprised of 37 guest rooms. A private staff is available between 6:30am and 10pm. Those staying on the Royal Beach Club floors receive a complimentary lei and champagne greeting on arrival, a complimentary Japanese robe, daily newspaper, upgraded bath amenities, and hair dryers. In the Beach Club Lounge guests may enjoy a continental breakfast buffet, afternoon tea, and early evening cocktail service.

Every Friday there are Hawaiian arts and crafts displays, hula shows and lessons, lei-making and ti leaf skirt-making instruction, and a poolside Aloha Show at Cook's at the Beach.

Dining/Entertainment: Sound of the Falls is the hotel's most romantic evening dining spot. Pacific bistro cuisine is offered in the open-air dining room that is surrounded by cascading waterfalls. A pianist tickles the ivories nightly. Reservations are recommended. (For further details, see Chapter 7, "Maui Dining.") The **Villa Restaurant** serves fresh island seafood nightly amid the beautifully landscaped lagoons and waterfalls. The **Villa Terrace** is a casual spot that offers a full all-you-can-eat seafood buffet (served seasonally in a 21-foot outrigger canoe). The poolside **Cook's at the Beach** serves breakfast, lunch, and dinner daily, and six nights a week you'll be treated to Hawaiian music and a hula show. The **Garden Bar,** with a 25-inch TV, serves the breakfast, lunch, and dinner menus from Cook's at the Beach. In the morning the **Colonnade Lounge** offers take-out coffee and Danish, and in the evening it serves as a meeting place where hotel guests may gather for cocktails. The Garden Bar is open daily and offers a poolside menu, cocktails, and entertainment six nights a week.

Services: Guest Services will help plan activities and tours of the hotel, and will provide information about various points of interest on the island. American Express and Hertz Rent-a-Car have desks in the hotel lobby. Japanese Guest Services provides translations of hotel information, as well as reservations and assistance with any activities that might be planned. Secretarial services are available to all guests upon request. Nondenominational church services are held every Sunday.

Facilities: The hotel's beauty salon—The Stylists—is located on the mezzanine level of the Beach Tower. There are also eight retail shops on the hotel's lobby level.

Westin's Kids' Club Keiki Kamp is the Westin's children's program. Counselors supervise children up to 12 years old from Monday through Friday on and off the property (in 1995 a new facility was added for the Keiki Kamp). Activities might include movies, a ride on the Sugar Cane Train, or a trip to the Hawaii Experience Domed Theater (see Chapter 8, "What to See & Do on Maui," for details).

There are five swimming pools available for guest use, three of which are joined together by a series of water slides and a swim-through grotto. There is also an outdoor swim-up Jacuzzi, organized water games, and aquacise classes. Scuba lessons for beginners (or refresher courses) are offered in the hotel's pool. After your first dive in the pool, you'll probably be ready and able to take a guided ocean beach dive or attend a scuba certification course.

The Westin's health club has weight training, aerobic, and exercise rooms, men's and women's locker rooms, a Jacuzzi, massage therapy by appointment, and several classes offered daily. Hotel guests have access to the Kaanapali golf courses. The Westin also has its own 64-foot catamaran.

The Whaler on Kaanapali Beach

2481 Kaanapali Pkwy., Lahaina, Maui, HI 96761. ☎ **808/661-4861** or 800/367-7052. Fax 415/283-3129. 360 units, 150 managed by Village Resorts. A/C TV TEL. High season (Dec 20–Apr 7) $180 garden-view studio, $195 ocean-view studio, $225 garden-view 1-bedroom/1-bath, $275 ocean-view 1-bedroom/1-bath; $230 garden-view 1-bedroom/2-bath, $285 ocean-view 1-bedroom/2-bath, $355 oceanfront 1-bedroom/2-bath, $295 garden-view 2-bedroom/2-bath, $385 ocean-view 2-bedroom/2-bath, $465 oceanfront 2-bedroom/2-bath. Low season (Apr 8–Dec 19) $10 to $35 lower. Rollaway $10. Crib $5. AE, MC, V. Free underground parking.

Not only does the Whaler on Kaanapali Beach have one of the best locations of any condominium on Maui, but it has some of the most spacious rooms as well. It's located right on the beach, nestled between the Kaanapali Beach Hotel and Whalers Village Shopping Center and just across Kaanapali Parkway from the Kaanapali golf courses. All of the individually owned units are tastefully decorated and come equipped with a full kitchen, marble-tiled bathrooms, VCRs, safes ($1.50 a day), and first-day coffee setups. Units range from studios (for up to two people) to two-bedroom units (up to six people), and all have private, blue-tiled lanais. There are laundry facilities on each floor (although a laundry service is available), and there's an exercise room and sauna on the property (open 7am to 9pm daily). Guests may also use the large oceanfront heated pool and barbecue grills. There are no restaurants on the property, but guests have charge-back privileges to several restaurants in the Whalers Village Shopping Center and other nearby restaurants. Court fees for tennis are $7 a day, and guests of the Whaler receive discounts at the Kaanapali resort golf courses. The lobby area houses a minimarket for last-minute grocery shopping and video rentals. There is a 24-hour front desk with 24-hour phone service.

MODERATE

Kaanapali Beach Hotel
2525 Kaanapali Pkwy., Lahaina, Maui, HI 96761-1987. ☎ 808/661-0011 or 800/262-8450. Fax 808/667-5978. 422 rms, 8 suites. A/C TV TEL. $145 garden; $165 courtyard view; $175 partial ocean view; $190 ocean view; $225 oceanfront; $190–$535 suites. Extra person $25. Special packages are available. AE, CB, DC, MC, V. Free parking.

Built in 1964 and renovated most recently in 1991, the Kaanapali Beach Hotel is one of the least expensive hotels in the Kaanapali Beach resort, but it doesn't scrimp on guest activities and aloha spirit. Rooms here are spacious, and all feature minirefrigerators and a shower or tub/shower combination. Rooms also have lanais, and all face inward toward the courtyard and the beach. The gardens in the courtyard are beautifully landscaped with plumeria and palm trees, and the lawn is well manicured. The central feature of the gardens is the whale-shaped swimming pool. Chaise longues are placed invitingly around the pool and are scattered throughout the gardens for those who would rather sit in the shade of a palm tree. The hotel property borders a great rock formation, affording guests excellent snorkeling opportunities. A unique feature of this hotel is the giant checkerboard in the courtyard.

The Kaanapali Beach Hotel is known for its Hawaiian activities program where guests can learn to cut pineapple, make ti leaf skirts and leis, weave lauhala (pandanus leaf), and participate in lau-printing. Guests are also entitled to receive some of the island's most authentic hula lessons. Every evening there is a complimentary hula show and other Hawaiian entertainment, including a nightly torchlighting ceremony. Every Friday there's a craft fair and lobby show. The hotel employees are well educated in Hawaiiana and show great pride in their hotel (even the hotel brochure was designed by hotel employees).

Dining/Entertainment: The **Kaanapali Mixed Plate** restaurant serves an all-you-can-eat breakfast, lunch, and dinner buffet daily. The **Tiki Terrace** is open daily for breakfast and dinner and serves a Sunday champagne brunch. The **Tiki Grill** is the hotel's poolside grill where guests can order sandwiches and hot dogs. The **Tiki Bar,** also poolside, specializes in tropical cocktails.

Services: United Airlines desk; babysitting; daily maid service; activities desk; free scuba and snorkeling lessons.

Facilities: Swimming pool; children's programs offered seasonally ($15 per child, including lunch); coin-op laundry facilities; beauty salon; beach equipment rentals (boogie boards, snorkeling and scuba equipment, sailboats, windsurfers, and catamarans); access to 11 tennis courts (six lit for night play) and Kaanapali golf courses; Tropical Breeze Clothing Store (featuring resort and active wear); sundry shop; jewelry store.

Maui Eldorado Resort

2661 Kekaa Dr., Kaanapali, Maui, HI 96761. ☎ **808/661-0021** or 800/535-0085. Fax 808/667-7039. 204 units (106 for rent through resort). A/C TV TEL. High season (Dec 21–Mar 31) $160 studio garden, $190 studio ocean view; $200 1-bedroom garden, $230 1-bedroom ocean view; $275 2-bedroom garden, $315 2-bedroom ocean view. Low season (Apr 1–Dec 20) $145 studio garden, $165 studio ocean view; $170 1-bedroom garden, $200 1-bedroom ocean view; $240 2-bedroom garden, $280 2-bedroom ocean view. Rollaway or crib $15. Special packages and weekly and monthly discounts are available. AE, MC, V. Free parking.

You might not think about staying at the Eldorado because it's located inland from the hotels that line Kaanapali Beach, and the exterior is a bit dated, but if you're trying to save some money, you shouldn't pass it by. The condominiums were some of the first accommodations built in the Kaanapali Beach resort (in the late 1960s). Back then, larger parcels of land were easier for developers to acquire, so rather than the high-rises that are so typical today, architects were free to design sprawling hotels and condominiums that blended with the landscape. The Eldorado is comprised of 12 separate buildings covering 10 acres, which gives visitors a greater sense of privacy. The studio and 1- and 2-bedroom units are larger than average, and the furnishings are adequate. A typical studio is somewhat like a hotel room with small living and dining areas and a kitchenette. Washer/dryer combinations are standard for each unit, and all condos have private lanais with outdoor furniture. One- and two-bedroom units have the same amenities but are larger and have more than one bathroom. The maximum number of guests allowed in a studio is two, a one-bedroom can accommodate four, and a two-bedroom can hold six. Most of the units look out over the Kaanapali golf courses. The ocean is a fair distance away, so when you book your condo, keep in mind that an "ocean-view" unit means only that it will be located on the second floor where you'll be able to get a glimpse of the water. All of the condos have beautiful views of the golf course, however.

A shuttle service will transport guests to the Eldorado's private Beach Club located on the beach right near Black Rock, a lava formation where snorkelers and scuba divers can amuse themselves for hours in a wildlife preserve. Every Friday night there is a complimentary Manager's Cocktail Party at the Beach Club. There are three swimming pools on the property (one heated) as well as a small gourmet grocery store. Barbecues and snorkeling equipment are available on request.

Maui Kai

106 Kaanapali Shores Place, Lahaina, Maui, HI 96761. ☎ **808/667-3500** or 800/367-5635. Fax 808/667-3660. 80 units, 60 in rental pool. A/C TV TEL. High season (Dec 18–Mar 31) $135 studio; $155 1-bedroom, $165 1-bedroom corner; $205 2-bedroom. Low season (Apr 1–Dec 18) $115 studio; $135 1-bedroom, $145 1-bedroom corner; $185 2-bedroom. Extra person $10. Minimum stay of 1 week during Christmas. MC, V. Free parking.

Because the Maui Kai is small and set off the main road, many people don't even know it's there. All the studio, 1-, and 2-bedroom units at the Maui Kai are oceanfront, but they're a little smaller than some of the units at other properties (don't let that scare you off, though—the views are worth it). Each of the condos is individually decorated in light color schemes, making the units pleasant and cheerful. Kitchens are fully equipped, and private lanais are either enclosed or open-air. Included in the rates listed above is twice weekly maid service, but daily maid service is available at an additional cost. A pool and Jacuzzi are located on the property, and guests can use an outdoor cabana with a kitchen (to prepare a quick lunch if you'd rather not return to your room). Other facilities include gas barbecues, laundry facilities, a Guest Activity Service, Ping-Pong table, and a lending library. You can't go wrong here.

Paki Maui at Kaanapali

3615 Lower Honoapilani Rd., Lahaina, Maui, HI 96761. ☎ **808/669-8235** or 800/535-0085. Fax 808/922-2421. 110 units, 77 in rental pool. TV TEL. $149 studio; $159–$179 1-bedroom; $219–$249 2-bedroom. Extra person $15. Children under 18 stay free in parents' room. Weekly discounts and special packages available. AE, DC, DISC, MC, V. Free parking.

The Paki Maui is located right on the water; although the beach isn't sandy, a rolling strip of lawn runs down to the water's edge. Sunbathing is a favorite activity of Paki Maui guests, but swimming, sandcastle building, and snorkeling are best saved for the sandy beaches located just a few minutes away. Studios and one- and two-bedroom apartments offer mountain, garden, ocean, or oceanfront views, and rates vary according to what you'll see from your private, fully furnished lanai. Naturally, ocean and oceanfront rooms are excellent, but if you want to save a little money, ask for the mountain- or garden-view suites. If you choose the garden view, you'll feel like you're living in Old Hawaii as you look out into the courtyard with its lagoon falls and koi pond. Each unit is fully furnished and individually decorated. All have microwaves and VCRs. There is daily maid service and daily continental breakfast. Relax in the outdoor pool or jet spa, and prepare a cookout using the barbecue facilities on the property. The manager hosts a weekly Mai Tai party for hotel guests, and the activity and travel desk will help you plan your day.

✪ Royal Lahaina Resort

2780 Kekaa Dr., Lahaina, Maui, HI 96761. ☎ **808/661-3611** or 800/44-ROYAL. Fax 808/661-6150 or 800/432-9752 for reservations. 540 rms, 26 suites. A/C TV TEL. $175–$195 garden view; $215–$235 ocean view; $275–$295 oceanfront; $235–$255 garden cottage; $295–$315 oceanfront cottage; $500–$1,500 suite. Extra person $20. AE, CB, DC, DISC, JCB, MC, V. Self-parking $1 per day.

The newly redecorated Royal Lahaina Resort is said to be located on a site "chosen by the monarchs of the Islands" because it was the "best location on the beach." Though there are more than 500 rooms here, the accommodations are spread over 27 acres in moderately sized buildings or cottages, affording guests a greater feeling of privacy than would be the case in a high-rise hotel with the same number of rooms. The low-rise cottages that dot the carefully landscaped grounds lend an air of serenity, and as you wander along the pathways between palm trees bent by trade winds, you'll be treated to a potpourri of scents from salt water and sun to plumeria blossoms and coconut oil. One of the best buys in the Kaanapali Beach resort, the Royal Lahaina offers tastefully decorated rooms with traditional Hawaiian appointments, such as bedspreads with Hawaiian quilt appliqués. The furnishings are wicker and rattan with floral, solid, or striped cushions, and the color schemes are neutral with touches of teal, peach, green, and light blue. All rooms have minirefrigerators, private lanais, and in-room safes, as well as ironing boards (housekeeping will supply the iron). Some rooms and all cottage suites have ceiling fans. Specialty suites are oceanfront, have two bedrooms, three baths, a living room, kitchen, private garden, pool, whirlpool, and waterfall (the price tag is high, though).

Guests may rent beach and water-sports equipment, including Hobie Cats, windsurfers, ocean kayaks, paddleboats, and snorkel gear. The traditional hula and lei-making classes are also offered here, and you might also have an opportunity to participate in Hawaiian quilt-making classes and ukulele lessons. There is a shopping arcade on the property where you can get everything from film to fine jewelry.

Dining/Entertainment: The **Royal Ocean Terrace Restaurant** is an open-air restaurant featuring Hawaiian and American cuisines. Breakfast and dinner are served there daily. Beachcombers Restaurant features Asian and Pacific Rim cuisine. **Basil Tomatoes,** overlooking the Kaanapali golf courses, serves up Italian cuisine. The **Royal Ocean Terrace Lounge** offers Hawaiian specialty drinks, poolside service, and Hawaiian-style entertainment daily. The **Chopsticks** lounge features a large imported beer selection as well as exotic drinks. The **Royal Scoop Ice Cream Parlor** serves pastries and sandwiches in addition to a selection of ice creams. The Royal Lahaina Luau (see Chapter 8, "What to See & Do on Maui," for details) takes place nightly at 5:30pm from September 1 to April 30 and at 6pm from May 1 to August 31.

Services: Room service, valet laundry and dry cleaning, babysitting referral service; daily complimentary introductory scuba lessons; Pleasant Hawaiian Holidays Travel Desk.

Facilities: Three swimming pools; Jacuzzi; a world-class tennis facility featuring 10 courts (six lit for night play), tennis stadium that seats up to 3,500, pro shop, snack shop, and one resident pro; two golf courses are adjacent to the property—the Kaanapali North Course and the Kaanapali South Course, pro shop, driving range, and one resident pro; beach and boating center; shuffleboard court; volleyball facility; croquet setup. There's also a beauty salon and a guest laundromat.

LAHAINA
EXPENSIVE

Embassy Suites Resort
104 Kaanapali Shores Pl., Lahaina, Maui, HI 96761. ☎ **808/661-2000** or 800/462-6284. Fax 808/667-5821. 413 suites. A/C TV TEL. 1-bedroom suite $240 scenic view, $300 ocean view, $375 deluxe ocean view; 2-bedroom suite $450; Presidential Suite $1,200. Extra person $20. AE, CB, DC, DISC, JCB, MC, V. Parking $5 per day.

With its pink exterior and stepped-back architecture, this all-suite 12-story hotel is difficult to miss as you drive along the Honoapilani Highway. It's one of the last hotels built on Kaanapali Beach before you reach Honokowai. If you take advantage of the room capacities (four people for the one-bedroom and six people for the two-bedroom), the rates are extremely reasonable. The large rooms are attractively furnished. Neutral color schemes set the backdrop for blue and white wide-striped pull-out couches in the living rooms and blue and white floral print bedspreads with shell-shaped, fabric-covered, padded headboards. The living room features a VCR, AM/FM radio and cassette stereo system, kitchenette (with microwave, minirefrigerator with automatic ice-maker), wet bar, and coffeemaker. Complimentary Kona coffee is replenished daily. All bedrooms have a second TV and private lanais. Spacious white-tiled bathrooms are equipped with double vanities, soaking tubs, and separate showers. There is a complimentary breakfast buffet (omelets are made to order) and a daily two-hour cocktail reception. Snorkeling, windsurfing, and scuba lessons are also available to guests.

Dining/Entertainment: The **North Beach Grill,** the hotel's oceanfront restaurant, features local seafood as well as steak, pasta, and a large salad bar. Poolside, you'll find the **Ohana Grill,** which serves pizza and light meals. The **Deli Planet** in the lobby

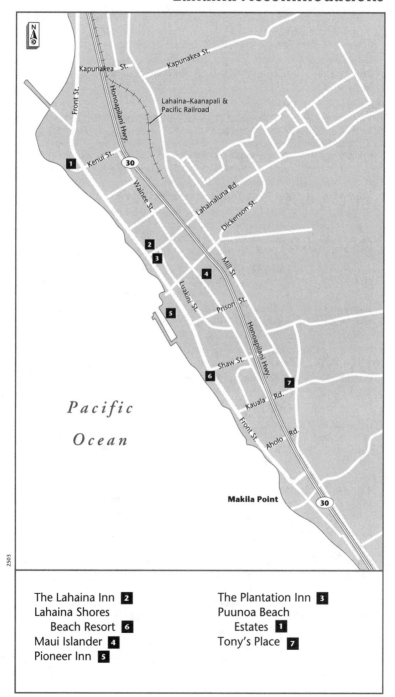

The Lahaina Inn 2
Lahaina Shores
    Beach Resort 6
Maui Islander 4
Pioneer Inn 5

The Plantation Inn 3
Puunoa Beach
    Estates 1
Tony's Place 7

makes sandwiches and picnic baskets to go. **Moonbeams Bar** serves mixed drinks, wine, beer, and soda.

Services: Room service; year-round children's program.

Facilities: One-acre swimming pool with 24-foot water slide, exercise room, hair salon, spa and massage, video arcade, 18-hole miniature golf, retail shops, self-service laundry facilities.

Puunoa Beach Estates

45 Kai Pali Place (write to 50 Nohea Kai Dr. for reservations), Lahaina, Maui, HI 96761. ☎ **808/ 667-5972** or 800/642-MAUI. 10 units. A/C TV TEL. High season (Jan 5–Apr 15) $580 standard 2-bedroom unit, $695 2-bedroom unit with loft; $730 standard 3-bedroom unit, $800 3-bedroom unit with loft. Low season (Apr 16–Dec 15) $550 standard 2-bedroom unit, $580 2-bedroom unit with loft; $605 standard 3-bedroom unit, $665 3-bedroom unit with loft. Minimum stay of 3 nights. Rates include full-size rental car. AE, MC, V. Free parking.

The exclusive Puunoa Beach Estates is perhaps one of the island's most unexpected and delightful properties. In spite of Puunoa's central location, it is amazingly private. The five two-story buildings are situated on three lovely acres of oceanfront property, and each building houses two condominium units. The units range in size from 1,700 to 2,100 square feet and are appointed with modern but elegant furnishings. Special touches such as fine Oriental carpets and beautiful ceramic pieces make each of the "estates" unique. Kitchens are fully equipped, and all master bathrooms have oversized Roman Jacuzzi tubs. Every unit also has a wet bar, full-sized washer and dryer, two TVs, and a VCR. Upstairs apartments have vaulted ceilings, which make the apartments seem even more spacious.

The property is bordered by a lovely strip of white-sand beach, and the pool is relatively private. A sauna is available for guest use, and if you feel like exploring the rest of the island, the concierge will arrange your activity schedule. When you arrive, you'll find a "Maui Mornings" grocery package waiting for you, and the *Wall Street Journal* and a local newspaper will be delivered daily to your home away from home. If you can afford it, Puunoa Estates is unbeatable.

The Sands of Kahana

4299 Lower Honoapilani Rd., Lahaina, Maui, HI 96761. ☎ **808/669-0400** or 800/367-7052. Fax 510/283-3129. 196 units, 129 in rental pool. TV TEL. $105–$175 1-bedroom; $165–$205 2-bedroom; $195–$260 3-bedroom; $195–$300 2-bedroom penthouse unit. AE, MC, V. Free parking.

There are scores of condominium complexes between Kaanapali and Kapalua, but there aren't many that offer spacious accommodations, ample recreational activities, and a beach perfect for swimming, sunning, and snorkeling. The Sands of Kahana has all of that and much more. The characteristic blue-tiled roofs are easy to spot from the road, and the sand-colored stucco exteriors blend nicely with the landscape in spite of their height. Near the entrance there's a well-stocked koi pond, and palm trees line the pathways leading to each of the condominium buildings. Pineapple-cutting and lei-making demonstrations are held in the courtyard just outside the lobby area, and there's a lovely beachfront pool and spa. Barbecue grills are centrally located for guest use, and there's even a separate pool, playground, and activities program for children. Three lighted tennis courts and a putting green are available for guest use. There's an open-air poolside restaurant on the property.

One-, two-, or three-bedroom condo units have large living rooms, many of which open directly into a bedroom (they can be closed off any time with accordian doors). Washers and dryers are standard, and the kitchens are roomy with more than enough storage space for those who plan on an extended stay. Private lanais feature bougainvillea-filled window boxes and functional outdoor furniture (usually enough for outdoor dining). Rates are higher here than at other properties, but so are the standards.

MODERATE

Honokeana Cove Resort Condominiums

5255 Lower Honoapilani Rd., Lahaina, Maui, HI 96761. ☎ **808/669-6441** or 800/237-4948. 38 units, 33 in rental pool. TV TEL. $105 1-bedroom unit; $105–$115 1-bedroom loft unit; $147 2-bedroom unit; $175 3-bedroom unit; $165 2-bedroom townhouse. Extra person in loft unit $15, lower units $10. Weekly and monthly discounts available. Minimum stay of 3 nights. MC, V. Free parking.

Love to snorkel? Well, at Honokeana Cove you'll find great snorkeling in the condominium's own private cove. All the one-, two-, and three-bedroom units are just steps away from the ocean; even though the shoreline is rocky, a sandy strip of beach is just a 5-minute walk away on a shoreline path. Each apartment is individually owned and decorated—some are a little better than others. All units are outfitted with dishwashers and fully equipped kitchens. Laundry facilities and barbecue grills are available for guest use. Near the ocean's edge across a beautifully manicured lawn, you will find the swimming pool where pupu parties are held weekly.

✪ The Lahaina Inn

127 Lahainaluna Rd., Lahaina, Maui, HI 96761. ☎ **808/661-0577** or 800/669-3444. Fax 808/667-9480. 12 rms. A/C TEL. $89 mountain view; $99 harbor view; $129 Makai Room; $129 Mauka Room; $129 Lahainaluna Room. Wedding packages available. AE, MC, V. Parking $5 per day.

The Lahaina Inn comes as something of a surprise in the middle of one of Maui's busiest and most commercial towns. It's a haven that takes you away from tourist traps, fast-food restaurants, and the busy wharf. In 1938, what is now the Lahaina Inn opened as a general store. After several different owners, and a stint as the Lahainaluna Hotel, Rick Ralston (the current owner, who also owns Crazy Shirts, Inc.) bought the structure and began an extensive restoration project.

Plush Oriental rugs, a Victorian camelback couch, and a rich walnut staircase welcome you into the hotel's lobby. At the top of the stairs you'll find the guest rooms, all of which are individually decorated with antiques from Ralston's own collection. Each room has a private lanai offering either an ocean or mountain view. Antique leaded glass lamps, fine fabrics, hand-done needlework pillows, floral wallpapers, intricately carved wood furnishings, lace curtains, and period paintings are just some of the lovely details that are scattered throughout the small hotel. Ralston thought of everything, down to the antique lock sets on guest-room doors, and no expense was too great—when the wooden floors didn't creak authentically, Ralston had the carpenters rip them up and lay them down again so they would whine and squeak as guests walked around the hotel. There's a room here to suit anyone's taste. All accommodations are air-conditioned, and continental breakfast is included in the room rate.

Adjoining the lobby is David Paul's Lahaina Grill (see Chapter 7, "Maui Dining," for details) serving New American cuisine.

Lahaina Shores Beach Resort

475 Front St. (reservations office 50 Nohea Kai Dr.), Lahaina, Maui, HI 96761. ☎ **808/661-4835** or 800/628-6699. 199 units, 154 in rental pool. A/C TV TEL. $100–$160 studio; $135–$190 1-bedroom; $170–$225 penthouse oceanfront unit. Rollaway or crib $10. AE, MC, V. Free parking.

This resort hotel bills itself as "Right on the Beach. Right in the Town. Right on the Money," and it's exactly that. In fact, this is the only hotel in Lahaina town that is located right on the beach. The individually-owned studios and one-bedroom units are comfortable. One-bedroom units sleep up to five (most have queen-size or two twin beds, and some have Murphy beds), and all have fully equipped kitchens. About one-third have microwaves, and all have VCRs. Laundry facilities for studios and one-bedroom units are located in the hall, but irons and ironing boards are standard in each condo. The six penthouse units have washers and dryers, king-size beds, and sofa sleepers. For the money, penthouse condos are probably your best bet. In general, bathrooms are small but serviceable. Just off the hotel's newly renovated lobby you can relax in the whirlpool spa or the hotel's swimming pool. There are no restaurants on the property, but complimentary breakfast is offered at the daily island orientation, and poolside lunch service is provided by Hecocks restaurant next door. Video tape rentals are available at the front desk.

Napili Sunset

46 Hui Dr., Lahaina, Maui, HI 96761. ☎ **808/669-8083** or 800/447-9229 (8am–5pm Hawaiian time). Fax 808/669-2730. 42 condo units. TV TEL. $90 garden-view studio for two; $169 1-bedroom beachfront apartment for two; $269 2-bedroom beachfront apartment for four. Minimum stay of 3 nights. MC, V. Free parking.

Built in the 1970s, the Napili Sunset enjoys a great beachfront location where the swimming is excellent, and the views from oceanfront studios, one-, and two-bedroom units are spectacular. These units are some of the most spacious on the island in this price category. The fully equipped kitchens are also outfitted with microwaves. Ceiling fans, complimentary in-room safes, and irons and ironing boards are standard. Local telephone calls are free. Some studios look out over the small kidney-shaped swimming pool. Maid service is provided daily, beach towels are available, and there is a coin-op laundry facility for guest use. There is a small convenience store on the property where guests can pick up groceries for a picnic or a beachside barbecue.

Napili Surf Beach Resort

50 Napili Place, Lahaina, Maui, HI 96761. ☎ **808/669-8002** or 800/541-0638. Fax 808/669-8004. 53 units. TV TEL. Apr 1–Dec 18: $79 garden-view studio, $125 ocean-view studio, $150 1-bedroom condo. Dec 19–Mar 31: $95 garden-view studio, $130 ocean-view studio, $155 1-bedroom condo. Room/car packages, 7-night, 14-night, and monthly discounts available. Rates are based on double occupancy. Extra person $15. Children 12 and under stay free in parents' room. No credit cards. Free parking.

Of all the condominium complexes in the area in this price range, the Napili Surf is probably the most suitable for those seeking a quiet Hawaiian vacation. Its beautiful, sandy crescent beach is great for sunbathing and ocean swimming. There's also a snorkeling reef just offshore. Even the least expensive unit is nicely furnished, comes with a fully equipped kitchen (including a microwave and dishwasher), has ceiling fans, and is serviced daily by the housekeeping staff. Laundry facilities are available to guests, as are barbecues. There are two swimming pools, and the beautifully manicured grounds with winding pathways are dotted with plumeria trees and other tropical flora.

Papakea Resort

3543 Lower Honoapilani Rd., Lahaina, Maui, HI 96761. ☎ **808/669-4848** or 800/367-7052. Fax 510/283-3129. 364 units, 120 in rental pool. A/C TV TEL. High season (Dec 21–Jan 3 and Feb 1–Apr 19) $150 partial ocean-view studio, $171 oceanfront studio; $160 partial ocean-view 1-bedroom suite, $203 oceanfront 1-bedroom suite; $224 partial ocean-view 2-bedroom suite, $273 oceanfront 2-bedroom suite. Low season (Jan 4–Jan 31 and Apr 20–Dec 20) $134 partial ocean-view studio, $155 oceanfront studio; $144 partial ocean-view 1-bedroom suite, $187 oceanfront 1-bedroom suite; $209 partial ocean-view 2-bedroom suite, $257 oceanfront 2-bedroom suite. Minimum stay of 2 nights. Rollaway $15. Crib $10. AE, MC, V. Free parking.

Papakea is a wonderful resort condominium property. Several four-story buildings are spread out over 13 acres and are surrounded by beautifully landscaped gardens, freshwater lagoons, and impeccably manicured lawns. There are even two Japanese fish ponds. Oceanfront units offer gorgeous views—you'll feel as though you can jump right off your lanai into the water. Don't, however, because the only drawback to this property is the fact that there is no sandy beach here. Never fear, though—you won't have to go far to find one. Chances are that you'll be completely content at Papakea, especially if you enjoy sports. There are two oceanfront pools and spas, two 12-hole putting greens, three lighted tennis courts (complimentary), and shuffleboard courts. Through the guest activities service you can find out about aquacise classes, scuba and surfing classes, and tennis clinics; if you want to relax, head for the cabana and hop in the sauna.

Large studio, one-, and two-bedroom condo units offer such standard features as fully equipped kitchens plus microwaves, washer/dryer combinations, and full daily maid service. Papakea offers just about everything you could possibly need on your long-awaited Hawaiian vacation.

Polynesian Shores

3975 Lower Honoapilani Rd., Lahaina, Maui, HI 96761. ☎ **808/669-6065** or 800/433-MAUI from the U.S. mainland, 800/488-2179 from Canada. Fax 808/669-0909. 52 units, 35 in rental pool. TV TEL. $85–$105 1-bedroom unit; $95–$120 2-bedroom loft; $140–$160 2-bedroom end unit; $160–$175 3-bedroom unit. Extra person $10. Minimum stay of 3 nights. DISC, MC, V. Free parking.

If you're looking for a small, private condominium property with a guaranteed ocean view, Polynesian Shores fits the bill. A rolling lawn leads to the heated swimming pool, and guests will find excellent snorkeling right at the edge of the property. Swimming is better a short walk down along the shoreline, but if all you want to do is sunbathe, the pool deck and the shoreline tiki lanai (outfitted with barbecues) are good bets. The one-, two-, and three-bedroom units are handsomely furnished, and have fully equipped kitchens. Coin-op laundry facilities are available. The hotel's well-maintained tropical gardens are a delight.

The Plantation Inn

174 Lahainaluna Rd., Lahaina, Maui, HI 96761. ☎ **808/667-9225** or 800/433-6815. Fax 808/667-9293. 18 rms and suites. A/C TV TEL. High season $119 standard, $149 deluxe, $159–$179 superior, $209–$219 suite; low season $104 standard, $129 deluxe, $145–$157 superior, $185–$195 suite. AE, DISC, MC, V. Free parking.

Just about a block from the waterfront you'll find another surprise—the Plantation Inn. As soon as you pass through its doors you'll forget that you're right in the heart of one of Maui's busiest towns. One reason is that all the rooms have been soundproofed. Each guest room has been individually decorated and is outfitted with amenities that are likely to please nearly any traveler. Your room might have a canopy or four-poster bed, floral prints or stripes, Oriental rugs, wall-to-wall carpeting, or hardwood floors. Color schemes might be pastel or of deeper, richer tones. For instance, Suite 8 has a separate living room with a roomy couch, an armchair, dividing doors with stained-glass art featuring humpback whales, a beautiful rice four-poster bed, lace-covered lampshades, and floral fabrics. Room 10, on the other hand, has an Asian theme—the walls are a deep Chinese red, a lacquered four-poster bed is the room's centerpiece, and Oriental rugs cover hardwood floors. Many of the furnishings in other rooms were handcrafted in Thailand, and beautiful stained-glass creations are scattered throughout. All rooms are equipped with VCRs, refrigerators, private bathrooms, and verandas. Suites feature additional amenities, including full cooking facilities.

Water-sports equipment and a tiled swimming pool are also available for guest use. **Gerard's** restaurant (see Chapter 7, "Maui Dining," for details), which features fine French cuisine by a chef who was voted "Best Chef on Maui" two years in a row, is located on the ground floor.

INEXPENSIVE

⑤ Hale Maui Apartment Hotel

3711 Lower Honoapilani Rd., (P.O. Box 516), Lahaina, Maui, HI 96767. ☎ **808/669-6312.** Fax 808/669-1302. 12 units. TV. $65–$95 apartment for two. Minimum stay of 3 nights. Extra person $10. MC, V. Free parking.

This tiny apartment building almost gets lost amid the larger condominium complexes that line the beach in this area, but if you're looking for a bargain, you shouldn't miss it. There's no swimming pool, but the building is just steps from the beach, and all units have private lanais. Even though there's no air-conditioning, the trade winds that blow through the apartments keep them amazingly cool (one side is cooler than the other, but you won't suffer no matter where you are). All the rooms have been refurbished, and the kitchens are fully equipped.

Maui Islander

660 Wainee St., Lahaina, Maui, HI 96761. ☎ **808/667-9766** or 800/367-5226. Fax 808/661-3733. 372 rms and condo units. A/C TV TEL. $75 standard double; $87 studio with kitchen; $95 deluxe studio with kitchen; $105 1-bedroom suite with kitchen; $157 2-bedroom suite with kitchen. Dec 20–Apr 1 add $9 to all rates. Room-and-car packages available. AE, DC, DISC, MC, V. Free parking.

Located just a couple of blocks from Lahaina's busy Front Street, the Islander affords the budget-minded traveler the opportunity to stay near some of Maui's most beautiful beaches—which are all public, by the way—in clean, comfortable accommodations. At the Islander you'll have a choice of a standard hotel room with a minirefrigerator, a studio, or a one- or two-bedroom suite with a full kitchen. The hotel has just completed a two-year renovation, and all accommodations have new furnishings, draperies and upholsteries, and carpeting. There is daily maid service, cable TV, in-room safes ($2.50 a day), air conditioning, and ceiling fans. The one-bedroom suites are large enough to accommodate four, and the two-bedroom suites are large enough for six.

The hotel's kidney-shaped outdoor swimming pool, lighted tennis court, and barbecue area are available for guest use, and there's an activities center that can help you plan your day. The activities center also sponsors free hula and lei-making lessons, scuba and snorkel lessons, as well as a Maui orientation with complimentary coffee and rolls each morning at 8am. A coin-operated laundry facility is available for guest use.

⑤ Noelani Condominium Resort

4095 Lower Honoapilani Rd., Lahaina, HI 96761. ☎ **808/669-8374** or 800/367-6030. Fax 808/669-7904. 50 units, 44 in rental pool. TV TEL. $87 studio; $110 1-bedroom; $140 2-bedroom; $170 3-bedroom. Extra person $7.50. Special room/car packages and weekly or monthly discounts available. Minimum stay of 3 nights. AE, MC, V. Free parking.

You won't get stuck in a condo with an undesirable view at Noelani because all units are oceanfront. A sandy beach is adjacent to the property, but if you don't want to get sand in your shoes, you can relax by one of the two heated oceanfront swimming pools where Mai Tai parties are held a few times monthly. Orientation continental breakfasts are included in the rates. Studios provide full kitchens, queen-size beds, plus a dressing area off the bathroom, so you're getting a good deal more space than you would in the average hotel room. The kitchens in all the units are furnished with microwaves and dishwashers. One-, two-, and three-bedroom units are equipped with washers and dryers (there are laundry facilities on the property for those staying in studio units), and the three-bedroom condos are bilevel (one bedroom downstairs and two bedrooms on the upper floor). The decor in most of the units is bright and airy, with floral or Hawaiian print fabrics. You'll be well entertained here, but if you feel like getting out, there's full concierge service, and if you'd rather stay in, all of the units have VCRs (the video library is located in the guest reception area). There are also barbecue grills and an oceanfront picnic area. There is weekly maid service.

Pioneer Inn

658 Wharf St., Lahaina, Maui, HI 96761. ☎ **808/661-3636** or 800/457-5457. Fax 808/ 667-5708. 50 rms. Standard $90, deluxe $135. Extra person $20; Children under 10 $10. AE, CB, DC, JCB, MC, V. No parking available on-site; free parking on street; otherwise, about $8 to $10 a day in a nearby lot.

The Pioneer Inn—a Lahaina landmark—has been the center of action since it opened as a hotel and wholesale and retail liquor business in 1901. Back then it offered sailors clean but Spartan accommodations, and it does the same today. Thus, the room rates here are the lowest you'll find in Lahaina. In the past critics have praised the hotel's low prices and historic atmosphere, but complained about noise levels from the downstairs saloon. Well, there's nothing to complain about now! The one-time rough-and-ready saloon is now a dining room (there's still a bar), and its atmosphere and clientele are greatly subdued from the old days of the Pioneer Inn. In addition, most of the rooms, all of which have private baths and lanais and air-conditioning, have been renovated and newly redecorated, making this one of the island's best buys.

Tony's Place

13 Kauaula Rd., Lahaina, Maui, HI 96761. ☎ **808/661-8040.** 3 rms (none with private bath). $50 single, $60 double. All rates include taxes. MC, V. Free parking.

If you're looking for really inexpensive accommodations right in Lahaina and just steps away from the beach, give Tony Mamo a call. He rents clean, comfortable rooms right in his own home. Two of the bedrooms share a bath and one shares a bath with Tony's room. The public spaces are communal, and guests may use the refrigerator, telephone, television, and rather extensive library. Tony spent 17 long, cold years in Alaska, and he moved to Maui to warm up and relax—he expects his guests to do the same.

KAPALUA
EXPENSIVE

Kapalua Bay Hotel

One Bay Drive, Kapalua, Maui, HI 96761. ☎ **808/669-5656** or 800/367-8000. Fax 808/ 669-4694. 194 rms, 3 suites, 125 villas. A/C MINIBAR TV TEL. Hotel $260 garden view; $325 ocean view; $375 ocean-view prime; $450 oceanfront; $760–$1,260 suite. Extra person $35. AE, DC, DISC, JCB, MC, V. Free valet parking.

Before the Ritz-Carlton appeared on the scene a couple of years ago, the 17-year-old Kapalua Bay Hotel and Villas (see also below) was the only hotel in the Kapalua resort, and it was considered to be one of the island's best. In recent years, the hotel has gone through some ups and downs due to frequent changes in ownership, but now the Kapalua Bay Hotel has made a comeback.

If you're looking for peace, quiet, a little tennis, and a lot of golf, the Kapalua Bay Hotel and Villas are for you (see Chapter 9, "Maui Sports & Recreation," for full descriptions of golf courses). The Kapalua resort is made up of 1,500 landscaped acres on a 23,000-acre pineapple plantation. When you check in, a member of the hotel's efficient staff will escort you to the skylit lobby, where you can relax with a cold glass of juice while they check to see that your room is ready.

Most of the rooms at this hotel offer ocean views, but some have golf course or gardens views. Rooms in the prime garden-view category typically afford a view of the ocean as well, but it's not a *full* ocean view. Each room has a long, narrow bathroom with a separate bathtub and shower, and two sinks (one at each end of the room). There are closets in the bathroom as well. A guest room renovation was completed in the summer of 1995. Each room has a private, spacious lanai with patio furniture for outdoor dining.

Dining/Entertainment: The **Bay Club** restaurant is one of the jewels of the Kapalua resort. Set on a promontory overlooking the bay, it is open for lunch and dinner daily and serves fresh island seafood (see Chapter 7, "Maui Dining," for details) in a romantic setting; a pianist provides quiet music nightly from 6:30 to 10:30pm. Hotel guests may also dine alfresco in the **Garden** at breakfast and dinner daily. There is live entertainment in the lobby terrace every evening. The **Pool Terrace** is the hotel's poolside, casual restaurant where continental breakfast is served; at lunch there are salads, sandwiches, burgers, and main dishes. A pianist entertains hotel guests who gather for drinks in the evening at the **Bay Lounge.**

Services: Limited room service; twice-daily maid service; ice service (ice is delivered to your room late every afternoon, and on request); resort shuttle service; complimentary airport transfer to the Kapalua West Maui Airport; church services; daily tea service; secretarial services; babysitting services on request; complimentary introductory scuba lessons.

Facilities: Two swimming pools on hotel grounds, nine others throughout the Kapalua villa and condo complexes (see below for descriptions of Kapalua condos), exercise facility with one-on-one fitness training (for a fee) and aerobics and aquacise classes. The Kapalua resort also has three fine golf courses (each with its own pro shop) and 10 plexi-pave tennis courts for day and night play. Villa guests have access to two additional tennis courts. Children between the ages of 5 and 12 might want to take advantage of Kamp Kapalua where they can enjoy snorkeling, surfing, tide pool exploration, lei-making, and cookie-baking, among other activities. Adults can plan similar activities (except for the cookie-baking) through the hotel's Beach Activity Center. The Kapalua Shops (see Chapter 8, "What to See & Do on Maui," for more details) are located within easy walking distance of the hotel.

Kapalua Villas

500 Office Rd., Kapalua, Maui, HI 96761. ☎ **808/669-8088** or 800/545-0018. Fax 808/669-5234. A/C TV TEL. Special packages available. 1-bedroom $185 fairway view, $215 ocean view, $245 oceanfront; 2-bedroom $245 fairway view, $305 ocean view, $365 oceanfront. Free parking.

The Kapalua Bay, Ridge, or Golf Villas are an excellent choice for travelers who want both the independence and economy of a condominium, plus the serenity of Kapalua and its beautiful golf courses and excellent tennis facilities. The villas are arranged in three private clusters: bay, ridge, and golf. All of the condominiums are privately owned, and therefore individually decorated, but are managed by the Kapalua Land Company, developer of the Kapalua resort. Villa guests have access to all of the resort's amenities and enjoy the privilege of special golf rates, advance tee times, and complimentary tennis. Each cluster of villas has private swimming pools and outdoor barbecues. A resort shuttle is available to transport guests to and from resort beaches and facilities, and those staying at the villas have charge-back privileges at some of the facilities located in the nearby Ritz-Carlton Hotel. There is twice weekly maid service.

The Ritz-Carlton

One Ritz-Carlton Dr., Kapalua, Maui, HI 96761. ☎ **808/669-6200** or 800/262-8440. Fax 808/ 665-0026. 550 rms, 58 suites. A/C MINIBAR TV TEL. $285 golf view; $325 partial ocean view; $400 ocean view; $455 oceanfront; $495 Club level; $625–$1,250 suite. Extra person over 18 years of age $40. Children under 18 stay free in parents' room. AE, DC, JCB, MC, V. Valet parking $10 per night; self-parking is available.

Located only 10 miles from historic Lahaina amid ancient Cook pines and ironwood trees, the Ritz-Carlton is the most recent jewel in the crown of the 1,500-acre Kapalua resort community. The original architectural plans called for building the hotel closer to the beach than it is today, but during preliminary construction it was discovered that the projected building site was over an ancient Hawaiian burial ground, so the plans had to be changed. The Ritz-Carlton has been appointed the caretaker of the burial site, which is now on the State Register of Historic Places.

In keeping with the Ritz-Carlton's dedication to the preservation of culture and art, the walls display 18th- and 19th-century European paintings as well as work by local artists. There are some beautiful landscapes of Haleakala Crater, Hana, and Upcountry. George Allan, Joyce Clark, Betty Hay Freeland, and Fred Ken Knight are among the local artists whose work graces the walls of the Ritz. The enormous ceramic vases and pots you'll see as you walk through hallways and other public spaces are the work of local artist Tom Faught.

The guest rooms further illustrate the Ritz's dedication to excellence with features such as full marble bathrooms with separate showers, double vanities, and an extra telephone. All rooms have complimentary in-room safes, AM/FM clock radios, hair dryers, and incredibly plush terrycloth robes. Private lanais are outfitted with a table and chairs, and most of the rooms provide ocean views. Ritz-Carlton Club Level rooms, located on the top three floors of the Napili wing, offer guests additional amenities, personal attention, and more privacy. Access to the Club Level floors is by elevator key. A concierge can be found in the Club Level lounge, which is set with food and beverage presentations throughout the day.

You can easily walk to the beach from the hotel, but there is a complimentary golf cart shuttle service to and from the strip of white sand at the end of the path.

During your stay here you might want to lie on the beach or by the pool working on your tan; otherwise you can take advantage of the hotel's jogging and walking trails, complimentary scuba lesson, snorkeling, sunset sails, windsurfing, or deep-sea fishing. Whatever your desire, the hotel's gracious and efficient staff will try to help you fulfill it.

If you're traveling with youngsters, I can't think of a better place for them. The children's program, Ritz Kids, offers supervised activities that include learning about Hawaiian culture. Each day features a specific environmental theme. For example, on Monday—Maui Day—children take escorted walks through the tropical flower and herb gardens and learn the Hawaiian names of various plants. Other activities include playing on the 9-hole putting green, croquet lawn, and tennis courts; children's aerobics classes; swimming in the three-tiered pool; and games and storytelling in the private Ritz-Kids Room. The Ritz Kids package includes a membership card, access to the international pen-pal program, and a twice-yearly newsletter about Hawaii and Ritz Kids friends. The full-day program costs $60 per child and includes a T-shirt and lunch. The half-day program is $40.

Dining/Entertainment: The **Anuenue Room** serves Hawaiian Provencal cuisine featuring a new signature dinner menu (see Chapter 7, "Maui Dining," for details). While having dinner or just a cocktail, guests can enjoy a jazz duo in the Anuenue Lounge (adjacent to the Anuenue Room). The **Terrace Restaurant,** which serves breakfast and dinner daily with indoor and outdoor seating, features traditional Hawaiian music nightly. The **Banyan Tree Restaurant** specializes in Mediterranean cuisine for lunch and serves lunch and cocktails poolside. The **Beach House** is the hotel's beachside cafe where guests can have a quick sandwich amid swaying palm trees. In the early evening, you might have a cocktail in the **Lobby Lounge and Library** while enjoying solo Hawaiian guitar music and a beautiful dramatic sunset.

Services: 24-hour room service; transportation to and from the airport; secretarial services; babysitting; shuttle to and from golf courses; same-day laundry service; car rental agency on property.

Facilities: 10,000-square-foot swimming pool; 10 tennis courts (five lit for night play); nine-hole putting green; guided hiking tours; full health center with outdoor aerobics classes, exercise and weight equipment, spa treatments and massage; full hair salon services.

MODERATE

○ Kahili Maui

5500 Lower Honoapilani Rd., Kapalua, Maui, HI 96761. ☎ **808/669-5635** or 800/786-7387. Fax 808/669-2561. 34 units, 30 in rental pool. A/C TV TEL. $109 studio suite; $149 1-bedroom suite. Rollaway $16. Crib $5. Children under 18 stay free in parents' room with existing bedding. AE, DC MC, V. Free parking.

Only a 5-minute walk from Napili and Kapalua Beach, the Kahili is surrounded by mango, papaya, and banana trees, which make up for the lack of ocean views. The studio and one-bedroom units are small, but absolutely spotless, attractively and individually furnished. Each unit has two bathrooms, queen-size sofa bed in the living room, a washer/dryer, and fully equipped kitchen. Guests also have full use of the condo's pool and Jacuzzi.

NAPILI
EXPENSIVE

Napili Kai Beach Club

5900 Honoapilani Rd., Napili Bay, Maui, HI 96761. ☎ **808/669-6271** or 800/367-5030 (line is open Mon–Fri, 6:30am–4:30pm Hawaii time). Fax 808/669-5740. 163 units. TV TEL. $180 luxury garden-view studio; $215 luxury ocean-view studio; $195 deluxe ocean-view studio; $205 deluxe beachfront studio; $230–$250 luxury oceanfront studio; $230–$270 deluxe ocean-view suite; $245–$280 deluxe beachfront suite; $300–$450 luxury garden-view suite; $365–$520 luxury ocean-view suite; $250–$475 luxury oceanfront suite. Rates based on double occupancy. Crib, rollaway, or extra person $5. MC, V. Free parking.

Located right on a beach between Lahaina and Kapalua, the newly remodeled Napili Kai Beach Club bills itself as "Maui's Most Hawaiian Resort." As a guest you will be given a guest membership in the Beach Club, which includes morning coffee or tea, a weekly putting party on the property's 18-hole putting green with 50¢ cocktails (except during high season), a weekly Mai Tai party, lei-making and hula lessons, afternoon tea, and access to beach towels, beach chairs, snorkels and masks, tennis rackets, and putters.

Rooms vary in size according to location. A studio is a large hotel-like room with the added bonus of a fully equipped kitchenette. The two-room suites, which accommodate up to four people, provide one or two baths and a fully equipped kitchenette. The three-room suites, which sleep up to six, offer two bedrooms and an additional bed in the living room. Each of the units has a private lanai. If you'd rather not stay in one of the high-rises in Kaanapali, but want to be on the beach on the island's west side, the Napili Kai could be what you're looking for.

> ## 👪 Family-Friendly Hotels
>
> Virtually all of the resorts on Maui offer a children's program, but several are exceptional.
>
> **Four Seasons Resort** *(see p. 111)*   This resort has one of the island's best children's programs. Kids 5 to 12 can participate in Hawaiian arts and crafts classes, marine life demonstrations, and sand sculpting, among other things. Scuba and windsurfing lessons for children over 12 are complimentary.
>
> **Grand Wailea** *(see p. 112)*   Camp Grande, the Grand Wailea's children's program, features a children's restaurant, pool, arts and crafts room, game room, computer learning center, and theater. Besides the comprehensive children's program, kids will love the hotel's 2,000-foot-long action pool with mountains, grottoes, waterfalls, slides, rapids, and even a rope swing.
>
> **The Ritz-Carlton** *(see p. 101)*   At the Ritz, children between 4 and 12 are entertained with scores of supervised activities. Lei-making, hula lessons, and coconut-leaf weaving are all popular with the kids.

Dining/Entertainment: The **Beach Pagoda** serves fast food, including burgers, hot dogs, fries, shakes, and nonalcoholic beverages. The **Sea House Restaurant,** which serves breakfast, lunch, and dinner daily, features nightly Hawaiian entertainment and dancing. The **Whale Watchers' Bar** is also available to guests.

Services: Daily maid service; activities desk.

Facilities: The Hankipanki Whirlpool (the Beach Club boasts that it's "Hawaii's largest heated whirlpool"); four swimming pools; barbecue facilities; shuffleboard; gift shop and boutique; nearby tennis courts with pro on duty ($10 fee to use the courts); two 18-hole putting greens.

2 Central & South Maui

Central Maui's main attraction is its inexpensive accommodations—mostly youth hostels that are not near a beach. South Maui, Kihei, Wailea, and Makena offer a variety of hostelries in a wide price range. Maui's south shore appeals to visitors because the weather is usually always sunny—Kihei has the lowest average rainfall on the island. Kihei's shore is lined primarily with affordable condominiums plus a few full-service hotels. More upscale hostelries can be found in Wailea, another of the island's planned resorts. Guests who stay in the Wailea resort have access to all resort facilities, including world-famous golf courses. With some of the island's most beautiful coastline, Makena remains undeveloped except for the Maui Prince.

CENTRAL MAUI
INEXPENSIVE

Maui Banana Bungalow

310 N. Market St., Wailuku, Maui, HI 96783. ☎ **808/244-5090.** Fax 808/248-2219. 27 rms (none with bath). $15 per person in shared accommodations; $38.95 double. Weekly and monthly discounts available. MC, V. Free parking on street.

One of several Wailuku youth hostels/hotels, the Maui Banana Bungalow is a favorite with windsurfers and European travelers. Shared accommodations house three or four beds (twins or bunk beds), single rooms have double beds, and double rooms have either twins or one queen-size bed. There is a common lounge area where hostel guests gather around the TV. There are communal refrigerators, a pay phone, and a laundry room. Guests may play volleyball and Ping-Pong or toss horseshoes. A barbecue grill is available for guest use, as are picnic tables and hammocks. There is a guest kitchen, and free videos are screened every night. Airport and beach transfer are complimentary services, and group trips are frequently arranged. There is also a windsurfer storage shed.

Maui Seaside Hotel

100 Kaahumanu Ave., Kahului, Maui, HI 96732. ☎ **808/877-3311** or 800/367-7000. Fax 808/922-0052. 190 rooms. A/C TV TEL. $70–$100 single or double. Extra person $12. AE, MC, V. Free parking.

If you've got to stay in Kahului because you have an early flight and want to be near the airport, your choices are limited, and none of them equals the island's other hostelries. The best choice is probably the Maui Seaside Hotel. The rooms are small and somewhat outdated, but they are clean, and the prices are good. The least expensive rooms face the garden. Above the ground level, the rooms face the pool; the most expensive rooms are both larger and situated in the Towers. Some of the rooms have kitchenettes. The hotel's restaurant, **Vi's,** serves a variety of cuisines, including Asian, American, and Italian; its entrées are in the inexpensive range.

All in all, the Maui Seaside is a bargain, but it's not a first choice for spending more than a night or two.

Northshore Inn

2080 Vineyard St., Wailuku, Maui, HI 96793. ☎ **808/242-8999.** Fax 808/244-5004. $12.95 per night shared accommodations; $36.95 double. Weekly discounts are available. AE, MC, V. Free parking.

This is one of the best hostels I've ever seen. It's clean and comfortable; there's a lounge area with a TV and VCR, laundry facilities, a communal kitchen, and a porch overlooking Vineyard Street. Owner Tina Dang strives to make the Northshore Inn a "home away from home" for all her guests, many of whom are windsurfers and Europeans. She's so in tune with the needs of her guests that she decorated certain rooms specifically for men and others specifically for women. There is a nominal one-time charge for a towel, top sheet, and blanket. The rooms that are classified as "shared accommodations" have five or six beds each, but there are also single and double rooms for those who would like more privacy. Van pickups at the airport can be arranged, and the Northshore Inn also sponsors several bus tours around the island (frequency varies according to the number of people who want to go, and the charges vary according to the distance traveled). There is no curfew, but the gate is locked at 9pm for safety reasons (guests are given keys to the gate). There is no smoking indoors, but it's allowed on the outdoor porch. Nightly movies are included in the room rate.

KIHEI/MAKENA
EXPENSIVE

Maui Hill

2881 S. Kihei Rd., Kihei, Maui, HI 96753. ☎ **808/879-6321** or 800/922-7866 from the U.S. mainland or 800/445-6633 from Canada. 51 units. A/C TV TEL. High season (Dec 22–Mar 31) $190 1-bedroom unit; $210 2-bedroom unit; $300 3-bedroom unit. Low season (Apr 1–Dec 21) $160 1-bedroom unit; $185 2-bedroom unit; $270 3-bedroom unit. Extra person $12. Ask about special promotions when making your reservation. AE, CB, DC, JCB, MC, V. Free parking.

Kihei-Wailea Coast Accommodations

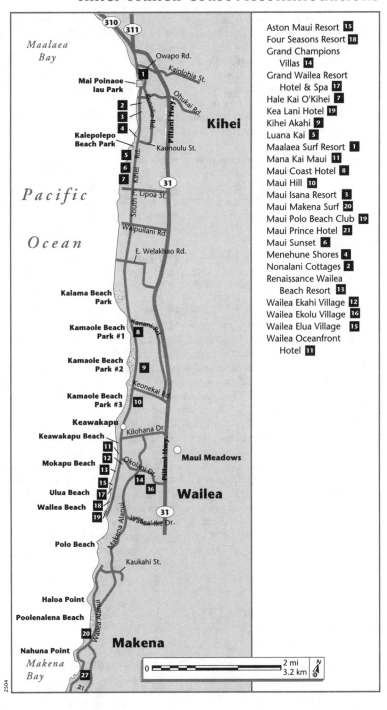

Aston Maui Resort **15**
Four Seasons Resort **18**
Grand Champions
Villas **14**
Grand Wailea Resort
Hotel & Spa **17**
Hale Kai O'Kihei **7**
Kea Lani Hotel **19**
Kihei Akahi **9**
Luana Kai **5**
Maalaea Surf Resort **1**
Mana Kai Maui **11**
Maui Coast Hotel **8**
Maui Hill **10**
Maui Isana Resort **3**
Maui Makena Surf **20**
Maui Polo Beach Club **19**
Maui Prince Hotel **21**
Maui Sunset **6**
Menehune Shores **4**
Nonalani Cottages **2**
Renaissance Wailea
Beach Resort **13**
Wailea Ekahi Village **12**
Wailea Ekolu Village **16**
Wailea Elua Village **15**
Wailea Oceanfront
Hotel **11**

As you might have guessed from its name, the Maui Hill is not an oceanfront property—on the contrary, its buildings are nestled into a hillside. When it was built almost 15 years ago it was one of the few properties constructed away from the oceanfront, and some people wondered if it would survive. Well, it has, in spades. In fact, it's probably the best deal you'll find on South Kihei Road; its only drawback is its distance from the beach.

The hotel consists of 12 three-story Spanish-style buildings with red-tile roofs and stucco exteriors. The suites, or apartments, are all spacious; although the owners' tastes in decorating vary greatly, each is pleasantly appointed. The upstairs units all have lofts, and the lodgings all have ocean views. Gourmet kitchens are an added feature for those who'd rather cook than go out to eat, and there's a barbecue area on the property for those who'd rather not be tied to the stove. Guests have access to the Maui Hill tennis court, shuffleboard, putting green, and freshwater pool and jet spa. There is daily maid service, and concierge service is available for those who need help with reservations or activities. Each week the manager hosts a cocktail party for all guests.

Maui Prince Hotel

5400 Makena Alanui, Kihei, Maui, HI 96753-9986. ☎ **808/874-1111** or 800/321-MAUI. Fax 800/338-8763. 310 rms, 20 suites. A/C TV TEL. $240 partial ocean view; $295 ocean view; $340 prime ocean view; $395 oceanfront; $440–$840 suite. Special packages, including golf packages, are available. No extra charge for third person provided existing bedding is used. $25 for rollaway or crib. AE, CB, DC, JCB, MC, V. Free parking.

The Maui Prince is the only hotel in the Makena resort, and its location is perfect. Somewhat removed from the hustle and bustle of Kihei and Wailea, the Prince offers its guests beaches and amenities as magnificent as many of the other full-service hotels in the area, but with a lot less hoopla. At check-in all guests are greeted by friendly staff members expressing their warmest aloha with a refreshing juice drink. Guest rooms are reached via open-air promenades that overlook the lobby. Each of the rooms has an ocean view, private lanai, and a large bathroom with a hair dryer and telephone. In your room you'll also find a complimentary sample of Hawaiian treats, and your minirefrigerator will be stocked with fruit juices and bottled water (restocked daily). In addition, all rooms have VCRs (videos can be rented in-house). The hotel gardens are immaculately maintained, and if you wander the grounds you'll find waterfalls that lead into carp-stocked ponds dotted with yellow and white water lilies. Every evening brings light to the Japanese lanterns that line the walk ways and a halt to the waterfalls in the courtyard so that classical musicians may set the mood for dining under the stars.

Dining/Entertainment: The hotel's main dining room, the **Prince Court,** offers Hawaiian regional cuisine, and **Cafe Kiowai** serves light meals in an open-air setting. Both restaurants offer spectacular views of the ocean and neighboring islands.

Services: Room service from 6am to 10pm daily.

Facilities: Pool; resort access to 36 holes of golf; six plexi-pave tennis courts; pro shop.

MODERATE

Luana Kai

940 S. Kihei Rd., Kihei, Maui, HI 96753. ☎ **808/879-1268** or 800/669-1127. Fax 808/879-1455. 113 units, 70 in rental pool. TV TEL. High season (Dec 20–Mar 31) $110 1-bedroom garden view, $125 1-bedroom ocean view; $130 2-bedroom garden view, $155 2-bedroom ocean view; $210 3-bedroom garden view. Low season (Apr 1–Dec 19) $75 1-bedroom garden view, $100 1-bedroom ocean view; $95 2-bedroom garden view,

$130 2-bedroom ocean view; $160 3-bedroom garden view. Room/car rates are available. AE, DC, MC, V. Free parking.

Luana Kai has a great location and some exceptional facilities. The beach is just a short walk across the lawn from the condominium units; there are four tennis courts, an impressive putting green, a sauna, and a fenced-off private pool and whirlpool area. One-, two-, and 3-bedroom units come fully furnished, and all have ceiling fans in lieu of air-conditioning. The upstairs units have loft bedrooms, and most are equipped with VCRs. Furnishings are generally contemporary, and color schemes are neutral or a combination of pastel and neutral tones. The only drawback here is that some of the condos haven't been redecorated recently, and they're beginning to show their age.

Maalaea Surf Resort

12 S. Kihei Rd., Kihei, Maui, HI 96753. ☎ **808/879-1267** or 800/423-7953. Fax 808/ 874-2884. 33 units in rental pool. A/C TV TEL. High season $175 1-bedroom unit; $237 2-bedroom unit. Low season $155 1-bedroom unit; $206 2-bedroom unit. MC, V. Free parking.

Located just off the "beaten path" in Kihei, the Maalaea Surf Resort is a nice surprise. All the one- and two-bedroom units in a series of low-rise buildings are individually owned, and most of them have recently been upgraded. Well-equipped kitchens have the added luxury of a microwave and dishwasher. Air-conditioning is standard and so are ceiling fans and VCRs. Most of the two-bedroom apartments have twin beds in one room for those traveling with children. There are laundry facilities in each building, and a housekeeping staff services the condos daily (except Sunday and holidays). Each unit offers a full ocean view, and 5 miles of beach begin almost right outside your door.

There are two swimming pools, two tennis courts, shuffleboard, and basketball courts on the property. The 5 acres on which the Maalaea Surf is situated are beautifully landscaped, and as you wander around the property you're likely to find a variety of fruits ripening on the trees, including kumquats (which taste like a cross between a lemon and an orange—you can eat the whole thing, including the peel) and avocados.

Mana Kai Maui

2960 S. Kihei Rd., Kihei, Maui, HI 96753. ☎ **808/879-1561** or 800/525-2025 (Mon–Fri 5:30am–3pm Hawaiian time). Fax 800/477-2329. 98 units, 67 in rental pool. TV TEL. High season (Dec 22–Mar 31) $115 hotel unit; $185–$225 1- and 2-bedroom condo units. Low season (Apr 1–Dec 21) $105 hotel unit with breakfast; $165–$205 1- and 2-bedroom condo units. Family plan and low-season discounts are available. AE, CB, MC, V. Free parking.

If you're traveling on a tight budget, the Mana Kai Maui might be just the thing for you. Hotel units are equipped with a divider for separating the sleeping area from the living area at night, and the one- and two-bedroom units, which are a little more pricey, include full kitchens. A two-bedroom apartment will sleep up to six. There are laundry facilities on every floor, and daily maid service is standard for all accommodations. Nestled in among the palm trees is a large swimming pool, and the mile-long stretch of beach that borders the property is great for swimming. The ground floor of the complex is devoted to commercial space, including a restaurant, beauty salon, boutique, activities desk, and a minimart. All things considered, the Mana Kai Maui is one of the best deals on the island.

Maui Coast Hotel

2259 S. Kihei Rd., Kihei, Maui, HI 96753. ☎ **808/874-6284** or 800/426-0670. Fax 808/ 875-4731. 260 rms. A/C TV TEL. Terrace $119 standard, $139 alcove suite; $179 standard 1-bedroom suite, $180 deluxe 1-bedroom suite; $225 standard 2-bedroom suite, $250 deluxe 2-bedroom suite. Room/car packages available. AE, MC, V. Free parking.

Opened in February 1993, the Maui Coast is one of Kihei's newest properties. The rates here are slightly lower than at some of the other hotels in the area because it's located across South Kihei Road from the beach, and none of the rooms offer the spectacular views that could be found at a beachfront property. However, you won't be disappointed with the accommodations.

The spacious and graciously designed lobby is representative of what you'll find in your room; each room is large and pleasantly decorated in a pastel green, purple, and pink color scheme. No matter what type of room you choose, you'll be more than comfortable. With a standard room you'll have a choice of twin, two double, or one king-size bed. The alcove suites (Junior Suites) offer king-size or two double beds as well as a pull-out couch; they are also equipped with a wet bar and an oversized whirlpool tub. The one-bedroom suite is furnished with a king-size bed and an extra TV. The two-bedroom suites sleep up to six adults. All deluxe suites offer whirlpool tubs, and all rooms are equipped with sitting areas with modern furnishings, minirefrigerators, clock radios, coffeemakers with complimentary coffee each morning, scales, hair dryers, complimentary in-room safes, individually controlled air-conditioning, and ceiling fans. In each room sliding glass doors open onto a private lanai outfitted with patio furniture.

Dining/Entertainment: The hotel's **Kamaole Bar & Grill Restaurant** serves three meals daily in a casual setting. The **Oasis** poolside bar features nightly entertainment, and the **Kamaole Sushi Bar** is open every night except Monday.

Services: Room service; activities desk.

Facilities: Complimentary laundry facilities (you need to supply the detergent); heated swimming pool; children's wading pool; two outdoor Jacuzzis; two tennis courts—both lit for night play; gift shop.

Menehune Shores

760 S. Kihei Rd. (P.O. Box 1327), Kihei, Maui, HI 96753. ☎ **808/879-3428** and 808/879-5828 or 800/558-9117. Fax 808/879-5218. 89 units. TV TEL. High season (Dec 15–Apr 15) $100 1-bedroom unit; $120–$130 2-bedroom unit; $140–$160 3-bedroom unit. Low season (Apr 16–Dec 14) $85 1-bedroom unit; $98.50–$110 2-bedroom unit; $130–$150 3-bedroom unit. Extra person $7.50. Minimum stay of 5 nights. Monthly discounts available. No credit cards. Free parking.

The stuccoed exterior of this horseshoe-shaped building is decorated with whimsical modern petroglyphs. Due to the condominium's unique shape, all the units face the ocean (some more directly than others). Inside you'll find agreeably decorated one-, two-, and three-bedroom units with full kitchens and private lanais. The two- and three-bedroom condos offer two full bathrooms, and all apartments are outfitted with washers and dryers. Menehune Shores is situated adjacent to the 16th-century Ali'i (Royal) Fish Pond of Kalepolipo, a great "swimming hole" for those who'd rather stay out of the heavy surf on this side of the island. The swimming hole, which is protected by a coral reef, is an excellent place for children to get their feet wet. If you'd rather swim in a freshwater pool, however, the condominium complex has a large oval-shaped pool surrounded by a large patio. Shuffleboard and barbecue areas are available for guest use. If you get tired of cooking for yourself and your family, you can try the Menehune Shores' oceanfront cocktail lounge and restaurant.

INEXPENSIVE

Ann & Bob Babson's Vacation Rentals

3371 Keha Dr., Maui Meadows, Kihei, HI 96753. ☎**808/874-1166** or 800/824-6409. Fax 808/879-7906. 2 rms, 1 apt., 1 cottage. TV TEL. $70–$85 double room in main house (including breakfast); $85 1-bedroom apartment; $105 2-bedroom/2-bath cottage. Extra person $10. Minimum stay 3 nights. 10% discount for seven nights or more. MC, V. Free parking.

It's not likely that you'll ever find more congenial and attentive hosts than Ann and Bob Babson. Their lovely home, cottage, and beautifully landscaped grounds—replete with bougainvillea, plumeria, papaya, bananas, palms, night-blooming jasmine, and even pineapple—are located about 400 feet up the mountainside in South Maui, just above the grand resort community of Wailea. Their Maui Meadows property, with 180-degree ocean views, is just moments away from some of the island's best white-sand beaches, not to mention the shops and restaurants in Kihei and Wailea. The Sunset Cottage, which is separated from the other accommodations, has two bedrooms with private baths, a living room with a sofa bed (the cottage can easily sleep six), a full kitchen, and a large deck offering fantastic views. The Hibiscus Hideaway apartment, on the ground floor of the main house, is perfect for a couple. It has a private entrance, living room, bedroom, bath, and kitchenette. In addition, there are two bed-and-breakfast units in the main house. The Bougainvillea Suite has a queen-size bed and private bath, while the Molokini Master Suite is equipped with its own deck (ocean view) and a Jacuzzi in the private bathroom. It must be the tub that makes this room so popular with honeymooners! The two rooms in the main house each have minirefrigerators. All of the accommodations are comfortably furnished and spotlessly clean. The Babsons go to great lengths to make their guests feel at home here. They encourage main house guests to make use of their own living room, dining room, and deck (spectacular views are enjoyed here as well). They have an extensive resource library and will provide guests with written reviews of their favorite restaurants, adventures, and shops, as well as helpful hints on seeing the island. Beach towels, mats, chairs, coolers, boogie boards, and even frisbees are available for guest use. The cottage has its own washer and dryer, and laundry facilities are available for other guests at a nominal fee.

Ann and Bob operate their own reservation service so they can arrange car rentals for you and bed-and-breakfast reservations elsewhere on Maui (as well as on other islands).

Hale Kai O'Kihei

1310 Uluniu Rd. (P.O. Box 809), Kihei, Maui, HI 96753-0809. ☎ **808/879-2757** or 800/457-7014. 40 units. TV TEL. High season (Dec 16–Apr 15) $660 1-bedroom unit; $835 2-bedroom unit. Low season (Apr 16–Dec 15) $455 1-bedroom unit; $625 2-bedroom unit. Rates based on double occupancy for 1-week minimum stay. Extra person $10 per day. Monthly discounts available. No credit cards. Free parking.

From the outside, the Hale Kai O'Kihei looks like your average cement-block apartment building, but don't be fooled. The interiors are actually rather charming, and the building manager is welcoming and extremely friendly. Apartments must be booked for at least a week, so during your stay you'll probably begin to feel right at home with your neighbors and other guests. By the time you leave you'll probably be gathering a group together for an evening barbecue and a game of shuffleboard. The beach out front is great for swimming, snorkeling, and surfing, and since the weather on this side of the island is almost always sunny, you'll get more than your money's worth.

All units feature full kitchens (with microwaves) and private lanais with outdoor furniture. Bathrooms are large, and the decor in all the apartments is bright and fresh. There's no air-conditioning, but the ceiling fans are adequate. Coin-op laundry facilities are centrally located.

Kihei Akahi

2531 S. Kihei Rd., Kihei, Maui, HI 96753. ☎ **808/879-2778** or 800/367-5242 from the U.S. mainland, 800/663-2101 from Canada. Fax 808/879-7825. 70 units. TV TEL. High season (Dec 15–Mar 31) $85 studio; $100 1-bedroom; $135 2-bedroom. Low season (Apr 1–Dec 14) $65 studio; $70 1-bedroom; $95 2-bedroom. Rates are per night for 4–6 nights. Extra person $12. Special air/car/condo packages and weekly and monthly discounts are available. Minimum stay is 4 nights. No credit cards. Free parking.

Not to be confused with Ekahi, located in the Wailea resort, Kihei Akahi is located directly across the street from one of Kihei's best beaches—Kamaole Beach Park II. A small grouping of low-rise buildings is complemented by nicely landscaped grounds. There are also two eight-story buildings in the complex. Most of the apartments have rattan furnishings with modern light fixtures, silk flower arrangements, and floral print fabrics. Each is also outfitted with a full kitchen, washer and dryer, ceiling fans, and a private lanai. Although you must cross the street to get to the beach, you'll be happy to know there are two pools on the property for guest use. Other facilities include barbecues and a tennis court.

Maui Sunset

1032 S. Kihei Rd., Kihei, Maui, HI 96753. ☎ **808/879-9272** or 800/367-2954. 225 units. TV TEL. High season $115–$135 1-bedroom; $145–$155 2-bedroom; $205–$245 3-bedroom. Low season $95–$115 1-bedroom; $115–$145 2-bedroom; $175–$200 3-bedroom. Extra person $8. AE, MC, V. Free parking.

The condominiums at the Maui Sunset were refurbished in 1989, so most of the furnishings are modern, and the color schemes are currently fashionable—neutral tones and rattan furnishings with pastel floral and striped accents. Many of the units come with sporting gear (such as boogie boards), stored in the closet for guest use. The Maui Sunset is one of the area's most popular condominiums because it's situated on a relatively large site and offers a beachfront location. Guests enjoy an abundance of on-site activities, including the swimming pool, sauna, exercise room, hot tub, croquet, putting green, shuffleboard, and tennis courts. There are barbecue areas as well. All units have ocean or garden views, and there is ample parking.

Nonalani Cottages

455 S. Kihei Rd., Kihei, Maui, HI 96753. ☎ **808/879-2497** or 800/733-2688. 8 cottages. High season (Dec 15–Mar 31) $80 cottage for two. Low season (Apr 1–Dec 14) $68 cottage for 2. Extra person $7. Minimum stay is 4 nights during low season. Weekly and monthly rates available. No credit cards. Free parking.

Perhaps you're not interested in staying in a youth hostel, and you can't afford to stay in a condominium (and certainly not one of the luxury hotels in Wailea). Well, how about one of these eight one-bedroom cottages equipped with a full kitchen, set on a small but lushly landscaped site? The cottage interiors and furnishings here are somewhat eclectic, but they're still a step above a youth hostel. Hammocks are strung from tree to tree, and a beautiful white-sand beach is only a short walk across the street. Each of the cottages has an outdoor deck where you can watch the sun set between plumeria, palm, and citrus trees. For reservations call one of the two numbers listed above or contact Dave and Nona Kong, P.O. Box 655, Kihei, Maui, HI 96753.

WAILEA
EXPENSIVE

Aston Wailea Resort

3700 Wailea Alanui, Wailea, Maui, HI 96753. ☎ **808/879-1922** or 800/367-2960. Fax 808/875-4878. 516 rms and suites. A/C MINIBAR TV TEL. $199 garden view, $219 mountain view,

$239 ocean-view tower, $269 ocean view, $269 oceanfront tower, $319 oceanfront. Suites $319–$2,000. AE, CB, DC, JCB, MC, V. Complimentary valet- and self-parking available.

Opened in 1976 as the first hotel in the Wailea resort, the Aston Wailea Resort (formerly the Maui Inter-Continental Resort) is a first-class choice for any traveler. A series of seven low-rise buildings and one seven-story tower surrounded by 22 acres of painstakingly maintained lawns and gardens have been designed to provide as many guest rooms as possible with ocean views. Not long ago, the hotel's public spaces were renovated to the tune of $40 million, and it shows. Large, comfortable sitting areas in the open-air lobby afford guests beautiful views of the ocean and neighboring islands. Artifacts from the hotel's Pacific Rim art collection are scattered throughout. In the lobby alone there's a wooden Tahitian outrigger canoe, Thai spirit houses, wooden Japanese chests, calabashes, raku ceramic sculptures, original oil paintings, and a plumeria design quilt. All of the hotel's spacious rooms have recently been renovated and upgraded. Each features separate dressing and bath areas with marble-topped sinks, and all rooms have private lanais with sliding glass doors. Complimentary guest activities include hula, scuba, snorkel, and windsurfing lessons. There are also lei-making and exercise classes, and you can arrange to go deep-sea fishing or take a trip on a catamaran.

The children's program consists of supervised activities for children ages 5 and older. Besides swimming lessons and arts and crafts classes, kids will learn about Hawaiian culture and the environment.

Dining/Entertainment: Hula Moons, located poolside, offers fresh seafood and meat specialties, as well as a great salad bar. **Lanai Terrace,** open daily for breakfast and dinner, permits gorgeous ocean views. Lanai Terrace offers a different cuisine each day of the week. Guests gather for live entertainment at **Inu Inu,** or enjoy sunset cocktails at **Kai Puka Lounge.** The Aston also has its own luau on Tuesday, Thursday, and Friday (see Chapter 8, "What to See & Do on Maui," for more details).

Services: 24-hour room service; same-day laundry and valet service; multilingual concierge; poolside beverage service; babysitting.

Facilities: Three swimming pools; gift shops, sundry shops, and a newsstand; beauty salon and barber shop; licensed massage therapist available by appointment.

✪ Four Seasons Resort

3900 Wailea Alanui, Wailea, Maui, HI 96753. ☎ **808/874-8000** or 800/334-MAUI. Fax 808/ 874-2222. 380 rms, 83 suites. A/C MINIBAR TV TEL. $295 mountain view, $320 garden view, $375 partial ocean view, $450–$570 ocean view, $490–$610 ocean-view prime; $541–$5,500 suite. Children under 18 stay free in parents' room (except on the Club Level where children pay an extra $60). AE, DC, JCB, MC, V. Free valet- or self-parking.

The moment you enter the lobby of the Four Seasons you'll be swept into a world of elegance, opulence, and decadence. In addition to providing an unobstructed view of the ocean, the lobby is graced with an abundance of tropical flowers, oversized wicker furnishings, and an extensive art collection. From the commissioned Art Screen behind the registration desk to the antique Chinese wedding baskets at the coffee table near the fountain to the ceiling murals, the Four Seasons is a virtual museum. Just on the other side of the open-air lobby are all the things that probably attracted you to Hawaii in the first place—the blue waters of the resort's fountained swimming pool, bright white cabanas, lanky palm trees, a strip of the most exquisite white-sand beach, and the brilliant turquoise Pacific Ocean. That's only the beginning.

Your room here will be equally luxurious. Although the color schemes (neutral with peach and green highlights) vary from room to room, the basic amenities are the same. In addition to private lanais, all rooms are outfitted with ceiling fans, rattan and wicker furniture, and wooden shutters. You'll also find a fully stocked minibar, VCR (the hotel has a movie library for guest rentals), clock radio, in-room safe, terry robes, and teak patio furniture on the lanai. The marble-tiled bathrooms are elegantly appointed with enormous framed mirrors, separate showers, oversized bathtubs, and separate makeup areas with vanity mirrors. The attention to detail here is unsurpassed. The management is so concerned about guests' comfort that it instituted a unique housekeeping policy. This is the only hotel where you will never ever see a housekeeping cart in the hallways. The cleaning staff works in teams—some clean, some go for supplies, and some restock minibars. They move swiftly (15 minutes) through each room, leaving not a speck of dust behind; thus, you won't be disturbed by staff members more than once a day. If you plan to stay for 10 nights or more, the hotel will also inquire in advance (by mail) about any special needs you might have. And, if you just can't stand looking at your suitcases the entire time you're on vacation, unpack them and have them stored. The utmost in decadence is the poolside service—an Evian spritz and cold oshibori towels for those who get too warm while soaking up the sun's rays.

If you want even more privacy and certain special privileges (such as free movie rentals, complimentary continental breakfast, afternoon tea, sunset cocktails and hors d'oeuvres, and after-dinner liqueurs and desserts), you should book a room on the Four Seasons Club Floor.

Traveling with children? Well, the Four Seasons takes great pride in its children's facilities, which are open year-round from 9am to 5pm. Activities available for kids 5 to 12 years old include lei-making lessons; hula classes; Hawaiian arts, crafts, and games; beach games; marine life demonstrations; sand sculpting; and tennis. The indoor facility is chock-full of toys, games, and books, and the best thing about the children's program is that it's complimentary. For older children there's a teen recreation center that features pool tables, a jukebox, table shuffleboard, and a big-screen TV. All children over 12 are also entitled to complimentary scuba and windsurfing lessons, and kids 13 and over may use the health club facility for an hour every day. There's a children's pool and Jacuzzi, and there's even a kids' rate for laundry service.

Note: At press time, the Four Seasons was undergoing a $4.2 million renovation.

Dining/Entertainment: Seasons (see Chapter 7, "Maui Dining," for details), open for dinner only, is the hotel's formal dining room specializing in Mediterranean cuisine. Dine at candlelit tables indoors or out while enjoying the sounds of a jazz trio. The **Pacific Grill** serves breakfast, lunch, and dinner daily. **Seaside,** located poolside, is open daily for lunch and dinner.

Services: 24-hour room service; twice-daily maid service; afternoon ice service; complimentary evening shoe-shine service; 24-hour medical service.

Facilities: Full health facility with separate men's and women's locker rooms, exercise and weight equipment; two on-site tennis courts, both lit for night play, as well as access to the 14-court Wailea Tennis Center; access to Wailea resort golf courses; putting green; complimentary Ping-Pong, volleyball, croquet, badminton, and biking equipment and facilities; the beach pavilion provides guests with scuba and snorkeling gear, boogie boards, kayaks, and paddleboats; use of the hotel's 60-foot catamaran for snorkeling, whale-watching, and sunset sails.

✪ Grand Wailea Resort Hotel & Spa

3850 Wailea Alanui, Wailea, Maui, HI 96753. ☎ **808/875-1234** or 800/888-6100. Fax 808/874-5143. 767 rms, 53 suites. A/C MINIBAR TV TEL. $380 terrace, $445 premier, $495 deluxe ocean, $1,100–$2,000 suite; $580 Napua Club, $1,400–$10,000 Napua Suite. Extra person in standard rooms is $30; in Napua Club rooms and suites $50. AE, DC, JCB, MC, V. Complimentary valet- and self-parking available.

Whether you're a hotel guest or simply visiting for the day, the moment you pass the Grand Wailea's grand waterfall at the hotel's entrance you'll be transported to another world. The secrets of the Grand Wailea's success are its six themes of genuine Hawaii feeling: flowers, water, trees, sound, light, and art. There are more flowers on this property than on any other on the island. Besides the ocean, you'll find waterfalls, pools, a lagoon, and smaller waterways throughout the property. The only sounds you'll hear evoke serenity. And the light is the best nature can provide. The $30 million collection of commissioned artwork by notables such as Fernard Leger, Fernando Botero, Zou Ling, Satoru Abe, Herb Kane, and Jan Fisher is testimony to the hotel's dedication to the preservation of classical elegance. All things considered, the Grand Wailea is the grandest of them all.

Even the most basic guest rooms here are elegantly furnished. Beautifully polished wood furniture and Oriental-style area rugs are standard, and fine artwork is scattered throughout the guest rooms. Basic amenities include in-room safes, ironing boards and irons, three telephones, and a basket of fresh fruit that is replenished daily. All rooms provide private lanais with teak outdoor furniture. Bathrooms come with oversized marble tubs, separate showers, and hair dryers. The exclusive Napua Club is comprised of 100 rooms and suites on floors accessible only by elevator key. Guests on these floors receive complimentary breakfast, hors d'oeuvres, and butler-style VIP service.

Spa Grande, at 50,000 square feet, is Hawaii's largest spa, and one of the Grand Wailea's most luxurious features. Treat yourself to a massage in one of the spa's oceanfront rooms, get a facial, take a Japanese bath, or relax under a waterfall massage. The choices are legion: aromatherapy, parafango (mud and seaweed), saunas, cold dips, shiatsu massage, herbal wraps, lomi lomi massage. Better yet, go for the Terme Wailea Circuit. The Circuit begins with a choice of exfoliating and cleansing treatments—a loofa scrub by a spa technician or a Japanese bath, including a "sitting shower" and a Japanese furo tub with a cool dip. The next phase might consist of a limu bath for detoxification or a Maui mud bath for balancing hormones and remineralizing the body. Phase three might consist of a tropical enzyme bath for toning and softening the skin. The cascading waterfall massage is followed by the jet shower. From there guests can either head upstairs to the private treatment rooms where they'll receive a massage or facial, or indulge in the Hawaiian Salt Glo treatment which uses rock salt and kukui nut oil to exfoliate and soften the skin. Finally, head to the Sonic Relaxation Room where you'll sit on a lounge chair wrapped in blankets listening to soothing music (which comes from the "hood" of the lounge chair and vibrates through the chair) while watching nature videos. If you're not relaxed after all of that, you probably never will be. In the event that you'd rather work up a sweat using your muscles, the spa also features weight training, aerobics, and racquetball.

The New England–style floating Seaside Chapel, with its stained-glass windows depicting a traditional Hawaiian wedding, and bell and clock tower, is one of the island's most popular places for wedding ceremonies. Even if you aren't getting married, you'll appreciate its quaintness as you sit in one of the gazebos enjoying the surrounding gardens.

Dining/Entertainment: The **Grand Dining Room Maui** is the hotel's classical dining establishment with an international menu, where guests can enjoy breakfast, Sunday brunch, and dinner (at press time, the Grand Dining Room was serving only breakfast). There is live entertainment in the evenings and during brunch. **Kincha** is one of the country's most authentic Japanese restaurants (see Chapter 7, "Maui Dining," for details). In the center of the restaurant there's a stage where authentic tea ceremonies and flower arranging are often performed. There's also a sushi bar, tempura bar, and three private tatami rooms. **Cafe Kula** serves country spa cuisine, low in fat, salt, and cholesterol, but packed full of flavor (see Chapter 7 for details). **Humuhumunukunukuapua'a** (it'll take you a while to learn to pronounce this one), named for the official fish of the state of Hawaii, is made up of a series of thatched-roof huts all "floating" on a stocked, saltwater lagoon. Appropriately, Humuhumunukunukuapua'a serves seafood. **Bistro Molokini,** named for the crescent-shaped sliver of an island located just in front of Kahoolawe, is an open-air bistro serving Italian specialties, many of which are cooked in a woodburning oven. The **Volcano Snack Bar** is a convenient poolside spot for a quick breakfast, sandwich or salad, and the occasional tropical drink. There are 12 bars scattered around the property, but **Tsunami** is the hotel's nightclub that features laser light shows, a hydraulic dance floor, and 20 video monitors—it's also a favorite with locals.

Services: Room service; babysitting; concierge.

Facilities: The 2,000-foot-long Action Pool sweeps swimmers through mountains and grottoes, drops them about 35 feet (gradually, of course), and takes them through waterfalls, slides, and rapids. There's even a rope swing bordered by authentic-looking rubber "rocks" in case you chicken out and don't drop into the water as you swing out. The 15,000-square-foot formal pool, inlaid with glass and mosaic tile, is bordered by 60-foot royal palms. The section of pool closest to the beach, inlaid with a floral design, is for adults only. Guests have access to five golf courses, and the tennis courts at the Wailea Resort Tennis Club.

The children's program, Camp Grande, is unsurpassed. Facilities include a children's restaurant, pool, arts and crafts room, game room, computer learning center, and a children's theater. The program is fully supervised.

There is also an elegant shopping arcade for those who simply cannot survive without a little window shopping.

✪ Kea Lani Hotel

4100 Wailea Alanui, Wailea, Maui, HI 96753. ☎ **808/875-4100** or 800/882-4100. Fax 808/882-4100. 413 suites, 37 villas. A/C MINIBAR TV TEL. 1-bedroom suite $265 scenic view, $350 ocean view, $450 deluxe ocean view; ocean-view villa $795 1-bedroom, $895 2-bedroom, $1,095 3-bedroom. Oceanfront villas are $100 more. Rollaway $25. Children under 18 stay free in parents' room (with existing bedding). AE, CB, DC, DISC, JCB, MC, V. Complimentary self-parking.

You can't miss the Kea Lani Hotel. Architecturally it looks as if it belongs somewhere in the Middle East. With its spotlessly white exterior, the Kea Lani ("white heaven") is unique among all the hotels on the island. As you pass the small fountain in the entryway, you'll enter the marble-floored lobby, to the left of which is a small bamboo "forest." You'll know as soon as you walk in and are greeted by the unassuming, but beautifully trained staff that you've made the right choice.

The suites, decorated in various shades of white, are all equipped with VCRs, laser disc/compact disc players, full stereos, microwaves, coffeemakers, and complimentary Kona coffee. The greatest thing about any of the rooms here is their size—they're extraordinarily large and filled with furniture that matches the scale of the rooms. No one will feel uncomfortable here. You'll love to return to your room to relax after a hard day of sightseeing or ocean activities. Each suite has a pullout couch in the living room, which is perfect if you're traveling with your kids. Families love this place (and parents appreciate the fact that there are coin-operated washers and dryers on every floor). Bathrooms are appointed with elegant oversized pedestal sinks, oversized Roman bathtubs, walk-in showers, telephones, and hair dryers. In addition, all bathrooms are stocked with top-quality oversized Neutragena products. Ironing boards and irons are standard amenities in all suites.

To get to the more private Kea Lani Villas you'll need to pass through the pool area where guests are relaxing in cabanas or on chaise longues around the 20,000-square-foot lagoon-style swimming pool with a water slide. White plumeria trees abound on the spacious grounds. Tropical plant life is clearly labeled.

Though the villas are located at the back of the hotel in front of the beach, they are low to the ground and don't obstruct the ocean views from the suites. The villas have all the same amenities as the standard suites; however, they also have private swimming pools (a bit larger than a large Jacuzzi), teak outdoor furniture, and full kitchens (with dishwashers, microwaves, and coffeemakers). Cooks can be hired through the hotel if you would like to be pampered, and washers and dryers are standard. All are oceanfront or offer ocean views. The two- or three-bedroom villas also have daily maid service and complimentary daily newspaper. Yellow-and-white-striped kimonos are available for guest use in all rooms. Overall, no matter which type of accommodation you choose, Kea Lani is absolutely a top choice.

Dining/Entertainment: The **Kea Lani Restaurant** features Pacific Rim cuisine in addition to daily specials. **Caffe Ciao** is a great little spot (see Chapter 7, "Maui Dining," for details) for fresh pastries, breads, and deli specials. The **Polo Beach Grille & Bar** serves lunch and snacks from 11am to 7pm. The **Lobby Bar** features Hawaiian entertainment.

Services: Daily maid service; concierge; Keiki Lani (children's camp) is available 9am to 3pm daily.

Facilities: Fitness center; separate adult and children's pools; florist; Jacuzzi; video library; activities desk; rental equipment—snorkeling gear, air mattresses, boogie boards, and beach towels.

Maui Makena Surf

3750 Wailea Alanui, Wailea, Maui, HI 96753. ☎ **808/879-1595** or 800/367-5246. Fax 808/874-3554. 100 units, 50 in rental pool. A/C TV TEL. High season (Dec 20–Apr 15) $320 1-bedroom ocean view, $345 1-bedroom oceanfront, $370 1-bedroom oceanfront ground floor; $385–$425 2-bedroom ocean view, $415–$455 2-bedroom oceanfront, $445 2-bedroom oceanfront ground floor; $525 3-bedroom oceanfront. Low season (Apr 16–Dec 19) $285 1-bedroom ocean view, $310 1-bedroom oceanfront, $335 1-bedroom oceanfront ground floor; $330–$370 2-bedroom ocean view, $370–$400 2-bedroom oceanfront, $395 2-bedroom oceanfront ground floor; $460 3-bedroom oceanfront. Extra person $20. Romance, golf, and tennis packages available. Minimum stay is 3 nights. AE, MC, V. Free parking.

Probably one of the most luxurious condominiums on Maui, the Makena Surf is also one of the most isolated properties on the island. Located between the Wailea and Makena resorts, the Makena Surf offers centrally air-conditioned units with spacious interiors. All apartments are individually (and in most cases exquisitely) decorated and offer full kitchen facilities, wet bars, washers and dryers, and a Jacuzzi tub in the master bathroom. All of the apartments provide at least an ocean view and large, private lanais. Because of the way the low-rise buildings were constructed (some in 1983, the new ones in 1992), the ground-floor units are more spacious and therefore more expensive. The facilities for guest relaxation and exercise include not only an incredible white-sand beach, but two pools, two whirlpool spas, four tennis courts, barbecue areas, and a tropical garden. Daily maid service is standard, and there is a concierge on duty to help you plan activities ranging from snorkel/sails to biking down Haleakala. Besides a resident manager, there is a rental manager to assist you with any problems or questions you might have about your apartment (though it's unlikely you will have any). If you're looking for a condominium that offers great facilities, access to resort golf courses and tennis courts, privacy, and elegance, you'll find it at the Maui Makena Surf.

Maui Polo Beach Club

3750 Wailea Alanui, Wailea, Maui, HI 96753. ☎ **808/879-1595** or 800/367-5246. Fax 808/874-3554. 71 units, 34 in rental pool. A/C TV TEL. High season (Dec 20–Apr 15) $270 1-bedroom oceanfront, $320 1-bedroom prime oceanfront; $330 2-bedroom oceanfront, $380 2-bedroom prime oceanfront. Low season (Apr 16–Dec 19) $235 1-bedroom oceanfront, $275 1-bedroom prime oceanfront; $285 2-bedroom oceanfront, $325 2-bedroom prime oceanfront. AE, MC, V. Free underground parking.

Although the exterior provides no clues, the Maui Polo Beach Club offers some of the most spacious, exquisitely appointed, privately owned condominium apartments on the island. Situated on about 2^1/$_2$ acres bordering the Wailea resort, all of the Polo Beach Club's condominiums are oceanfront. Each apartment has koa wood and marble accents, elegant furnishings, and vast windows and glass doors that look out over the neatly trimmed lawn and perfectly smooth white-sand beach. Private lanais are so spacious that you might not want to leave. Of course, you'll need to do some grocery shopping to stock the fully equipped kitchen (there's even a microwave), and you should take advantage of the pool and whirlpool spa; otherwise, there's really no reason to leave. Daily maid and concierge services are included in the rates.

✪ Renaissance Wailea Beach Resort

3550 Wailea Alanui, Wailea, Maui, HI 96753. ☎ **808/879-4900** or 800/992-4532. Fax 808/874-5370. 347 rms, 12 suites. A/C MINIBAR TV TEL. $275 mountain view; $315 oceanside; $380 ocean view; $485 Mokapu Beach Club; $760 1-bedroom Makai suite. Extra person $35. Children 18 and under stay free in parents' room. AE, CB, DC, DISC, ER, JCB, MC, V. Free valet- or self-parking.

From the moment you walk into the lobby of the Renaissance Wailea Beach Resort, you'll know that you've discovered pure gold. Indeed, shafts of golden light bathe the open-air lobby, and brass accents are polished to a high shine. You'll be greeted by welcoming employees carrying fresh leis. Though the room views vary, the quality of all rooms are eqully good, due in part to a recent $43 million renovation. The decor is neutral in tone and light in feeling. Wicker and rattan furnishings might include a loveseat, glass-topped coffee table, armchair, and ottoman. Each room is outfitted with a VCR (movies are complimentary). Two of the three telephones in guest rooms have modem capability. Minibars are fully stocked with beverages and snacks, and the use of in-room safes is complimentary. Light sources are more than adequate, and louvered doors, which lead to oversized private lanais, are easily opened to allow sunlight. Lanai furniture is sturdy and stylish.

The well-lit bathrooms feature a marble-topped double vanity, telephone, hair dryer, lighted makeup mirror, vanity stool, coffeemakers, and recessed glass shelves (for bathroom amenities). "Hapi" coats (robes) are also provided for guest use. If you would like extra-special service, stay in a room that's part of the Mokapu Beach Club; this entitles you to the exclusive services of the club manager, VIP check-in, complimentary continental breakfast served on your lanai (or in your personal blue cabana), and terry robes (in addition to Hapi robes). The best part about the Beach Club rooms is their location. You couldn't get much closer to the beach, and nothing could be better than relaxing just outside your room in a hammock strung between palm trees.

The site of the resort has been split by a lava formation, which created two quite distinct crescent-shaped beaches, thus giving all guests the added air of privacy and seclusion. The lava formation is an excellent place to snorkel, and there are endless nooks and crannies in which to capture a private moment.

Dining/Entertainment: For fine dining, **Raffles** is open Tuesday through Saturday and serves Pacific Rim cuisine. The **Palm Court Restaurant,** which offers American specialties and a plentiful buffet, features ponds and waterfalls and a spectacular ocean view. **Hana Gion** is the hotel's Japanese restaurant, and the poolside **Maui Onion** offers light meals daily. Thursday evening brings the hotel's luau, and the **Sunset Terrace** offers contemporary entertainment nightly.

Services: 24-hour room service; multilingual concierge and hotel staff; Avis car rental desk; complimentary hula and lei-making lessons, and pineapple-cutting demonstrations. Camp Wailea, a supervised children's program, is available for a nominal fee; complimentary shuttle service within the Wailea resort; babysitting; massage therapy clinic; check-cashing service; complimentary incoming fax service (small charge for outgoing fax service).

Facilities: Two swimming pools; four whirlpool spas; complimentary health club and fitness center; two on-site complimentary tennis courts with access to the 14 courts at the Wailea Tennis Club; access to Wailea resort golf courses with special guest rates; jogging paths; complimentary scuba lessons daily; beauty salon; self-operating laundry facilities; shopping boutique; nonsmoking floors.

Wailea Elua Village

3750 Wailea Alanui, Wailea, Maui, HI 96753. ☎ **808/879-1595** or 800/367-5246. Fax 808/ 874-3554. 152 units, 63 in rental pool. A/C TV TEL. High season (Dec 20–Apr 15) $225 1-bedroom garden view, $275 1-bedroom ocean view, $335–$350 1-bedroom oceanfront; $310 2-bedroom garden view, $360 2-bedroom ocean view, $425–$450 2-bedroom oceanfront; $435 3-bedroom garden view, $540 3-bedroom oceanfront. Low season (Apr 16–Dec 19) $190 1-bedroom garden view, $275 1-bedroom ocean view, $280–$300 1-bedroom oceanfront; $260 2-bedroom garden view, $305 2-bedroom ocean view, $360–$380 2-bedroom oceanfront; $360 3-bedroom garden view, $475 3-bedroom oceanfront. Special romance, golf, and tennis packages available. Minimum stay is 3 nights. AE, MC, V. Free parking.

Located on Ulua Beach between the Grand Wailea Resort and the Renaissance Wailea Beach Resort, Wailea Elua Village is unsurpassed among condominium properties. As you drive up to the Elua, you'll pass through the security gate and by the guard house and enter the 18 acres of landscaped grounds that surround the condominiums. With a purchase price of $500,000 or more, you can be sure that the privately owned units are superbly decorated and strikingly appointed. The one-, two-, and three-bedroom apartments will be oceanfront or have ocean or garden views. However, no matter what the view, you'll be just steps away from an excellent snorkeling reef, two pools (one with whirlpool spa), a paddle tennis court, putting green, and beachfront promenade to the major hotels in the area (and some of the island's finest restaurants). All of the condos are centrally air-conditioned and furnished with a washer and dryer, VCR, full kitchen, and gas barbecue on the lanai.

Wailea Grand Champions

3750 Wailea Alanui, Wailea, Maui, HI 96753. ☎ **808/874-3554** or 800/367-5246. Fax 808/ 874-3554. 188 units, 28 in rental pool. A/C TV TEL. High season (Dec 20–Apr 15) $169 1-bedroom garden view, $189 1-bedroom partial ocean view; $209 2-bedroom garden view, $229 2-bedroom partial ocean view. Special romance, golf, and car packages available. Minimum stay is 3 nights. AE, MC, V. Free parking.

Set on 11 acres between the Wailea Tennis Court and the Wailea Blue Golf Course, Wailea Grand Champions is one of many properties managed by Destination Resorts. Mostly residential, Grand Champions is a great place for couples who want a quiet apartment not far from the beach and away from the hubbub of the luxury resort hotels. All of the one- and two-bedroom units are air-conditioned and provide large, fully outfitted kitchens. Washers and dryers are standard, and a housekeeping service is offered daily. All guests have access to the property's two pools, barbecue area, and two whirlpool spas. There is a private guard at the entrance; however, I saw him there only once during my stay. The condominiums were built in 1989, so they are still new and freshly decorated, but unless you're a tennis or golf fanatic, you might prefer another resort property closer to the beach.

MODERATE

Wailea Ekahi Village

3750 Wailea Alanui, Wailea, Maui, HI 96753. ☎ **808/879-1595** or 800/367-5246. Fax 808/874-3554. 294 units, 59 in rental pool. TV TEL. High season (Dec 20–Apr 15) $139–$149 garden-view studio, $159–$169 ocean-view studio; $179–$199 1-bedroom garden view, $199–$219 1-bedroom ocean view; $289–$299 2-bedroom garden view, $309–$319 2-bedroom ocean view. Low season (Apr 16–Dec 19) $129–$139 garden-view studio, $149–$159 ocean-view studio; $159–$169 1-bedroom garden view, $179–$189 1-bedroom ocean view; $239–$259 2-bedroom garden view, $259–$279 2-bedroom ocean view. Special romance, golf, and tennis packages available. Minimum stay is 3 nights. AE, MC, V. Free parking.

In the late 1970s when the Wailea resort was still relatively new, three luxury condominiums were built and named one, two, and three in Hawaiian—Ekahi, Elua, and Ekolu. Since the Wailea Ekahi Village was the first built, it is situated on an enormous, prime land site within the Wailea resort. The 34 acres upon which the Ekahi was built used to be scrubland, but it has since been transformed into lush tropical gardens. The condominiums, which include individually owned studio, one-, and two-bedroom apartments, are set back from Keawakapu Beach, but the walk through the gardens to reach them is so pleasant that you hardly notice. From the beach you can walk 1 1/2 uninterrupted miles to the Kihei area. Most of the units are equipped with window air conditioners, but even those without them stay fairly cool. Since the apartments are privately owned, the decorating style varies from unit to unit, but you probably won't have any objections. The second-floor units provide high ceilings, and all offer private lanais (many of which are shaded by a canopy of bougainvillea). All units provide such amenities as a washer and dryer, fully equipped kitchen, and daily maid service. Outdoor facilities include four swimming pools, two paddle tennis courts, shuffleboard, and a beach pavilion with a barbecue area.

Wailea Ekolu Village

3750 Wailea Alanui, Wailea, Maui, Hi 96753. ☎ **808/879-1595** or 800/367-5246. Fax 808/874-3554. 148 units, 33 in rental pool. TV TEL. High season (Dec 20–Apr 15) $159 1-bedroom garden view, $179 1-bedroom ocean view; $199 2-bedroom garden view, $229 2-bedroom ocean view. Low season (Apr 16–Dec 19) $139 1-bedroom garden view, $159 1-bedroom ocean view; $169 2-bedroom garden view, $189 2-bedroom ocean view. Special romance, golf, and tennis packages available. Minimum stay is 3 nights. AE, MC, V. Free parking.

The Wailea Ekolu (meaning "three") is the least expensive of the group, due in part to the fact that it's not right on the beach. Also, the accommodations aren't as spacious or as elegant as some of the others in the Wailea resort. Several of the units do provide ocean views, but keep in mind that you'll be a good distance from the beach. Few of the apartments are air-conditioned, but all are equipped with ceiling fans, washers and dryers, and full kitchens. The decor in some of the units is a bit out of date, but all are spotlessly clean and well kept. In the two-bedroom condos, the master bathroom has only a bathtub (no shower); showers are available in the second bathroom. Besides the recreation pavilion, there are two solar-heated swimming pools and several barbecue areas.

INEXPENSIVE

⑤ Wailea Oceanfront Hotel

2980 S. Kihei Rd., Kihei, Maui, HI 96753. ☎ **808/879-7744** or 800/367-5004. Fax 808/874-0158. 88 rms. A/C TV TEL. $90 standard; $95 superior; $105 deluxe; $110 ocean view; $165 1-bedroom family unit. AE, MC, V. Free parking.

The rooms here are very small, but some are practically on the beach—in fact, Carelli's on the Beach, one of the island's best Italian restaurants, is located right next door. You'd be hard-pressed to find an oceanfront property this close to the Wailea resort for less money. All rooms, which have recently been renovated, come equipped with alarm clocks and a minirefrigerator. The tropical floral bedspreads give the rooms a bright, fresh look. Coin-operated laundry facilities are available for guest use. Complimentary coffee and doughnuts are served daily in the lobby. So long as you don't plan to spend too much time in your room (I can't imagine why anyone would on Maui!), Wailea Oceanfront Hotel is a good choice.

3 Upcountry & Hana

Most visitors to Maui don't think about booking accommodations Upcountry because of its distance from the beach, but you might want to spend a couple of days and nights living like a true Maui native (most Mauians actually live Upcountry because rents are less expensive). There are no major hotels (except the Hotel Hana Maui) in Upcountry Maui, but there are scores of small bed-and-breakfasts hidden away among the trees on the slopes of Haleakala. Most of these are rooms in residents' homes, or guest cottages on residents' properties. If you're considering staying Upcountry for a night or two, try booking a room in one of the places listed below, or contact **AA Paradise Network Maui,** P.O. Box 171, Paia, HI 96779, ☎ 808/579-8500 or 800/942-2242. **Bed and Breakfast Hawaii** (P.O. Box 449, Kapaa, Kauai, HI 96746 ☎ 808/822-7771 or 800/733-1632) is also an excellent reservation service.

UPCOUNTRY
MODERATE

✪ Kula Lodge

R.R. 1 (Box 475), Kula, Maui, HI 96790. ☎ **808/878-2517** or 800/233-1535. Fax 808/878-2518. 5 chalets. $150 Chalet 1 and 2; $120 Chalet 3 and 4; $100 Chalet 5. Extra person $30. AE, MC, V. Free parking.

So, you've spent some time on the beach, which is probably why you came here, but now you'd like to escape the crowds and spend time amid pine trees and eucalyptus. You want to hear birds (other than the ever-sociable mynah and the smart-alecky parrot) singing, and you long to see some flora other than plumeria and birds of paradise. In this case, Kula Lodge is just the place you're looking for. At 3,200 feet above sea level, nestled on the slopes of Haleakala, the lodge is surrounded by flower farms that cultivate carnations and the intriguing protea. You'll probably have an incredible view from your chalet, and after the sun drops below the horizon and a chill is in the air, you'll be able to retreat to your rustic home and bask in the light of the fire. (*Note:* not all rooms are equipped with fireplaces.) Chalets 1 and 2 offer queen-size beds, a fireplace, private lanai, and loft area with two twin beds. Chalets 3 and 4 also have queen-size beds and a sleeping loft, but the beds in the loft are futons. Chalet 5, a one-story structure, is equipped with a double bed, studio couch, and private lanai.

As you may have guessed, Kula Lodge is quite popular with locals, so if you're considering a stay here you need to book well in advance—just because it's not on the beach doesn't mean its rooms are readily available!

Adjacent to the chalets is the hotel's Hawaiian restaurant, The Kula Lodge & Restaurant (see Chapter 7, "Maui Dining," for details), which is popular among both locals and tourists.

INEXPENSIVE

Haikuleana Bed and Breakfast

555 Haiku Rd., Haiku, Maui, HI 96708. ☎ **808/575-2890.** 4 rms. $85 double. Discounts for stays longer than 5 days. Free parking. From Kahului Airport follow the signs to Hana Highway, Route 36. Go through the town of Paia along the coast, past Hookipa Beach Park. At mile marker 11 turn right onto Haiku Road, continue about 1 mile to 555 Haiku Rd. on the left. You won't see a sign because they're not allowed on Maui, so look for the number on the mailbox.

Haikuleana Bed and Breakfast is set on 1¹/₂ acres of Upcountry land. Built in 1870, the home's main purpose was to attract a doctor to the Haiku pineapple plantation. Since then it has been home to one doctor after another—in fact, patients used to wait on what is now the screened porch. In 1947 Dole acquired the Haiku Pineapple Company. Miss Lindsay then took up residence here along with her servants. The property later became a pig or chicken farm (no one remembers which), and it fell into disrepair. Denise and Clark Champion began renovations, and the last owner (Fred Fox) finished the job. The current owners are Jeanne and Ralph Blum.

When you walk in the front door the common area is off to your right, and straight ahead is where guests gather in the mornings for breakfast. There's a TV in the living room, which is tastefully appointed with Oriental rugs and floral-patterned fabrics. The first room (to the left), decorated with blue-and-white-striped accents, was the original doctor's office. It's a twin-bedded room, but the beds can be pushed together to form a king-size bed. Another room is paneled in cedar. All have showers, and some of the original woodwork and wood floors have been redone. Antiques are scattered throughout the inn, and some of the bathroom sinks came from the old Lake Placid Inn. All the rooms have ceiling fans and electric blankets to provide comfort in any weather. Another guest room has a separate entrance and painted wood furnishings. In the breakfast area guests can make use of a small refrigerator stocked with juices and sodas. Full breakfast includes a hot dish, such as pancakes with macadamia nuts and coconut, topped with coconut syrup; homemade breads, coffee, tea, and juices are always available. Every evening guests are treated to complimentary pupus.

Kuau Cove Plantation Bed & Breakfast

2 Waa Place, Kuau, Paia, Maui, HI 96779. ☎**808/579-8988.** Fax 808/579-8710. 2 rms, 2 studio apts. $85 double room (including breakfast), $100 studio double ($8 extra for breakfast). Extra person $20. Weekly and monthly discounts. Free parking. From Kahului Airport follow the sign to Hana Highway (Rte. 36). Go through the town of Paia. Continue for 1¹/₂ miles and turn left on Waa Place (one block before the Kuau Mart). Kuau Cove Plantation Bed & Breakfast is the first house on the left. There will not be a sign since signs for bed-and-breakfasts are not permitted on Maui.

Nestled near a quiet tropical ocean cove on the north shore of Maui, Kuau Cove Plantation offers the unique charm of an old Hawaiian plantation home with the convenience of a central location (near Paia town). Also, it's only steps from the ocean and sandy beaches. Built around 1939 as a doctor's home next to the old Paia Sugar Plantation hospital on Baldwin Avenue, the house was moved to this location in 1958 when the new hospital was built in Kahului. This renovated home is furnished with antiques and period wicker and rattan. There are two large bedrooms in the main house, each with private bath. One room is twin-bedded, but the beds can be made into a king-size bed. The other has a queen-size bed. All rooms have ceiling fans, refrigerators, and cable TV outlets. The guest dining room overlooks the garden, and guests also have access to a sunny veranda. In addition, there are two separate, large studio apartments with private bathrooms and kitchens. Here, guests can add breakfast to their room rate. One studio overlooks the garden, while the other has an ocean view. Breakfast includes coffee, tea, juice, fresh fruit, and a variety of hot dishes.

Kuau Cove Plantation is situated on beautifully landscaped grounds (there are two gigantic monkeypod trees and one rubber tree). In the garden a Jacuzzi is available for guest use. Guests may also use the barbecue grill and outdoor tables. A private walkway leads to a secluded ocean cove. Although there is no sand beach here, sandy beaches are within a short walk. Hookipa Beach is just 1 mile away. Fred Fox (the owner) is a delightful host.

✪ Olinda Country Cottage and B&B

536 Olinda Rd., Makawao, Maui, HI 96768. ☎/Fax **808/572-1453.** 1 cottage, 2 rooms. TV TEL. $95 cottage (including first morning's breakfast), $85 double (including breakfast). 2-night minimum stay. No credit cards. Free parking.

Up the hill from Makawao town, at the top of Olinda Road, which winds through a forest of 150-foot tall blue-gum euycalyptus trees, Olinda Country Cottage and B&B sits at an altitude of 4,000 feet above sea level. Owners Ellen Unterman and Rupa McLaughlin have turned what was always a beautiful property into a breathtaking one. Ellen owned an antique shop in Santa Monica for 15 years, and her incredible country collection is scattered throughout the beautifully restored Tudor mansion (which houses the bed-and-breakfast rooms) and the romantic cottage. The antiques are complemented by designer accoutrements. The cottage, which is quite private, can accommodate up to five people. Inside you'll find a living room with fireplace, a fully equipped kitchen, a queen-bedded room, a washer and dryer, and a TV and VCR—all the comforts of home and then some. The views from this elevation are incredible. The top floor of the main house offers guests a full 5,000 square feet of luxury. Each room has a private bath, and guests share an enormous living room. Breakfast is served in the living room each morning. Olinda is surrounded by 8 acres of land.

A GAY B&B

Camp Kula—Maui B&B

P.O. Box 111, Kula, Maui, HI 96790. ☎/Fax **808/878-2528.** 2 rms. $65–$78 double.

Camp Kula is "where happy campers play." Proprietors D.E. and Ray say there's no need to pitch a tent at this camp. They've opened the doors of their home and the cabinets of their kitchen to gay and lesbian visitors to Maui. Located in Upcountry Kula on the slopes of Haleakala, Camp Kula is a slice of paradise; because it's not on the beach, a stay here will make you feel like a real local. You can relax in one of the hammocks or on the koa swing while dozing to the tinkling sound of wind chimes. D.E. and Ray will help you find popular local beaches, waterfalls, hiking trails, and snorkeling spots. If you're traveling alone, the Prince Kuhio Jr. Suite, with its own entrance, is perfect. Queen Emma's room, which is larger, is "suitable for a king or two queens." There's a king-size bed, TV, and separate sitting area. All rooms have shared baths. Rates include a "help yourself" continental breakfast, including fruit, fresh-baked breads, coffee, tea, and juice. Camp Kula is a member of the International Gay Traveler Association.

HANA
EXPENSIVE

Hotel Hana Maui

Hana Hwy., Hana, Maui, HI 96713-0008. ☎ **808/248-8211.** Fax 808/248-7202. 96 rms and cottages. MINIBAR TEL. $335 standard garden room; $395 garden Junior Suite; $550 Garden Suite; $450 Sea Ranch Cottage; $815 Sea Ranch Cottage Suites. Honeymoon, wellness, family, and extended stay packages available. AE, DC, MC, V. Free parking.

The Hotel Hana Maui is the best hotel in town—actually, it is the only hotel in its price category in Hana. When you check in you will receive a lei greeting, fresh fruit, and a glass of juice before you're driven to your room in a golf cart by a staff member. The Hotel Hana Maui was originally opened in 1946 by Paul Fagan, a major figure in the sugar trade who decided to turn his sugar plantation into a cattle ranch with a small hotel to attract visitors to Hana. Paul Fagan also owned a baseball team, which he brought to the Kauiki Inn (now the Hotel Hana Maui) for spring training. After sportswriters began mentioning the new luxury resort in Hana, it wasn't long before wealthy tourists began arriving at an airstrip in Hamoa for their stay at the 10-room Kauiki Inn. Today the Hotel Hana Maui, which underwent a major renovation in 1989, is a haven for many celebrities who come here seeking privacy. (Privacy is exactly what you'll get here.) There's nothing to distract you from enjoying your time in Hana—no TV or other reminders of the outside world.

The cottage-style buildings housing the guest rooms are spread out over 66 acres. All rooms feature bleached hardwood floors, oversized furnishings, traditional Hawaiian quilt bedspreads, ceiling fans, and fully stocked minibars with built-in automatic ice makers. The spacious tiled bathrooms all have large soaking tubs with views of private gardens; there are terry robes and a variety of tropically scented soaps, shampoos, and body lotions. Each room is equipped with a coffeemaker and grinder as well as fresh coffee beans. All units have sliding glass doors that open onto landscaped patios. The very private Sea Ranch Cottages, a new addition to the hotel on a coastal bluff, feature sundecks (most with hot tubs) and huge picture windows.

The hotel's new Wellness Center, a major part of the Hana Health and Fitness Retreat, sponsors a daily schedule of activities including nature walks, aquacise, and low-impact aerobics. The 25-meter heated pool and Jacuzzi are available to all guests, as are the stair-climbers, stationary bikes, and multistation weight-training machine. The program is designed to enhance awareness of the relationship among mind, body, and spirit. A modified yoga class (called Inner Rhythmns) works on breathing techniques to calm the mind and tune into the body.

Although the hotel has a restaurant (for which reservations are necessary), room service is not available to guests. In addition to a beauty salon for men and women, there are several shops within the hotel. Your room rate includes transportation to and from Hana Airport, tennis, practice golf (Hana has no golf course), and use of bicycles, snorkeling, and beach equipment. Car rentals can be arranged by the hotel.

Note: As of mid-1996, the owners of Hotel Hana Maui were looking for a prospective buyer for the property. Otherwise, the hotel is functioning normally.

MODERATE

Hana Kai-Maui Resort

1533 Uakea Rd. (P.O. Box 38), Hana, Maui, HI 96713. ☎ **808/248-8426** or 800/346-2772. Fax 808/248-7482. 12 units. $125 studio for 2; $125–$150 1-bedroom apartment. Children 8 and under stay free in parents' room. Extra person $10. Weekly and monthly discounts available. AE, MC, V. Free parking.

So, you survived the switchbacks on the way to Hana, and you want a comfortable studio or one-bedroom apartment to call home while you explore this beautiful area. The Hana Kai-Maui, tucked away in a cove on Hana Bay, is the perfect choice. Since restaurants in Hana are hard to come by, you'll want the comfort of your own fully equipped kitchen if you plan to spend more than a couple of days in town; this is what you'll get at the Hana Kai-Maui. Nearly all of the apartments offer reasonable views. In most cases, private lanais overlook Popolana Beach. All units are decorated in neutral tones with pastel tropical floral print fabrics and rattan furnishings. Wall-to-wall carpeting is standard. There is a barbecue area outside for guest use.

✪ Hana Plantation Houses

P.O. Box 248, Hana, Maui, HI 96713. ☎ **808/923-0772** or 800/228-HANA. 12 units. TV TEL. $80 Lani Makaalae Studio, $110 Lani Makaalae Too; $100 Hale Kipa Downstairs, $135 Hale Kipa Upstairs; $70 Garden House (downstairs), $140 Garden House (upstairs); $160 Waikoloa Beach Cottage; $150 Hale Ainahau. Extra person $10. AE, MC, V (with 4% service charge). 10% discount for stays of 7 days or longer. Free parking. The Hana Plantation Houses office is located off Hana Highway, in the Hana Gardenland Botanical Gardens. You'll see a sign on your right at the Kalo Road intersection.

If you're looking for a true home away from home where you can rest and enjoy complete privacy, you might want to contact the folks who run Hana Plantation Houses. They manage a group of houses and studios scattered around the town of Hana, and they'll do everything in their power to make your stay as relaxing and rejuvenating as it can be. One choice is Hale Kipa ("House of Hospitality"). Located in the town of Hana, this is a two-story plantation-style house on manicured grounds with its own private hot tub. The upstairs section sleeps four; the downstairs sleeps two. If there are just two of you, ask about the beautiful Hale Ainahau. Built in 1992, it is located on Waikoloa Point, surrounded by 4 acres of tropical landscaping. Papaya and banana trees dot the property (you can pick the bananas and papaya), and you'll find a duck pond, hiking trails, and views of Hana Bay. Hale Ainahau is powered by solar energy. Since the floor plan of Ainahau is open, it is a perfect romantic retreat for a vacationing couple. Other options include the Lani Makaalae Studio and Lani Makaalae Too, a tropical-style studio and a tropical-style cottage, respectively. Although there are too many choices to be listed here, believe me—there is something for everyone at Hana Plantation Houses.

INEXPENSIVE

⑤ Aloha Cottages

73 Keawa Place (P.O. Box 205), Hana, Maui, HI 96713. ☎ **808/248-8420.** 5 cottage units. $60–$90 double. Extra person $10–$20. No credit cards. Free parking.

If you're watching your expenses, your choices in Hana are somewhat limited. However, Mrs. F. Nakamura, proprietress of the Aloha Cottages, offers two-bedroom cottage units for a fraction of the price of some of the other accommodations in town. Each cottage can easily accommodate up to four people, and two units can accommodate larger groups. If you're looking for the current rage in decorator fashions, the Aloha Cottages aren't for you. However, they are perfect if you want clean, comfortable lodgings with a fully equipped kitchen, sizable living room, and bathroom with a full tub/shower combination. Also available is a studio with a two-burner hot plate, toaster, refrigerator, adequate kitchen supplies, and a bathroom with a shower. Three of the units have TVs, but there are no telephones in the rooms (messages will be taken for you). There are barbecue grills. Aloha Cottages are centrally located near the grocery store and town restaurants. Beaches are nearby.

Cabins

⑤ Waianapanapa State Park

Off Hana Hwy. (Contact the Department of Land and Natural Resources, Division of State Parks, 54 S. High St., Wailuku, Maui, HI 96793.) ☎ **808/243-5354.** 12 cabins. $14 for 2 in a 2-room cabin; tent camping free. Maximum stay is 5 nights in cabins and camping. No credit cards. Free parking. Approximately 4 miles before you reach the town of Hana, you'll see the entrance to Waianapanapa State Park on your left.

The cabins at Waianapanapa State Park are so popular with locals and tourists alike that reservations need to be made up to six months in advance. You can't just stop by and expect to get one, but if you call ahead for a reservation, you can camp year-round for free. The two-room cabins (accommodating up to six) are located not far from a black-sand beach, and some even overlook the ocean. Close by are several different hiking trails that will take you along the coastline. Towels, bedding, kitchen equipment (including a refrigerator and cooking utensils), and electricity are provided. (Several of my friends who have stayed in the cabins here say that you should bring your own sheets and towels if possible; bug spray is also advisable in the summer.) This is not only the least expensive way to see Hana, but also one of the most interesting. *Note:* Although swimming is permitted at the black-sand beach, the ocean conditions can be treacherous at times.

The first time I visited Maui, more than 12 years ago, the dining scene really left something to be desired. I'm happy to report that today the situation has changed for the better. Chefs are taking advantage of the island's natural resources, especially fish found in Hawaiian waters such as *opakapaka* (pink snapper), *ahi* (yellowfin tuna), *ono* (another mackerel or tunalike fish), *lehi* (orange snapper), and *onaga* (long-tail red snapper). Island-grown fruits, vegetables, and herbs provide unbelievably creative, health-conscious chefs a veritable cornucopia with which to work. Since virtually every cuisine is represented somewhere on the island, there's something to suit nearly everyone's taste.

For help with food terms that may be unfamiliar to you, see "Glossary of Island Foods" in the Appendix of this book.

Most restaurants on Maui are informal. Only a handful require men to wear jackets, and only a couple insist on ties and jackets. In upscale restaurants, you'll see diners in resort wear (a nice shirt and pants for men, and nice pants or a dress for women); in more casual eateries, you'll see diners wearing shorts. Even though the dining scene is generally informal, you need to determine if reservations are necessary.

To help you choose where to eat, the restaurants listed below are categorized first by area, then by price. **Expensive** refers to restaurants where most main courses are $20 or higher; **moderate** are those where the main courses range from $15 to $19; **inexpensive** are those where most main courses are $14 and under.

1 Restaurants by Cuisine

AMERICAN

Cheeseburger in Paradise
(Lahaina, *I*)
David Paul's Lahaina Grill
(Lahaina, *M*)
The Grill & Bar (Kapalua, *M*)
Hamburger Mary's
(Wailuku, *I*)

Pavillion (Kaanapali, *M*)
Peggy Sue's (Kihei, *I*)
Pineapple Hill Restaurant
(Kapalua, *E*)
Stella Blues Cafe & Deli
(Kihei, *I*)
Tasty Crust Restaurant
(Wailuku, *I*)

Key to abbreviations: *E*=Expensive, *I*=Inexpensive, *M*=Moderate

BARBECUE

Smokehouse BBQ (Lahaina, *I*)

CAFE

Cafe Kula (Wailea, *M*)
Cafe Kup à Kuppa (Wailuku, *I*)
Crossroads Caffe (Makawao, *I*)
Grandma's Coffee Shop (Keokea, *I*)
Maui Coffee Roasters (Kahului, *I*)
Pauwela Cafe (Haiku, *I*)

CHINESE

Ming Yuen (Kahului, *I*)

CONTINENTAL

The Bay Club (Kapalua, *E*)
The Maalaea Waterfront Restaurant
   (Kihei, *E*)
Swan Court (Kaanapali, *E*)

DELI

The Courtyard Deli (Makawao, *I*)
Dollie's Pub & Cafe (Between
   Kaanapali and Kapalua, *I*)
Juicy's Healthy Food Deli
   (Lahaina, *I*)
Pic-nics (Paia, *I*)
The Sand Witch (Kihei, *I*)

FRENCH

Chez Paul (Lahaina, *E*)
Gerard's (Lahaina, *E*)

GERMAN

Wunderbar (Paia, *E*)

GREEK

Greek Bistro (Kihei, *M*)

HAWAIIAN

The Anuenue Room (Kapalua, *E*)
Avalon Restaurant & Bar
   (Lahaina, *M*)
Haliimaile General Store
   (Makawao, *E*)
Hana Gardenland Cafe (Hana, *I*)
Kula Lodge & Restaurant (Kula, *M*)
Old Lahaina Cafe (Lahaina, *I*)
A Pacific Cafe Maui (Kihei, *E*)
The Plantation House Restaurant
   (Kapalua, *M*)
Sam Sato's (Wailuku, *I*)

SeaWatch Restaurant at Wailea
   (Wailea, *E*)

INTERNATIONAL

The Class Act (Kahului, *I*)
Lahaina Coolers Restaurant & Bar
   (Lahaina, *I*)
Roy's Kahana Bar & Grill (Between
   Kaanapali & Kapalua, *E*)

ITALIAN

B.J.'s Chicago Pizzeria (Lahaina, *I*)
Bistro Molokini (Wailea, *M*)
Caffe Ciao (Wailea, *M*)
Carelli's on the Beach (Kihei, *E*)
Casanova Italian Restaurant
   (Makawao, *E*)
Longhi's (Lahina, *M*)
Pizza Paradiso (Kaanapali, *I*)
Scaroles Ristorante (Lahaina, *M*)
Scaroles Village Pizzeria (Lahaina, *I*)
Spats Trattoria (Kaanapali, *M*)

JAPANESE

Kincha (Wailea, *E*)
Kobe Japanese Steak House
   (Lahaina, *M*)
Nikko (Kaanapali, *M*)

MEDITERRANEAN

The Garden Restaurant (Kapalua, *E*)
Seasons (Wailea, *E*)

MEXICAN

Aloha Cantina (Lahaina, *I*)
Compadres Mexican Bar & Grill
   (Lahaina, *M*)
Margarita's Beach Cantina (Kihei, *I*)
Maui Tacos
   (Between Kaanapali & Kapalua, *I*)

PACIFIC

Kea Lani (Wailea, *E*)
Pacific Grill (Wailea, *E*)
Pacific'O (Lahaina, *M*)
Sound of the Falls (Kaanapali, *E*)

SEAFOOD

Alexander's Fish, Chicken & Ribs
   (Kihei, *I*)
Erik's Seafood Grotto (Between
   Kaanapali & Kapalua, *E*)
Kimo's (Lahaina, *I*)

Lokelani (Kaanapali, *M*)
Mama's Fish House (Paia, *E*)
Paia Fish Market Restaurant (Paia, *M*)

STEAKS

Lahaina Provision Company
(Kaanapali, *E*)
Makawao Steak House (Makawao,*E*)

THAI

Royal Thai Cuisine (Kihei, *I*)
Saeng's Thai Cuisine (Wailuku, *I*)
Siam Thai (Wailuku, *I*)

VIETNAMESE

A Saigon Cafe (Wailuku, *I*)

2 West Maui

West Maui is home to most of the island's best restaurants. You'll find some of them on or just off Front Street in Lahaina. Many more are in the major hotels in the Kaanapali resort area, and you'll find a few scattered between Kaanapali and Kapalua. Finally, even though Kapalua is home to only two hotels, you'll find still more in that resort area. If you're staying anywhere on the west side, you won't have to go very far for good food.

KAANAPALI
EXPENSIVE

Lahaina Provision Company

200 Nohea Kai Dr. (in the Hyatt Regency). ☎ **808/661-1234.** Reservations not necessary. Main courses $18–$30. AE, DC, MC, V. Daily 11:30am–2pm and 6–11pm. STEAK/SEAFOOD.

An open-air garden restaurant and cocktail lounge, Lahaina Provision Company is a less expensive and more casual alternative to the Hyatt's elegant Swan Court restaurant. The lunchtime bill of fare includes several standard sandwich offerings as well as a few more substantial entrées. There's something on the lunch menu for the whole family. The kids will probably love the soft ice cream. The dinner menu is more sophisticated. The Shrimp Nokekula—beer-battered coconut shrimp with a delectable orange-horseradish sauce—is a delicious way to begin your meal. Sweet Maui onion rings with Hawaiian barbecue sauce are also excellent as an appetizer. My recommendations for entrées are the seafood mixed grill or the surprisingly flavorful vegetarian black bean and tofu cake. Among the steaks are a tasty filet mignon with roasted Maui onions, top sirloin steak, prime rib, and grilled New York steak. All entrées come with a vegetable and potatoes or rice. A word of advice: Save room for dessert. The Lahaina Provision Company is known for its Chocoholic Bar, loaded with irresistible chocolate desserts.

Sound of the Falls

2365 Kaanapali Pkwy. (at the Westin Maui). ☎ **808/667-2525.** Reservations recommended. Main courses $24–$37. AE, DC, JCB, MC, V. Mon–Wed and Fri–Sat 6pm–9:30; brunch Sun 10:30am–2pm. PACIFIC BISTRO.

This is the Westin's signature restaurant and one of Maui's most romantic dining spots. The open-air dining room, fronted by the ocean, as well as a beautiful paddling pool for the resident swans, is a great venue for watching the spectacular sunset every evening. All of this, plus the restaurant's Pacific bistro cuisine, promise an evening you won't soon forget.

As a first course here, I would recommend the tangled tiger prawns served with a chili cilantro garlic sauce. Escargot lovers (and even those who generally avoid these delectable gastropods) should enjoy the provincial snails in a crispy phyllo with Boursin cheese and roasted Kula tomato sauce. If you've come to love ahi sashimi during your stay on the island, the sesame-seared sashimi with straw mushrooms, chiso, and Japanese mustard is terrific. If you'd rather begin your meal with a salad, the rainbow of baby mixed greens in crisp rice paper, served with a passion fruit vinaigrette is an excellent choice. Everything on the main-course menu looks so good that you'll probably have a difficult time making a decision. Not to worry—the waiters here are exceptionally friendly and will eagerly recommend their favorites. Seafood dishes include sake-glazed Pacific salmon with black sesame seeds and a green onion pancake; and the pan roast of Pacific seafoods in a light lobster-lemongrass essence. Other menu offerings include guava-basted rack of lamb served with garlic potato purée and peppered venison chops served with a sesame citron sauce. Desserts change daily, but if you're lucky you might be dining at a time when the Chocolate Kona Bomb is on the menu. It's vanilla and Kona coffee ice cream wrapped in a hard chocolate shell and drizzled with an incredible sauce. Soufflés are always an option, but be prepared for a 25-minute wait. Sunday brunch ($26.95 per person) at Sound of the Falls is one of the best on the island. Live piano music is featured, and champagne is on the house. Children are welcome here, and smaller portions for them are available at half price.

Swan Court

200 Nohea Kai Dr. (in the Hyatt Regency). ☎ **808/661-1234.** Reservations required. Main courses $26–$39. AE, DC, MC, V. Mon–Sat 7–11:30am, Sun 7am–12:30pm; daily 6–10pm. CONTINENTAL.

The setting at Swan Court couldn't be more romantic. In fact, *Lifestyles of the Rich and Famous* named it one of the top 10 most romantic restaurants in the world. Elegant swans glide through the water only a few feet from your table, and the comforting sounds of rushing waterfalls calm your spirit at any time of the day. Breakfasting here will quietly coax the sleep from your bones without your awareness, and the food will awaken your senses in a most agreeable fashion. Relax with a glass of fresh-squeezed juice and a bowl of fruit while you wait for your main course. Perhaps you're in the mood for a breakfast classic like eggs Benedict or an omelet with three cheeses (in this case, Boursin, Mozzarella, and Brie). Or, maybe you'd rather try the macadamia nut griddle cakes drizzled with a warm coconut syrup. For those who want a little of everything, the Court Buffet is an excellent choice. You will be able to choose from a variety of fresh island fruits, breakfast pastries, pancakes, French toast, and omelets.

Later in the day, Swan Court will affect your senses and those of your partner in a way that is equally pleasurable but quite different from the morning hours. By candlelight choose hot or cold appetizers such as smoked salmon or lobster potstickers (with lilikoi and black bean sauce), or even Szechuan duck wontons. Featured entrées include Hunan marinated rack of lamb with haricots verts, Maui onion confit, and potato galette and grilled swordfish served with crab tortellini. When I last dined at Swan Court, the Cuisine Naturelle offering was grilled salmon with a sweet miso glaze and ginger spiced vegetables. For dessert try the chocolate and Kaanapali coffee mousse tower or the raspberry soufflé served with a dark chocolate and Chambord sauce.

MODERATE

Lokelani

100 Nohea Kai Dr. (in the Maui Marriott). ☎ **808/667-1200.** Reservations recommended. Main courses $15–$19. Sundowner menu $19.75. AE, DC, MC, V. Wed–Sun 6–9pm. Proceed on Kaanapali Parkway following the signs to the Maui Marriott. Nohea Kai Drive is on your left. REGIONAL SEAFOOD.

Kaanapali Coast Dining

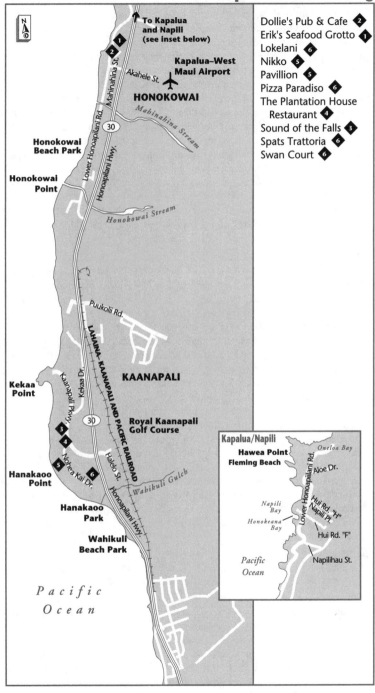

Dollie's Pub & Cafe 2
Erik's Seafood Grotto 1
Lokelani 6
Nikko 5
Pavillion 5
Pizza Paradiso 6
The Plantation House
    Restaurant 4
Sound of the Falls 3
Spats Trattoria 6
Swan Court 6

Named for one of the island's beautiful flowers, Lokelani is the Maui Marriott's fine dining room. Overlooking the hotel's courtyard and gardens, the dining room has a comfortably elegant atmosphere. Before you order, tempt your palate with French bread or Lavosh and seasoned olive oil delivered to your table by your waiter. Every dish is prepared with the freshest of ingredients—so fresh that Chef Lou Trope often plucks herbs out of his own private garden just outside the restaurant at the near edge of the courtyard. The menu changes frequently, but choices might include the Maui onion soup (three onions and three cheeses baked and served in a whole onion) or Dungeness crab cakes (served with a Chinese garlic black bean sauce, Lahaina mango coulis, and ginger mayonnaise). For an entrée, the pan-seared herb-crusted ahi with sautéed shiitake mushrooms, baked eggplant, oven-dried Kula tomatoes, and goat cheese, is an excellent choice. You might also chance to be there on a night when the chef is serving sesame pepper-crusted char sui rack of lamb. Another good choice is the Hunan barbecued wild boar served with a ginger soy mustard sauce, fresh mango chutney, and wok-seared vegetables. Desserts change daily, but anything the pastry chef whips up will be worth the indulgence. You're sure to leave Lokelani feeling contented, relaxed, and supremely satisfied.

Nikko

100 Nohea Kai Dr. (in the Maui Marriott). ☎ **808/667-1200.** Reservations required. Dinner selections $18.95–$39. AE, DC, MC, V. Daily 6–9pm. JAPANESE STEAK HOUSE.

In Japanese, nikko means "sun's rays," and it is also the name of one of Japan's most well-known and loveliest parks, hence, the word has become synonymous with magnificence. The Maui Marriott strives for magnificence in its own version of Nikko—an authentic Japanese restaurant with teppanyaki-style cooking. Appetizers include breaded scallops, deep-fried and glazed with a teriyaki sauce; Japanese dumplings stuffed with seafood and vegetables, served with a spicy sauce; shrimp and vegetable tempura; and teriyaki fish tidbits. Don't forget to order the sake or plum wine, another Japanese favorite. In addition, there's a selection of Japanese beers and wines by the glass. Each dinner selection includes shrimp or scallops, miso soup or tori soup (clear broth with chicken, mushrooms, scallions, and daikon), a fresh island salad, steamed rice, teppanyaki vegetables, and green tea. You might choose the sesame chicken or the Nikko shrimp. If you can't decide, it might be best to order the chicken and New York sirloin dinner. Menu choices always include a chef's special and a vegetarian stir-fry. For dessert try Nikko's fried ice cream (a vanilla ice-cream ball rolled in a crunchy coating, deep-fried, and topped with honey or chocolate sauce). If you're a fan of green-tea ice cream, it's available here. There is a children's menu, and if you feel like dining early the Samurai Sunset Menu ($13.50–$18.50) is served between 6 and 6:30pm.

Pavillion

200 Nohea Kai Dr. (in the Hyatt Regency). ☎ **808/661-1234.** Reservations not necessary. Main courses $4.75–$15. AE, DC, MC, V. Daily 6am–6pm. AMERICAN.

If you've spent all day on Kaanapali Beach but don't feel like dining in bustling Whalers Village, the Pavillion at the Hyatt Regency is an excellent alternative. I recently enjoyed a lovely late breakfast in the poolside, open-air restaurant and was happy to find "Cuisine Naturelle" (low in sodium, cholesterol, calories, and fat) on the first page of the menu. You'll find fresh juices, seasonal fruits, and assorted hot or cold cereals with or without fruit. For the calorie-conscious with a heartier appetite, there's an egg-white omelet, apple cinnamon oatmeal with dried fruit and cinnamon apples, or chicken hash Florentine (sautéed chicken hash on a bed of spinach, served with whole-wheat toast). If you're less concerned about calories, the

Leilani waffle with fresh fruit or seasonal berries or the Kaanapali pancakes with macadamia nuts and warm maple syrup are both excellent. There are several choices for egg lovers, including the No Ka Oi omelet with Cheddar or Monterey Jack cheese, ham, bacon, mushrooms, and green onions. There's even a Japanese Bento breakfast with all the traditional accompaniments. At lunch, begin with a fruit smoothie (papaya, coconut, banana, pineapple, strawberry, or peach), "rummed up" or virgin. Other tropical drinks are available as well. Lunch appetizers include sashimi, Cantonese pot-stickers, and Philippine Lumpia (thin-skinned egg rolls with plum sauce and hot mustard). Salad entrées, such as the Kalani with chicken, avocado, egg, tomato, bacon, and greens with bleu-cheese dressing, are very filling. An excellent sandwich choice is the Heavenly Hana—macadamia-nut bread spread with cream cheese and topped with sliced banana, papaya, pineapple, and other seasonal fruits. The cheesecake with fresh seasonal berries and the double-fudge Kahlua cake are scrumptious.

Spats Trattoria

200 Nohea Kai Dr. (in the Hyatt Regency). ☎ **808/661-1234.** Reservations recommended. Main courses $15–$26. AE, DC, MC, V. Tues–Sat 6:30–10pm. ITALIAN.

For northern Italian cuisine in an intimate setting, try Spats, one of the Hyatt's award-winning restaurants. Traditional appetizers include *prosciutto con melone fresco* (thinly sliced prosciutto with fresh melon) and *calamari fritti* (fried calamari). I enjoyed the *involenti di polenta,* a tasty, light, rolled polenta with mushrooms, chicken, tomatoes, and Mozzarella. There's also a good hearty minestrone soup. As is customary at the Hyatt, there are also several Cuisine Naturelle offerings on the menu. Try the *capesante e verdure alla griglia* (grilled scallops and vegetables in tomato sauce) or the *insalata d'espinachi* (a salad of spinach, carrots, and mild onions tossed in a horseradish yogurt dressing). To help you out, the Cuisine Naturelle dishes on the menu indicate the number of calories, carbohydrates, cholesterol, sodium, and fat. The *ravioli d'aragosta* (lobster ravioli in a seafood sauce) and the *fettuccini speciale* (fettuccine, mushrooms, sun-dried tomatoes, garlic, roasted peppers, olive oil, and fresh herbs) are good pasta choices. There are also several meat and fish dishes. The *tagliato di filetto* (marinated fillet of beef with a light herb Chianti sauce) is excellent, as is the *filetto di salmone* (grilled salmon fillet with roasted red peppers in a light balsamic vinaigrette). After dinner try the Spatstick (espresso with Baileys and Tuaca) or the Cocoa Mac Cafe (crème de cacao and macadamia-nut liqueur served with Kona coffee, whipped cream, and sprinkled with macadamia nuts). For dessert (no, the Cocoa Mac Cafe is not the dessert), consider the white and dark chocolate mousse or the fresh seasonal fruits and berries served with warm port wine zabaglione.

INEXPENSIVE

✪ Pizza Paradiso

Whalers Village Food Court, 2435 Kaanapali Pkwy. ☎ **808/667-0333.** No reservations. Pizza $3.20–$4.95 by the slice, $16–$20 whole pie. No credit cards. Daily 11am–9pm. ITALIAN.

If you're looking for "a big slice of heaven for just a little dough," Pizza Paradiso will fit the bill (and then some). Maui may not be a place you'd expect to find New York–style pizza, and Whalers Village might be the last place you'd think of looking for it, but it's there, and this is some of the best pizza I've ever had. There's a three-cheese pizza (Mozzarella, Parmesan, and Cheddar), a Jimmy Hoffa ("spicy pepperoni buried under tons of Mozzarella"), the Maui Wowie (Maui pineapple and Canadian bacon), the Veg Wedge (roasted eggplant, bell peppers, onions, olives, tomatoes, and "shrooms"), the Paradiso (a combination of pepperoni, sausage, bell peppers, onions,

⊕ Family-Friendly Restaurants

Scaroles Village Pizzeria *(see p. 139)*   This is a good place to take the kids in Lahaina—they'll welcome the change from seafood and hamburgers.

Kimo's *(see p. 138)*   Located in the center of Lahaina, this family-style eatery has a childrens' menu as well as a pleasant view.

Maui Tacos *(see p. 141)*   If your kids like Mexican food, they will probably like this fast food–style restaurant for lunch or early dinner. The traditional menu offers extremely healthful dishes, and the atmosphere is rather casual.

olives, and shrooms), and my personal favorite, the God Father (roasted chicken, artichoke hearts, sun-dried tomatoes, olives, bell peppers, onions, fresh basil, and shrooms). One slice was enough for me—in fact, each slice weighs in at nearly *a pound,* but if that doesn't satisfy, you can also get a whole pie. Besides pizza, Pizza Paradiso offers subs, salads, and spaghetti and meatballs. Everything here is made with the freshest ingredients, such as Kula produce, and part-skim-milk Mozzarella is used on all pizzas. Pizza Paradiso is located in a small food court in Whalers Village.

LAHAINA
EXPENSIVE

Chez Paul
Honoapilani Hwy., Olowalu Village. ☎ **808/661-3843.** Reservations necessary. Main courses $21–$32. AE, DC, MC, V. Two seatings nightly at 6:30 and 8:30. From Central Maui, follow Honoapilani Highway until you come to Olowalu Village, where the speed limit drops and you'll see a small grouping of businesses on your right—Chez Paul is among them. FRENCH.

I love Chez Paul. Perhaps that's because it's both quaint and elegant, or perhaps because it's reminiscent of French restaurants I've frequented in the past. Whatever the reason, I know that Chez Paul (open since 1968, a rarity on the Maui food scene) serves some of the island's best French cuisine.

Traditional appetizers such as *bloc de foie gras* (goose-liver pâté) with toast points and escargots bourguignons, and entrées such as *canard lapernousse* (boneless roast duck with Dijon mustard and a breaded Swiss-cheese crust over a cream-sherry sauce) are common menu offerings. You might also find a *fond d'arichaud à la framboise* (sliced artichoke with raspberry vinaigrette) to start or *poisson et hommard à façon* (fresh island fish served over a duxelle of mushrooms and sliced Maine lobster served in a sorrell sauce). The *noisette d'agneau des préss salés* (sautéed sliced lamb flank with a thyme-raspberry sauce topped with a garlic cream) is excellent, as are the *médaillons de veau normande* (thin slices of white veal over a duxelle of mushrooms in a Madeira wine sauce). Naturally, the desserts are spectacular, and the wine list is extensive and very well-selected. Chez Paul is a local favorite, so if you're planning to dine there, call a couple of days in advance for reservations.

✪ Gerard's
174 Lahainaluna Rd. ☎ **808/661-8939.** Reservations recommended. Main courses $24–$29. AE, MC, V. Daily 6–10pm. FRENCH.

For truly authentic French cuisine in a lovely, Hawaiian plantation–style setting (indoors, on the patio, or in the garden), Gerard's can't be beat. In business on Maui for more than a decade, Chef Gerard Reversade hails from the Gascony region of France where he learned to cook at the tender age of 10 (by 12 he was baking croissants from scratch—no small feat for a person of any age, I assure you). Still a

Lahaina Dining

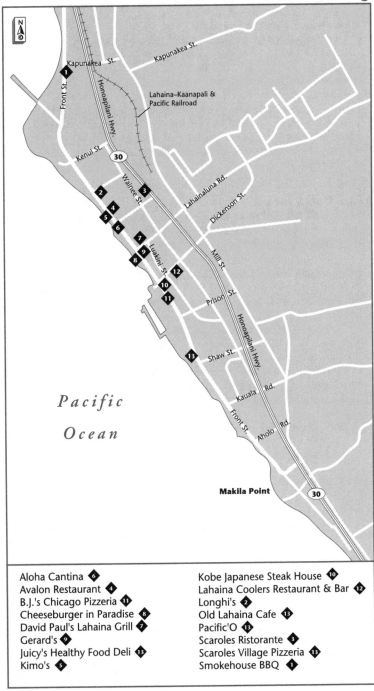

Aloha Cantina **6**
Avalon Restaurant **4**
B.J.'s Chicago Pizzeria **11**
Cheeseburger in Paradise **8**
David Paul's Lahaina Grill **7**
Gerard's **9**
Juicy's Healthy Food Deli **13**
Kimo's **5**

Kobe Japanese Steak House **10**
Lahaina Coolers Restaurant & Bar **12**
Longhi's **2**
Old Lahaina Cafe **13**
Pacific'O **13**
Scaroles Ristorante **3**
Scaroles Village Pizzeria **13**
Smokehouse BBQ **1**

true lover of food and cooking, Chef Gerard can almost always be found in the kitchen whipping up incredible dishes.

I would highly recommend a full three-course meal here. You might begin with shiitake and oyster mushrooms in puff pastry or ahi tartare with taro chips. Follow that with the rack of lamb with roasted garlic and potato and carrot purée or the roasted opakapaka with Hawaiian peppers. If you like venison, this is the place to try it—Chef Reversade prepares an excellent noisette of venison saddle served with a sauce Poivrade, poha berry compote, and sweet potato galette. A fresh island fish of the day is always on the menu, and desserts (many of which feature Hawaiian chocolate from the Big Island) are simply not to be believed. In addition to Gerard's ever-changing array of deserts, you can always find the crème brûlée or homemade sorbets on the menu.

MODERATE

Avalon Restaurant & Bar

844 Front St. ☎ **808/667-5559.** Reservations recommended. Main courses $10.95–$27.95. AE, MC, V. Daily 11:30am–10:30pm. HAWAII REGIONAL.

Located right in the center of Lahaina on Front Street, Avalon is one of the island's most popular eateries. A friend aptly describes the decor here as "tropical madness," and personally, I wouldn't expect anything but tropical madness from a self-taught chef/restaurateur who once owned a catering company called "Can't Rock and Roll, But Sure Can Cook." In both the indoor and outdoor dining areas, you'll find tables laid with tropical print cloths. Walls are hung with the works of local artists.

The menu is exotic, innovative, and healthful. To start, try Chef Mark Ellman's Avalon seared sashimi, fresh Hawaiian ahi (yellowfin tuna) that's quickly seared, sliced thin, and served with a shiitake mushroom and ginger sauce. Also excellent are the Avalon summer rolls with shrimp, avocado, rice noodles, and fresh herbs (including island-grown cilantro and fresh mint) wrapped in rice paper and served with Thai peanut sauce. Main courses run the gamut from barbecued lamb chops (marinated with palm sugar, coarse grain mustard, mint, and garlic, and served with mashed potatoes) to Chinese duck (sake-roasted duck served with plum sauce and Chinese steamed buns). My personal favorite is something that has been referred to by some as "the Jell-O mold of the nineties," the chile-seared salmon tiki-style. It's Avalon's signature dish—a layered salad of salmon, greens, mashed potatoes, eggplant, and mango and tomato salsa drizzled with a plum vinaigrette. A waiter will tell you how to mix the towering salad when it arrives at your table. Don't miss Avalon's inspired dessert: the Caramel Miranda. It's a scoop of macadamia nut ice cream surrounded by fresh fruit (raspberries, blueberries, strawberries, mangoes), accented with baby coconuts, all surrounded by a marvelous, light caramel sauce.

Avalon also has an award-winning wine list and a full bar.

Compadres Mexican Bar & Grill

1221 Honoapilani Hwy. (at Lahaina Cannery). ☎ **808/661-7189.** Reservations not necessary. Main courses $7.99–$12.99. AE, DC, MC, V. Daily 8am–10pm. MEXICAN.

When Compadres first opened in Honolulu in 1984, it was so well received and became so popular that owners Richard J. Bradley and Richard M. Enos decided to expand their business. Since then they have opened restaurants in the Napa Valley, Palo Alto, and Lahaina. Indoor and outdoor dining is available, and the furnishings are casual and comfortable. Rattan and weathered pine furniture, Mexican artifacts, a fountain, an aviary, and lots of greenery are charmingly accented by the wall paintings of Peggy Chun.

Lovers of authentic Mexican cuisine will find traditional favorites on the menu, as well as some variations. Carnitas—lean pork that is fried, slow-roasted, shredded, and served with soft flour tortillas and salsa Navarro—originated in Jalisco and are popular here. The nachos are good, as is the taco salad, which is served on refried beans in a flour tortilla boat. Several fresh fish entrées are always offered, and if you're watching your caloric intake, look for the Compadres 400 menu items—all of which have 400 calories or less. Sandwiches and burgers are also available. Breakfast features specialties such as huevos rancheros and a variety of omelets. The bar, which remains open until about 1am, offers a full selection of Mexican beers and the bartender mixes a fantastic margarita. The complete menu and appetizers are also available at the bar.

✪ David Paul's Lahaina Grill

127 Lahainaluna Rd. ☎ **808/667-5117.** Reservations recommended. Main courses $7.95–$24.95 at dinner; $5.95–$8.95 late-night bistro dinner. AE, MC, V. Daily dinner 6–10pm; late night bistro menu 10–11pm summer, 10pm–midnight winter (except Sun). NEW AMERICAN.

Chef/co-owner David Paul Johnson has a gold mine in this restaurant. Located just off Front Street next door to the Lahaina Inn, David Paul's is one of the island's most popular eateries. Casually elegant with black-and-white tiled floors, plain black chairs, green marble-topped tables, changing artwork, and a beautiful pressed-tin ceiling, David Paul's offers a constantly changing selection of innovative dishes, the likes of which you'd be hard-pressed to find anywhere else. An absolutely delectable appetizer that's almost always on the menu is the spicy crab cake (Dungeness crabmeat, chili peppers, and capellini pasta pan fried in corn oil and trimmed with sesame mustard sauce and local avocado relish). Another excellent starter would be the Yukon gold potato cakes with house smoked salmon. The buttery potato cakes, topped with a nicely seasoned crème fraîche, seem to melt in your mouth, while flakes of smoked salmon tease your palate with the flavor imparted during the macadamia smoke process used by the chef. Another incredible dish—an entrée—is the Kona coffee–roasted lamb (lamb chops marinated in Kona coffee and herbs, lightly roasted, and then grilled over kiawe wood); forget the mint sauce, this lamb is served with a unique, rich Kona-coffee sauce. Another excellent choice for seafood lovers is the Maui onion–crusted seared ahi served with vanilla bean rice, apple cider–soy vinaigrette, chive infused olive oil, and caramelized onions. The late-night bistro menu is similar to the regular menu. Desserts change daily, but two favorites are the triple berry pie and the chocolate macadamia nut brittle flan. Cheesecake lovers would probably like the black-and-white cheesecake if it's on the menu. Don't be afraid to try something new here; David Paul Johnson is truly an inspired chef, and I guarantee that you won't be disappointed.

Kobe Japanese Steak House

136 Dickenson St. ☎ **808/667-5555.** Reservations accepted. Full dinners $13.90–$25.90. AE, JCB, MC, V. Daily 5:30–10pm. JAPANESE.

You might be surprised to find an authentic Japanese steak house just off Front Street. The moment you enter Kobe you'll be carried right out of the hustle and bustle of Lahaina into a traditional Japanese country inn setting. Heavy wood tables are surrounded by beautiful Japanese wall hangings and other rare artifacts and antiques such as a 300-year-old kimono, porcelain hibachis, and emperor dolls. Begin your meal here with a warm sake. If you're in the mood for some sushi (Kobe boasts "Hawaii's most beautiful sushi bar"), the sashimi is excellent here. If you choose a teppanyaki dinner, you'll get teppan shrimp and shabu-shabu soup to start. The chef will prepare your choice of meat or fish with a variety of vegetables on the teppanyaki-hibachi grill right at your private table (or a communal one). Some of the choices might include teriyaki chicken, hibachi steak, sukiyaki steak, a lobster and steak combo, filet mignon, Kobe emperor steak, or chicken and shrimp. Rice and hot tea accompany your dinner. All the beef served here has been prepared and raised in traditional Japanese fashion (the cows are even massaged). Try the green tea ice cream for dessert. A children's menu is available.

Longhi's

888 Front St. ☎ **808/667-2288.** Reservations accepted, but not required. Main courses $7.50–$16 at lunch, $13–$26 at dinner. AE, DISC, MC, V. Daily 7:30–11:30am, 11:45am–4:45pm, and 5–10pm. ITALIAN.

Proprietor Bob Longhi has been in business here for more than 17 years, and his restaurant, Longhi's, is still going strong. People from all walks of life seem to enjoy the way the waitstaff recites the constantly changing menu from memory (be careful though—the bill might mount up without warning, since it's difficult to keep track of the prices as your waiter announces them). The open-air first floor dining room with tile floors and koa wood tables is a pleasant and welcoming spot for breakfast or lunch, and it's great for people-watching since there's a constant flow of tourists passing by. The slightly more elegant upstairs dining room is available for dinner. Breakfast choices include fresh-squeezed juice, an assortment of fresh fruit, various types of pastry, and more substantial items such as frittatas, quiches, eggs Benedict, pancakes, omelets, and bagels and lox. At lunch imported Italian cold cuts make great (huge) deli sandwiches, and fresh pasta or seafood are big sellers. The dinner menu, most of which has an Italian twist, offers a variety of meat and poultry, seafood, and of course, pasta. The fettuccini Lombardi and porcini is excellent, as is the shrimp Longhi. Desserts here are divine. Longhi's employs a full-time pastry chef to create everything from cakes and tortes to cold soufflés and eclairs. In fact, over the years, more than 1,000 different desserts have been served (and enjoyed) at Longhi's. Live entertainment is offered every Friday and Saturday evening, and complimentary valet parking is available every night.

✪ Pacific'O

505 Front St. ☎ **808/667-4341.** Reservations recommended. Main courses $15–$22. MC, V. Sun–Wed 11am–10pm, Thurs–Sat 11am–midnight. CONTEMPORARY PACIFIC.

Located right on the beach, this restaurant is a relatively new addition to the Lahaina scene. Those who dine here enjoy their meals at floral-clothed tables in the shade of white canvas umbrellas against a backdrop of sea and sand. I would call the cuisine here "Hawaiian regional," but the chef prefers "contemporary Pacific." What it's called matters less than how it tastes, and so far, Pacific'O seems to be faring rather well. The shrimp pot-stickers with fresh coriander Tobiko sauce are a tasty way to start your meal, and so is the lobster and papaya salad. One of my favorite appetizers is the pizza pupu with a smoked shrimp, goat cheese, and eggplant caviar topping. Pacific'O offers some delicious entrées as well. Try the fish grilled in a banana leaf and smothered with a lemongrass pesto and vanilla-bean sauce. The sesame-crust lamb is also an excellent choice. It's covered with a blackened sesame crust, drizzled with a roasted macadamia-nut sauce, and complemented by a mango/pineapple chutney. Furthermore, Pacific'O recently won second place at the Seafood Festival on Oahu with their coconut-and-macadamia-nut-crusted fish with a sweet-and-sour glaze and Thai peanut sauce; they took first place in the seafood category in 1995 at the Taste of Lahaina. Sunsets here are spectacular, and there's live jazz on the beach every Thursday, Friday, and Saturday evening from 9pm to midnight.

Scaroles Ristorante

930 Wainee St. ☎ **808/661-4466**. Reservations recommended. Main courses $14.95–$24. AE, MC, V. Mon–Fri 11:30am–2pm; daily 5:30–9:30pm. ITALIAN.

Billing itself as "the New York side of Lahaina," Scaroles Ristorante is tucked away in an inconspicuous corner on the mauka side of Wainee Street. You'll recognize it by the awnings and black trellis fence with white trim outside. There are also some outdoor tables with black-and-white-checked cloths and fresh flowers in black bud vases. The interior decor mirrors the exterior but with an abundance of hanging plants and a number of prints hanging on the walls. The large windows at the front and side of the restaurant can be opened, providing diners with the open-air feeling that is typical of the beachside restaurants.

Begin your meal with Scaroles's cold antipasto or Mozzarella marinara. The baked, stuffed clams are excellent, as is the homemade pizza bread. If you love pasta, give the pasta Scarole a try; it's served in a cream and Gorgonzola sauce with sun-dried tomatoes, pine nuts, and mushrooms. The chicken saltimbocca, with prosciutto and Fontina cheese, is one of several chicken dishes on the menu. Of course, there's veal parmigiana, but my recommendation for veal would be the veal calvados, which is sautéed in apple brandy with cream, shallots, and apples. There are several traditional seafood offerings as well. For dessert try the tiramisù, cannoli or ricotta cheesecake, and a nice dark cup of espresso.

INEXPENSIVE

✪ Aloha Cantina

839 Front St. ☎**808/661-8788**. No reservations. Main courses $5.95–$15.95. AE, MC, V. Daily 8am–11pm. MEXICAN/SOUTHERN CALIFORNIAN.

How does dining on great-tasting, well-priced, Mexican food in an indoor "tropical oasis" sound to you? What if I told you that there would be a simulated hurricane blowing through every hour or so? If that isn't enough to entice you, the food should be. Maui fish tacos (fresh fish grilled with spices and served in a flour tortilla with cabbage, special sauce, and fresh fruit on the side) are quite good, as are the flautas (flour tortilla filled with chicken, fried until crispy, and served with homemade pineapple dipping sauce). Other menu offerings include tortilla soup, lobster tacos, Lahaina fajitas, taquitos, and breakfast dishes (for example, huevos rancheros and breakfast burritos). Naturally, frosty tropical drinks flow freely, and every day from 4:30 to 6:30pm there's a complimentary Nacho Bar in Hurricane McShane's Coconut Bar. Outdoor dining is available.

B.J.'s Chicago Pizzeria

730 Front St. ☎ **808/661-0700**. Reservations only for parties of 10 or more. Pizzas $5–$22. AE, MC, V. Mon–Thurs 11am–11pm; Fri–Sat 11am–midnight. ITALIAN.

Deep-dish Chicago-style pizza is the draw at B.J.'s (the open-air dining room and ocean views haven't hurt business either). Bring your appetite (and a few extra people); the pizzas are big here, but if you arrive between 11am and 4pm you'll be able to get the 6-inch individual lunchtime version of your favorite pie. Besides pizzas, B.J.'s offers salads, pasta, and sandwiches.

☉ Cheeseburger in Paradise

811 Front St. ☎ **808/661-4855**. No reservations. Main courses $5.95–$9.95. Daily 11am–11pm. AE, MC, V. AMERICAN.

If you've been on Maui for a while and suddenly discover that you're tired of eating fish and would like a big, fat, juicy hamburger—that sounds familiar to the owners of Cheeseburger in Paradise, Laren Gartner and Edna Bayliff. They first visited Maui on vacation and had exactly that experience. At that time, however, there was no place to get that burger. They decided to come back to Lahaina and open—with absolutely no restaurant experience at all—Cheeseburger in Paradise. Of course, everyone thought they were crazy to try to open a restaurant with no prior experience, but the critics quit laughing pretty quickly when they discovered that Edna and Laren were bringing in millions of hamburger dollars after only a year in business. In fact, in 1993, Cheeseburger in Paradise served an average of 165 pounds of beef a day (that's close to 500 burgers a day). Everybody who dines at this waterfront burger joint has a great view, but what keeps packing them in is the incredible "three-napkin" burgers and cheeseburgers. For those who don't eat meat there are vegetarian selections, as well as a variety of salads. You can also get all sorts of tropical drinks. This is a great place.

Juicy's Healthy Food Deli

505 Front St., #142. ☎ **808/667-5727.** No reservations. Menu items $1–$6.25. MC, V. Mon–Fri 9am–7pm, Sat–Sun 10am–6pm. VEGETARIAN.

One of many establishments located at 505 Front Street, Juicy's Healthy Food Deli is a great spot for breakfast, lunch, or an early light dinner. Not much more than a hole in the wall, the restaurant is jam-packed with goodies, a deli counter, and a few tables (more tables with umbrellas are outside). For breakfast try the low-fat baked goods or the fruit with low-fat granola, cinnamon, yogurt, and raisins. A good "healthy" lunch or dinner dish here is the vegetarian chili made with fresh vegetables, tomatoes, beans, tofu, and some serious spices served over brown rice and topped with melted cheese. Other choices might include the hummus platter or the ultimate Bogie Burrito (an enormous flour tortilla stuffed with beans, melted cheese, avocado, tomato, lettuce, salsa, and sour cream). Try the garden burger—a vegetarian cheese patty served warm with tomato, onions, lettuce, sprouts, and mayonnaise. There are also salads and "wicked sandwitches," as well as daily entrées (made without meat or meat products). The fresh-squeezed juices and fruit smoothies are excellent.

Kimo's

845 Front St. ☎ **808/661-4811.** Reservations recommended. Main courses $7.95–$19.95. AE, MC, V. Downstairs, daily 11am–2pm; upstairs, daily 5–10:30pm. Bar daily 11–midnight. SEAFOOD/STEAKS.

Located on Front Street right on the waterfront, Kimo's is something of a Lahaina landmark. Tired of exotic foods? Kimo's offers a simple surf-and-turf menu in a congenial atmosphere. The oceanfront view is the biggest draw, however. As with many other restaurants on Maui, Kimo's offers a variety of fresh fish prepared in several ways. Fish options for the day might include ono, ahi, onaga, a'u (broadbill swordfish), mahimahi, opakapaka, ulua (pompano), or lehi, depending on what the day's catch brings in. Once you decide on the fish, you can choose the preparation. Fish baked in the restaurant's orange-ginger sauce (fresh ginger, orange zest, and macadamia nuts) is tasty, or you can simply have it sautéed in seasoned bread crumbs and Parmesan cheese and topped with lemon butter. If you want to avoid additional fat, you can have it broiled without oil or butter and served with tropical salsa. If shellfish is your favorite, try spiny lobster served with drawn butter or shrimp Tahitian (sautéed in butter and wine with garlic and cheese). Steak and prime rib are other popular dishes, and the menu also offers some island favorites, such as kalua pork ribs and Polynesian chicken. Dessert options are limited; however, Kimo's original hula pie is delicious. There is a children's menu.

Lahaina Coolers Restaurant & Bar

180 Dickenson St. ☎ **808/661-7082.** Reservations not necessary. Main courses $5.50–$10.50 at lunch, $7.25–$14.50 at dinner. AE, DC, MC, V. Mon–Sat 7–11:15am, Sun 7am–noon; daily 11:30am–midnight. INTERNATIONAL.

With the following motto, ". . . because life is too short to eat boring food," how could anyone pass up Lahaina Coolers? The atmosphere is casual and inviting. Small Formica-topped tables are surrounded by white plastic chairs, and surfboards hang from the ceiling. The largest marlin ever caught in Hawaii by a woman hangs (stuffed, of course) inside the restaurant as well. The breakfast menu includes eggs Benedict, bagels and lox, various kinds of omelets, and pancakes. The varied lunch and dinner menu is offered all day. On the pupu list, the fresh fish tacos are excellent. A familiar dish with a twist is the mini crab cakes with pineapple-cilantro aioli. Favorites on the menu include the Evil Jungle Pasta and the Evil Jungle Pizza. Both are topped with grilled chicken and a spicy Thai peanut sauce. There's also a locally inspired pizza topped with Portuguese sausage, pineapple, tomato, and onion. Among the salads, an excellent choice would be the papaya chicken salad with papaya seed dressing. The menu category "More Stuff" includes a bistro burger with bacon, mushrooms, and Gorgonzola cheese and the standard cheeseburger and french fries. For dessert, give the tropical taco filled with tropical fruit and berry "salsa" or the Mousse that Roared (the flavor changes daily) a whirl.

Old Lahaina Cafe

505 Front St. ☎ **808/661-3303.** No reservations. Main courses $5.95–$21.95. AE, MC, V. Mon–Sat 7:30am–3:30pm, Sun 8am–3:30pm; daily 5:30–10pm. HAWAIIAN/ AMERICAN.

This restaurant, located on the beach side of the 505 Front Street complex, is a delightful spot for a low-key breakfast, lunch, or sunset dinner. The spacious dining room, with its blue-and-white-clothed tables, overlooks the beach and the grounds of the Old Lahaina Luau (see Chapter 8, "What to See & Do on Maui," for details). Breakfasts are substantial but inexpensive. My favorites include the Molokai French toast (Molokai sweetbread grilled in an egg batter and drizzled with maple syrup) and the macadamia nut pancakes. The paniolo breakfast includes two eggs; a choice of sausage, bacon, or papaya wedge; Molokai sweetbread toast; and rice or home fries. Lunch offerings include standard sandwiches and burgers as well as more interesting alternatives (for example, kalua pig sandwich or kiawe-broiled mahimahi). Dinner is heavy on seafood with some beef, chicken, and vegetarian selections as well. You might also enjoy the Old Lahaina Luau dinner: kalua pork (baked in the beachside imu), kalbi ribs, chicken long rice, lomi lomi salmon, sweet potato, rice, and poi. Dive into a Chocolate Suicide for dessert.

Scaroles Village Pizzeria

505 Front St. ☎ **808/661-8112.** Reservations not necessary. Main courses $5.95–$11.95; pizzas $11.50–$24. AE, MC, V. Sun–Thurs 11am–10:30pm; Fri–Sat 11am–midnight. ITALIAN.

The owners of Scaroles Ristorante opened a New York–style pizzeria serving thin- or thick-crust pizzas, sandwiches, appetizers, calzones, and pastas. It's a more casual version of the restaurant on Wainee Street, but the food is equally delicious. Pizza toppings run the gamut from homemade sausage to pineapple and pesto. The house special is the clam and garlic pizza, which is, without a doubt, some of the best pizza you'll ever have. You can order a whole pizza (14 or 16 inches) or just a slice or two. If you're not in the mood for pizza, there's a full selection of appetizers, including baked stuffed mushrooms and Mozzarella marinara. The sandwich menu includes a sausage and pepper sandwich and a meatball hero, both of which I can recommend highly. Calzones of every variety are offered—just choose two of your favorite pizza toppings and the chef will make you a "pizza sandwich" to order. There are also baked ziti, spaghetti, lasagne, and ravioli.

Not to be forgotton, of course, are the desserts, coffees, beer, wine, and cocktails.

Smokehouse BBQ

1307 Front St. ☎ **808/667-7005.** No reservations. Main courses $4.95–$17.95. MC, V. Daily 11am–9pm. BARBECUE.

Located just across the street from the backside of the Lahaina Cannery Shopping Center, Smokehouse BBQ is considered by many to be the best barbecue on Maui. After more than 10 years in the business, the cooks here have developed a technique for smoking meat and then broiling it over kiawe wood (a relative of mesquite). The result is a taste treat of naturally sweet, supremely tender meat coated in Smokehouse BBQ's own sauce. Those who like it hot can ask for the Dragon BBQ Sauce. Kiawe-smoked beef ribs are available as an appetizer, à la carte, or as a complete dinner with french fries, coleslaw, and baked beans. Pork ribs are also a specialty of the house. Other choices here include hamburgers, fish sandwiches, and several rib and chicken or Louisiana hot-link combinations. Vegetarian offerings include the California-style avocado burger and the charbroiled veggie burger. There is a short children's menu.

BETWEEN KAANAPALI & KAPALUA
EXPENSIVE

Erik's Seafood Grotto

4242 L. Honoapilani Hwy. ☎ **808/669-4806.** Reservations accepted. Main courses $13.95–$20.95. AE, MC, V. Daily lunch 11:30am–2pm, dinner 5–10pm. SEAFOOD/CONTINENTAL.

Located at the Kahana Villas, this restaurant might be a little out of the way for some, but if you love seafood you might want to make the trip because Erik's offers one of the largest selections of fresh seafood on the island. Before you get started on the menu, enjoy one of Erik's cocktails, such as the Lava Flow (made with fresh bananas, pineapple juice, coconut syrup, cream, and rum topped with grenadine) or Leslie's Libation (a blend of blackberry brandy and fruit juices). (Happy hour is from 11:30am to 4:30pm daily.) If you can still walk after one of these, check out the menu. Appetizers include clams casino, escargots bourguignon, sashimi, and smoked salmon. There are up to nine different fish offered daily (and they're all displayed nightly), including a'u (broadbill swordfish), mahimahi, ono (a delicious game fish), ahi (yellowfin tuna), ulua (Hawaii's pompano), uku (Hawaii's gray snapper), hapupu'u (Hawaiian sea bass), and onaga (red snapper). Each will be prepared as listed on the menu, but all can be cooked with Cajun spices. House specialties include a tasty bouillabaisse, scampi Olowalu (shrimp sautéed in garlic butter and drizzled with a creamy caper sauce), and Hawaiian saltwater prawns (sautéed with fresh basil, thyme, and anisette and served on a bed of fettuccine). Shellfish choices include barbecued shrimp, coquilles Ste-Jacques, and king crab. Rack of lamb, filet mignon, and New York steak are also offered. There are several desserts and a limited children's menu.

✪ Roy's Kahana Bar & Grill

4405 Honoapilani Hwy. (at Kahana Gateway Shopping Center). ☎ **808/669-5000.** Reservations recommended. Main courses $6.50–$26.95. AE, DC, JCB, MC, V. Daily from 5:30pm. (usually closes around 10pm). EURO-ASIAN.

The original Roy's Kahana Bar & Grill opened in Honolulu in 1988 and proved to be such a success that chef/owner Roy Yamaguchi decided to open a second restaurant on Maui (a third opened in Tokyo in 1992). Today it's one of the island's hottest upscale eateries. The atmosphere in the large dining room is upbeat, vibrant, and convivial. In fact, it can be rather noisy at times, but that's all part of the fun. In the center of it all is an open kitchen that rises to the ceiling in a brilliant flash of copper. Local art decorates the walls, picture windows treat diners to lovely views, and elegant floral arrangements dot the room. And the food? Well, simply put, it's amazing. Part of the menu is fixed, while the rest changes according to the whims and creative inspiration of the chef. Some appetizers that might tempt your tastebuds are the island-style pot-stickers with a spicy miso sauce, the roasted garlic escargots with carmelized onions, polenta croutons and citrus butter, and Roy's grilled Szechuan-style baby back pork ribs. Individual imu pizzas are an excellent choice if you're not too hungry—especially the Chinese pork sausage pizza with ginger hoisin sauce and wild mushrooms. Other excellent main-course dishes include the spicy rimfire shrimp and Asian vegetables (served with a wonderful spicy sweet chili sauce); smoked and peppered duck accompanied by gingered sweet potatoes and a Mandarin orange sauce; and roasted banana pork loin served island-style with a Chinese black bean hoisin sauce. The desserts, which change frequently, are all good; however, if the dark chocolate soufflé (which has a liquid chocolate center) is on the menu, I would recommend it.

Next door to Roy's Kahana Bar & Grill is Roy's Nicolina (☎ 808/669-5000); it offers the same basic menu with additional unique specialties by the chef. Both restaurants are worth a visit.

INEXPENSIVE

Dollie's Pub & Cafe

4310 L. Honoapilani Hwy. (in Kahana Manor). ☎ **808/669-0266.** Reservations not necessary. Main courses $3.95–$19. MC, V. Mon–Sat 10am–midnight, Sun 8am–midnight; brunch Sun 8am–1pm. SANDWICHES/PIZZA.

A sign outside Dollie's Pub & Cafe announces "Dollie's, home of the $1 draft." Perhaps best known for its selection of beer and wine, Dollie's Pub & Cafe is a festive spot for a quick bite at lunch. There are 20 varieties of sandwiches, including pastrami and provolone, tuna salad on pita bread, teriyaki beef, and meatball and Mozzarella in a marinara sauce. On the pupu menu there are potato skins, chili and rice, hot chicken wings, nachos, and garlic bread. The main dishes are more substantial. The vegetarian lasagne with three cheeses, carrots, and spinach is good, as is the fettuccine Alfredo. Dollie's will also make small, medium, and large pizzas to order, and from 10am to 4pm you can order individual 5-inch pizzas. Thirty-six different beers are available, including Red Stripe (Jamaica), Steinlager (New Zealand), Bass Ale (England), and Guinness Stout (Ireland). Every day there is a focus on one special drink, for example, Tequila Tuesday and Long Island Iced Tea Day.

Maui Tacos

Napili Plaza. ☎ **808/665-0222.** No reservations. All menu items under $7. No credit cards. Mon–Sat 10am–9pm, Sun 11am–7pm. MEXICAN.

Another one of Mark Ellman's (of Avalon fame) creations, Maui Tacos promises the island's freshest Mexican food. Ellman wanted to establish a restaurant with authentic yet healthy Mexican fast food, and he seems to have achieved it. You can order everything from chili relleños to tacos, nachos, and burritos. Try a bean or potato tostada or a fresh fish soft taco. Burritos come stuffed with the following: beans, beans and rice, potatoes and beans, and chili verde. There are two kinds of breakfast burritos: one with salsa, potatoes, rice, beans, and scrambled eggs; the second one has all of the above plus chorizo (Mexican sausage).

All dishes are prepared with 100% vegetable oil. You can either eat on the premises (there are about a dozen seats), or buy food to go. Two additional Maui Tacos are located in Lahaina Square (☎ 808/661-8883) and Kamaole Beach Center (☎ 808/ 879-5005).

KAPALUA
EXPENSIVE

✪ The Anuenue Room
One Ritz-Carlton Dr. (in the Ritz-Carlton Hotel). ☎ **808/669-6200.** Reservations recommended. Main courses $16.50–$40. AE, DC, MC, V. Tues–Sat 6–9:30pm. HAWAIIAN PROVENÇAL.

In keeping with traditional Ritz-Carlton standards, the Anuenue Room offers fine dining in a classically elegant setting. One needn't worry too much about a dress code here—after all, it is Hawaii—but shorts, T-shirts, and jeans are definitely out of the question. Comfort reigns supreme here, and the beautiful view of the Pacific Ocean and the island of Molokai coupled with the light of a flickering candle will guarantee you a relaxing and romantic dining experience. If you like sashimi, start with the assortment of island sashimi, a plate of ahi, onaga, and blue marlin served with zested orange and miso vinaigrette. Another superb appetizer is the seared goose foie gras with Kona lobster and Chinese cabbage in a five-spice lobster broth. If you'd rather start with a soup, I strongly recommend the lobster ginger consommé if it's on the menu. During my last visit to the Anuenue Room, I ordered the grilled rare ahi with crispy potato layers, papaya prawn compote, and a fresh chili-tomato butter sauce— I couldn't have been happier. I also tasted the herbed veal loin with a lavender salsify confit. It was served with braised white beans and a tomato essence. The flavors in this dish were multilayered and complemented one another. There is a separate vegetarian menu. For dessert, I would recommend a special soufflé or the chocolate macadamia nut toffee torte. (The torte is served with a cinnamon sauce which gives the sweetness of the chocolate and toffee a little kick.)

✪ The Bay Club
One Bay Dr. (in the Kapalua Bay Hotel & Villas). ☎ **808/669-5656** or 808/669-8008 (after 5pm). Reservations required at dinner, recommended at lunch. Main courses $7.75–$12.95 at lunch, $7.75–$29 at dinner. AE, DC, MC, V. Daily 11:30am–2pm and 6–9:30pm. SEAFOOD/ CONTINENTAL.

If you choose to dine at the Bay Club, you'll be treated to one of the most spectacular dining views on the island. At lunch the atmosphere is nautical, but at dinner the restaurant is full of romance as the lights are dimmed and the sun falls below the horizon. This is a perfect place for a quiet dinner for two on any night of your Maui vacation.

I began my meal here with the sashimi. It comes with wasabi and pickled ginger and is superb. Other appetizers include the smoked salmon with herb cream cheese and escargots sautéed with garlic and wild mushrooms. For entrées there are meats and poultry, including a filet mignon in a Madeira and black truffle sauce and an herb-crusted rack of lamb with rosemary jus. The shellfish is also excellent— choices include sautéed prawns and sea scallops served over angel hair pasta and topped with a creamy basil sauce and the South Pacific bouillabaisse. My favorite dishes, however, are the fresh island fish, which can be prepared in several ways. It can be sautéed, broiled, poached, or blackened, and there are a variety of sauces as well. Try the artichoke and shiitake mushroom sauce or the tropical salsa. If you'd rather have a more Asian touch, request the ginger, cilantro, shiitake mushroom, and sesame sauce or the ginger and leek sauce. Whatever you choose, it will be a taste sensation.

At lunch the menu choices are less exotic but equally delicious. For starters there's baked onion soup or (if you need a little cooling off) the chilled cucumber soup. The Cobb salads (both seafood and traditional) are very good. There are fish and pasta-of-the-day specials, as well as a nice variety of sandwiches.

The Garden Restaurant

One Bay Dr. (in the Kapalua Bay Hotel). ☎ **808/669-5656.** Reservations accepted. Main courses $19–$29. Fixed-price dinner $37 without wine, $49–$51 with wine. AE, DC, MC, V. Mon–Thurs 6–10pm; Fri–Sat buffet 5:30–9:30pm, Sun brunch 9:30am–1:30pm. Follow Honoapilani Hwy. past Lahaina town, the Kaanapali Beach resort, Kahana, and Napili. On your left you'll see the sign for the Kapalua resort. Go left and follow the signs to the Kapalua Bay Hotel. The restaurant is located within. MEDITERRANEAN/PACIFIC RIM.

If you've already visited the Bay Club (see listing above), you know that the Kapalua Bay Hotel (and its restaurants) are known for their sweeping ocean views. The Garden Restaurant is a lovely spot for dinner (and somewhat less formal than the Bay Club). While dining you'll be surrounded by tropical foliage and lulled by the sound of a gentle waterfall. At dinner you might choose one of the fixed-price menus, which includes an appetizer, salad, entrée, and dessert, plus the sommelier's selection of wines. Of course, there's the à la carte menu as well. Start with a seasonal salad of mixed Kula greens and Belgian endive or a salad of fresh Mozzarella, sun-ripened tomatoes, and marinated eggplant with a garlic basil vinaigrette. Main courses include steamed ono Oriental-style with shiitake mushrooms, cilantro, and ginger; or the delectable sautéed mahimahi served with fresh tomatoes and a shallot-herb sauce. Other choices might include a tenderloin of beef with garlic potatoes, confit of onion, and horseradish mustard sauce; or osso bucco Milanese-style with white beans, tomato, and garlic. For dessert don't miss the Manjari chocolate cake with a vanilla sauce or the strawberries with almond cream and mint. On Friday night there's a seafood buffet, Saturday night features an Oriental buffet, and Sunday brings an elaborate brunch.

Pineapple Hill Restaurant

1000 Kapalua Dr. ☎ **808/669-6129.** Reservations recommended. Full meal $12–$30 per person. AE, DC, MC, V. Daily 5–8pm (last seating is at 8pm). AMERICAN/POLYNESIAN.

At the end of a mile-long row of exquisite pines, you'll find Pineapple Hill Restaurant, once the home of the late David Thomas Fleming, one of the first to introduce pineapples, mangoes, lichee nuts, and a variety of other plants and trees to the Maui landscape. He called his home Maka'oi'oi, or "sharp eyes," probably because of its beautiful views of the Pacific and the rolling landscape that is now home to the Kapalua Golf Courses and the Ritz-Carlton Hotel. Today you can dine on fine seafood and choice-cut meats in this historic building. To begin, treat yourself to a bucket of fresh steamer clams or mushrooms stuffed with shrimp and crab. The house specialty on the list of appetizers is Nehms, an "Oriental delight." Continue with filet mignon and lobster or shrimp. There's also a Hawaiian teriyaki steak. If you prefer seafood, shrimp Tahitian (large prawns seasoned and baked in the shell with wine and cheese) is the house specialty, and the king scallops Provençale is delicious. Of course, several kinds of fresh fish are available to be poached, sautéed, or broiled to your liking. The menu also offers several poultry and pasta dishes, as well as a veggie plate for those who prefer a light meal. All dinners are served with the house soup or garden salad, fresh vegetables, and bread. Pineapple Hill's baked papaya Tahitian (with

Tahitian vanilla beans and coconut milk) is the best way to end a meal here—in fact, it won first prize in the dessert category at Taste of Lahaina in 1994.

MODERATE

The Grill & Bar

200 Kapalua Dr. (between the Tennis Garden and the Golf Club). ☎ **808/669-5653.** Reservations recommended at dinner. Main courses $4.25–$9.95 at lunch, $7.50–$23.95 at dinner. AE, MC, V. Daily 11am–3pm and 5–10pm; bar open until midnight or 1am. AMERICAN/INTERNATIONAL.

Part of the Kapalua resort, the Grill & Bar offers full lunch and dinner menus, as well as cocktails, in an open-air, country-club setting. Small birds fly in and peck around by diners' feet hoping to pick up a crumb or two, but most people don't even notice because they're too busy taking in the beautiful views of the Kapalua Golf Course, Kapalua Bay, or the West Maui Mountains. I prefer the tables that look out over the ocean. Many people stop here after their morning tennis matches or a round of golf for a light luncheon. The Thai chicken salad with strips of chicken served on Kula greens with a variety of vegetables and drizzled with peanut dressing is a regular favorite. The veggie pizza (on the café menu) with sliced eggplant, sun-dried tomatoes, roasted peppers, and Puna goat cheese is excellent also. If you're in the mood for something more substantial, there are burgers, deli sandwiches, and fish sandwiches. Dinner appetizers might include sashimi; J.J.'s baked artichoke; or Thai shrimp summer rolls in rice paper with mint and a spicy dipping sauce. My personal favorite is the Portuguese bean soup. Entrées include a choice of fresh fish prepared in one of the following ways: grilled with lemon butter sauce; sesame-crusted and baked with spicy lilikoi sauce; or coriander-dusted and dry sautéed with fresh basil and Romano cheese. The naturally raised Waianae chicken (herb-roasted with a shiitake-Chardonnay sauce) is among the poultry selections. If you like lamb, try the Australian rack of lamb marinated in garlic, Dijon mustard, and herbs and served with a Madeira and mint sauce. The grilled tournedos served in a béarnaise or mint béarnaise sauce is also a good choice. A few vegetarian selections are always on the menu, and a children's menu is available on request. For dessert try the Kimo's Hula Pie or the passion fruit sorbet.

✪ The Plantation House Restaurant

2000 Plantation Club Dr. ☎ **808/669-6299.** Reservations recommended. Main courses $5.95–$9.95 at lunch, $14.95–$23.95 at dinner. AE, DC, MC, V. Daily 8am–3pm and 6–10pm; last dinner reservation 9pm. HAWAII-MEDITERRANEAN.

The moment you enter the Plantation House Restaurant, you'll fall in love with its casual Old World elegance, and you'll be drawn in by the walls of windows that provide—according to islanders—the "best and most spectacular dining views." Unfortunately, many restaurants that offer an intimate dining experience also force you to be intimate with those sitting next to you and behind you; they also seem to confuse intimacy with sitting virtually on top of your dining partner. Not so at the Plantation House. The dining room here is light and spacious, the heavy wood tables are large, and the dining chairs are roomy and comfortably upholstered. You may dine near the central, double-sided fireplace; down a couple of steps and closer to the windows; or out on the lanai. Owners Michael Hooks and Roy Dunn, with a great deal of experience in the restaurant business, have perfectly blended that experience and their innate talents with the expertise and creativity of Chef/co-owner Alex Stanislaw, whose cuisine is known island-wide. Stanislaw has successfully blended the flavors of Mediterranean cuisine with those of the Asia-Pacific islands (using island-grown produce) to create his own personal variety of Hawaiian regional cuisine.

My favorite dinner appetizer is the crab cakes, served with a red pepper pesto and a Pacific Island herb mayonnaise. The honey guava-scallops (Atlantic sea scallops wrapped in guava-smoked bacon and broiled in a lehua honey-guava glaze) and the Hawaiian-style sashimi (sliced ahi on a bed of shredded cabbage, pickled ginger rose, daikon, and hot wasabi) are also delicious. House specialties include the incredible sesame-shichimi–crusted opakapaka (crusted in black sesame seeds, seared, and sake-glazed) served on a somen kaiware sprout salad in black bean sauce—you won't soon forget the taste. Other fish can be prepared in a variety of styles. One of my favorites is blackened on baby Kula greens with a warm Kona crab vinaigrette. It's light but packed with flavor. Other great main courses include double-cut lamb chops broiled and served with a wild rosemary-shallot bordelaise, and "Duck under the influence." If you've still got room for dessert, try the Da Kine Brownie.

In addition to dinner, the Plantation House serves an excellent breakfast of fresh fruit, omelets, and French toast. Lunch consists of salads and sandwiches. Both lunch and dinner are reasonably priced.

3 Central & South Maui

It's most likely that you'll be in Central Maui in the morning or afternoon, and all of the restaurants I've listed for Kahului and Wailuku are good choices for lunch. Some are also nice spots for dinner, but if you don't happen to be in the area at dinner time, there's no reason to make a special trip.

South Maui is another story, however. While Kihei is known for its fast-food establishments, there are also quite a few excellent places for dinner, including Carelli's on the Beach and the Greek Bistro. The Wailea resort area is positively loaded with superb dining establishments.

KAHULUI
INEXPENSIVE

☺ The Class Act
Maui Community College, 310 Kaahumanu Ave. ☎ **808/242-1210** (Reservations are taken Wed and Fri between 8:30 and 10:30am). Reservations strongly recommended (accepted up to 2 weeks in advance). Full 4-course lunch $10. No credit cards. Lunch only Wed and Fri 11am–1:30pm. Closed mid-May to mid-Sept. INTERNATIONAL.

If you want a different type of dining experience while getting a four-course gourmet meal for $10, make a lunch reservation at the Class Act, Maui Community College's student-operated restaurant. Here you'll have a glimpse into the world of culinary training, and you can help these up-and-coming chefs by filling out a "report card" at the end of your meal. Students are responsible for both cooking and table service. Each week brings a taste of a different country or region. Students of the Class Act put together Italian, Japanese, French, Mexican, Chinese, Austrian, Thai, and regional American four-course menus. Diners have a choice of two entrées (often one of the choices, designated "Heart Healthy," is low in sodium and cholesterol). Everyone who dines here enjoys the experience (if you're looking for ambience, this isn't the place). It's a local favorite.

Maui Coffee Roasters
444 Hana Hwy. ☎ **808/877-2877.** No reservations. Bakery items $1.20–$2.40; other menu items 48¢–$7.95. MC, V. Mon–Fri 7am–6pm, Sat 8am–5pm, Sun 9am–3pm. CAFE/BAKERY/DELI.

If you happen to be passing through Kahului at breakfast or lunchtime and you don't feel like stopping at one of the many fast-food places, Maui Coffee Roasters offers a nice alternative. Inside there are several round, café-style, handpainted tables for two. Overhead hangs a large, inflatable Godzillalike creature who has apparently swept Barbie off her feet. Superman, also suspended in midair, is in hot pursuit. Bright posters and various other artwork adorn the walls, and tall directors' chairs line the front of the coffee bar. Aside from coffee by the pound, there are teas, coffee-making paraphernalia, coffee mugs, T-shirts, and greeting cards for sale. Breakfast items include the veggie egg bagel (eggs, tomatoes, cream cheese, sprouts, and on-ions on a choice of bagel) and the turkey egg bagel (same as the veggie egg bagel, with the addition of turkey). At lunch there is a variety of sandwiches, such as the basmoto sandwich (basil, Mozzarella, and tomato drizzled with a balsamic vinaigrette, served on French bread). The Ultimate Veggie burger is the most popular lunch item. The Nicky salad is composed of brown and wild rice, melted Cheddar cheese, lettuce, tomatoes, cucumbers, and a balsamic vinaigrette served with French bread. There is always a daily soup and several daily specials. There are about 30 different coffees and teas on the menu.

☺ Ming Yuen

162 Alamaha St. ☎ **808/871-7787.** Reservations recommended. Main courses $3.50–$37; lunch buffet $8.50 per person. DISC, MC, V. Mon–Sat 11:30am–5pm; lunch buffet Mon–Fri 11am–1:30pm; dinner daily 5–8:30pm. CANTONESE/SZECHUAN.

I am extremely picky when it comes to Chinese food, but I must admit that Ming Yuen is an excellent choice—some even think it's the best Chinese restaurant on the island. The spacious interior is decorated in a traditional red-and-black scheme, and the atmosphere is relaxed and comfortable. From the moment you enter, the well-trained staff is attentive and congenial, and all dishes are artfully presented. Appetizers of note include the Crispy Gau Gee and the hot-and-sour soup. As in most Chinese restaurants, there are a variety of listings under the categories of duck, chicken, pork, beef, and seafood. Notable are the chicken with sugar snaps, crispy roast chicken, mu shi pork, Mongolian and Hunan beef, and the chile shrimp. Grandma's tofu is a spicy, Szechuan-style vegetarian dish (there are about 17 other vegetarian offerings on the menu). Try the Mandarin mousse for dessert.

WAILUKU
INEXPENSIVE

☺ A Saigon Cafe

1792 Main St. ☎ **808/243-9560.** Reservations recommended at dinner. Main courses $6.50–$16.95. DISC, MC, V. Daily 10am–9pm. VIETNAMESE.

I must acknowledge that I wasn't expecting much the first time I ate here. The de-cor is plain—tables fill the center of the dining room, while booths line the walls—but the restaurant is comfortable and clean. When you see how many people pack into this place on a daily basis (mostly local customers), you begin to realize that owner Jennifer Nguyen has got something up her sleeve. Simply put, the food here is wonderful. The menu is extensive, and you'll probably be as overwhelmed as I was, so I'll give you a few suggestions to get you started. The fresh summer rolls (goi cuon) are light and flavorful. Filled with shrimp, seasoned pork, fresh mint, bean sprouts, lettuce, and rice noodles, they are served with a peanut sauce. Don't be put off by the fresh mint—the dish would be lost without it. I also enjoyed the shrimp pops (ground, marinated shrimp served steamed and grilled on a sugarcane stick—accompanied by noodles, lettuce, mint leaves, and peanut or sweet-and-sour garlic sauce), which are a bit like the shrimp toast you find in some Chinese restaurants, only better. As an entrée I would recommend the Rice in a Clay Pot (sliced chicken breast with shrimp, shiitake mushrooms, baby corn, peas, carrots, and onions sautéed in a blend of spices and poured over jasmine rice and simmered in a hot clay pot) or the Vietnamese "burritos." The tofu dishes here are fantastic. There are so many dishes on the menu here, it's impossible to list very many. Be adventurous and sample a variety of dishes. This is a great place for lunch or dinner.

Cafe Kup à Kuppa

79 Church St. ☎ **808/244-0500.** Reservations accepted for parties of 7 or more. All items under $6. No credit cards. Mon–Fri 7am–3pm. INTERNATIONAL CAFÉ.

Cafe Kup à Kuppa is a popular espresso bar that serves both breakfast and lunch; the atmosphere is comfortable and friendly. The decor is sparse, but the white walls are hung with the works of local artists. Regular breakfast dishes include Farmer's eggs (eggs scrambled with veggies and cheese), homemade quiche, bagels and lox, and breakfast burritos. Lunch brings 10 daily specials, including salads, pastas, curries, sandwiches, and local-style plate lunches. Also available are desserts, "real" milkshakes, and fresh-fruit smoothies.

Hamburger Mary's

2010 Main St. ☎ **808/244-7776.** Reservations not necessary. Main courses $3.95–$8.95. MC, V. Mon–Fri 9–10am, Sat–Sun 8–10am; daily 10am–10pm. AMERICAN.

Though Hamburger Mary's attracts a large gay following in the evening when the lights go down and the music is turned up, during the day the crowd is mixed. The decor is eclectic; among other things, there are neon bar signs and celebrity posters. Naturally, most people come here for hamburgers such as the "Meaty Mushroom" (a charbroiled burger topped with Cheddar and cream cheese and smothered with sautéed mushrooms) or the "Famous Chili Size" burger (topped with chili, onions, and whatever kind of cheese you like). Vegetarians can order the veggie garden burger or "Meatless Mary" (with cheese, pineapple, and mushrooms). Breakfast dishes include the Lahaina breakfast (two eggs any style, served with rice and toast) and the Hawaiian breakfast (three eggs any style served with charbroiled ham and fresh pineapple slices). However, my favorite is "Hawaiian Toast" (choice of multigrain or Hawaiian sweetbread dipped in egg batter, and flavored with vanilla, nutmeg, and cinnamon); topped with maple syrup, it's divine. Mary's bar and dance floor are open until 2am.

Saeng's Thai Cuisine

2119 Vineyard St. ☎ **808/244-1567** or 808/244-1568. Reservations recommended. Main courses $5.95–$11.95. MC, V. Mon–Fri 11am–2:30pm; daily 5–9:30pm. THAI.

Locals flock to Saeng's Thai as much for the atmosphere as for the cuisine. The setting is pleasant and gardenlike—in contrast with Siam Thai (see below), Wailuku's other excellent Thai restaurant. The mildly spicy satay shrimp or broccoli served with a peanut sauce are excellent starters, as are the fresh spring rolls stuffed with shrimp, somen noodles, lettuce, basil, and mint leaves served with bean sauce. If soup is what you're looking for, there's a great chicken coconut soup on the menu, and the tom-yum soup (lemongrass, kaffir lime leaves, green onion, and Thai parsley simmered in a spiced bouillon) with chicken is one of the tastiest I've ever had. Saeng's Thai offers several specialties as well, including Kai Yang (marinated cornish hen with lemongrass and kaffir leaves, grilled to perfection) and shrimp asparagus (stir-fried shrimp with green onion, asparagus, and mushrooms sautéed in a delectable sauce). One of my particular favorites is the honey shrimp, deep-fried shrimp with sesame seeds served on a bed of broccoli. Red, green, and masman curries with beef, chicken, or pork are prepared according to your level of tolerance for spicy food. There are about

20 vegetarian offerings, as well as fixed-price family dinner selections (including appetizer and dessert) for two, three, or four. Try the Thai tapioca pudding for dessert (special desserts are served on the weekend).

Sam Sato's

The Mill Yard, 1750 Wili Pa Loop. ☎ **808/244-7124.** No reservations. Plate lunches $4.90–$5.75. No credit cards. Mon–Sat 7am–2pm. HAWAIIAN.

Unfortunately for visitors, local-style eateries are a dying breed on Maui; however, if you happen to be in Wailuku and would like to experience some real local color, stop by Sam Sato's for a plate lunch or a bowl of saimin. Sandwiches and burgers are also available. If you're feeling adventurous, try the manju pastries. Don't expect anything fancy in the way of food or decor here.

Siam Thai

123 N. Market St. ☎ **808/244-3817** or 808/242-4132. Reservations recommended. Main courses $5.95–$13.95. AE, MC, V. Mon–Fri 11am–2:30pm; daily 5–9:30pm. THAI.

Siam Thai is another local favorite, and it's no wonder. The food is delicious and surprisingly inexpensive. The black-and-white exposed brick walls are accented by black booths that line the left side of the restaurant. On the right there are tables next to which is a reclining Buddha and a tropical fish tank. There's a bar at the rear of the restaurant, and piped-in music plays softly in the background. One of my favorite appetizers is mee krob (Thai crispy noodles) with bean sprouts, green onions, and a sweet sauce. Siam Thai also offers boneless chicken wings stuffed with carrots, long rice, mushrooms, green onion, and egg—a tasty treat, especially for those who don't care for spicy dishes. The tom-yum soup (chicken, lemongrass, and kaffir lime leaves simmered in a spiced bouillon) and the chicken coconut soup are also excellent. You can specify the degree of spiciness. The Siam Thai fried chicken is excellent (Cornish game hen deep-fried and served with a sauce of garlic and black pepper). Equally delicious is the Evil Prince, your choice of beef, chicken, or pork sautéed in hot spices with fresh basil and served on a bed of cabbage. Of course, you'll find the traditional red, yellow, green, and masman curries on the menu, and my favorite fish dish, *Pla Raad Prig* (deep-fried whole fish topped with the chef's special spicy sauce). There are also a number of vegetarian offerings.

Tasty Crust Restaurant

1770 Mill St. ☎ **808/244-0845.** No reservations. Breakfast items $1.10–$3.75; lunch and dinner items $1.50–$7.94. No credit cards. Daily 5:30am–1:30pm; Tues–Sun 5–10pm. AMERICAN/HAWAIIAN.

Ask anyone on the island where you should go for hotcakes, and the answer is always the same—Tasty Crust. With a reputation like that and some of the lowest prices around, it should come as no surprise that Tasty Crust is about as local as they come. The diner-style interior, complete with video games, is a little run-down but clean, and the place is nearly always packed. The hotcakes are so popular that they're served all day. Of course, there are other menu offerings as well, such as plate lunches and dinners served with rice and a salad. And you can't go wrong with a grilled cheese or a hamburger deluxe, but I'd put my money on those hotcakes.

KIHEI
EXPENSIVE

✪ A Pacific Cafe Maui

1279 S. Kihei Rd. (in Azeka Place II shopping center). ☎ **808/879-0069.** Reservations recommended. Main courses $11.50–$23. AE, DC, MC, V. Daily 5:30–10:30pm. HAWAII REGIONAL.

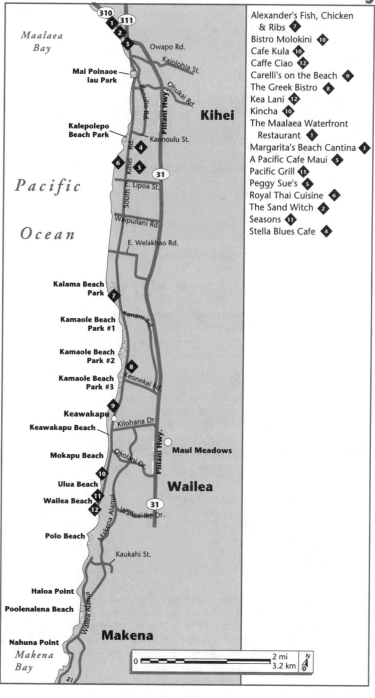

Kihei-Wailea Coast Dining

Maalaea Bay

310
311
1
2
3

Owapo Rd.

Kaiolohia St.

Mai Poinaoe Iau Park

Ohukai Rd.

Kanolio Rd.

Pilani Hwy.

Kihei

Kalepolepo Beach Park

Kihei Rd.

Kaonoulu St.

6
4
5

31

E. Lipoa St.

Pacific

South Kihei Rd.

Waipuilani Rd.

Ocean

E. Welakhao Rd.

Kalama Beach Park 7

Kanani Rd.

Kamaole Beach Park #1

Kamaole Beach Park #2 8

Keonekai Rd.

Kamaole Beach Park #3

Keawakapu 9

Keawakapu Beach

Kilohana Dr.

Maui Meadows

Mokapu Beach

Okolani Dr.

Pilani Hwy.

Ulua Beach 10

Wailea Beach 11
12

Wailea

Wailea Alanui

31

Wailea Ike Dr.

Polo Beach

Kaukahi St.

Haloa Point

Poolenalena Beach

Wailea Alanui

Makena

Nahuna Point

Makena Bay

21

0 ——— 2 mi / 3.2 km

N

Alexander's Fish, Chicken & Ribs 7
Bistro Molokini 10
Cafe Kula 10
Caffe Ciao 12
Carelli's on the Beach 9
The Greek Bistro 8
Kea Lani 12
Kincha 10
The Maalaea Waterfront Restaurant 1
Margarita's Beach Cantina 3
A Pacific Cafe Maui 5
Pacific Grill 11
Peggy Sue's 5
Royal Thai Cuisine 6
The Sand Witch 2
Seasons 11
Stella Blues Cafe 4

Every once in a while a really great restaurant pops up in an unexpected location. A Pacific Cafe Maui, created by Jean-Marie Josselin (A Pacific Cafe Kaua'i) and George Gomes (resident chef on Maui), is such a restaurant, and Azeka Place II is the unlikely location. Terra-cotta–colored walls and copper accents make the interior of this unusually shaped restaurant warm and inviting, and hand-painted china hints of the originality and creativity of the culturally diverse menu that has been inspired by the cuisines of Hawaii, India, and the Mediterranean. Start with the Kalua pork and mustard cabbage pot-sticker. It's served with a flavorful sweet and sour chili dip. Another great appetizer is the pizza topped with shoyu-ginger glazed chicken, sweet chili sauce, goat cheese, scallions, and shiitake mushrooms—the unusual combination of flavors will delight you. As an entrée I would recommend the Tandoori smoked and barbecued pork loin with grilled vegetables, green apple and leek chutney, and quinoa salad or the grilled opah served with banana salsa and Thai coconut curry sauce. In addition, each day brings a variety of unique specials. Desserts change regularly, but on my last visit I enjoyed a flavorful tropical fruit tart. Be sure to make reservations, since this is a very popular place.

Carelli's on the Beach

2980 S. Kihei Rd. ☎ **808/875-0001.** Reservations required. Main courses $13–$33. AE, MC, V. Daily 5:30–10pm. ITALIAN/SEAFOOD.

Kihei's most popular restaurant to date, Carelli's boasts a long list of celebrity diners, including Jack Nicholson and Joe Montana. It's no surprise, really, since Carelli's has a great location and sophisticated ambience. Owner Tony Habib designed the restaurant in the style of his grandfather, Rocco Carelli. Tiles have been imported from Italy, and beautiful murals grace the restaurant's walls. Even Rocco's original wood-burning pizza oven has been imported for baking Carelli's daily specialty pizzas. Antipasti runs the gamut from fresh seared Hawaiian ahi mostarda (served with a Torinese mustard sauce) to the always welcome calamari fritti (fried calamari served with chipotle aioli), and the staff will assemble any combination you request from the seafood bar. The specialty of the house is Carelli's zuppa di mare cioppino— clams, mussels, scallops, prawns, lobster, squid, and crab in a spicy tomato sauce. The rest of the menu changes frequently, but you can count on a variety of pastas, meats, and a fish of the day. Desserts also change often. Although there's a minimum charge in the main dining room, none exists at Rocco's Mangia Bar, where you can enjoy a light meal and a drink.

The Maalaea Waterfront Restaurant

On Maalaea Bay. ☎ **808/244-9028.** Reservations recommended. Main courses $16.50– $24.95. AE, MC, V. Daily 5–8:30pm (last seating is at 8:30pm). CONTINENTAL/SEAFOOD.

A family-run business located at the Kihei end of the Maalaea Harbor, this restaurant was voted by the *Maui News* to have the best seafood and service on the island in 1992 and 1993. Needless to say, it's one of Maui's most popular dinner spots, so be sure to make a reservation a couple of days in advance. Dining here is a lovely experience. The view is marvelous, the service impeccable, and the ambience romantic. Red crescent-shaped booths are comfortable, and fresh flowers grace each table. Begin your meal with chilled colossal shrimp or crab-stuffed mushroom caps au gratinée. The Maine lobster chowder is excellent, as are the sautéed Alaskan king crab cakes. For your entrée, choose a cooking method for your favorite fresh fish. If you're in the mood for something on the lighter side, try your fish poached or broiled and topped with steamed straw mushrooms, julienne bell peppers, snow peas, fresh leeks, carrots, chopped watercress, and Chilean shrimp served with white wine. How about Italian? Go for the Sicilian-style Provençal, a sauté of red and green bell peppers, black olives, artichokes, fresh mushrooms, tomatoes, garlic, olive oil, rosemary, and nutmeg. Other entrées include scallops au gratinée, live Maine lobster (steamed or stuffed), roasted rack of lamb (served with a delectable Szechuan peppercorn sauce), and tournedos of beef au poivre in a light cognac cream demi-glace. In addition, Chef Ron offers a "Game du Jour" (wild game prepared in traditional and contemporary styles). The wine list here is extensive.

MODERATE

The Greek Bistro

2511 S. Kihei Rd. (in Kai Nani Village). ☎ **808/879-9330.** Reservations recommended. Main courses $11.95–$18.95. AE, MC, V. Daily 4–9:30pm. CONTINENTAL/GREEK.

Located at the rear of Kai Nani Village, the Greek Bistro is one of Maui's hidden surprises. The restaurant has an authentic Mediterranean feeling—in fact, the place is so charming that a friend of mine drives all the way from Haiku (which is a long way to residents of Maui) just to dine here. Start your meal with a Greek salad, or better yet, the Macedonian salad (a salad of kalamata olives, cucumbers, tomatoes, onions, and feta cheese dressed with a mixture of olive oil and "Grecian spices"). The leg of lamb kabob is excellent, as is the *spanikopita* (layers of filo dough, spinach, onions, and cheese). The moussaka is authentically prepared with chopped lamb and baked with sliced eggplant, potatoes, onions, herbs, and wine topped with béchamel sauce. The menu lists a few continental specialties such as chicken and mushroom pasta or filet mignon cooked with mushrooms, wine, and Grecian herbs. What's for dessert? Baklava, what else?

INEXPENSIVE

Alexander's Fish, Chicken & Ribs

1913 S. Kihei Rd. ☎ **808/874-0788.** No reservations. Menu items $4.95–$15.95. No credit cards. Daily 11am–9pm. SEAFOOD.

Located in Kihei—"across from the whale at Kalama Park"—is this local fish and chips joint. Opened in 1990, Alexander's quickly became popular for good food at very reasonable prices. Six years later, it's still going strong. My favorite dishes here are the fish-and-chips and the fish-and-shrimp combo meals. When you order fish and chips, you'll have a choice of ono, mahi, or ahi, and you can order it broiled or fried (in 100% canola oil). In addition, the restaurant offers oysters, chicken, and delectable ribs. If you want to put together a picnic for the family, the menu lists a 13-piece basket of fish, chicken, shrimp, calamari, oysters, and ribs, as well as a variety of sandwiches. If you would like to eat on the premises, Alexander's offers covered lanai seating.

Margarita's Beach Cantina

101 N. Kihei Rd. (in Kealia Beach Plaza). ☎ **808/879-5275.** Reservations recommended. Main courses $6.95–$17.95. AE, MC, V. Daily 11:30am–10pm. Bar 11:30am–midnight. MEXICAN.

This restaurant is located on the upper level of this commercial complex. Once inside the festive Mexican restaurant, you can dine on the large outdoor deck overlooking the ocean, or indoors amid the strings of chili lights, neon beer signs, and hanging plants. The menu offerings are fairly standard as far as Mexican restaurants go—nachos, tostadas, tacos, enchiladas, burritos, and chili rellenos. To start, try the jalapeño poppers (jalapeño peppers filled with Cheddar or cream cheese). The fiesta tostada is a crispy flour tortilla filled with beef, chicken, or tofu, lettuce, tomatoes, cheese, olives, sour cream, and guacamole. Combination plates of two or three separate menu items are served with rice and beans, and there are several sandwich offerings, including charbroiled fish or barbecue chicken sandwiches. A popular burger is the Mexican burger topped with cheese, guacamole, and pico de gallo sauce. House specialties include the fajita platter, carnitas, homemade beef tamales, and New York steaks. Desserts change daily. Happy hour is from 2:30 to 5pm; during that time you can get 96¢ margaritas ($4 per liter). Live entertainment is available some evenings, and there is never a cover charge.

Peggy Sue's

1279 S. Kihei Rd. #303 (in Azeka Place II shopping center). ☎ **808/875-8944.** Reservations not necessary. Main courses $3.95–$9.95. Daily 11am–10pm. AMERICAN.

Though Peggy Sue's is a modern establishment, it will take you back in time to the Malt Shops of the 1950s—there's even a vintage jukebox. Hamburgers of all kinds (bacon and cheese, chili-cheese, and even a pineapple-and-cheese teriyaki burger), french fries, and fantastic milk shakes make Peggy Sue's a local favorite. You can also get hot dogs, salads, and sundaes. A children's menu is available.

Royal Thai Cuisine

1280 S. Kihei Rd. ☎ **808/874-0813.** Reservations not necessary. Main courses $5.95–$13.95. AE, MC, V. Mon–Fri 11am–3pm; daily 5–9:30pm. THAI.

This little Thai restaurant has a big reputation here on the south shore. Its focus is not on the decor (the green vinyl booths and bent-cane chairs around small tables are plain and unadorned), it's on the food. The menu is packed with noodle, curry, seafood, and vegetable dishes. You might begin with the marinated shrimp satay or the delicious green papaya salad. For a main course, try the Thai red curry with chicken, beef, or shrimp, or the chili shrimp (shrimp marinated with spices and sautéed in a chili sauce with bamboo shoots and green onion). The sweet-and-sour fish (deep-fried mahimahi with vegetables in a sweet and sour sauce) is tasty, as is the Thai garlic or the Thai ginger (both with your choice of chicken, beef, or pork). Vegetarian dishes range from satay broccoli and tofu to cashew nut vegetables. Everything at Royal Thai Cuisine is reasonably priced. You get great food without denting your wallet.

The Sand Witch

145 N. Kihei Rd. ☎ **808/879-3262.** No reservations. Sandwiches $3.95–$6.95. AE, MC, V. Daily 11am–10pm. SANDWICHES/SALADS.

Located adjacent to the Sugar Beach resort condominium complex near the end of North Kihei Road, the Sand Witch is a cozy spot for a quick, inexpensive lunch or dinner. Pupus include nachos topped with melted Cheddar cheese, jalapeño salsa, onions, and guacamole and potato skins filled with ham, chili, salsa, Cheddar and Parmesean cheese, and guacamole—it tastes much better than it sounds. Under the heading "Sheer Witchery Sandwitches," you'll find the Witch Hoagy with turkey breast, roast beef, baked ham, Cheddar cheese, onions, tomatoes, sprouts, and romaine lettuce, all served on French bread. Standard offerings include ham and cheese, corned beef, or tuna salad. If you love hot dogs, this is the place for you. There are several varieties of "Warlock Weiners" (1/4-pound beef hot dogs). The Wild Dog is topped with beef and bean chili, melted Cheddar, onions, and salsa, and the Poor Man's Reuben is smothered with sauerkraut, Cheddar, onions, and "the Sorcerer's special dressing." The Sand Witch has a large bar and is well known for its selection of tropical drinks. Take-out is available.

Stella Blues Cafe & Deli

1215 S. Kihei Rd. (in Long's Center). ☎ **808/874-3779.** Reservations are accepted. Sandwiches $4.75–$7.50. DISC, MC, V. Daily 8am–9pm. AMERICAN/INTERNATIONAL.

The plain plastic tables and chairs that flank the front window of Stella Blues Cafe & Deli do not hint at what you'll find inside one of Kihei's trendiest gathering spots. Multicolored Hawaiian floral-print tablecloths will probably be surrounded by groups of hip Mauians engaged in animated conversation. Breakfast choices include: Quickstart (two eggs any style with home fries and toast), South of the Border (two eggs scrambled with Cheddar cheese, onions, jalapeño peppers, a side of salsa, served with home fries and a warm flour tortilla), pancakes, or yogurt and granola served with fresh island fruit. Stella's Caffe Latte, a mocha with cinnamon, orange, and whipped cream, is great with anything. At lunch, salads and sandwiches are standard fare. Try the curried chicken salad or Toby's Tofu Tia Extraordinaire (a soft flour tortilla wrapped around seasoned, sautéed tofu, sprouts, Kula onion, tomato, avocado, sour cream, and topped with salsa). Dinner highlights include the vegetarian lasagne, Alaskan crab cakes, and Thai sweet chili chicken. The ever-changing desserts and pastries are baked fresh daily, so be sure to check the pastry case. Stella's occasionally offers live entertainment, so check the local listings or call for information.

WAILEA
EXPENSIVE

Kea Lani
4100 Wailea Alanui (in the Kea Lani Resort). ☎ **808/875-4100.** Reservations recommended. Main courses $24–$36. AE, CB, DC, DISC, JCB, MC, V. Daily 5:30–10pm. PACIFIC RIM.

The open-air Kea Lani restaurant is simple but graciously elegant with its low lighting, white-cloth tables, straight-backed chairs with a carved pineapple motif, and large tropical flower arrangements. Diners may choose a table indoors or outside on the lanai. Since the menu changes monthly, there's no telling what delicacies you'll find when you're there; on my last visit, the menu included the following appetizers: chicken-coconut soup with kaffir lime leaf and kha ginger, and crispy smoked Ulupalakua Ranch elk summer rolls with three dipping sauces. Entrées included Maui onion–crusted New York sirloin with herb butter and Pompeii potatoes; Muscovy duck with sweet jalapeño barbecue sauce and cast-iron-skillet corn bread; and the day's fresh Hawaiian fish (my fish was served pan-seared with spicy Thai green curry and kabocha pumpkin).

✪ Kincha
3850 Wailea Alanui (in the Grand Wailea). ☎ **808/875-1234.** Reservations necessary. Main courses $20–$85; fixed-price meals $58–$500. AE, DC, MC, V. Daily 6–10pm. JAPANESE.

Enter Kincha (meaning "teapot") and you're in another world. Greeted by the sight of a 24-karat gold Japanese teapot, you'll feel as though you're entering a quiet cave. In fact, 800 tons of rock from the base of Mount Fuji were used for the construction of this restaurant, a brilliant work of art, which only hints at the artistic presentation of its authentic Japanese cuisine. The restaurant, which somewhat resembles a teahouse in Kyoto, was actually built in Japan, shipped in pieces to Maui, and then reconstructed by a master Japanese craftsman. From the corner pillars to the bridges that cross koi ponds, not one nail is visible. One of the central features of this cultural oasis is a stage where nightly flower arranging and tea ceremonies are performed.

Diners can sit at the sushi or tempura bars, at Koagari or Zashiki table seatings, or in one of the three private tatami rooms. The tatami rooms (which open onto beautiful gardens and waterways) are for those who choose Kaiseki dining, a very expensive but extraordinarily beautiful way to enjoy Japanese cuisine. A Kaiseki dinner consists of at least 14 courses made from the freshest and highest-quality foods available. Vegetables are carved into elaborate flowers, and fresh lobster or sashimi might be served in a small ice igloo. Tiny quail eggs are often served with handpainted faces, and everything is served on matching, handcrafted dinnerware. The Miyabi (meaning "elegance") dinner consists of an appetizer, clear broth soup, sashimi, hassun, broiled fish, boiled vegetables, steak, onmono, a vinegar course, shokuji, seasonal fruit, dessert, and green tea. Also included in the Miyabi dinner is a homemade fruit wine. This meal will cost about $300 per person. Advance reservations are required for the tatami rooms. Of course, you can dine à la carte as well. Try the Japanese-style chicken steak with the chef's special sauce, or the hamachi shioyaki, broiled salted yellowtail tuna. You could also order assortments of sashimi, sushi, and tempura. Excellent hot appetizers are the agedashi tofu (fried tofu with sweetened shoyu sauce) and the chawan mushi (bits of shrimp, bamboo shoots, ginkgo nuts, and mushroom in an egg custard). The seaweed salad served with a vinegar-miso dipping sauce, and the cha soba (tea-flavored buckwheat noodles), also served with a dipping sauce, are excellent choices as well. If you order dessert à la carte, you'll have a choice of ice creams (including green tea, azuki bean, and ginger). Hiyashi zenzai (sweet azuki red beans) served with ommatcha ceremonial green tea, is a taste treat.

Pacific Grill

3900 Wailea Alanui (in the Four Seasons Resort). ☎ **808/874-8000.** Reservations recommended for dinner. Main courses $9.25–$15.75 at lunch, $9.25–$28 at dinner. AE, DC, MC, V. Daily 6am–2:30pm and 5:30–9:30pm. PACIFIC RIM.

Also located in the elegant Four Seasons Resort, the Pacific Grill is a comfortable breakfast and lunch stop, as well as a casual yet traditional dinner spot. In the morning two breakfast buffets are available—one with island fruits, cereals, granola, yogurt, fresh pastries, health foods, juice, and coffee; the second includes all of the aforementioned choices plus omelets, made-to-order eggs, and an assortment of breakfast meats. You can also order from the à la carte menu. Start your lunch with the island sashimi with soyu sauce and pickled ginger or the saimin Wailea with Oriental vegetables, char-sui chicken, and dim sum. There is a great salad bar with a changing assortment of island greens and vegetables, as well as a daily selection of previously prepared salads, and soup. On the sandwich menu, the grilled swordfish sandwich on a dill kaiser roll with pesto aioli and new potato salad is a good choice. A great specialty item is the poached island fish with a miso-ginger broth and somen noodles (it's good for you, too). If you're up to it after lunch, head over to the Pacific Grill dessert buffet.

The dinner menu lists Pacific Rim, as well as North American specialties to start, including Vietnamese spring rolls or a Caesar salad with herb-laced croutons. Main courses include such specialties as the wok-fried Pacific salmon with a sesame-seed vinaigrette, vegetables, and wonton egg noodles. The Korean beef (thinly sliced sirloin) with hot chili oil and a garlic sesame soy sauce, and the Thai coconut curry with lobster, shrimp, scallops, and stir-fried Oriental vegetables served in a crispy lumpia basket are both worth a try. There are also several pasta options, and a menu of lighter fare (including sandwiches). There is a fairly extensive children's menu.

The SeaWatch Restaurant at Wailea

100 Wailea Golf Club Dr. ☎ **808/875-8080.** Reservations recommended. Main courses $18–$24. AE, MC, V. Daily 8am–10pm. HAWAII REGIONAL.

SeaWatch owners Roy Dunn and Mike Hooks have a knack for picking great restaurant locations (see the Plantation House Restaurant), and this one is no exception. If you want to dine out on the lanai, you'll be treated to views of Maalaea, Molokini, and Kahoolawe. The interior dining areas, decorated in pastel shades and dotted with fan palm and banana trees, are spacious and inviting. On my last visit, I started off with the Chinese five-spice crab cakes, which were superb. I also sampled the unusual spinach salad (served with warm grilled shrimp sate), which is tossed with a Lehua honey-sesame vinaigrette. I chose fish as my main course and had it wok-seared with spicy Thai lemongrass and served with a black bean sauce. I wasn't disappointed. Also on the menu were spicy Szechuan barbecued chicken breasts, kiawe-grilled rack of lamb, filet mignon, and New York steak. SeaWatch also offers breakfast (a variety of omelets, muffins, cereals, and French toast) and lunch (there's a sandwich menu), but dinner is the best.

Seasons
3900 Wailea Alanui (in the Four Seasons Resort). ☎ **808/874-8000.** Reservations recommended. Main courses $27–$40. AE, DC, JCB, MC, V. Daily 6–9:30pm. MEDITERRANEAN.

The view of the ocean from Seasons' orchid-filled terrace is magnificent, especially at night as the sun falls smoothly and swiftly below the horizon. The decor is light and airy, allowing the diner to appreciate the view as well as the food. Seasons is fine dining at its best. Begin with the consommé of duck accompanied by a porcini spaetzle or the sauté of foie gras and wild mushroom layer cake with a Madeira sauce. The grilled vine-ripened tomatoes and marinated onions dressed with a warm balsamic vinaigrette are a more healthy alternative. Main courses include a selection of pastas, such as the tagliatelle with rare-seared ahi and a lemon caper sauce, and a variety of meats and fish. The sautéed opakapaka with a saffron-celeriac purée and fennel essence is flavorful, as is the peppered beef tenderloin with garlic bread pudding and an oven-dried tomato relish. For dessert, chocoholics will be intrigued with the Chocolate Enchantment. Fruit lovers will enjoy seasonal berries with crème fraîche or crème anglaise or the almond crêpes with sautéed bananas and caramel nougat ice cream. There is a short list of dessert wines by the glass.

MODERATE

Bistro Molokini
3850 Wailea Alanui (in the Grand Wailea). ☎ **808/875-1234.** Reservations recommended. Main courses $9.50–$17 at lunch, $14.50–$29 at dinner. AE, DC, MC, V. Daily 11:30am–4pm (light lunch 4–6pm) and 6–10pm. ITALIAN.

Even if you're not in the mood for Italian food, you may be tempted to enter Bistro Molokini—it's hard to pass up the spectacular dessert presentation at the entrance to the restaurant. While dining here you'll enjoy lovely views and catch a glimpse of the chef (who hails from northern Italy) at work in the restaurant's exhibition kitchen. Lunch antipasti are fairly standard—*insalata caprese* (tomato and fresh Mozzarella cheese salad) and fried calamari. *Carpaccio malatesta* (thin slices of raw beef with vegetables in a light lemon dressing) is an interesting addition. The *fusilli alla plinio* (pasta spirals with chicken, wild mushrooms, and sun-dried tomatoes) is a good choice for an entrée, and pizzas with a variety of toppings are available. The *straccetti alla romana* (sliced, marinated, grilled beef served on a warm garlic bruschetta) is excellent. The dinner menu offers many of the same appetizers, pastas, and pizzas, but the meat and fish dishes are a bit different. Try the *galletto alla diavola,* a mustard-marinated baby chicken that's clay-baked and served with fresh tomatoes. The grilled lamb chops in balsamic vinegar and basil sauce *(costolette d'agnello)* and the sautéed veal chops with porcini mushrooms and Fontina cheese *(nodino di vitello alla piemontese)* are both excellent choices. For the calorie-conscious, the lunch and dinner menus also list several spa suggestions. And those spectacular desserts? Well, if you're lucky, you might get the *torta di mele alla milanese* (thin, apple tart with vanilla gelato and an amaretto sauce) or the *torta al cioccolato amaro* (a flourless chocolate tart with fruit sorbet and a raspberry coulis). If either of those seems too extravagant, you can order the *caffè semi freddo* (espresso with white chocolate gelato and chocolate truffle liqueur).

Cafe Kula

3850 Wailea Alanui (in the Grand Wailea). ☎ **808/875-1234.** Reservations not necessary. Main courses $8.50–$13. AE, DC, MC, V. Daily 6am–3pm. NATURAL FOOD.

Recently featured in *Vegetarian Times* magazine, Cafe Kula is one of my favorite restaurants on the island. Even if you're not a guest at the Grand, you might want to make a trip to Cafe Kula. The open-air setting is exceptionally pleasant. Some of the tables have been placed under a covered portico, while others stand, cabana-covered, outside on the lanai. Ceiling fans whir silently overhead, cooling patrons as they dine at marble-topped tables. The coral-and-turquoise-colored floor tiles are complemented by brightly striped seat cushion covers. The goal of Chef Kathleen Daelemans "is to offer food for better living." She has daily contact with Upcountry farmers, who keep her informed about which organically grown fruits, vegetables, and herbs are ready to be harvested so she can plan her menus. The produce is picked about 6:30am and arrives in the kitchen by 10:30am. All fish are local, meat and poultry are the freshest available, and each dish is low in sodium, fat, and cholesterol.

When I dined at Cafe Kula, I began with crostini spread with Maui sun-dried tomato paste and a light but tasty homemade herbed ricotta cheese. The Kula and toybox tomato salad with fresh island herbs, topped with thinly sliced reggiano Parmesan cheese and drizzled with a delicate but flavorful balsamic vinaigrette, is also a superb way to begin a meal here. Follow either of those appetizers with the spicy black bean chili served with a mango salsa and a delectable sweet Maui corn bread (all breads are homemade). The Hawaiian ahi tuna sandwich (served with a sampling of homemade pickles) is prepared on the kiawe wood-fired grill, as is the Cafe Kula grilled vegetable sandwich with slow-baked tomatoes, caramelized Maui onions, roasted peppers, and delicious herbed ricotta cheese. Flavorful but healthy desserts include Hawaiian blueberry almond torte with orange coulis, tropical fruit tart, chocolate raspberry crêpes with mango yogurt, and fruit plate.

Cafe Kula also serves such breakfast items as fresh-fruit smoothies; the Spa Power drink (a combination of tropical fruit juices and protein); muesli with fresh and island-dried fruit; homemade granola with fresh fruit; Haiku apple-banana pancakes with pecans; eggs; muffins; and pumpkin bread. It's a great way to start the day.

✪ Caffe Ciao

4100 Wailea Alanui (in the Kea Lani Resort). ☎ **808/875-4100.** No reservations. Main courses $17–$29. AE, CB, DC, DISC, JCB, MC, V. Daily 6:30am–8pm. GOURMET ITALIAN DELI.

It's hard not to fall in love with Caffe Ciao, a charming authentic Italian gourmet deli. The tiled floors and black-and-white tiled walls (up to the chair rail) are lined with small metal tables and chairs where you can grab a quick bite or linger over a cup of cappuccino while reading one of the many available newspapers. In addition to pasta salads and deli items, the menu includes a fresh fish of the day prepared to order. You might like to have it grilled with arugula and sun-dried tomatoes or pan-seared with grilled shrimp and chow mein vegetables. Other entrées include cappellini with grilled scallops in a basil broth, grilled boneless lamb chops in a wild cherry ginger sauce, crispy crab pancit with seared scallops, and barbecue shrimp and New York steak in a spicy peanut sauce. Desserts here are spectacular—from tortes and tarts to cakes and cookies. The menu changes monthly; the café also sells various specialty food items (such as oils, vinegars, and sauces).

4 Upcountry

Dining choices Upcountry are somewhat more limited than those in West Maui, and the drive can take up to an hour and a half depending on where you're staying (if you're staying in Hana, it will take you a lot longer), but you won't be disappointed with any of the restaurants listed below. Although some are more upscale than others, they are all local favorites and serve excellent, high-quality food.

MAKAWAO
EXPENSIVE

Casanova Italian Restaurant and Deli
1188 Makawao Ave. (P.O. Box 1166). ☎ **808/572-0220.** Reservations recommended. Main courses $8–$24. CB, DC, DISC, MC, V. Deli daily 8:30am–7:30pm. Restaurant, lunch Mon–Sat 11am–2pm, dinner daily 5:30–9:30pm. Bar stays open until 1am. ITALIAN.

At some point when you're exploring Upcountry Maui you'll probably find yourself in the old paniolo town of Makawao, home of Casanova Italian Restaurant and Deli. You might be surprised, but this is an authentic Italian restaurant (owned by Stefano Segre, Francesca LaRue, and Steven Burgelin—who hail from Milan). In this cowboy town you'll still find hitching posts and men wearing 10-gallon hats, but don't let that stop you from heading inside for a bite to eat.

All meals here begin with warm, fresh focaccia which has been baked in the central kiawe wood–fired pizza oven (imported directly from Italy) at a temperature of 700° F. The focaccia practically melts in your mouth. Combine it with an antipasto of *spinaci saltati al burro e parmigiano* (fresh Kula spinach sautéed with garlic, butter, and Parmesan cheese) or the antipasto *misto all'Italiana* (a selection of fine deli meats, marinated seafood, roasted peppers, and a variety of cheeses), and you'll think you've died and gone to heaven. It only gets better when the entrées arrive. You might choose a pasta dish. Casanova reputedly has the best homemade pasta on the island (they even supply pasta to some of the island's finest hotels and other restaurants). Try the *gnocchi strozzapreti* (ricotta and spinach dumplings in a tomato and Gorgonzola sauce) or the *paglia e fieno aii funghi* (linguine with a variety of mushrooms in a creamy garlic sauce). There is always a fresh fish (and veal chop) of the day, and if you can spare a half-hour, I'd recommend the *pesce intero al forno,* a whole fish oven-baked with white wine, fresh herbs, and garlic (this dish takes a while to prepare). Bread is only one thing they cook to perfection in that enormous pizza oven, so if you crave a really fine pizza, now's the time to satisfy it. The pizza Greca with tomato sauce, feta cheese, Greek olives, and oregano is recommended, as is the Vulcano with baked eggplant, smoked Mozzarella, and fresh tomato. You can also create your own pizza by choosing from the list of toppings. Since the desserts are baked fresh daily, be sure to look at the dessert tray. Homemade gelato is available every day. Stay on after dinner and enjoy an evening of dancing and live entertainment—your cover charge will be waived if you're dining.

The original deli next door to the restaurant serves an excellent breakfast, sandwiches at lunch, coffees, and mouth-watering pastries any time of the day.

✪ Haliimaile General Store
Haliimaile. ☎ **808/572-2666.** Reservations recommended. Main courses $13–$24. MC, V. Lunch Mon–Sat 11am–2:30pm, dinner daily 5:30–10pm, brunch Sun 10am–2:30pm. Five miles up Highway 37 (Haleakala Hwy.), turn left at the Haliimaile cut-off sign. Continue 1¹/₂ miles to Haliimaile General Store. HAWAII REGIONAL/AMERICAN/INTERNATIONAL.

First of all, you're probably wondering how to pronounce the name of this wonderful restaurant, right? Well, it goes something like this: hi-lee-ee-meye-lee, and roughly translated, it is "a covering of the fragrant maile twining shrub." This whole area was once overgrown with the aromatic maile plant, which was often used in the making of redolent leis. Today the restaurant is surrounded by about 1,000 acres of pineapple fields. Owners Bev and Joe Gannon have transformed the General Store (which first opened in 1929) into one of Maui's best restaurants. Originally, they planned to open a gourmet deli/catering business, but on their first day when scores of people showed up looking for a place to sit down and enjoy their meal, the Gannons decided they'd better turn the place into a restaurant. With the presence of lofty pine shelves that hold ceramics, glassware, gourmet foods, and basketry, you'll still feel as if you're in a general store. There are two dining rooms here—one for more casual dining up front, and an intimate room at the back. Local artwork, including the bartop and the bas-relief next to the bar (both by Tom Faught, whose work is also on display in the Ritz-Carlton Kapalua), is displayed throughout. I love this restaurant for several reasons, including the fact that it offers some of the finest food on Maui in a casual setting.

Begin your meal with the incredible leek and goat cheese tart, served with crispy pancetta and smoked tomato coulis; or the unique Brie and grape quesadilla served hot with a sweet-pea guacamole. Their "Famous House Salad" is reminiscent of something my mother used to make with fresh mixed greens, onions, mandarin oranges, and walnuts in a balsamic vinaigrette topped with crumbled bleu cheese. For a main course, try the Italasian shrimp and scallops—they're sautéed with shiitake mushrooms and served in a cilantro pesto cream sauce over angel hair pasta. The Szechuan barbecued salmon, topped with a sauce of caramelized onions, garlic, orange zest, Szechuan peppercorns, and fresh herbs, is absolutely out of this world. You might also like to try the Australian rack of lamb Hunan style. It's marinated in hoisin sauce, sesame, and Oriental black beans and then grilled to perfection. The wine list here is extensive, and Joe Gannon will help you find a bottle that will complement your meal perfectly. Desserts change daily, but Haliimaile General Store's own signature dessert (which appeared on the cover of *Food & Wine* in March 1992), piña colada cheesecake, is superb.

Makawao Steak House

3612 Baldwin Ave. ☎ **808/572-8711.** Reservations recommended. Main courses $15.50–$24.95. MC, V. Lunch Mon–Fri 11am–2pm; dinner daily 5–10pm. AMERICAN.

Opened in 1990 and located right in the center of Old Makawao Town, the Makawao Steak House is exactly what you might picture it to be—it is, after all, right in the heart of paniolo country. Wood-paneled walls, a working fireplace, and comfortable wooden chairs have all been carefully chosen by owner Dickie Furtado, who designed his restaurant specifically with the diner's comfort in mind. It is exactly as cozy as you might expect, and there's even a blue-plate special. Start with a seafood sampler or the appetizer they call "Dynamite" (scallops and fresh vegetables baked in a firecracker sauce). The Portuguese bean soup is good, and there are several salad selections. Entrées include fresh seafood (there's even a calamari steak), as well as items from the kiawe broiler and from the barnyard. Among seafood dishes, there's a bouillabaisse, baked scallops, crab legs, and shrimp scampi. Most diners come for the steak, though, and there are several choices here. Two recommendations are the filet mignon and the porterhouse steak. There's a nice teriyaki steak as well, and lamb lovers will be happy to find rack of lamb on the menu. The Greek chicken is boneless chicken breast filled with spinach, feta cheese, and black olives, served with a lemon sauce. Something with a more Hawaiian twist might be the chicken in phyllo (boneless chicken breast filled with a macadamia nut herb dressing, butter, and encased in phyllo pastry) or the boneless breast basted in a ginger and teriyaki sauce. That blue-plate special is a 16-ounce porterhouse steak, kiawe-broiled and served with a caper-and-garlic-flavored olive oil sauce. It is served with rice and sautéed spinach. Try the white chocolate mousse or the mud pie for dessert.

INEXPENSIVE
The Courtyard Deli
3620 Baldwin Ave. ☎ **808/572-3456.** No reservations. Menu items $4.95–$5.50. AE, MC, V. Sun–Wed 7am–5pm, Thurs–Sat 7am–8pm. DELI.

The first thing you'll notice about this place is that it smells divine. The menu quotes such literary greats as George Bernard Shaw, who believed that, "There is no love sincerer than the love of food"; and James Beard, who once said, "Too few people understand a really good sandwich." The people at the Courtyard Deli seem to be in agreement with Mr. Shaw and Mr. Beard. Offerings here include the king of deli sandwiches—the pastrami melt; a weekly variation on the chicken salad sandwich; and everyone's favorite, the tuna melt. More unusual menu listings include the "Garden Burger with Da Works," a blend of mushrooms, herbs, and oatmeal topped with Mozzarella cheese served on a whole-wheat bun; or the "Fakin' Bacon BLT," slices of "fakin' bacon" topped with tempeh, avocado, mayonnaise, and Maui onion. You can also request a sandwich made to order, and there's always a soup of the day. Desserts are made fresh daily and are constantly changing, so don't forget to ask what they are. If you're in Makawao in the morning, stop by for breakfast. Try Claire's cinnamon custard French toast (croissants baked in custard and served with syrup) or the Belgian waffles (served with maple syrup and fresh fruit). There are several variations of scrambled eggs, and the Mauka Morning Burrito (scrambled eggs, cheese, and salsa wrapped in a whole-wheat chapati) should satisfy even those with the healthiest of appetites.

Crossroads Caffe
3682 Baldwin Ave. ☎ **808/572-1101.** No reservations. Menu items $1.50–$5.50. No credit cards. Mon–Sat 8–10:30am and 11am–4pm. CAFE/DELI.

Located directly across the street from Casanova (see above), the Crossroads Caffe is a great place to stop for a bite between shops and art galleries. Small marble-topped tables surrounded by metal versions of the more traditional bent-cane chairs flank the walls of this tiny café. A few tables are outdoors as well. Breakfast choices range from bagels and English muffins to Belgian waffles and breakfast burritos. Lunch options include the popular Boboli pizza of the pesto and veggie varieties, a turkey melt, "dolphin-safe" tuna sandwiches, grilled cheese, and a veggie burger with cheese. Lunch specials are available daily. Beverages include natural juices and sodas, as well as many varieties of coffee. Check the pastry case for the day's bakery selections, which might include muffins, croissants, and more elaborate choices (for example, the delicious Kona mocha cheesecake). If nothing on the menu strikes your fancy, maybe the frozen yogurt will.

HAIKU

Ⓢ Pauwela Cafe
375 W. Kuiaha Rd. (Old Pauwela Cannery). ☎ **808/575-9242.** No reservations. All items under $8. No credit cards. Mon–Sat 7am–6pm, Sun 9am–2pm. INTERNATIONAL.

Haiku is not the center of culinary activity on Maui, but Pauwela Cafe is such a great little place I thought you might find it worthwhile if you were planning to spend some time Upcountry (especially if you're on the way up to Hana). Owners Becky and Chris Speere both have loads of professional cooking experience. Chris spent some time as executive sous chef at the Maui Prince Hotel and now is an instructor at Maui Community College's Food Service Program, and Becky, whose strong suit is baking, was responsible for providing some of the island's best restaurants with delectable desserts. The brightly colored interior of Pauwela Cafe is as inviting as the great food and low prices. The frequently changing menu has an international theme—for instance, at breakfast you might find Cuban burritos (flour tortillas filled with scrambled eggs, black bean chili, and sour cream) or pain perdu (French toast topped with an orange- and vanilla-flavored custard). The lunch menu might bring such specialties as Thai sausage sandwiches, Hawaiian ceviche, or Moroccan stew. You can also order fresh-fruit smoothies, scones, muffins, cakes, and pies of all shapes and varieties. In my opinion, the Pauwela Cafe is a culinary adventure that shouldn't be passed up.

KULA
MODERATE

Kula Lodge & Restaurant
Rte. 377 (R.R. 1, Box 475), Kula. ☎ **808/878-1535** or 808/878-2517. Reservations recommended at dinner. Main courses $3.50–$7.75 at breakfast, $6.75–$22 at lunch and dinner. MC, V. Daily 6–11:30am breakfast; 11:45am–4:30pm lunch; 4:45–10pm dinner. HAWAII REGIONAL/CONTEMPORARY.

While sea and sand is probably why you came to Maui in the first place, you might get a little homesick for a cooler climate and that fireplace you left behind. If that's the case, head Upcountry to the Kula Lodge & Restaurant. The views are spectacular. Lunchtime brings a mixed crowd of local businesspeople and early-rising tourists who made the journey to Haleakala Crater to watch the sun rise. At dinner the lights are dimmed, and a fire in the hearth sets the scene for an intimate, candlelit, relatively inexpensive dinner for two. A good lunch or dinnertime appetizer is Grandma's Thai spring rolls (fresh vegetables, mint, marinated tofu, and soba noodles wrapped in rice paper and served with a Thai peanut sauce). If you love onion soup, you've come to the right place. The Kula onion soup is prepared with sweet onions sautéed in a rich broth with just a touch of sherry and a topping of garlic croutons and Swiss cheese. Notable sandwiches include the mahimahi fish burger with tartar sauce and the meatless garden burger served with lettuce, tomato, and onion on honey wheatberry bread. Naturally, there is a large selection of fresh fish and shellfish, and—true to the Upcountry theme—several varieties of steak, and a delicious roasted rack of lamb Dijonnaise, in a mustard breadcrumb crust, served with ratatouille. On the pasta menu a good choice is the homemade salmon ravioli served with a basil tomato coulis. Breakfasts, from the whole-grain cereals to buttermilk griddle cakes, are hearty and delicious. There's also a children's breakfast menu.

INEXPENSIVE

Grandma's Coffee Shop
Hwy. 37, Keokea. ☎ **808/878-2140.** No reservations. Menu items $1.75–$6.95. No credit cards. Mon–Sat 7am–5pm. AMERICAN.

Grandma's Coffee Shop is an excellent place to stop for coffee and pastry on your way up to Haleakala Crater, that is, if you're not headed there for the sunrise. If so, you could stop by on your way back down. Several years ago Alfred Franco began learning the fine art of coffee roasting. His teacher? You guessed it—his grandmother. Although the cafe is only about 8 years old, the Franco family has been roasting coffee on Maui for almst 80 years; today you can buy the coffee by the pound right here in Grandma's Coffee Shop. Alfred says that people often ask him why his coffee is so expensive, and he simply explains that it's of a much higher quality. If you know your java, you'll understand that you're getting your money's worth at Grandma's. There are café tables available for eating in, but you can order various food items to go (this is great if you're planning a picnic on the crater). In the morning there is a large variety of freshly baked, homemade pastries from coffee cake to cinnamon rolls or even banana bread. At lunch there are several sandwiches and perhaps a piping-hot chili. If you can get a table and you're not in a hurry, eat in the coffee shop—you'll get an idea of just what it's like to live on Maui. Local patrons come and go greeting their friends. You'll envy them and their island lifestyle. In case you're wondering, the artwork displayed on the walls of Grandma's is local.

PAIA
EXPENSIVE

Mama's Fish House

799 Poho Place (on Rte. 36). ☎ **808/579-8488.** Reservations recommended at dinner. Main courses $19.95–$28.95. AE, DISC, MC, V. Daily 11am–9:30pm. SEAFOOD.

One of the oldest restaurants on the island, Mama's is located just 1¹/₂ miles from Paia. You'll have no trouble finding it because the entrance is marked by a ship's flagpole and a couple of vintage vans. On one of Maui's prettiest beaches, Mama's is actually a converted beach house that belongs to the restaurant's namesake, "Mama" Doris Christiansen, who decided to open her home as a fresh fish house in 1973. Everybody—locals and tourists alike—enjoys dining at this beachfront establishment. The interior, plastered with items that are reminiscent of Old Hawaii (for example, kapa cloth, grass skirts, and old photos), is inviting and comfortable. All the fish served at Mama's is brought in on Mama's own fishing boats, and fresh herbs are grown in the Christiansens' backyard. At dinner, the house salad topped with smoked fish is delicious. Try one of the day's fresh catches sautéed in white wine and sprinkled with macadamia nuts. You can't leave here without having Mama's famous macadamia nut cheesecake.

Wunderbar

89 Hana Hwy. ☎ **808/579-8808.** Reservations recommended. Main courses $3.95–$12.95 at lunch, $7.75–$21.95 at dinner. AE, MC, V. Daily 7:30am–2pm and 5–10pm; appetizers 2:30–6pm. Bar stays open until about 1am. GERMAN/INTERNATIONAL.

Though Wunderbar is furnished only with plain wooden tables and chairs, it's an upbeat and friendly spot. A piano in the center of the restaurant and an abundance of beer signs hanging on the walls liven the place up. The bar is almost always hopping, and the TV above it is always on. The breakfast menu includes a variety of egg dishes, pancakes (including coconut banana and chocolate), Belgian waffles, and a few southwestern favorites (for example, huevos rancheros and breakfast burritos). The lunch menu offers a soup of the day, sandwiches, salads, seafood specials, and several pasta dishes. You can order a regular ground-beef burger, or choose something a little more interesting, such as Kalbsrahmgulasch mit spaetzle ("chunks" of veal in a spicy, creamy paprika sauce served with homemade spaetzle noodles). At dinner the menu is much more extensive, including pastas, several seafood specialties (such as blackened ahi served with a sweet Thai basil sauce), several hearty entrées (for

---

Breakfast

If you're an early riser in need of a light breakfast, try the **Sunrise Cafe** at 693A Front St., (☎ **808/661-3326**) in Lahaina, where you can get coffee and great pastries starting at 5:30am. **Marie Callendar's** in the Lahaina Cannery Mall (☎ **808/667-7437**) also opens early (7am) and serves full breakfasts; try the macadamia nut and banana waffles. If you're Upcountry in Paia, the **Peaches and Crumble Cafe and Bakery** (2 Baldwin Ave., ☎ **808/579-8612**) is an excellent choice for baked goods. Looking to try something new? Head for the **Komoda Store and Bakery** (☎ **808/572-7261**) in Makawao. It opens at 6:30am, and people line up to get their masaladas and cream buns. If you simply can't live without your morning bagel, **Maui Bakery Bagelry & Deli,** at 201 Dairy Rd. (☎ **808/871-4825**) in Kahului, will satisfy you.

---

example, zuri gschnetzlets, sliced veal with a creamy mushroom sauce), and a variety of classic French dishes (steak au poivre, filet mignon, and rack of lamb). Desserts might include chocolate mousse cake, macadamia nut ice cream, or Fire & Ice (Haagen-Dazs Macadamia Nut Brittle ice cream, fresh pineapples and bananas, flambéed with dark Island Rum). Most people, however, come for the large variety of beers and for the nightlife, which typically begins at 10pm.

MODERATE

Paia Fish Market Restaurant

100 Hana Hwy. ☎ **808/579-8030.** No reservations. Main courses $3–$13.95. No credit cards. Daily 11am–9:30pm. SEAFOOD.

Paia is known for its offbeat restaurants, and the Paia Fish Market is no exception. If you eat in, you can sit at one of a few heavy wood picnic tables; otherwise, you can take food out—whatever suits your fancy. No matter what you do, you'll have an opportunity to meet some of the locals, many of whom rave about the fish market. Menu offerings include all varieties of charbroiled seafood—snapper, mahimahi, swordfish, ahi, opah, salmon, and ono—to name a few. Fish and chips (cooked in cholesterol-free oil and lightly coated in a beer batter) is served at lunch and dinner. If you prefer, there are scallops and chips, shrimp and chips, and calamari and chips. Several pasta options are available, as well as some Mexican dishes (fajitas and quesadillas). The Fish Market also serves steak (filet mignon or New York steak) together with home fries or Cajun rice and cole slaw. You will also find a decent selection of beers and wines.

INEXPENSIVE

Pic-nics

30 Baldwin Ave. ☎ **808/579-8021.** No reservations. Menu items $1.25–$15.95. No credit cards. Daily 7am–7pm. SANDWICHES/BURGERS.

If you stay on Maui long enough, you'll become curious about Pic-nics' spinach nut burgers because everyone on the island is singing their praises. The tropical decor is cheerful and inviting, and the food is delectable. The spinach nut burger, made of spinach, chopped nuts, sesame seeds, and spices, is served topped with Cheddar cheese on a whole-wheat bun. It is so well known that it has been featured in major magazines and newspapers all over the country. Other popular sandwiches include the picnic burger supreme— lean ground beef topped with Cheddar and Swiss cheeses, two strips of bacon, tomato, lettuce, sweet Maui onion, and mayonnaise. The Windsurfer is a variation on the spinach nut burger—it's topped with bacon, Swiss and Cheddar cheeses, lettuce, tomato, sprouts, and dressing on a whole-wheat bun. There are other sandwiches—ham and Swiss, turkey, roast beef, and BLTs. At breakfast try the Paia Plantation Breakfast—scrambled eggs topped with Cheddar cheese on buttered toast served with papaya-pineapple jam and Kona coffee (all for only $3.95!). There's also an assortment of fresh-baked pastries and muffins, and a number of coffees and frozen yogurt treats (shakes and sundaes).

If you're headed out on an excursion and know you'll be passing Pic-nics (for example, on your way to Hana), give them a call in advance and order a picnic lunch so you can pick it up on your way.

HANA

Hana Gardenland Cafe

Kalo Rd. ☎ **808/248-8975.** No reservations. Breakfast items $2.25–$4.75; lunch and snack items $2.75–$6.95. MC, V. Daily 9am–8pm. SANDWICHES/REGIONAL SPECIALTIES.

The Hana Gardenland Cafe is the best place in Hana to stop for breakfast or lunch, and it's a favorite choice for celebrities such as Mary Steenburgen, Bob Weir, and Tom Robbins. Hillary Clinton stopped here three mornings in a row during a visit to Maui. Order your food at the window and enjoy your surroundings in the palm frond–covered patio, or wander through the art gallery and gift shop located adjacent to the restaurant (to your right as you entered). Favorites here include the guacamole (served with taro chips) and enormous sandwiches at lunch. Breakfast specialties include homemade granola, banana bread, and a variety of egg dishes (served with Maui Crunch toast). There's an espresso bar. The art gallery displays the work of local and regional artists, and the gift shop is full of wonderful local souvenirs (none of which are trashy or plastic).

8

What to See & Do on Maui

Most visitors to Maui have only a few things in mind—salt water, sand, sun, and tropical drinks. While all of those are perfectly legitimate vacation expectations, Maui offers much more. From the slopes of Haleakala to the Iao Valley and all the way to Hana, the vistas and varieties of plant and animal life are unequaled anywhere else in the United States. There are art galleries and museums, as well as a brand-new cultural center. This chapter will cover all of the above, as well as shopping and nightlife.

SUGGESTED ITINERARIES

If You Have 1 Day

What a horrifying prospect! First and foremost, get an early start. Before you head to the beach you might want to make a reservation for an evening luau. Most hotels hold their own luaus, so check with your concierge. If your hotel doesn't have a luau, the Old Lahaina Luau would be an excellent choice. If you've been touring the other islands for some time and have had your share of luaus, try a sunset sail instead (many hotels offer their own).

Since it generally takes a long time to get from one town to another, a major excursion (such as a trip to Haleakala or Upcountry) probably wouldn't be worth the effort. Instead, I'd recommend that you spend the morning and early afternoon on the beach near your hotel. For lunch, head to Lahaina. Try dining at Avalon or David Paul's Lahaina Grill. After lunch, take a walk along Front Street, where you can visit some interesting shops and art galleries. You might also enjoy taking the walking tour that has been prepared by the Lahaina Historical Foundation. It will take you to all the historically significant sites in Lahaina; later in this chapter you can read more about some of the stops on the tour.

After exploring Lahaina, you'll probably be ready to give your weary feet a rest. Head back to the hotel and get ready for that luau!

If You Have 2 Days

If you have only two days on Maui you'll still have to hustle, but you should be able to squeeze in a major excursion.

Day 1   Spend Day 1 as described above, but try to go to bed early, because you'll need to get up early on your second day in order to take an excursion.

Day 2   Most of the island's major excursions will take a full day, so plan carefully. If you want to see the sun rise atop Haleakala, you'll have to get an early start because it could take up to three hours to reach the summit. If you simply can't get up that early, another possibility is a trip to the Iao Valley in the morning. Save time by asking your hotel to prepare a picnic lunch—this will enable you to take a short hike through the valley without having to head back to town when you get hungry.

Later in the day, if you still want to go to the top of Haleakala, you could try to catch the sunset (which is also spectacular). Be sure to take a sweater or jacket because the temperature drops dramatically on Haleakala when the sun goes down.

If you finish your hike fairly early in the afternoon, but are not interested in driving to the top of Haleakala, you could take a trip Upcountry. En route you might want to make a quick detour to the Alexander & Baldwin Sugar Museum. After that, head for Hana Highway and drive up to Paia, where you'll find some unique boutiques and excellent restaurants. If you want to see some incredible windsurfing (or do some of your own), go just beyond Paia town on Hana Highway to Hookipa Beach Park. When you're finished there, turn around and go back to Paia town and go left on Baldwin Avenue through Paia into the town of Makawao. Here you'll find some interesting shops, several wonderful art galleries, and some of the island's finest restaurants (which you might want to keep in mind for dinner—you could even make a reservation while you're in town).

If you still have time (and energy) after you've visited Makawao, there's one more stop you might make before driving back to your hotel. Check to see if Tedeschi Vineyards is still open. If it is, drive up there and enjoy a taste of Maui blanc (the famous pineapple wine) or even the pineapple-passion fruit wine they just started making.

By the time you've done all (or most) of the above, you're probably ready for a substantial dinner. If spectacular views are more important to you than great food, try the Kula Lodge. If you'd rather have Italian food, return to Makawao and see if you can get a table at Casanova. Or, if seafood is what you crave, return to Paia and give Mama's Fish House a try.

If You Have 3 Days

Days 1 and 2   If you came to Maui to relax, then I'd recommend spending your first day on the beach. Go snorkeling, take a scuba-diving or surfing lesson, and if you're feeling particularly adventurous, go parasailing or take a helicopter ride. If you came to Maui to explore, then you could start your trip by following the itinerary presented under Day 2.

On your second day, follow the itinerary for Day 1 or Day 2, depending on what strikes your fancy. If you've already done the Upcountry tour (or Haleakala), take the other trip suggested for Day 2.

Day 3   If you're still energized, now's the time to take a trip to Hana. Start early: It will take you at least three hours to get there and three hours to return; if you're not a confident driver, you need to make every effort to leave Hana well before dark because the road is very very curvy and can be dangerous. You'll probably want to spend several hours exploring the waterfalls and blue pools in the area, and if you're a hiker, you'll find much to do in Hana. There are no restaurants along the way, but if you leave early you won't be ready for lunch until after you get to Hana. The Hana Gardenland Cafe is an excellent spot for lunch. Otherwise, pack a picnic.

If you want to spend your last night in Hana, there is an airport where you can catch a plane that will get you to Kahului in time for your departure from Maui (you will even have time to spare). If you've never driven to Hana before, don't be tempted to fly there—the drive is most of the fun.

If You Have 5 Days or More

If you've got at least 5 days, you can take it easy

Days 1–3 Spend a couple of mornings on the beach and do only one activity a day. Take one afternoon to explore Lahaina and another to hike in the Iao Valley or visit Paia, Makawao, and the winery. On the third day, try to make it to the top of Haleakala for the sunrise and then spend the afternoon relaxing on the beach.

Days 4–5 On Day 4, go to Hana and spend the night. On Day 5, either continue exploring Hana or head back down and take a trip you didn't have time for on Days 1 through 3 (perhaps a trip to Iao Valley).

1 West Maui

West Maui is the island's playground: Great restaurants and interesting shops stand side by side, and beautiful resorts stand majestically along the coastline. If there's an activity in which you would like to participate during your stay on Maui, it probably originates somewhere in West Maui. Many locals refer to Maui's western shore as the "New York City" of Maui.

LAHAINA

Lahaina, meaning "merciless sun," is one of the hottest spots on the island—and not just because of its temperature. From the founding of this small town, Lahaina has been one of the centers of activity on Maui. Maui's King Kahekili called Lahaina home until King Kamehameha's troops defeated him in the Iao Valley in the late 1700s. Then it was Kamehameha I who set up his power base in Lahaina. Today, during your stay in Lahaina, you can still visit the ruins of Kamehameha I's brick palace. It remained the seat of Hawaiian power until Kamehameha III moved it to Honolulu in the mid-1800s.

In 1819 the whaling men arrived in search of humpback whales, and they found much more than they could have hoped for—Hawaiian women, grog shops, and plenty of hospitality. They turned Lahaina on its ear for about 5 years before the missionaries arrived and began to put an end to their lawless ways. The missionaries prohibited the sale of alcohol and helped build a jail to hold unruly sailors (see below for details). Rev. William Richards built his home in Lahaina (which the sailors, angered by the meddlesome missionaries, tried to destroy with cannonball fire), and more missionaries, such as Rev. Dwight Baldwin, followed. The Lahainaluna School was built in the West Maui Mountains, overlooking Lahaina town, and the island's first printing press was delivered to Lahaina, making it the point of origin for the very first newspaper in the Hawaiian Islands. When Lahaina's days as the whaling capital of the Pacific came to an end, Mauians turned their attention away from the ocean and back to the land to boost the economy. At that time the island's abundant growth of wild sugarcane became important. Soon thereafter, the sugar industry came to Maui in full force, but it didn't revive Lahaina's economy. Lahaina reverted to its sleepy ways and remained that way until the mid-1960s, when tourism became the town's major draw.

HISTORIC LAHAINA ATTRACTIONS

In the pamphlet *Lahaina Historical Guide,* obtainable at virtually any hotel or at the Maui Visitors Bureau, you will find a walking tour of the town of Lahaina. Each of

Lahaina Attractions

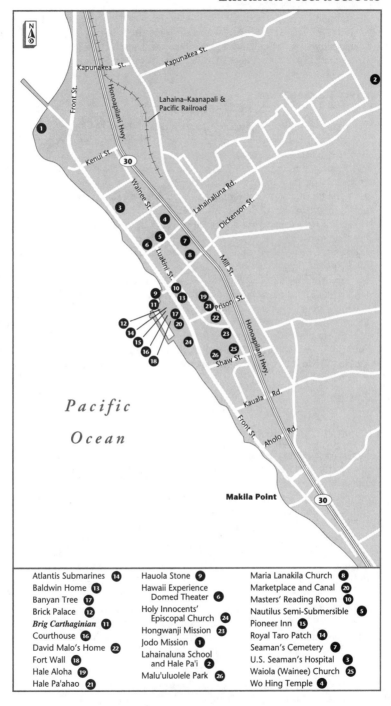

Atlantis Submarines **14**

Baldwin Home **13**

Banyan Tree **17**

Brick Palace **12**

Brig Carthaginian **11**

Courthouse **16**

David Malo's Home **22**

Fort Wall **18**

Hale Aloha **19**

Hale Pa'ahao **21**

Hauola Stone **9**

Hawaii Experience
   Domed Theater **6**

Holy Innocents'
   Episcopal Church **24**

Hongwanji Mission **23**

Jodo Mission **1**

Lahainaluna School
   and Hale Pa'i **2**

Malu'uluolele Park **26**

Maria Lanakila Church **8**

Marketplace and Canal **20**

Masters' Reading Room **10**

Nautilus Semi-Submersible **5**

Pioneer Inn **15**

Royal Taro Patch **14**

Seaman's Cemetery **7**

U.S. Seaman's Hospital **3**

Waiola (Wainee) Church **25**

Wo Hing Temple **4**

the stops on the tour is marked with a signposted number so you can find your way around easily. I have elaborated on some of the information you will find in the guide to enhance your understanding of the various sites. Though I have left out several sites covered in the pamphlet, those I have written about here appear in order by number following the walking tour.

Masters' Reading Room
Corner of Front and Dickenson Sts. ☎ **808/661-3262.**

When ships first began landing at Lahaina Wharf in the early 1800s, sailors had virtually unlimited access to anything they might need or want—fresh water, grog, hogs, and fresh produce; and women would swim out to the ships as they arrived. Seamen looked forward to stopping in Lahaina, but all that changed shortly after the arrival of the missionaries in 1823. By 1825 the 23 grog shops that once lined the streets were shut down due to the prohibition of prostitution and the distribution, production, and sale of alcohol. Sailors who made return visits to their own private piece of paradise were shocked to find that all of their pleasures/vices had been banned. At this time the Masters' Reading Room was conceived as a "shore retreat for both officers and seamen." Many of the town residents and the seamen themselves donated funds and building materials to the reading room. The lower floor served as a storage area, while the upstairs, with its observation deck, was purely for the comfort of the masters and officers. For about 10 years the Masters' Reading Room was an extremely popular onshore gathering spot for the men who docked their ships in Lahaina Harbor, but by 1844, with the increase of traffic on the waterway, hotels and bars began reopening and the reading room lost its appeal. In 1846 Dr. Dwight Baldwin (who lived in the building next door) bought the reading room at an auction for $70 to accommodate his growing family. In 1855 he divided the room in two and took tenants.

Baldwin Home
Front St. ☎ **808/661-3262.** Admission $3 adults; $2.50 seniors; $1 children. Daily 9am–4:30pm.

In 1830 Rev. Dwight Baldwin and his young bride Charlotte left their New England home and sailed for the Hawaiian Islands where Rev. Baldwin was to serve as a doctor at a "medical station" in Waimea on the Big Island. In 1835 he was transferred to Lahaina's Wainee Church, where he hoped to continue full-time in his missionary pursuits. It soon became clear that he was the only missionary in Maui County qualified to practice medicine, and thus continued his work as a doctor in Lahaina.

The oldest building standing in Lahaina today, the Baldwin Home was built in 1834. The walls were constructed of coral, stone, and timber. Today visitors may view the original construction through a cutout section of the inner wall in the back room. Though the house was built in 1834, the Baldwins did not occupy it until 1838, but they remained there until 1871. The original building consisted of only one floor, but as the family grew, a bedroom and study were added, and finally a second story was built. At one time a total of six children were housed within the coral walls of this modest home; as you tour the interior, you'll get an idea of what their lives were like. You'll also be able to view some of Rev. Baldwin's medical tools, old photos, furnishings, books, and kitchen implements.

Royal Taro Patch
From the Baldwin Home, cross Front Street and head between the buildings on Market Street (which dead-ends rather quickly) and the Lahaina Library. The Royal Taro Patch used to be on the *makai* side of the library. Taro, which is a staple of the

Hawaiian diet and is used to make poi, also plays an important role in Hawaiian mythology. It is said that Wakea's firstborn son (Wakea being the god, "the sky father," from which Hawaii's ali'i were said to have been descended), Haloanaka, was born somewhat prematurely and died shortly after birth. He was buried at one end of Wakea's house, and from his body grew a taro plant. The leaf of the taro was named *laukapalili*, or "quivering leaf," while the stem was called *haloa*. The second child born to Wakea was named Haloa, and it is believed that Haloa was the father of humankind.

The making of a taro patch was quite an undertaking. Taro was best grown on land that could easily be irrigated (some of the land was considered *malo'o*, or "dry"). Once a good patch of land was found, banks of earth were formed and packed down (trampled by the farmer's own feet) around it. Water was then allowed to flow freely into the patch. After a period of time, when the patch became dry, the earthen dams that surrounded the patch were strengthened with stones, palm leaves, and sugarcane plants until the banks were watertight. The soil was then turned, wetted, and packed down. Rows were marked, and taro tops were planted in each row. From that point forward the taro patch would be watered regularly. About a year after the planting the taro would be ready for picking.

There are many varieties of taro, ranging from kai (said to yield excellent poi) to the *haokea* (which has a blander flavor than kai when mashed into poi). Both of the aforementioned types, which are in the "blue" taro family, represent the top and bottom of the scale—there are, in fact, scores of other varieties in the same family that fall between kai and haokea. One very special taro, the *pi'iali'i* (or "king's choice"), was known by its pink-purple coloring and is believed to produce a superb poi. In addition to poi, taro was also used in the manufacture of a medicinal drink.

Several historical accounts that include references to this particular taro patch state that King Kamehameha himself could often be seen working in the taro patch in an effort to teach his people that there is dignity to be found in heavy physical labor. One account documenting these activities says that, "The king and his wife, the queen, his trusted friend and official, John Young, and his wife, and several others in the party . . . were without shoes and stockings and hats . . . and no more clothes than necessary. They were as happy as any children playing in summer showers."

Hauola Stone

From the taro patch, head toward the water, then proceed to your right, and soon you will see the Hauola Stone (Healing Stone), located in the water on your left (look for the Hawaii Visitors Bureau marker). Stones played a large role in the life of early Hawaiians. They were fashioned into tools such as axes, poi pounders, and squid-fishing implements and were even used to polish wooden bowls and canoes. Some stones (more likely, boulders) were worshiped for their healing properties.

Ancient Hawaiians believed that an ill person needed only to sit on this Healing Stone, while their submerged legs were being washed by the waves, to be cured.

The Hauola Stone was also used as a hiding place for *piko*, or the umbilical cords of newborns. It was traditional for Hawaiian families to hide the umbilical cords, and if they were left completely undisturbed, the child whose piko had been hidden would one day become a chief. The Hauola Stone was a logical place to hide these precious items because it was a sacred place; thus, it was unlikely that anyone would try to violate the stone's secret crevices.

Brick Palace

Just across Wharf Street from the Pioneer Inn, near the library, is a site that is extremely important in the history of Maui. In 1802, when King Kamehameha came to Maui on his way to conquer Kauai, he decided to remain in Lahaina for more than a year. Several years earlier, a brick house had been constructed for the king in Lahaina by two Australian bricklayers; King Kamehameha made this building his headquarters during his stay on Maui while he was busy consecrating temples, collecting taxes from other islands, and planning his attack on Kauai. The palace is no longer standing, but it managed to survive for about 70 years after it was built—quite a feat for the islands' first brick structure.

Brig *Carthaginian*

Lahaina Wharf. ☎ **808/661-8527.** Admission $3. Daily 10am–4:30pm.

The brig *Carthaginian* is an authentic replica of a 19th-century whaling vessel. The original *Carthaginian* was built under the direction of Captain Allan Villers, an expert on square-rigged ships, for the filming of a movie and was later docked and used as a museum. During a trip to Honolulu for drydock in 1972, the ship was unfortunately lost at sea. Luckily, a new brig (the one you see today) was found in Europe, and a crew from Lahaina sailed the ship from Europe to its new home port at the Lahaina Wharf. During the hurricane a few years back that devastated Kauai, residents feared that the *Carthaginian* would once again be lost at sea, but as you can see, the brig was spared.

Currently operated by the Lahaina Restoration Foundation, the *Carthaginian* museum features audiovisual displays that do an excellent job of informing visitors about whales and 19th-century whaling life. Though the ship looks large from the outside, the spaces within are rather small and cramped. Don't let that deter you, however; going into the ship is the best way for you to gain an understanding of how the whaling men lived while they were at sea.

Pioneer Inn

658 Wharf St. ☎ **808/661-3636.**

On October 9, 1901, the Pioneer Hotel Company, Ltd., came to Lahaina to open a hotel and a liquor business. Within a year the Pioneer Hotel had opened and begun what was to be a very prosperous enterprise. When prohibition was enforced by the missionaries, almost two decades after the hotel opened, business slacked off because a large part of the hotel's profit was came from the sale of alcohol, especially in its saloon. At that time, George Freeland, the hotel's general manager, bought out the stockholders and became sole owner of the establishment. The main building of the hotel served Lahaina residents and visitors in its original form up until the mid-1960s, when tourism to the island began to grow significantly. In 1966 a new wing was added to accommodate these new guests, and with the new wing the hotel formed a C shape around a lovely courtyard. Most casual observers cannot tell which part of the building is the addition because the architectural details were duplicated so carefully. Today the Pioneer Inn, which still stands on its original site, is one of the island's least expensive accommodations. For decades the Pioneer Inn's saloon was one of Lahaina's favorite watering holes, which often created problems for those who wanted to sleep in the rooms on the upper floors. Since the recent renovation (and new limited bar hours), noise is less of a problem.

Banyan Tree

The first time I visited Lahaina I was very young, and so my memories of Maui were somewhat clouded, but one recollection has always remained perfectly clear. It is my memory of this wonderful banyan tree *(Ficus benghalensis)*. With branches that cover almost an acre of land and rise to a height of about 50 feet, and about 12 trunks, it's not easy to forget.

A member of the fig family, the tree came all the way from India and was presented as a gift to Lahaina's Smith family in the early 1870s. William Owen Smith was the sheriff of Lahaina, and he planted the tree here in this central location on April 24, 1873. The banyan tree got its name from Hindu traders (banyans) who used to hawk their wares in the shade of the tree's canopy. Throughout history banyans have been gathering places for townspeople and visitors, and the tradition continues in Lahaina. Everything from luaus to children's festivals have taken place here, and the benches scattered among the aerial roots are almost always filled with tired tourists or residents on a lunch break. In the evening, hundreds of mynah birds perch on the tree's branches and serenade visitors with a cacophonous and unrelenting tune.

The banyan tree produces a small red fruit that is edible but not very tasty.

Note: If you are traveling with children, please try to keep them from swinging on the tree's aerial roots because repeated stress weakens the roots and, eventually, the tree itself.

Courthouse

On the other side of the banyan tree on Wharf Street is the old courthouse. Like his predecessor, Kamehameha I, Kamehameha III built himself a palace on Maui. It was called *Hale Piula* (or "House with the Tin Roof"), and like the Baldwin Home, it was built of coral bricks. Though the two-story palace was said to be under constant repair, it was supposed to have been very comfortable for guests who received the "royal" treatment. One visitor's account states that after a long and satisfying lunch, Kamehameha's servants brought an enormous bed into the "dining room," and they all laid down together for an afternoon nap.

In January 1848 the dilapidated palace was restored and converted into a courthouse. For 10 years it served Maui's judges, but in 1858 a meteorological event—known as the Kauaula wind—blew through town and toppled the courthouse. Rebuilt in 1859, the courthouse building contained a jail (now used by the Lahaina Art Society as a gallery and museum), a post office (in operation since the new courthouse opened), and a police station.

Fort Wall

Adjacent to the courthouse, you'll see the "ruins" of the old Fort Wall. Built between 1831 and 1832 by order of Maui's governor Hoapili as a show of force against the antics of the wild and woolly whaling men who wintered in Lahaina, the old fort reportedly had 20-foot walls and covered 1 acre. Every evening a soldier would march upon the ramparts beating a drum as a warning to the sailors to return to their ships or be jailed. The fort, which housed about 60 fighting men, was well equipped with rifles, bayonets, and swords. The government ordered the destruction of the coral block fort in 1854, and the coral bricks were moved to Prison Street and used in the building of the prison, Hale Paahao. Today, the ruin you'll see is not an actual ruin; it is a modern, partial reconstruction. Had the entire fort been rebuilt, considerable damage would have been inflicted on the banyan tree, so the restoration specialists opted to reconstruct only a small section of the fort.

Marketplace and Canal

On the other side of Canal Street from Banyan Tree Square, there was once an interesting marketplace and canal that breathed life into the daily comings and goings of Old Lahaina. During Lahaina's whaling days there was a canal that ran between the waterfront and Front Street. Whaling men would board their ships' boats, which were loaded with supplies that they used for bartering in the government-regulated canal marketplace. The market, which was probably established before 1833, was covered by a "large straw house" that ran the entire length of the canal. Along each side of the canal, stalls were set up and were rented by the governor to merchants who bid the highest price. Whalers would steer their boats through the canal, bartering for provisions along the way. Because native women were prohibited from visiting men on the whaling ships, women were not allowed anywhere near or inside the marketplace to ensure that they would not hitch a ride back with the sailors to the whaling ships. If any women were caught in the vicinity of the marketplace, they were fined $1. There were also strict rules of conduct for the merchants. They were not allowed to "overcharge, undersell, wrangle, break bargains, entice, or pursue" a purchaser. If they participated in any of these activities, their merchandise was taken from them.

Holy Innocents' Episcopal Church
561 Front St. ☎ **808/661-4202.**

Located off Front Street, not far from Prison Street, you'll find a quaint little Episcopal church. It was particularly important in Hawaii's history because it marked the beginning of the organized Anglican Church in the islands.

In 1861, Rev. Thomas Nettleship Staley was consecrated as the first bishop of Hawaii. The next year, Rev. Staley, along with King Kamehameha IV and a Rev. William R. Scott, arrived in Lahaina and began leading services in a schoolroom on December 14 (12 days after their arrival). Kamehameha had translated the first part of the *Book of Common Prayer,* and Rev. Scott found a residence. Scott remained in residence for one year and was replaced by Archdeacon George Mason. He and his wife headed up a school for boys and a school for girls, respectively.

Much later, in 1874, money for the procurement of the plot of land at the corner of Front and Prison Streets was raised, and in 1909 construction of the Church of the Holy Innocents began. (Incidentally, the site of the church was formerly the site of the home of Kamehameha I's daughter.) Today you can visit the church and see some rather interesting artwork, created in 1940 by DeLos Blackmar.

The Episcopal Cemetery, where a number of early Mauians are interred, is located on Wainee Street.

Waiola (Wainee) Church
535 Wainee St. ☎ **808/661-4349.**

The church you see today was built on the original site of the first Hawaiian Christian services, which took place in 1823. The first house of worship was built here in 1832, but it lost its steeple and half of the roof in a windstorm on February 20, 1858. Eventually, with the help of fund-raising Hawaiians, the sale of the old timber, and other donations, the church was rededicated on March 31, 1859. After the reconstruction, the stone church survived until June 28, 1894, when a group of Hawaiians, angered by the overthrow of the monarchy, set fire to it. S. E. Bishop reported that the pastor of the church at the time, Rev. A. Pali, was openly in favor of the overthrow of the monarchy and "had become obnoxious to a majority of his people on account of politics."

It was three years before the church was rebuilt, and though it remained intact for many years, it was once again damaged by fire on October 20, 1947. This time the fire was accidental, but, once more the church was reconstructed. Only a few years later, in January 1951, after termites had made sawdust of the church's foundation, a Kauaula wind blew through town at 80 miles an hour. It literally picked the church up off the ground and tossed it back to earth, where it landed in a heap of rubble and splintered timber. The church you see today was rebuilt and rededicated in April 1953: At that time the name was changed from Wainee Church to Waiola Church.

The church's cemetery is probably the most important burial site on the island, for it holds the remains of many of Maui's most prominent leaders. King Kaumuali'i, once the monarch of Kauai, is buried here. Queen Keopuolani and her daughter, Princess Nahi'ena'ena, as well as Governor Hoapili are all buried near one another. High Chiefess Liliha, granddaughter of King Kahekili, who led a rebellion with 1,000 soldiers while she was governor of Oahu, found her final resting place here. Finally, the Wainee Cemetery is also the burial site of Rev. Richards and some of his young family members.

Note: This cemetery is considered sacred by Hawaiians, so please be respectful while visiting.

Maluluolele Park

To me, Maluluolele Park is one of the most fascinating places in Lahaina—not because of the parking lot, baseball diamond, or tennis and basketball courts, but because of what used to be here. Instead of these playing fields, try to imagine a pond, and just at the edge of the pond, connected to Front Street by a small bridge, Mokuula, the residence of King Kamehameha III. The royal residence was nothing more than a hut, but it sat on an island surrounded by waters protected by the great dragon/lizard, Kihawahine. The royal family believed that Kihawahine had special powers, so when Kamehameha I took Maui into his kingdom, he claimed the island and the water around it as a sacred spot for Hawaiian royalty. The king also had a palace, but Mokuula was his own private sanctuary; very few outsiders were allowed the pleasure of visiting the king here.

It is reported that Mokuula was home to many Maui chiefs and three kings, and served as the final resting place for several members of the royal family. Unfortunately, in 1918, the pond was filled in and the island was razed.

David Malo's Home

Born around 1793 to Aoao and his wife, Heone, in North Kona, Hawaii, David Malo was a prominent figure in Maui's history. As a young man he became acquainted with High Chief Kuakini, brother of Queen Ka'ahumanu. Because of his connection with the royal family, Malo was in a position to be able to learn a great deal about the history, traditions, and legends that played such a large role in Hawaiian life. He observed and recorded everything he learned about Hawaiian lore; it is thanks to Malo that we now have some knowledge of Old Hawaiian traditions. Compiled under the title *Hawaiian Antiquities* (translated from Hawaiian in 1898), Malo's writings have aided in the resurrection of certain Hawaiian traditions, such as the hula and the art of making kapa cloth. David Malo's home used to stand not far from the corner of Prison Road and Wainee Street.

Hale Paahao (Lahaina Prison)
Prison Rd. ☎ **808/667-1985.**

From the early 1830s, Lahaina's prisoners were kept at the old fort (see above). However, in 1851 the fort's doctor reported that the prisoners were coming down with illnesses that could have been prevented. Inmates had to sleep on the ground, and the doctor believed that if they had a dry place to sleep, they would be less susceptible to illness. No one is absolutely certain if this request was the reason for the construction of Hale Paahao, but work on the new prison had begun by the end of the year. The site for the prison (which, today, is near the corner of Prison and Wainee Streets) was wrested under duress from the Hawaiian who owned it. The superintendent of public works in Honolulu requested that Lahaina authorities make every effort to "depreciate [the land's] value . . . letting [the owner] know at the same time that if the price is too high the Government will take it anyhow and pay him what they please."

Construction of a wooden prison house had begun in 1852, but it wasn't until 1853 that funds were appropriated to build a brick prison wall. When the old fort was demolished in 1854, some of the bricks were used in the wall's construction. The old prison cells were restored in 1959, and the rest of the structure was reconstructed in 1988.

Hale Aloha

When the Protestants arrived on Maui, they also built churches and meetinghouses. The Hale Lai, one of the original Protestant meetinghouses, was erected in the early 1800s for prayer groups, church meetings, and religious schooling. However, by 1855 it had fallen into a state of disrepair. Its most obvious problem was a leaky thatched roof, but when plans were made to reconstruct the roof using shingles, it was discovered that the walls were structurally unsound, so it was decided to tear down the old meetinghouse and build a new one.

Protestant leaders decided that the new house should be built in "commemoration of God's causing Lahaina to escape the smallpox, while it desolated Oahu in 1853, carrying off some 5,000 or 6,000 of its population." The new meetinghouse was to be called *Hale Aloha,* or "House of Love." The construction of Hale Aloha was completed in May 1858, almost exactly three years since the decision had been made to rebuild. By 1860 the government declared Hale Aloha fit to be used as an English school, and about 140 students were enrolled. Two years later the building was rented to the Anglican Church, which held the first Anglican services in Lahaina. In 1908 the building was repaired and became the parish house for Wainee (now Waiola) Church.

Maria Lanakila Church
712 Wainee St. ☎ **808/661-0552.**

Maria Lanakila Catholic Church (Our Lady of Victory) is the oldest Catholic church on Maui; it was dedicated on September 8, 1858. The present church was remodeled in 1928 and restored in 1995. The parish community began on April 21, 1846, with the arrival of permanent missionary priests from France.

Hongwanji Mission
551 Wainee St. ☎ **808/661-0640.**

Since 1910, the Hongwanji, members of Lahaina's largest Buddhist sect, have been meeting here on the grounds of the current Hongwanji Mission (erected in 1927). Originally, the Hongwanji built a small temple and started a language school. Today various Buddhist celebrations are held at the Hongwanji Mission.

Seamen's Cemetery

The original Seamen's Cemetery was located just adjacent to the one you see today on Wainee Street, between Dickenson and Paneawa Streets. In it were buried "the wandering sons of the ocean." Most of the headstones have long since disappeared, but the area is now maintained by the Lahaina Restoration Foundation, so—hopefully—there will be no further damage.

Lahainaluna School and Hale Pai
980 Lahainaluna Rd. ☎ **808/661-8384.**

When the Lahainaluna School was established in the early 1830s, there weren't many books around for the students to read, so an old Ramage printing press was sent from Honolulu to Lahaina in 1833. Not only did it print translations of school texts, but it also produced Hawaii's first newspaper, *Kalama Hawaii* ("Torch of Hawaii"), in 1834. When the school grew, a permanent structure, now known as Hale Pai, was built to house the printing press. Not long afterward the *Grammar of the Hawaiian Language and Dictionary of the Hawaiian Language* was printed.

Initially the press was operated by whaling men with printing experience. Around 1842, after the school's enrollment had more than quadrupled, students were instructed in the art of printing and binding books.

Today, visitors can go inside Hale Pai by appointment. Call the above number for information.

Wo Hing Temple

Front St. ☎ **808/661-5553.** Admission free. Daily 10am–4pm.

The Chinese came to Maui by the hundreds to work in the sugarcane fields and on the pineapple plantations; in the early 1900s some of them formed what we know as the Wo Hing Society. The Chinese, however, call it the Chee Kung Tong; this was a secret society that originated hundreds of years ago during the Manchu dynasty. Originally founded as a fraternal order, members of this society were considered equal and were sworn to protect and help each other according to need. Eventually, a chapter of the society was established everywhere that Chinese found themselves together in large numbers. The original group that attended the Wo Hing Temple numbered only about 100.

If you're interested in the history of the Chinese in Lahaina, head inside and look at the exhibit that has been set up by the Lahaina Restoration Foundation. Be sure also to visit the cookhouse, where you can see old movies of Hawaii shot by Thomas Edison in 1898 and 1903, as well as cooking displays.

U.S. Seamen's Hospital

1024 Front St. ☎ **808/661-3262** for information.

No one knows exactly when this hospital was established, but there is a notation by Herman Melville that one of his shipmates on the *Acushnet* died at the hospital in 1843. Built of coral blocks, much like the Baldwin House, the Seamen's Hospital is a two-story building with lanais that run the length of each floor. Some accounts say that the hospital was leased by the United States from King Kamehameha III in an attempt to get thousands of ailing American sailors off the streets and beaches. It was common practice at that time for ship captains to simply dump unwanted crew members off in the Hawaiian Islands before sailing onward to the Far East where they would do their trading.

In 1865 the Sisters of the Society of the Holy Trinity bought the old hospital for less than $1,000 and opened the St. Cross School for Girls. The school later moved to Honolulu, at which time the Episcopal minister took up a 30-year residence here with his family. In 1908 the old Seamen's Hospital was in horrible shape; not long thereafter, it became part of the Bishop estate. The Lahaina Restoration Foundation bought the building in 1974 and has restored it to its former glory. Visitors are most welcome.

Jodo Mission

Heading out of Lahaina in the direction of Kaanapali, you'll pass a sign that reads JESUS COMING SOON (immortalized in a song by the Eagles). Right after you pass the sign, turn left down Ala Moana Street. As soon as you make the turn, you'll see the pagoda. As you approach the pagoda you'll also see a giant, 3½-ton bronze Buddha. It was placed here in 1968 to commemorate the 100th anniversary of Japanese immigration to Hawaii, and it has the distinct honor of being the largest

Buddha in existence outside Japan. This is a perfect spot to get away from hectic Front Street and enjoy some peace and quiet.

OTHER LAHAINA ATTRACTIONS

Hawaii Experience Domed Theater

824 Front St. ☎ **808/661-8314.** Admission $6.95 adults, $3.95 children. Daily, with hourly showings 10am–10pm.

A relatively new addition to the Front Street scene is the Hawaii Experience Domed Theater, where visitors can view a 45-minute film on a 180-degree, 60-foot-long screen. The film, *Hawaii: Islands of the Gods,* is literally a journey around the islands. You'll feel as though you're piloting the helicopter as it takes you over the volcano on the Big Island, into canyons, and along the Maui coastline. A bicycle ride down the curvy road from Haleakala gives you the feeling that you're on the bike but have absolutely no control over which way you're turning. You'll go on an underwater scuba-diving expedition, and you'll see a sunset hula show. Basically, the Hawaii Experience Domed Theater is a great place for everyone to explore the hidden wonders of the islands without having to pay the high prices.

Note: If you're prone to motion sickness, you might want to skip this experience. If you want to give it a try anyway, and you begin to feel nauseous during the movie, look away from the screen for a few moments. Otherwise, motion sickness bags are provided at every seat in the theater.

Atlantis Submarines

665 Front St. ☎ **808/667-2224.** Admission to full Odyssey tour $79 adults, $38 children 12 and under (must be at least 3 feet tall); regular tour $59 adults, $28 children. Two dives daily between 9am and 6pm.

If you don't feel like snorkeling or scuba diving, but you want to see Maui's tropical fish up close, perhaps you might enjoy an excursion on a working submarine. Well, on Maui, this is possible. Atlantis Submarines offers the island's only fully submersible submarine rides. A small boat, departing from Lahaina Harbor, takes visitors out to sea where the 65-foot, 80-ton submarine will submerge to a depth of over 100 feet. The vessel will then glide above reef formations, out of which colorful fish and other sea creatures will swim to meet the submarine. Most of the dives are made during daylight hours, but there is also a twilight trip, which would give those who prefer to snorkel or scuba dive during the day the opportunity to view sea life at a time when most snorkelers and scuba divers are heading out of the water. There are two options for dive packages; ask for details when you make your reservation.

To make reservations, call ahead, or go over to the Atlantis office in the Pioneer Inn Arcade in Lahaina town. The line is almost always long, and the excursion takes about 2 hours, so you need to allot either an entire morning or an afternoon.

Nautilus Semi-Submersible

Slip No. 10, Lahaina Harbor. ☎ **808/667-2133.** Admission $29.95 adults; $15.95 children 6–12; 5 and under free (one free child per paying adult).

If you're a little nervous about diving 150 feet in a submarine, but still want to feel as if you're swimming with the fish, perhaps Nautilus Semi-Submersible is more your speed. Though the Nautilus vessels don't submerge entirely, they do have underwater viewing cabins. The hour-long tours of reef areas are narrated, and a professional diver spends time outside the vessel searching for interesting marine life. Nautilus is also a good choice if your budget is tight—its tours are less expensive than excursions with Atlantis.

NEAR LAHAINA

About 5 miles outside Lahaina, heading toward Central Maui, you will come to Olowalu, a small town with a big history. It's so small, in fact, that if you blink while you're driving by, you might miss it. Your first clue that you're approaching the site of the famed Olowalu Massacre will be a slight drop in the speed limit. Captain Metcalf was responsible for the clash that led to the massacre here; though the massacre was short-lived, its effect on the history of the Hawaiian Islands was profound (for more information, see "A Look at the Past" in Chapter 2).

To view the petroglyphs, park in the lot in front of Chez Paul and the general store, and head around to the back of the restaurant where you'll find a dirt pathway leading to an old wooden stairway. It's quite a hike, so be prepared. Before attempting the hike, it would be advisable if you could find someone who knows the way because there are two paths, but only one leads to the petroglyphs.

LAHAINA SHOPPING

Shopping on Maui is limited mainly to malls and shopping centers—but some island towns (for example, Lahaina) do have interesting boutiques and art galleries.

Malls & Shopping Centers

The **Lahaina Cannery Mall** (open 9am–9pm) is located just outside of town, in the direction of Kaanapali. There you'll find everything from sundries to shoes and sunglasses. You'll find necessities plus certain unexpected items (for example, Kona coffee, Chocolate Chips of Maui [chocolate-dipped Maui potato chips—fantastic!], and chocolate-covered macadamia nuts to take [or send] home at **ABC Discount Stores** and **Longs Drug Stores**). You'll find exclusively designed, 100% cotton hand-blocked batik fashions at **Blue Ginger Designs.** Another clothing store, for men and women, is **Reyns**—they have a great collection of T-shirts. There's a branch of **Superwhale Children's Boutiques** (Superwhale specializes in aloha wear and outrageous sportswear for children of all ages). Speaking of kids, they'll love **Kite Fantasy,** which sells kites of all sorts, shapes, and varieties. **Hobie Hawaii** offers beach and sportswear for the whole family. **Lahaina Printsellers Ltd.**, a shop that specializes in antique maps and engravings, is represented here. Artist Stephen Strickland (an intaglio artist/engraver) gives free demonstrations here several days a week. **Maui on My Mind,** a lovely shop, features handmade jewelry and other types of wearable art. The **Guy Buffet Collection** is also worth a stop. Buffet, a Frenchman, is a popular island artist whose work (whimsical renditions of life on Maui) has been reproduced on scarves, dinnerware, shirts, and calendars (among others).

Lahaina Center, at 900 Front Street, on the western edge of Lahaina, is home to the famous **Hilo Hattie's,** where you can get aloha print shirts, dresses, sportswear, "funwear," and much more. If you're staying in one of the resorts (Kapalua and Kaanapali as well as all West Maui hotels) and don't have a car, don't worry—Hilo Hattie's will pick you up and shuttle you to the store. And when you arrive there, you'll be given a shell lei and a refreshing glass of tropical juice. Also at Lahaina Center is Hawaii's biggest department store, **Liberty House.** There you'll find the usual assortment of men's and women's fashions, lingerie, and bathing suits, as well as some beautiful items made in Hawaii. **Front Street Theatre** is a multiplex cinema that's also located in the center. In addition, at 2pm on Wednesday and Friday free hula shows are presented here.

The **Wharf Cinema Center** (open 9am to 10pm) is, as its name suggests, where you'll find many of Maui's first-run movies, but it's also a great place to do some shopping, snacking, and people-watching. If you suddenly find yourself in need of a new bathing suit, try **Island Swimwear.** A great shop for the kids is **Little Polynesians,** which specializes in tropical wear. If you'd like to take a fashion trip back in time, **Gigi's Fashion Boutique** has classic design clothing from the 1920s, 1930s, and 1940s. If, for some reason, you're looking for something in leather, **Gigi's Leather Boutique** is the place to stop. There's also a branch of the very expensive **Crazy Shirts** at the Cinema Center. **Tropical Artware** is a great place to pick up some unique jewelry (including, but not limited to, ear cuffs and toe rings). They also carry basketware and ceramics.

Places to grab a quick snack include Song's Oriental Kitchen, Lani's/Gekko Japanese Restaurant, Chun's Korean Bar-B-Cue, Greek Zorba, Blue Lagoon Steak and Seafood, Subway, and Orange Julius. If you crave something cool and refreshing, Lahaina Towne Ice Cream and TCBY should do the trick.

In addition, the Wharf Cinema Center hosts "Hawaiiana Arts & Crafts Works in Progress" where you can watch demonstrations by Maui artisans. The artists welcome questions as they work on (and sell) their latest pieces. The Hawaiiana demonstration takes place on the theater level.

If you're staying in the Kaanapali resort and would rather leave the car behind, the Wharf Cinema Center offers a shuttle service aboard blue double-decker buses. Ask the concierge at your hotel for information.

Not far down Front Street (heading in the direction of Maalaea) you'll also find the **Lahaina Marketplace,** open from 9am to 9pm daily. Mauians sell their wares from outdoor carts while tourists browse and snack. **Kuku A'ala** (meaning "Sensual Fragrances"), is one of the best places to visit here. It has a variety of custom colognes in island scents such as plumeria, rain, gardenia, and tuberose. They also offer myriad bath and beauty products. A favorite is the mango body oil. Lahaina Marketplace is a good place to pick up an inexpensive souvenir for someone back home.

Still farther down Front Street is a shopping complex known as **505 Front Street.** Though there aren't nearly as many shops at 505 as in the Wharf Cinema Center, several are worth visiting. At Suite #107, you'll find **Foreign Intrigue,** a shop that features unique furniture (folding teak chairs, painted cat benches), clothing (batik silk sarongs), gift items, and artwork. Most of the merchandise is imported from Indonesia, but some of it comes from Thailand and Hong Kong. **Lei Spa** has a wide variety of fragrant soaps and a nice selection of women's clothing. Most of the shops at 505 Front Street are open Monday through Saturday from 9am to 9pm, and from 10am to 5pm on Sunday.

Front Street Shopping

Front Street in Lahaina is a shopper's wonderland. It's not a particularly long street, but there you'll find everything from tourist T-shirt shops to exquisite art galleries.

In addition to the galleries listed here, you might be interested in the following shops:

Tropical Blues at 754 Front Street is a good place to find unique T-shirts; they have been designed by the owners. The store also carries some interesting pieces of costume jewelry made by artists from all over the country. **Whalers Locker** at 780 Front Street is a "museum of a shop" with collectors' items, including netsuke figurines and Niihau shell leis. One of Lahaina's oldest shops is **The Whaler Ltd.,** at 866 Front Street. Everything here has a nautical theme—from jewelry and glasswork to sculpture and scrimshaw. Another great place is **Maui Island Coffee** at

658 Front Street. They sell all sorts of coffees in a wide range of flavors; try the Kona Peaberry or Maui coffee (grown on Maui).

Below is a list of galleries in Lahaina. The art scene here changes dramatically from year to year, so there will likely be other galleries of interest along Front Street when you're visiting Lahaina. The following have been around for some years:

Addi Galleries
844 Front St. ☎ **808/661-4900.**

This gallery has an interesting and diverse collection, including "organic colorfield" paintings by Mauian Elan Vital, impressionist John Cosby, marine bronze sculptures by Dale Evers, African wildlife works by Craig Bone and Kim Donaldson, clown paintings by Red Skelton, and marine life works by David Miller.

David Lee Galleries
712 Front St. ☎ **808/667-7740.**

This establishment features the stunning works of David Lee, a Chinese artist who has mastered the art of painting with natural powder colors on silk. His unique work has a luminescent quality. Even if you're not shopping, it might be worthwhile to stop by and have a look.

Galerie Lassen
844 Front St., Suite 101. ☎ **808/667-7707.**

Here you'll find the work of local artist Christian Riese Lassen, as well as works by Richard Stiers, Red Skelton, Ting and Lu Hong, and Sassone.

Lahaina Arts Society
649 Wharf St. ☎ **808/661-0111.**

Located adjacent to the banyan tree are two galleries that many of Maui's undiscovered artists call home. Here you'll find works in a variety of media. On weekends and holidays the Lahaina Arts Society sponsors arts and crafts events under the adjacent world-famous shade tree.

Lahaina Galleries
728 Front St. ☎ **808/667-2152.**

Here you'll get an up-close look at the work of Robert Lyn Nelson, who originated two- and three-worlds imagery (you'll understand what I mean when you see it), as well as paintings by (among others) the very talented Andrea Smith and Guy Buffet. Many of the artists represented at Lahaina Galleries are world renowned.

Madaline Michaels Gallery
816 Front St. ☎ **808/661-3984.**

Specializing in three-dimensional artwork, Madaline Michaels Gallery exhibits the work of notables such as Mexican sculptor Sergio Bustamente. His work is so bright and colorful that you won't soon forget it. The following artists are also represented here: Todd Warner, Reinhart, Michael Amman, Jack Dowd, Roark Garley, and Steven Smeltzer.

Martin Lawrence Gallery
126 Lahainaluna Rd. ☎ **808/661-1788.**

At Martin Lawrence you'll see representative modern works by Mark King, Michele Delacroix, Linnea Pergola, Andy Warhol, Keith Haring, Hiro Yamagata, and Susan Rios.

New York to Paris Art
505 Front St. ☎ **808/667-0727.**

Rather than marine life scenes by local artists, this gallery exhibits a collection of varied works by internationally acclaimed artists such as Ronnie Wood, Miles Davis, Alberto Vargas, Mati Klarwein, and John Lennon.

South Seas Trading Post
780 Front St. ☎ **808/661-3168.**

This establishment is, in my opinion, more of a gallery than a "shop." It's also one of my favorites. Here you'll find all sorts of treasures from the South Pacific, including masks, jewelry, wall hangings, and puppets. Much of the work has been imported from Borneo, Papua New Guinea, Thailand, and Kashmir.

Village Galleries
120 Dickenson St. ☎ **808/661-4402.**

Just off Front Street you'll find Village Galleries, my favorite art gallery in Lahaina. It displays the work of Hawaii's finest artists. Names you'll learn to recognize are George Allan and Macario Pascual.

Wyland Galleries
711 Front St. ☎ **808/667-2285.**

Here you'll find the work of Wyland, "The world's leading marine life artist," as well as pieces by a host of internationally acclaimed artists. There are two other Wyland Galleries in Lahaina (at 697 Front Street and at 136 Dickenson Street).

LAHAINA AFTER DARK

Old Lahaina Luau
505 Front St. ☎ **808/667-1998.** Tickets $57 adults, $28.50 children age 12 and under.

Unanimously the best luau on Maui's west side (perhaps on the whole island), the Old Lahaina Luau takes place right on the beach behind the shopping complex at 505 Front Street.

When you arrive you'll be given a flower lei greeting and a tropical drink, and then you'll be escorted to your seat. You may choose in advance whether to sit on mats in the more traditional fashion or to be seated at a table. Photographers stroll around during the Hawaiian crafts and lei-making demonstrations, so if you forget your camera you won't have to worry—just enjoy yourself. The feast is served buffet-style, and you'll be treated to a traditional imu (in-ground oven) ceremony and a taste of kalua pig. Poke, lomi lomi, and haupia cake are among the traditional Hawaiian offerings for dinner, but if those menu items don't strike your fancy, you can always choose teriyaki beef, fried rice, salad, and fresh fruit. There is an open bar all evening; after dinner authentically attired Hawaiian men and women perform traditional hulas, accompanied by chanting and music performed with ancient-style instruments. The price of admission includes the open bar, all-you-can-eat buffet, flower lei, and the hula performance.

Friday Night Is Art Night
Every Friday night from 7 to 9pm, several of Lahaina's art galleries stay open late, so visitors and locals alike can gather to admire the works of local and international artists. Refreshments may be served by individual galleries, and there is often live entertainment. Check the paper or call the Lahaina Town Action Committee (☎ 808/667-9175) for more information on what's happening while you're in town.

Blue Tropix

900 Front St., Bldg. A202. ☎ **808/667-5309** (for recorded information).

Blue Tropix features dance music with a DJ weeknights, and it frequently hosts live entertainment. There's usually a $5 cover after 9pm. (See Chapter 7 for full restaurant listing.) Open Thursday through Monday (nightclub) until 2am.

Moose McGillycuddy's

844 Front St. ☎ **808/667-7758.**

Moose McGillycuddy's regularly features live rock bands and attracts a young crowd. The cover charge varies according to performers but is usually only $2 or $3. Open nightly from 9:30pm to 2am.

EN ROUTE FROM LAHAINA TO KAANAPALI

You might be interested to know that along Honoapilani Highway (as you drive from Lahaina to Kaanapali) you'll pass the old site of the Royal Coconut Grove of Mala. Flanking both sides of the highway, the coconut grove was planted originally in 1827 by Hoapili Wahine, the wife of Governor Hoapili. Rev. William Richards suggested that she plant the coconut grove on her empty plot of land, but Hoapili didn't see the point—she knew she wouldn't live to see the trees grow to full maturity. He pointed out that her grandchildren would be able to enjoy them when they became adults. Hoapili Wahine was convinced and immediately sent one of her men to the Big Island for a load of coconuts. When he returned, they proceeded to plant what was to become the Royal Coconut Grove of Maui.

KAANAPALI

Located only a few miles west of Lahaina, just off Honoapilani Highway, is the Kaanapali resort area. It's hard to believe that this area, with its glitzy, high-class resorts and beautiful white-sand beaches offering unparalleled views of neighboring Molokai and Lanai islands, was once a sugar plantation owned and operated by the Pioneer Mill Company. At Black Rock, near the Sheraton Maui Resort, was a wharf from which sugar, molasses, canned pineapple, fuel, and various other products were shipped. Nearby there were two enormous storage tanks, one for molasses, the other for fuel, a sugar warehouse, a small cluster of homes for the wharf employees, and a plant whose purpose was to turn pineapple cores and skins into cattle feed. Just mauka of the wharf and the sugar plantation was an old racetrack, used only on weekends and holidays. It was also Maui's first commercial airport.

Today, the warehouses, fuel and molasses tanks, and the wharf are gone; in their place stand some of the island's most beautiful hotels and golf courses.

To get around the Kaanapali resort, you can hitch a ride on the free Kaanapali Resort Trolley. It services all hotels and runs all day. Pickup points are the Royal Lahaina, the Sheraton/Kaanapali Beach Hotel, Whalers Village and the Westin, the Marriott/the Hyatt, and the Kaanapali Golf Course.

If you'd rather leave your car parked in Lahaina Center, there are other ways for you to reach Kaanapali from Front Street. If you're on a budget, it might be best for you to take the **Lahaina Express,** which shuttles visitors from its stop at the Wharf Cinema Center to hotels in the Kaanapali resort, beginning at 9:07am. It runs approximately every 25 to 35 minutes and makes its last trip from Whalers Village in the Kaanapali resort area at 9:45pm, arriving at the Wharf Cinema Center at about 10pm.

If you'd like a little commentary on local history as you're making the trip and are willing to spend a little money, I'd recommend that you take the **Lahaina–Kaanapali**

& Pacific Railroad (☎ 808/661-0089), otherwise known as the Sugar Cane Train. Children especially love the songs and stories of the conductor as they take the 12-mile journey on a fully reconstructed turn-of-the-century train. The original locomotive was used to transport sugarcane from sugar plantations to the ships anchored off Kaanapali Beach. The one-way trip takes about 25 minutes. One-way prices are $9.50 for adults, $5 for children (ages 3 to 12); round-trip $13.50 for adults, and $7 for children. If you want to combine your round-trip train ride with a visit to the Hawaii Experience Domed Theater, you can buy a combination ticket for $17.50 adults, $7 children. A combination ticket that includes admission to the Baldwin House, the Wo Hing Temple, and the *Carthaginian* is $17.50 for adults, $7 for children. If you want to combine your train ride with a Nautilus tour, the cost is $39.50 for adults and $19.75 for children.

Before or after your trip on the Sugar Cane Train, don't forget to stop at the Depot Snack Shop, located at the Lahaina Kaanapali & Pacific Railroad station just off Honoapilani Highway. Actually, the shop is worth a stop even if you don't ride the train. Friendly and extremely knowledgeable Brad Reith has owned and operated the place for years; he sells treats you can't get anywhere else. Fresh, sweet, juicy sugarcane is $2.25 a package. You can also buy coconuts in different stages of development. Drink delicious coconut "milk" or enjoy coconut in a gourmet form called "spoonmeat ($3)." They don't call Brad "Coco B" for nothing!

Also at the depot is Sugar Cane Gifts, where you can buy T-shirts and a variety of other gifts.

KAANAPALI ATTRACTIONS

Other than the beaches and golf courses (see below for for details), there are very few real attractions in the Kaanapali resort area. A couple of interesting places to visit are the **Whalers Village Museum** (☎ 808/661-5992) and the **Hale Kohola** (House of Whales), located in Whalers Village at the center of the Kaanapali resort. The Whalers Village Museum will take you back to the "Golden Era of Whaling" through photographs, scrimshaw, and a re-created ship forecastle. In Hale Kohola, by contrast, you'll learn about the evolution of the whale. There are a number of hands-on exhibits (such as squeezable whale blubber) that are great for kids. Admission to both museums is by donation, and they're open daily from 9:30am to 10pm. Don't skip these museums if you've already been to the brig *Carthaginian*—they are all worth visiting if you're interested in the life and plight of the whale today and in undeerstanding how the current crisis developed.

Special Hotel Attractions

Even if you're not a guest at the **Hyatt Regency Maui** (200 Nohea Kai Dr.), you might like to stop by during the day to look at this beautiful $80 million resort complex. When you walk through the hotel's entrance, you might think that you've entered an unusual, open-air museum. That's because the Hyatt is home to an incredible Asian and Pacific art collection. The hotel's lush tropical gardens cover 40 beautifully maintained acres dotted with waterfalls and tropical fish pools. The grounds also function as a wildlife preserve and home to some extraordinary exotic birds—there are even some penguins. A half-acre swimming pool winds through streams, rock formations, and waterfalls, and is crossed by a rope bridge. There is also a 150-foot water slide. The Hyatt has a new attraction called Incredible Journeys! (☎ 808/661-0092). It's a VirtualTour of Maui in a "helicopter" that never leaves the ground. It's a good alternative for those who don't want to pay the high price of an actual helicopter ride. There are also 19 shops on the hotel's lobby level.

Maui Attractions

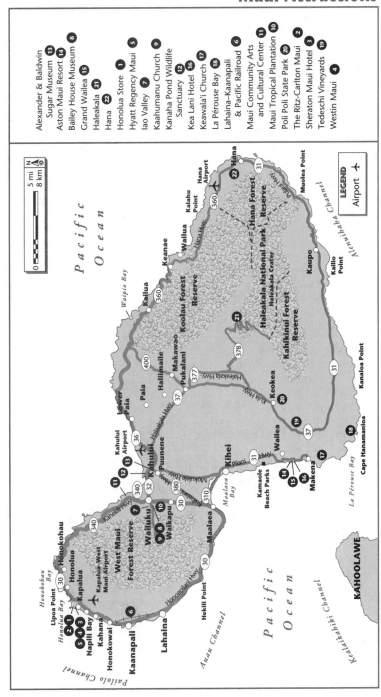

Alexander & Baldwin Sugar Museum **13**
Aston Maui Resort **14**
Bailey House Museum **8**
Grand Wailea **15**
Haleakala **21**
Hana **22**
Honolua Store **1**
Hyatt Regency Maui **5**
Iao Valley **9**
Kaahumanu Church **7**
Kanaha Pond Wildlife Sanctuary **12**
Kea Lani Hotel **16**
Keawala'i Church **17**
La Pérouse Bay **18**
Lahaina–Kaanapali & Pacific Railroad **6**
Maui Community Arts and Cultural Center **11**
Maui Tropical Plantation **10**
Poli Poli State Park **20**
The Ritz-Carlton Maui **2**
Sheraton Maui Hotel **3**
Tedeschi Vineyards **19**
Westin Maui **4**

183

If you have an interest in astronomy and know you're going to be near Kaanapali in the evening, make a reservation for the Hyatt's "Tour of the Stars"; here you can use the hotel's new computerized telescope, which has the capacity to chart and identify more than 1,000 different celestial objects. As the viewer focuses on a particular object or star, a recorded message describes its attributes. The program is offered nightly at 8, 9, and 10pm, and costs $12 for adults and $6 for children 6 and under. Call 808/661-4727 for viewing times and more information.

The Westin Maui (2365 Kaanapali Pkwy.) is another must-see hotel. The Westin also has an exquisite art collection, glorious gardens, and brilliantly colored birds. You can walk through the gardens on well-maintained pathways and even stand behind a waterfall. The pool is double the size of the one at the Hyatt; instead of stargazing, here you can take a wildlife tour led by the hotel's wildlife ranger. Call 808/667-2525 for more information.

If you're interested in a little bit of history, head over to the **Sheraton Maui Resort.** There you'll find a lava promontory known as Black Rock. This spot is believed to be the jumping-off place for the souls of Hawaii's dead, and it has also been a place from which an ancient Hawaiian king or chief would jump to prove himself to his army. Every evening, a young man employed by the Sheraton Maui makes the jump. It begins with the blowing of a conch shell, followed by the lighting of the torches along the path, and culminates in a spectacular dive. *Note:* The Sheraton is currently undergoing renovation, but it should be open by the time you read this. If the renovations have been completed, try to arrange a trip to see the evening jump from Black Rock.

KAANAPALI SHOPPING

Though there are scores of shops in hotel lobbies in the Kaanapali resort, the most popular shopping area is **Whalers Village,** located between the Westin and the Whaler Condominium complex. It can be reached via the Kaanapali Parkway or by way of the pathway that runs the length of the beach in front of the hotels. There are all kinds of shops located here—you'll find everything from books and sundries to scrimshaw and silks. A free hula show is staged in Whalers Village every Wednesday and Sunday at 1pm.

There's a small branch of **Waldenbooks** on the lower level, and there is also an **ABC Store** where you can get everything from tacky souvenirs to sodas and snacks. Next door to ABC is **Whalers Fine Wines & Spirits** in case you want to surprise someone with a nice bottle of wine or champagne one evening.

One of my favorite shops here is **Silks Kaanapali,** where you can get beautiful, unique, handpainted silk clothing and accessories. The **Dolphin Gallery** showcases some fine jewelry and so do **Jessica's Gems,** the **Pearl Factory, Maui Divers,** and **Classique Designs of Maui.**

If you are in the market for a unique (and expensive) T-shirt or beachwear for yourself or the kids, try **Crazy Shirts. Hobie Sports** and **Sgt. Leisure** also carry men's and women's apparel, and a special shop for children is the **Superwhale Children's Boutique** (parents will go wild at Superwhale).

Designer items more your speed? Well, **Louis Vuitton, Coach, Chanel,** and **Tiffany & Co.** are all represented here. In addition, **Sea & Shell Gallery** has some wonderful, locally handcrafted jewelry, as well as some interesting paintings. **Ka Honu Gift Gallery** features Hawaiian arts and crafts (here you can buy koawood bowls, pottery, and Hawaiian dolls and jewelry), and so does the **Nohea Gallery. Lahaina Printsellers** is popular island-wide for its antique maps and prints.

A unique addition to Whalers Village is the popular **Endangered Species Store,** where you can buy all kinds of things related to the world's endangered species. T-shirts are big sellers, but there are also beautiful animal figurines, as well as posters, crystals, tote bags, and books.

Note: You can ride the Kaanapali resort trolley to Whalers Village beginning around 7:30am and ending at 11pm.

KAANAPALI AFTER DARK

Nightlife in Kaanapali is alive and well. If you're a barfly, all of the major hotels have good bars, and several offer traditional luaus several evenings during the week. Remember that you must make reservations in advance to attend any of the following luaus.

The Maui Marriott Luau

100 Nohea Kai Dr. ☎ **808/667-1200.** Admission $55 adults; $20 children 5–12; under 5 free.

At the Marriott's beachside luau, you'll receive a shell lei greeting when you arrive, and from that point on you'll have access to the open bar. If you've got the stamina, you can drink Mai Tais all night long. Before dinner you'll be able to participate (or just watch others participate) in a variety of traditional Hawaiian crafts and games. The menu consists of kalua pig (baked in the traditional imu), teriyaki beef steak, Polynesian sweet-and-sour chicken, fresh mahimahi in lemon butter, fried rice, Hawaiian baked sweet potatoes, stir-fry vegetables, poi, papaya, pineapple, lomi lomi salmon, fresh baked poi rolls, haupia, and more. The after-dinner show, one of the island's most authentic, features Hawaiian fire dancers and traditional hula dancing. The luau begins at 5pm and ends at 8pm. Nationally recognized, the Marriott's luau is one of the island's best.

Drums of the Pacific

In the Hyatt Regency Maui, 200 Nohea Kai Dr. ☎ **808/667-4727.** Luau seating $55 adults; $15 children 6–12; 5 and under free. Cocktail seating (does not include dinner) $29 adults; $10 persons 20 and under.

The Hyatt Regency offers its own version of the traditional Hawaiian luau. Like the others, the Hyatt offers an open bar and an all-you-can-eat traditional luau buffet, featuring Hawaiian specialties and an imu ceremony. After dinner you'll be taken on a tour of the Polynesian islands as dancers perform authentic dances to the music of Samoa, New Zealand, Fiji, Tahiti, and Hawaii. The luau seating is Monday through Saturday at 5:30pm; the cocktail seating is at 6:45pm. The show begins at 7pm.

Sheraton Maui Resort Luau

2605 Kaanapali Pkwy. ☎ **808/661-0031.** Admission $42 adults, $19 children 6–12.

The Sheraton Maui has an excellent luau. Included in the cost of your ticket is a traditional lei greeting, open bar, and an all-you-can-eat buffet of Polynesian cuisine, including poi, pineapple chicken, kalua pig, island fish, and teriyaki steak. The after-dinner show features a fire-knife dance and the songs and dances of Hawaii, Tahiti, New Zealand, and Samoa. The three-hour luau takes place every Monday through Saturday, beginning at 5pm. *Note:* Again, the Sheraton Maui is currently undergoing a renovation. Be sure to call before heading over for the luau to make sure the hotel has reopened for business.

Royal Lahaina Luau

2780 Kekaa Dr. ☎ **808/661-3611.** Admission $55 adults; $28 children 5–12; under 5 free.

The Royal Lahaina Luau is offered seven nights a week in the hotel's luau gardens. The festivities begin with sunset cocktails, and entertainment begins with the traditional imu ceremony and a Hawaiian menu class (among other things). The feast is presented buffet style; the tables are laid with salads, teriyaki beef, pineapple chicken, island fish, and kalua pig. The live show tells the history of the Hawaiian Islands through traditional hula song and dance. The Royal Lahaina Luau was a recent winner of the prestigious Hawaii Visitors Bureau Kahili Award of Merit. September through April the seating is at 5:30pm; May through August it's at 6pm.

Hotel Entertainment

My personal favorite nightspot is the **Makai Bar** in the Maui Marriott. Here you can sit and watch the sun fall below the horizon (and catch a glimpse of the Marriott's luau) while sipping a tropical drink, munching on pupus, and listening to live entertainment. The Marriott's **Maui Comedy Club** is open every Monday evening, beginning at 8:30pm. At the **Royal Terrace Lounge** in the Royal Lahaina Resort, various entertainers perform several evenings a week from 7 to 10pm (call 808/ 661-3611 for current schedules). The **Garden Bar** at the Westin also frequently offers live entertainment throughout the week; call 808/667-2525 for details.

KAPALUA

Today, Kapalua is a beautiful oceanfront resort area with spectacular hotels, challenging golf courses, and well-maintained gardens, but it wasn't always so. In fact, the Kapalua area has an interesting history. It began as a Honolua Ranch with Henry P. Baldwin as its owner. By the late 1800s he had purchased most of the ranch, which was being managed by Richard Searle and used for cattle grazing and coffee growing. In 1911, Baldwin hired D. T. Fleming to run the ranch, and since Fleming had previously been cultivating pineapple in Haiku, he began planting pineapple at Honolua Ranch. H. P. Baldwin died that same year, and his son, Alexander Baldwin, took over. In 1924 Alexander Baldwin renamed his father's company Baldwin Packers, Ltd.; by 1929 pineapple production had grown to more than eight times that of cattle farming—2,500 acres had been planted with pineapple, while only 300 were being used for cattle raising. By 1946 cattle ranching had come to a standstill. Pineapple was cultivated at Honolua and then shipped by truck to waiting trains that would take the pineapple to the Lahaina Cannery to be canned. Later it was sent to Honolulu and then to the U.S. mainland. In 1962 Baldwin Packers merged with the Maui Pineapple Company and the Lahaina Cannery shut down since the canning operation had been moved to Kahului.

While pineapple was the major industry in Kapalua, coffee cultivation continued (without much success) until the late 1920s or early 1930s. Fleming also recognized the medicinal potential of aloe and planted 10 acres for the purpose of making a skin cream. Unfortunately, he never lived to see the product gain in popularity. Of course aloe is used today in every manner and form—from soaps to lotions to shampoos. Fleming didn't stop with coffee beans and aloe; he also planted watermelon and mango, avocado, citrus, lychee, and macadamia-nut trees between 1938 and 1940. Since the orchards didn't yield much profit compared to the pineapple plantation, they were eventually removed.

Filipino, Hawaiian, and Japanese plantation workers lived in camps along the shoreline (and a bit farther inland), and within each camp a tremendous sense of community developed. Together, they fished, swam, raised their own produce, and played on sports teams. Since the company provided them with all the provisions they needed, there was no need to leave the plantation.

In 1971 Maui Land & Pineapple Company announced plans to begin building the Kapalua resort. Today, it is home to the Kapalua Bay Hotel & Villas and the

Ritz-Carlton Hotel, but pineapple production continues. The resort covers less than 1,000 of the 23,000 acres owned by Maui Land & Pineapple Company.

Other than sporting activities and exceptional beaches, there aren't many tourist attractions in the Kapalua resort. You can visit the old **Honolua Store** (Honokahua Road) where plantation workers used to go for supplies—today its gift shop and small grocery store attract resort guests. **The Ritz-Carlton** (One Ritz-Carlton Drive) displays a wonderful collection of local art in its public spaces, and it's worth taking a look inside if you're in the area. The **Kapalua Bay Hotel** (One Bay Drive) also exhibits the work of several local artists, including Andrea Smith, and displays some feather leis in the lobby.

The Kapalua Shops on Kapalua Drive are within walking distance of the Kapalua Bay, and they include (among others) a branch of the **South Seas Trading Post** and **Haimoff & Haimoff**, both fine jewelry stores; a branch of the **Lahaina Gallery**; and **Mandalay**, which sells designer silks and cottons. There is also a **Kapalua Logo Shop** and another branch of **Lahaina Printsellers** represented here.

2 Central & South Maui

KAHULUI

Of all Maui's towns, Kahului is the one that has been most ravaged by the passage of time. It witnessed the early battles of Ka'ahumanu, the arrival of the Europeans, the development of the sugar and pineapple industries, and the coming of America's favorite fast-food restaurants. Today Kahului is home to more than one-third of all Mauians, the airport, and most of the island's shopping malls.

KAHULUI ATTRACTIONS

It might be something of a miracle that, in spite of all its problems, within this small city exists **Kanaha Pond Wildlife Sanctuary,** home to the Hawaiian stilt (ae'o). Located at the junction of Route 36 and Route 37, the pond and wildlife sanctuary are open to the public daily, and there is no admission charge. It's just you and the birds out there. You might see some ducks and geese, but what you really want to look for is the ae'o, a medium-sized bird with a black back, white underside, and long, thin, hot-pink legs. There is an observation deck off Route 37.

The only other tourist attraction near Kahului (actually in Puunene) is the **Alexander & Baldwin Sugar Museum** at 3957 Hansen Rd. (☎ 808/871-8058), next door to a still-operational mill. The museum, although small, is interesting since it documents some of the history of the sugar industry on Maui. The building that currently houses the museum was once the home of the mill's superintendent. You'll hear the recorded sounds of sugar production as you walk through, and you'll see photo murals of the early plantation workers and machinery. Some museum artifacts date back to the late 1870s. There are scale models and a working model of factory machinery. Children love this place. When you've finished going through the exhibits, have a look around the museum shop, which sells items relating to sugar production and plantation life. Admission is $3 for adults, $1.50 for children ages 6 to 17, free for children under 6. The museum is open Monday through Saturday from 9:30am to 4:30pm.

KAHULUI SHOPPING

Kahului's **Ka'ahumanu Center** (275 Ka'ahumanu Ave. ☎ 808/877-3369, ext. 21, for information), Maui's largest shopping mall, has nearly 100 shops and a six-plex theater. There is a food court on the second level, and the mall is anchored by **Sears,**

Liberty House, and a two-level **J.C. Penney.** Specialty shops include **The Gap, The Disney Store, Caswell-Massey,** and **Pocketbook Man.** The Queen's Market Food Court features American, Mexican, Italian, Chinese, and Korean eateries. The Center is open from 9:30am to 9pm Monday through Friday, 9:30am to 7pm on Saturday, and 10am to 5pm on Sunday. The **Maui Mall** at 52 Ka'ahumanu Avenue is an open-air shopping center with frequent outdoor entertainment (check local listings) and a variety of interesting shops. There's a supermarket located here, as well as **Maui Natural Foods**—a health food outlet, as you might have guessed.

KAHULUI AFTER DARK

If you want to hang out with a primarily local crowd, there are several options. The **Red Dragon Room** in the Maui Beach Hotel (170 Ka'ahumanu Ave. ☎ 808/ 877-0051) offers DJ entertainment on Saturday from 10:30pm to 2:30am. Next door (also at 170 Ka'ahumanu Ave. ☎ 808/877-0071) is the **East West Dining Room** where Thursday through Saturday a variety of entertainment (karaoke to Top 40) is featured, depending on the night. There is no cover charge at either place. **Luigi's Pasta and Pizzeria** ☎ 808/877-3761 in the Maui Mall also provides entertainment Thursday through Saturday evenings. Call for details.

Maui Arts & Cultural Center

Maui Central Park, off Kahului Beach Rd. ☎ **808/242-7469** or 242-SHOW for box office and information.

Until recently, Maui was without a performing arts venue. Performing arts groups were obliged to use shopping malls and school gyms as their stages. Artists and the people of Maui alike had to endure uncomfortable facilities with no rehearsal studios, poor lighting, and poor acoustics. Now, there is a $32 million Maui Arts & Cultural Center, which opened its doors in 1994 after more than a decade of planning and fund-raising by the community. During its first year of operation, nearly half a million people attended more than 2,000 different events at the center. Besides locally produced shows, Maui's new center hosted such notable artists as James Taylor, Steve Allen & Jayne Meadows, Tony Bennett, and the Vienna Boys Choir, plus rockers Santana and Hootie and the Blowfish. Most recently, the center hosted Blues Traveler.

Various Hawaiian and multicultural festivals and concerts under the stars are scheduled throughout the year in the Alexander & Baldwin Amphitheater. Castle Theater, the trilevel main stage hall, seats 1,200 and is considered to be one of the finest venues in the Pacific Rim, both acoustically and technically. The 4,000-square-foot Kazuma International Gallery has showcased the works of local artists, in addition to such international exhibits as the Golden Tea Room from Japan (this was the first time the exhibit was allowed out of the country) and East European Ceramics. Productions of the Maui Academy of Performing Arts and others can be seen in the 200-seat McCoy Studio Theater.

A free "behind the scenes" guided tour is given at 11am every Tuesday (call 808/ 242-ARTS to reserve a place for the tour). Tickets can be purchased by phone with a credit card and picked up before the show. The center is located within minutes from Kahului Airport, about 30 minutes from Wailea and 45 minutes from the Lahaina/Kaanapali resort area.

WAILUKU & ENVIRONS

Even though Wailuku today is a bit run-down and ramshackle, it is still one of Maui's most historic towns. For one thing, it was, as its name suggests (*wai* meaning "blood," *luku* meaning "massacre") the site of one of the bloodiest battles ever fought on Maui.

You'll probably be tempted to drive right by Wailuku on your way to the Bailey House Museum or the Iao Needle, but don't. Stop at Ka'ahumanu Church and try to imagine what Wailuku was like in the 1800s; then head over to Main Street for some browsing or shopping in the antique stores. There are also some great lunch spots here (see Chapter 7, "Maui Dining," for listings).

WAILUKU ATTRACTIONS

Ka'ahumanu Church
High St. ☎ **808/244-5189.**

Named for Queen Ka'ahumanu, one of Hawaii's most powerful and influential queens, Ka'ahumanu Church is the oldest stone church on Maui. The first structure that was built on this site was temporary, and when Ka'ahumanu attended services in that temporary church (she was at the forefront of the Hawaiian conversion to Christianity), she asked that when a new church was built, it be named for her. Her wish was granted with the building of a more permanent adobe structure on this site. The adobe church was replaced in 1837 by a large stone church. The one you see today (restored in 1975) is only part of the original stone church. You probably won't be able to go inside during the week, but it's worth stopping to have a look around.

Bailey House Museum
2375-A Main St. ☎ **808/244-3326.** Admission $4 adults; $3.50 seniors; $1 children ages 7 to 12. Mon–Sat 10am–4pm.

In the early 1820s American Protestant missionaries began settling in the Hawaiian Islands so that they might begin to "civilize" the native Hawaiian population by teaching them to read and write. They wanted to save the souls of the Hawaiian people with Christian values, which meant that Hawaiians needed to be educated so they could learn to read the Bible. The missionaries established schools for adults and children and then created an alphabet for the Hawaiian language so they could translate the Bible into Hawaiian.

In 1837 the Wailuku Female Seminary was established on Maui so that Hawaiian women could be taught the virtue of a good Christian home and family. The seminary founders, Rev. Jonathan and Theodosia Green and Miss Maria Ogden, were replaced at some point by Edward and Caroline Green; due to lack of funding, however, the seminary was forced to close its doors in 1849. After it closed, the Baileys purchased the building and made it their home for 40 years. Edward Bailey's contribution to Maui was enormous. He helped vaccinate Mauians against smallpox (an epidemic on Oahu devastated the population), built roads, surveyed land, designed churches, defined water rights for the sugar industry, grew his own sugarcane, built sugar mills, and helped establish Maunaolu Seminary for women in Makawao. Bailey was also an accomplished artist whose paintings and copper engravings are an invaluable source of information about 19th-century Maui. Many of his works can be seen on the first floor of the Bailey House Museum today. Visitors will also be able to view the museum's large collection of "precontact" Hawaiian artifacts, such as stone and shell implements, kapa cloth, and wood and feather work. Upstairs is the Bailey family parlor and a bedroom, where you can see period furnishings, clothing, quilts, children's toys, and more. There are also outdoor displays of some of the original varieties of sugarcane brought to Maui, stone artifacts, a koa-wood outrigger canoe, and a redwood surfboard. The museum shop has a great selection of books about Hawaii. The Bailey House Museum is owned and operated by the Maui Historical Society.

Maui Tropical Plantation

Highway 30 at Waikapu (1670 Honoapilani Hwy., Wailuku). ☎ **808/244-7643** or 800/
451-6805. Admission to the market, nursery, restaurant, and Plantation Village is free; Tropical Express Tour $8.50 adults, $3.50 children 5–12, under 5 free; Country Barbecue $48.95
adults, $19.95 children 5–12, children 1–4 free. Maui Tropical Plantation daily 9am–5pm;
Country Barbecue Tues–Thurs 4:30–7:30pm (reservations required).

Situated in the Waikapu Valley and covering 60 acres, Maui Tropical Plantation is
a working plantation of commercial crops—including sugarcane, pineapple, coffee,
bananas, mangoes, papayas, and macadamia nuts. Visitors may take a leisurely stroll
through the Agricultural Village, stopping to view pictoral displays of Maui agriculture and admire the Southern Cross Windmill, which captures the rainwater that
flows from the West Maui Mountains to irrigate sections of the plantation. After that,
guests might want to take a tram ride on the Tropical Express to see up close how
the crops are grown and harvested. The 40-minute tram tour is narrated and makes
a few stops along the way. A trip to the Tropical Nursery where visitors can see
hibiscus, orchids, and ginger is worthwhile. The Tropical Market is stocked with
breads, jams and jellies, T-shirts, macadamia nuts, chocolate, Maui In Maui ice
cream, books, and more. A luncheon buffet is available at the Tropical Restaurant,
but many people prefer to visit the Tropical Plantation on Tuesday, Wednesday, or
Thursday evening for the Hawaiian Country Barbecue. Included in the price of admission to the barbecue are select drinks throughout the evening, a sunset tram ride,
lei-making and pineapple-cutting demonstrations, dinner, and the Hawaiian Country
Show featuring "Rodney Arias." It's something like a luau with a paniolo/Upcountry
twist.

IAO VALLEY

Follow the signs from Wailuku toward the Iao Valley, and just a short distance from
town you'll come to **Kepaniwai Park and Heritage Gardens** (on the left side of the
road). The beautifully landscaped gardens are dotted with structures dedicated to the
people of Hawaii. The park is the brainchild of architect Richard C. Tongg. Here
you'll find a Chinese pagoda, New England salt box, Japanese teahouse and garden,
bamboo house, and Hawaiian grass shack. There is no admission charge. Next door
is the Hawaii Nature Center at Iao Valley where children and adults can participate
in nature activities. Call 808/244-6500 in advance to sign up for their special programs.

If you leave the gardens and continue up toward the Iao Valley, you'll soon come
to a sign that reads, BLACK GORGE PRESIDENT KENNEDY PROFILE. Pull over and have
a look at the rock formation. I didn't believe it either until I stopped and looked for
myself. You'll be amazed.

Continue on up, and after about another mile you'll arrive at the Iao Valley, at the
center of which is the **Iao Needle,** a 2,250-foot lava rock that is covered with a layer
of beautiful green foliage. This is where Kamehameha won the island of Maui by
driving local warriors and chiefs into the valley and "outgunning" them (they were
only equipped with spears) with his English cannons. It is said that the carnage was
so great that the waters of this stream (Kepaniwai) ran red with blood. Fortunately,
you'll find no trace of that today. Instead, you can park your car and follow one of
the many well-maintained paths through the valley, along which you'll find a couple
of nice swimming holes.

WAILUKU SHOPPING

Shopping options in Wailuku aren't the best, although there are a few interesting
antique shops on North Market Street in an area known as Antique Row. Take a walk

along North Market and poke your head into some of the shops. **Traders of the Lost Art** at 62 North Market is filled with primitive ritual art and ancestral carvings from New Guinea as well as some contemporary items from Asia and Hawaii. **Ali'i Antiques,** 139 N. Market Street, showcases Asian art from the Ming and Ch'ing dynasties; and **Memory Lane** (158 North Market St.) where you'll find myriad one-of-a-kind items. American artists are the specialty of owner Joe Ransberger. The **Iao Theater,** also located on North Market, is the oldest theater in the state and is currently undergoing a massive renovation. **Jovian Gallery** at 7 Market Street is home to the works of many of Maui's most talented artists as well as unique jewelry and stationery among other things. *Note:* This area of Wailuku may grow somewhat over the next few years, so by the time you read this there may be even more great shops there.

One of the more interesting shops in Wailuku is **Gima Designs** (2058 Main Street ☎ 808/242-1839), where you'll find the original silk designs of Elaine Gima. Her work is exquisite, and she makes items to suit everyone's budget. If you're planning a stop at Gima Designs, call ahead to be sure Elaine is there—she doesn't keep regular shop hours.

KIHEI, WAILEA & MAKENA

Maui's south shore isn't known for its sights and attractions, but if you're in the area for the day, a few stops are worth making.

ATTRACTIONS

Head through Kihei into the planned Wailea resort, where you'll find some of the island's most beautiful hotels. The **Grand Wailea,** off Wailea Alanui, has the most incredible art collection of all the hotels on the island, and it also has a fantastic 20,000-foot-long action pool. You might enjoy taking a ride in the hotel's elevator to Kincha, the Grand Wailea's Japanese restaurant (even if you do not plan to eat there). The **Aston Wailea Resort** has recently been refurbished, and the changes include some exquisite Pacific Rim artifacts. Finally, even if you don't go into any of the hotels, you might like to drive by the strange and wonderful **Kea Lani Hotel** for a look at its distinctive architectural design.

Just a bit farther down the road from Wailea is Makena. Continue on until you see a sign indicating Makena Landing. Turn right and you'll be on Honoiki Street. Follow it to the end, and then go left. Here you will find **Keawala'i Church,** which is built of coral and lava rocks. If you go back out to Makena Alanui Road (the main road you were on before you turned right at the Makena Landing sign) and turn right and follow the road until it ends, you'll be at **La Pérouse Bay** where you'll find Maui's last lava flow, which occurred at the end of the 18th century. There's a trail here that you can follow. You'll discover some beautiful coves and evidence of ancient Hawaiian villages. *Note:* Please don't stray from the trail because you might damage some of the ancient sites.

SHOPPING

Azeka Place and **Azeka Place II,** just off South Kihei Road, are loaded with tourist shops where you will find swimwear, alohawear, handcrafted Maui jewelry, postcards, and water-sports gear. Other shopping areas in Kihei include **Long's Center,** the **Dolphin Shopping Plaza, Rainbow Mall,** and **Kukui Center.** All are located just off South Kihei Road. None of these shopping centers offers much of interest to the discriminating shopper. Personally, my favorite places to shop in Kihei are the **Kihei International Marketplace,** off South Kihei Road between Foodland and the 76 gas station, and the Kihei Open Air Marketplace (located next door to McDonald's). Both are great flea markets where you can get everything from T-shirts and sarongs to work by local artisans. Kihei International Marketplace is open daily from 9am to 6pm, and Kihei Open Air Marketplace is open from 8am to 3pm.

The **Wailea Shopping Village** offers more upscale shopping, but the goods are quite similar to those found in Lahaina and Kapalua. There's a small market filled with tourist items as well as certain staple foods, a sunglasses shop, a couple of women's boutiques, and a beachwear shop. Most of the Wailea hotels also have shopping arcades.

AFTER DARK

The Aston Wailea Resort offers **Wailea's Finest Luau** (☎ 808/879-1922) on Tuesday, Thursday, and Friday evenings from 5 to 8pm. At an oceanfront setting, the luau includes a lei greeting, open bar, imu ceremony, authentic Hawaiian hula show, and a full luau buffet. The cost is $52 for adults and $26 for children. Parking is complimentary.

Renaissance Wailea Resort (☎ 808/879-4900) presents the **Wailea Sunset Luau** every Thursday beginning at 6pm (seating begins at 5:30pm). Set in the hotel's luau gardens, the Renaissance luau offers an extensive luau menu and a Polynesian show featuring traditional hula, Tahitian drums and dancing, and a spectacular fire-knife dance finale.

Another option would be to head for the hotel bars. **Tsunami** in the Grand Wailea has a DJ from 9pm to 2am on Tuesday and Thursday (no cover charge), as well as on Friday and Saturday (open 9pm to 4am, $10 cover). Sunday and Monday are karaoke nights from 9pm to 2am (no cover charge). For a more relaxing evening you might try the Grand Wailea's **Volcano Bar,** which features strolling Hawaiian entertainment nightly beginning at 5:30pm. Jazz musicians perform nightly at the **Kea Lani Hotel** in the lounge area of the restaurant.

3 Upcountry

Most people know about Haleakala, but very few know about the area on Haleakala's western slope known as Upcountry. A trip to Maui simply wouldn't be complete without at least a one-day excursion to Upcountry. Passing through on the way to the crater to see the sunrise or sunset isn't enough. It would be worthwhile if you planned a whole day to explore the area's lush countryside, parks, botanical gardens, shops, and even a winery. While you're in Upcountry you can see where the paniolos ride the range on Haleakala and Ulupalakua ranches, and you can visit the old cowboy town of Makawao where hitching posts are as common as the beautiful boutiques and fine restaurants that line the main street. A trip to Kula will reveal the things that make Maui unique. There you'll find an abundance of flowers (including unusual protea, jacaranda, and even fields and fields of carnations), Tedeschi Vineyards, and Polipoli State Park.

MAKAWAO

To reach Makawao from Kahului, take the Hana Highway (Route 36) to Haleakala Highway (Route 37). Follow Haleakala Highway to the junction of Route 40 (Makawao Road) and turn left. Follow Makawao Road into Makawao.

When you arrive in Makawao, you'll feel a noticeable change in temperature. For every 1,000 feet above sea level, the temperature on Haleakala drops about three degrees. If you're in the area on a winter evening, you won't be surprised to find out that many Upcountry homes have well-used fireplaces. Rather than a tropical scene, what you'll find in Makawao are pastoral scenes, with rolling fields, pine trees, fuschias, and proteas.

In the late 1700s, Captain George Vancouver presented King Kamehameha with several head of cattle. He then convinced the king to place a kapu on the cattle so they would have time to reproduce and become a food source for the Hawaiian people. At the beginning of the 19th century, Kamehameha imported three *españoles* (Mexican cowboys) to domesticate the cattle, which had grown into a wild herd. Over time, Hawaiian cowboys joined the españoles, and they became known as *paniolos.* Paniolos, who still ride the range up here, are responsible for providing Maui with much of its milk and beef. Of course, you can't have cowboys without a rodeo; in fact, there are several rodeo events in Makawao every year. Makawao celebrates the Fourth of July every year with a western twist; for example, the town's parade includes covered horse-drawn wagons.

Makawao's main street, **Baldwin Avenue,** was once home to simple barbershops, saloons, and general stores, but today it is lined with upscale boutiques, art galleries, and restaurants. **Collections** (☎ 808/572-0781), **Gecko Trading Co. & Boutique** (☎ 808/572-0249), and **Hurricane Ltd.** (☎ 808/572-5076) sell women's clothing and accessories; for men's fashions try **Tropo** (☎ 808/573-0356); **Holiday & Co.** (☎ 808/572-1470) also has clothing and gifts; **Goodie's** (☎ 808/572-0288), with tie-dye clothing and crystals, is for the hippie in all of us. **Upcountry Kids** (unique children's clothing) and **Upcountry Legends** (clothing) are both located in the restored Makawao Theater Building. **Miracles Bookery Too,** 3682 Baldwin Avenue in Makawao (☎ 808/572-2317), has a great selection of New Age books, as well as music, symbolic jewelry, and incense.

If you're looking for a snack or a quick meal, **Kamoda Store and Bakery** (☎ 808/572-7261) is where the locals line up every morning for fresh-baked cream puffs and malasadas on a stick; locals also like to stop at **Kitada's Kau Kau Korner** (☎ 808/572-7241) in the morning for saimin and coffee or later in the day for plate lunches. **The Rodeo General Store** (☎ 808/572-7841) stocks a little bit of everything. Their chicken is delicious, and they make great sandwiches and sushi as well. Rodeo General Store also has a selection of wines (some of which are very well selected).

Some of the more interesting local **art galleries** here include the **David Warren Gallery** (☎ 808/572-0344), which features the work of David Warren, and **Maui Hands** (☎ 808/572-5194), which sells and displays beautiful raku pots, jewelry, drums, rainsticks, baskets, watercolor paintings, and ceramics. **Viewpoints Gallery** (☎ 808/572-5979) is an artists' cooperative for 25 local artists. Everyone who has gallery space must spend some time tending the shop. The artists' two- and three-dimensional works are quite diverse and exciting. **Hot Island Glass** (☎ 808/572-GLASS) is a glassblowing studio and gallery in "The Courtyard," where you might be able to watch an incredibly talented husband-and-wife team at work. Incidentally, the temperature of molten glass is 2,000° Fahrenheit, the same as that of lava. **Ola's,** located at 1156 Makawao, is the realization of a dream for owners (and sisters), Shari O'Brien and Cindy Heacock. Their collection includes the work of more than 80 different artisans (from all over the country), and it's unique on the island of Maui. You'll find everything here from beautiful glasswork to jewelry and interesting art furniture. Furthermore, in 1996 Ola's began selling handmade chocolates purchased from a New York manufacturer. The concession is called "Bella's at Ola's," and the chocolates are a must. A brand-new spa, **Spa Luna** (1156 Makawao Avenue), which offers everything from facials to full body wraps and massages of all kinds at affordable prices, is a great place to stop during a trip to Makawao. In addition to overall body pampering, you can take yoga and chi kung (five day commitment required for chi kung) classes. Call 808/572-1300 and make an appointment before you head Upcountry. Spa Luna is a wonderful place.

A bit farther down Baldwin Avenue (you'll have to drive to get there) is the **Hui Noeau Visual Arts Center** (☎ 808/572-6560). The Hui Noeau was founded in 1934 by Ethel Baldwin and other Maui residents who wanted to stimulate an interest in art among Mauians. The Hui's goals were simply to support artistic talent among the local people and to educate the general public. Today the Hui sponsors educational programs in ceramics, painting, drawing, sculpture, printmaking, and jewelry making, to name just a few. There are art studios, and works by distinguished Hawaiian artists are always on display. There is also a gift shop.

If you're passing through Makawao in the evening, stop by **Casanova** (☎ 808/572-0220) for a night of dinner and dancing (see Chapter 7, "Maui Dining," for further details). From disco to blues to mambo and swing, there's always something going on at Casanova. A recent weekly calender included Country and Western dancing (with instruction) on Tuesday nights; Ladies Night is Wednesday; Thursday nights bring an ongoing fund-raising project (including a live show and DJ) to benefit the Maui AIDS Foundation; on Friday and Saturday there is live music. There is usually a $5 cover charge (unless you're dining), and entertainment begins at 9:45pm. Casanova closes at 1am.

KULA

Kula means "plain, field, or open country," and Kula is just that. Today it is home to the famous sweet Maui onion and most of the island's herb and flower farms, but its land was once covered with beautiful koa trees. Once the koa tree forests were cleared, Hawaiians began farming the land for vegetables, which they took down to the coastal towns to trade and sell. During the years of the whaling industry, Irish potatoes were one of the main crops here.

To reach Kula from Makawao, head back to Haleakala Highway (Route 37) and go left. Haleakala Highway turns into Kula Highway.

Soon after you turn onto Kula Highway, you can make a stop at **Enchanting Floral Gardens of Kula, Maui** (just off Route 37 across from the 10-mile marker ☎ 808/878-2531). The gardens display more than 900 species from around the world, including native Hawaiian flora. You'll see the spectacular blue and red jade vine, shell ginger, and the pincushion protea, among others. A small admission fee is charged at the door. Enchanting Floral Gardens of Kula, Maui is open daily from 9am to 5pm.

If you're hungry while you're in the area, visit **Grandma's Coffee Shop** (see Chapter 7, "Maui Dining," for details). Continue along Route 37. It's a bit of a drive, so don't think I've sent you in the wrong direction. It will be on your right. There's no parking lot, so just park on the roadside wherever you can find a space.

After you've had a bite at Grandma's, return to Route 37 and continue in the same direction you had been going. Just past Keokea you'll come to Ulupalakua Ranch (on your right), and then you'll see **Tedeschi Vineyards** (P.O. Box 935, Ulupalakua, Maui, HI 96790; ☎ 808/878-1266) on your left. In the mid-19th century, the area that is today known as Ulupalakua Ranch was a sugar plantation. It didn't last more than 10 years as a sugar plantation; then it was bought by whaling captain James Makee, who turned it into a working cattle ranch called Rose Ranch in honor of his wife's favorite flower. The cattle ranch was a great success for Makee, and as a result, it attracted many notable visitors, including King David Kalakaua, for whom Makee built a cottage on his ranch (you can still see it today). In 1963 when C. Pardee

Erdman bought the ranch, it had already been renamed Ulupalakua Ranch. In 1973, Erdman met Emil and JoAnn Tedeschi, Napa Valley wine makers who visited the ranch and decided to test different varieties of grapes here for wine making. One hundred and fifty varieties of grapes later, they discovered that the Carnelian grape adapted well to the climate on Maui, and they began making wine in a small winery on the ranch. It's only one of two working commercial wineries in the Hawaiian Islands (the other is on the Big Island), and currently five wines are being produced from the Carnelian grape: Maui Brut Champagne, Rose Ranch Cuvée, Maui Blush, Plantation Red, and Ulupalakua Red. Besides the grape wines, Tedeschi is famous for Maui Blanc, its pineapple wine, which has a light but distinctive flavor. Last time I visited they were also producing an interesting pineapple-passion fruit wine called Maui Splash! Another new addition is Pineapple Sparkling Wine. There's a tasting room and gift shop on the premises, which are open daily from 9am to 5pm. Free tours of the vineyards are offered daily from 9:30am to 2:30pm.

When you leave Tedeschi Vineyards, turn around and head back toward Makawao on Route 37. When you get to the junction of Route 377, take Route 377 (Kekaulike Ave.) to Waipoli Road, where you need to take a right to get to **Polipoli State Park.** A long series of switchbacks (in preparation for your drive to Hana) will lead you right into the park. You're likely to be awed by the park's magnificent redwood trees. If you'd like to get out and walk around, you can take the Redwood Trail, a 1.7-mile hike through the redwood forest. The trail stays among the trees. From the Redwood Trail you might veer off onto the Plum Trail, which will take you through sugi, cedar, and ash groves. There are many other trails in the park.

When you've finished poking around the park, return to Kekaulike Road (Route 377) and go right, following it until you get to the **Kula Botanical Gardens** (on your right). The gardens opened to the public in 1971 after 2¹/₂ years of planting and nurturing. Today you can take a nice, leisurely stroll here while looking at tropical and local Hawaiian plants of all varieties. The park is open daily from 9am to 4pm; admission is $4 for adults and $1 for children ages 6 to 12.

If you still haven't stopped for a bite to eat, now is your chance. Exit the Kula Botanical Gardens and continue in the direction of Makawao. Soon you'll come to the **Kula Lodge & Restaurant** (☎ 808/878-1535) where you can dine on Hawaiian regional and contemporary cuisine while enjoying the dining room's spectacular vistas. Afterward, you might like to stop at the **Upcountry Harvests** gift shop next door to Kula Lodge. There you can buy protea of all varieties, as well as koa wood bracelets and bowls and other Hawaiian products. It's open weekdays from 9am to 5pm.

4 Haleakala

Haleakala (pronounced "ha-lay-ah-ka-lah"), meaning "House of the Sun," is the world's largest dormant volcano, and it's like nothing you've ever seen before. To me, Haleakala seems omnipotent. The sheer force it must have had to climb 30,000 feet from the ocean floor is mind-boggling. It is easy to understand why ancient Hawaiians feared and respected this mountain. Only the kahuna were brave enough to live on the volcano. Others hoped only to appease the goddess Pele by making sacrifices to her at the crater's edge.

Today, visitors to Maui have much less to fear from the volcano than did the Hawaiians of old. Haleakala hasn't erupted for more than 200 years; although it is not extinct, geologists believe that the volcano will not erupt any time in the near future. Maui has shifted away from the "plume" that lies under the ocean, which had caused

Haleakala's eruptions; chances are slim that the volcano will become active again. Maui should continue to shift away from the plume, and the volcano will eventually become extinct. Since Haleakala's last eruption, the main activity seen on the mountain has been erosion. It is believed that over time, rainwater and flowing streams (combined with a slow collapse and sinking of the volcano) have eroded more than 3,000 feet off the mountain.

The 7-mile-long crater, large enough to hold the entire island of Manhattan, attracts visitors from all over the world, and it is protected as a national park. Its summit reaches a height of 10,000 feet, and the mountain stands 24 miles wide, covering most of the island's width and half of its length. Hundreds of thousands of island visitors trek to the summit of Haleakala every year to see the sun rise or set. Some enjoy hiking on its lush lower slopes or simply marveling at the beauty of its multi-hued cinder cones. Others come to see the much-talked-about silversword and unusual animal life.

A word of caution: As you are driving up to the summit, you'll probably see a number of bicyclists riding down the mountain. Chances are that none of them is an experienced biker, so be on your guard.

THE DRIVE TO THE SUMMIT

Before you get started there are a few things you should know. From wherever you are on Maui it will take you between 1 1/2 and 3 hours to get to the summit, so plan accordingly. Also it is typically much colder at the crater than it is near Maui's beaches, so take a jacket or sweater with you. The air at the top is rather thin, so it is advisable that anyone with a heart problem check with a doctor before setting out (it's probably not a good idea for heart patients to make the trip at all).

Most people drive up in the early morning or early evening because the afternoon cloud cover around the top of Haleakala obstructs the beautiful views. Make sure the weather is good before you start out (it would be a shame to get there and discover that you can't see or do anything); call 808/572-7749 for a weather report. Finally, there are no restaurants at the top, so if you want to see the sun rise, it would be advisable to pack a picnic breakfast or plan to stop at one of the restaurants or bakeries at the base of the mountain (Grandma's Coffee Shop, Kula Lodge, Kitada's Kau Kau Korner, or Komoda's Store; see Chapter 7,"Maui Dining," for details).

No matter what your point of origin, you'll begin the drive on Route 37 (Haleakala Highway), which you will follow until you get to Pukalani, where you will go right onto Route 377 (Upper Kula Road). Take Route 377 to Haleakala Crater Road (Route 378)—the road is well marked. Your starting elevation is about 3,700 feet above sea level, and 22 miles and 32 switchbacks later you'll reach the summit. There are several stops you will probably want to make along the way, the first of which is a lookout just under 5 miles from the beginning of the trail. It will be on the right side of the road; stopping here will afford you beautiful views of the neighboring islands, Kahoolawe and Molokini. On your right you'll see West Maui Volcano, which was actually the first active volcano on Maui. Eruptions of hot lava from both volcanoes joined together to form what you see today as the island of Maui. At one time all of the islands in Maui County, including Molokai, Lanai, and Kahoolawe were joined above sea level.

When you've finished taking pictures and admiring the view, hop back in the car and continue up the mountain. Shortly after you reach the park entrance (where you'll have to pay a fee of $4 for a car or $2 for a bicycle), you'll see a turnoff on your left. Don't take it here—it's easier and safer to make the turn on your way back down.

Haleakala National Park

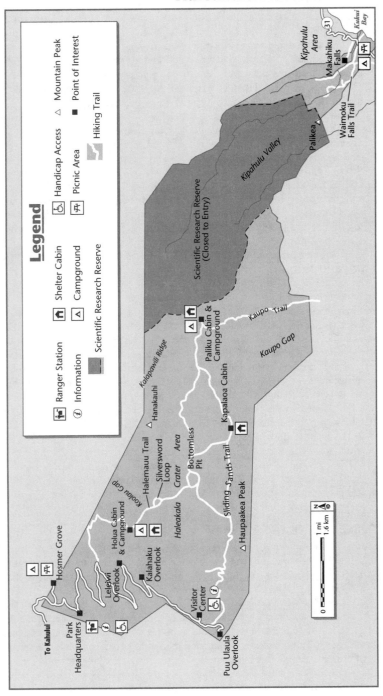

Park Headquarters will be your next stop (unless you're here for the sunrise, in which case you should stop on the way back down because it doesn't open until sunrise). Here you'll find a wide variety of books and general information (including the day's schedule for ranger-guided hikes and camping permit information). Outside Park Headquarters you might be able to see a nene or two.

After you leave Park Headquarters, keep an eye out for Leleiwi Overlook, at mile marker 17. The parking lot is about half a mile beyond mile marker 17 on your right. Park there and cross the road to the short trail that leads to the overlook, where you'll be treated to an incredible panoramic view of Haleakala Crater, which resembles a moonscape. You're now at an elevation of 8,800 feet. Notice how the colors of the cinder cones change as the clouds move across the sky. Aside from the view, the thing that really attracts visitors to this spot is a phenomenon known as the Specter of the Brocken. Sometimes, if conditions are just right (usually in the afternoon when it's rather cloudy and the view from here is obstructed), you can see your shadow, ringed by a rainbow, in the clouds below. If I were a scientist, I would probably know how to explain this phenomenon to you, but I'm not, so for the purposes of this book, it will have to remain a mystery. (If you're eager to understand the phenomenon, I'm sure one of the park rangers can explain it to you.) While you're at Leleiwi Overlook, notice the dramatic change in vegetation from the rolling meadows of Kula and the other towns at the base of the mountain.

Continue up the volcano and soon you will arrive at the Haleakala Observatory Visitor Center (a little over 3 miles from Leleiwi Overlook), where the views are unsurpassed. In clear weather you'll be able to see for more than 100 miles, and you'll really feel as though you're at the very edge of the earth. If you're here for the sunrise, you'll understand why the ancient Hawaiians named this place Haleakala, "House of the Sun," for the sun appears to rise directly out of the crater. As the sun rises and moves across the sky throughout the day, the giant cinder cones you see below seem to change colors. There are ecological, geological, and archaeological exhibits here that describe the volcano's history. In addition to the informational exhibits, you can buy books, gifts, and film here. There are also rest rooms.

The actual summit of Haleakala is a little more than half a mile from the visitor center, so don't turn around at the visitor center thinking you've seen all you've come to see. Continue on until you get to Puuulaula Summit (also known as Red Hill). At 10,023 feet, this is the volcano's highest point. Here you'll also see a cluster of buildings known as Science City. Much of the research that is done here can be performed nowhere else in the world.

DESCENT FROM THE SUMMIT

Now it's time to head down Haleakala. *Put your car in low gear to descend;* if you do that, you won't be among those who suddenly see smoke coming from the car and don't understand why. If you sit on the brakes the whole way down, you probably won't have any brakes by the time you reach the base of the mountain.

Along the way, you'll have two more stops—the first is Kalahaku Overlook (look for the sign on your right). It's the best place to see silversword, a plant that is unique to Hawaii. Over the centuries, it evolved from the sunflower family and is thought to live for 50 years before it blooms and then dies. (See Chapter 2 for more about silversword.) At one time this unusual plant virtually covered the area, but feral goats and curious visitors have virtually wiped it out. Haleakala National Park has now fenced off many areas where silversword still grows in an effort to protect one of Hawaii's rarest plants.

The second, and last, stop is at Hosmer Grove. There will be a sign on your right. The parking area is about a half mile from the turnoff; just off the parking lot there is a half-mile-long trail that will take you through a forest of trees introduced and planted by Ralph Hosmer in 1910. Here you will see eucalyptus, sugi pine (from Japan), deodar (from India), and a variety of pine trees. The park provides a brochure at the beginning of the trail that will help you to locate and identify the various trees. There's also a picnic ground here.

HIKING HALEAKALA

There are several hiking trails that vary in length and difficulty. The Halemauu Trail, which begins at an elevation of 8,000 feet—about 4 miles beyond the park headquarters—is a 10-mile hike that takes you from the west side of the volcano's rim down to the valley floor and into the east end of Haleakala. During the hike, which follows a series of switchbacks, you'll pass Holua cabin and the many cinder cones. The trail won't take you back to the parking lot where you began, so be prepared either to walk back up from the trail's end, or hitch a ride with someone who's going up. Sliding Sands Trail begins at 9,745 feet near the visitor center and follows the south rim of the volcano. This trail is also 10 miles long, and as you walk you'll pass Kapalaoa cabin, Paliku cabin, and loose cinder slides. As with the Halemauu Trail, you'll have to rely on the goodwill of others to get you back to your car. The third trail, known as the Kaupo Gap Trail, crosses the most difficult terrain. The area is covered with vegetation and rough lava. It is also extremely difficult to get back to the main road from the end of the Kaupo Gap Trail, so if you're planning to take that hike, you should also plan on camping somewhere in the area so you can walk back the next day. For information about camping in the park, write to Superintendent, P.O. Box 369, Makawao, Maui, HI 96768.

If you'd rather not take the self-guided hikes, ranger-guided hikes are usually scheduled during the summer months and take between $1/2$ and 2 hours. Check at park headquarters for a schedule. Other ways to see Haleakala are on horseback or by bike. See Chapter 9, "Maui Sports & Recreation."

A few words of advice: Never hike alone. Always carry enough water so you won't become dehydrated. Wear the proper shoes. Carry a sweater or jacket because the temperature drops here in the evening. Do not stray from established trails—you might damage the native flora without knowing it. Finally, do not remove anything, other than your trash, from Haleakala. Every year people take pieces of lava from the island, and every year they return them back with notes begging someone to return the lava to its rightful place. The reason? Well, some say that if you take lava from the island, you will have bad luck, and all those who have sent lava back to Maui have reported unusual bouts of bad luck.

5 Hana

Hana, together with its environs, is a lush tropical rain forest dotted with waterfalls and blue pools (it's famous for its Seven Sacred Pools, or Oheo Gulch). It's where you'll find red- and black-sand beaches, and it's where you'll find Hamoa Beach, a favorite of Mark Twain. In short, Hana is paradise. This may be what you came to Maui looking for, but it will take you at least 3 hours to get there. The first time I made the trip to Hana, I had no idea that I'd find myself confronted with 30 miles of bumpy, unpaved switchbacks and one-lane bridges. Today the road is paved (and was recently repaved), so the drive is a bit easier; however, if you have a tendency to get carsick, you should fly. Otherwise, drive: It's a trip you'll never forget—both for the challenge it presents and its beauty.

THE ROAD TO HANA

Before you begin the drive, there are a few things you need to know. First, the road to Hana is always crowded, and it's not unusual to find yourself driving in bumper-to-bumper traffic the entire distance. Because of the traffic, the winding (there are 617 curves) road, and the one-lane bridges (there are 56), it will take you about 3 hours to go from Kahului to Hana town. There are no gas stations or places to eat along the way, so it would be advisable to fill your gas tank before you leave and pack a picnic lunch. I would suggest that you begin the drive in the morning if you plan to return from Hana before it gets dark (the road is more dangerous at night). Otherwise, try to get a hotel room in Hana (see Chapter 6 for Hana accommodations) for at least one night. I've actually found the trip to be much more enjoyable if I stay overnight in Hana. If you're planning to hike, carry water with you—it's not a good idea to drink from most of the streams in the area. Do not attempt to drive if heavy rainstorms are predicted because mudslides are frequent and often block the road. Finally, don't forget to take your bathing suit; there are some wonderful pools fed by beautiful waterfalls where you can stop to swim during the drive.

Now we can begin. From Kahului, take Hana Highway (Route 36) in the direction of Upcountry. Your first stop along the way will be Paia. If you didn't already fill your gas tank, you can do so here. Paia is also a good place to buy things for that picnic lunch. You can purchase supplies at the **Paia General Store,** which will be on your left after the gas station, or you can go right on Baldwin Avenue to **Pic-nics** or the **Paia Fish Market** (see Chapter 7, "Maui Dining," for details). There are some great little shops here as well, including the ✪ **Maui Crafts Guild,** which is on your left just before you reach the center of Paia. The Guild is owned and operated by local Maui artists who are required to use only materials native to Hawaii in creating their artwork. Open daily, this is a great place to pick up an authentic souvenir. There are plenty of other shops on Baldwin Avenue and along Hana Highway that sell everything from women's fashions to swimwear and aromatherapy oils. **Just You & Me Kid** has great children's clothes (designed by owner Carol Ann), and the **Hana Hou Gallery** is another place to find the work of local artists. If you're still shopping for island-wear at this point, you might want to visit the **Summerhouse. Maui Girl Co.** is worth a stop, even if you're just looking because they have an interesting collection of silk and rayon aloha shirts from the 1930s, 1940s, and 1950s. With its unusual assortment of shops and its resident artists, Paia has gained a reputation for being something like Greenwich Village. After you've shopped around and stocked up on provisions, continue your drive.

The first point of interest after Paia is **Hookipa Beach Park,** where scores of windsurfers take advantage of Maui's best windsurfing beaches. Beyond Hookipa Beach Park is **Haiku,** known for its pineapple plantations. Many of Maui's permanent residents call Haiku home. Rents aren't so steep, the weather is good, and the beaches are nearby, which makes it one of Maui's more attractive residential areas. After you pass through Haiku civilization thins out somewhat; and now you may begin to think that I was lying about the curvy roads and the one-lane bridges, but enjoy the straight and spacious road while you can. You'll soon see a sign indicating the miles of curvy, bumpy road ahead. That's when the traffic will begin to look like the streets of Manhattan when the President is in town. It doesn't matter, though—you're in no hurry, and you'll be making lots of stops along the way.

Hana

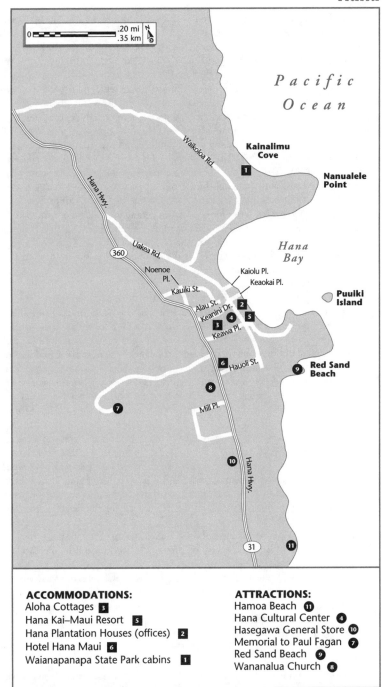

ACCOMMODATIONS:
Aloha Cottages **3**
Hana Kai–Maui Resort **5**
Hana Plantation Houses (offices) **2**
Hotel Hana Maui **6**
Waianapanapa State Park cabins **1**

ATTRACTIONS:
Hamoa Beach **11**
Hana Cultural Center **4**
Hasegawa General Store **10**
Memorial to Paul Fagan **7**
Red Sand Beach **9**
Wananalua Church **8**

By the time you reach **Kailua** (kye-loo-ah), your surroundings will have changed dramatically. Instead of scrub grass and sand, you'll begin to see guava trees (guavas are the yellow lemonlike fruits you'll see along the side of the road), heliconias, African tulip trees, ginger, and even bamboo (see Chapter 2, "Introducing the Valley Isle," for more information on the flora). Strangely enough, in the early part of this century, Kailua is where the island's criminals were sent, and beyond this town (which still has no grocery store) there was only a dirt path leading up to Hana.

As you round the bends to **Waikamoi,** the trees become more dense. You'll pass through a bamboo forest, and not long afterward (a half-mile after mile marker 9), you'll arrive at a maintained hiking trail. Stop here and take the 1-mile hike along the **Waikamoi Ridge Nature Trail,** which will lead you through groves of eucalyptus, ginger, heliconia, ti, and giant philodendron. Be on the lookout for lobster claw heliconia and the beautiful maidenhair ferns.

A couple of miles beyond Waikamoi you'll come to **Puohokamoa Stream.** If you're lucky, there will be space for you to park here so you can get out and take the short trail that leads to a double waterfall and a swimming hole, which can be seen from the bridge near where you'll park the car. Just over 1 mile from Waikamoi is **Kaumahina State Wayside,** where the dramatic coastal vistas are beyond your wildest imaginings. The bay, edged by a gorgeous black-sand beach, is known as **Honomanu Bay.**

Between 5 and 7 miles farther along the twisting, turning, increasingly beautiful road are the villages of **Keanae** and **Wailua,** which can be seen from the road. They're the last of the true old Hawaiian villages, in which taro farming and poi making are still done in the traditional fashion. When you get to mile marker 18 (actually Wailua), you'll be able to pull off the road and follow the signs to the **Coral Church** and the **Miracle of Fatima Shrine.** In the 1860s an unusually violent storm visited itself upon the island; when it was all over, the people of Wailua emerged to find that the storm had washed enough coral up onto the beach so that they could construct the church. Believing it to be a miracle, they constructed the Miracle of Fatima Shrine.

Drive back out to Hana Highway and continue toward Hana. Soon you will come to **Puaa Kaa State Wayside,** which is a great place to stop for a picnic if you haven't already had lunch. There are also two pools, each with a lovely waterfall, where you can have a quick swim before lunch. At this point some of you might be wondering if you're ever going to reach Hana, but I assure you, it won't be long now. Get back in that winding train of cars, steel yourself for the hairpin turns, and keep going.

The next side trip is really worthwhile—**Waianapanapa State Park**—where you can visit 120 acres of land that have been preserved by the State of Hawaii. You can camp here, but you need a permit in advance of your arrival (see "Hiking & Camping" in Chapter 9 for more information on camping, or Chapter 6, "Maui Accommodations," for information on the Waianapanapa cabins). Waianapanapa is dotted with the foundations of Old Hawaiian houses and temples, gravesites, and stone walls. There are also several freshwater caves in Waianapanapa that can be reached via a well-marked trail from the parking lot. One of the caves is said to turn red every year at the same time because of a deadly battle between a Hawaiian chief and his adulterous wife.

There's one more stop before you get to Hana. ✪ **Hana Gardenland,** on the right side of the road, is a tropical garden with a little cafe and a superb art gallery and gift shop attached. Many local artists are represented in the gallery. There are plans to expand the 3-acre botanical gardens to include large aviaries for tropical birds. The cafe is excellent; in fact, when Hillary Rodham Clinton visited Hana, she had breakfast at the Hana Gardenland Cafe three mornings in a row.

HANA

Most people are disappointed when they arrive in Hana because it's just a sleepy little town that happens to be situated between the rest of the island and Oheo Gulch, which is really what people come to Hana looking for. Hana might not be much to look at, but that's not important. Hana is a state of mind—a way of life. Things are slow and simple, and the people who have lived here for decades like it that way. For centuries, Hana was cut off from the rest of the island, but by the middle of the 19th century, civilization had made its way to this small town in the form of a sugar plantation, owned by George Wilfong. As with other sugar plantations on the island, Wilfong's plantation drew immigrants from Portugal, Japan, China, and the Philippines. Sugar production became the lifeblood of the Hana community, and this continued until about the middle of this century.

Around that time a man by the name of Paul Fagan bought several thousand acres of land right in the middle of Hana town. He brought in some cattle and began what would eventually become Hana Ranch. Fagan loved "Heavenly Hana" so much that he decided to live out the rest of his life here. He built the **Hotel Hana Maui,** hoping that it would be used primarily during the spring training of his baseball team (the San Francisco Seals) and as a place for his friends to stay when they visited. However, the first year the Seals came to train, scores of sportswriters and reporters came along with them, and then the word got out about this island paradise. From that point on, tourists have come to Hana in force. Today, the Hotel Hana Maui is still operating, and there's a memorial to Paul Fagan (he died in 1960) across the street from the hotel. It's a large, lava-stone cross set atop a hill.

Besides visiting the hotel and memorial, stop at the ✪ **Hana Cultural Center** (☎ 808/248-8622) on Uakea Road. Although it doesn't deserve a lot of time to visit, the Cultural Center holds some real treasures. There are Hawaiian quilts on display, poi boards (used for pounding taro into poi), brooms made of coconut fronds, old fish hooks, a coconut grater, stone lamps, and even some kapa cloth. It's open daily from 10am to 4pm, and admission is by donation. Next door is the tiny old Hana courthouse. Your admission fee to the cultural center entitles you to explore the courthouse and jail.

Hana Bay might be your next stop—there's excellent snorkeling and swimming here, as well as Tutu's, a hamburger/snack shop. In addition to Hana Bay, Hana is home to both a **red-sand beach** and the famous **Hamoa Beach** (located just outside the center of town). The **Hotel Hana-Maui** isn't far inland from Hana Bay, and on its far side is **Wananalua Church,** a beautiful coral stone church that was constructed in 1838. Before you leave Hana, stop by **Hasegawa General Store,** which sells absolutely everything: bread, butter, soup, candy, books, clothing, fruits, vegetables, bumper stickers, meat, hammers—the list goes on and on. Hasegawa's has established itself as something of a legend on Maui.

BEYOND HANA

The final stop on your trip to East Maui is **Oheo Gulch.** Although commonly referred to as the Seven Sacred Pools, they are neither sacred nor are there seven of them. Before you get there, however, you'll come to **Wailua Gulch,** a spectacular double falls. Oheo Gulch is located about 10 miles from Hana in Kipahulu. You'll know when you're there by the number of cars and the rather unattractive parking lot. The pools are like stepping-stones, each one flowing down into the next, and finally into the ocean. These are the lower falls, and you can frolic in them with the rest of the tourists who made the drive, or you can venture uphill from the parking lot (don't stop: The uphill trek is tough but short—it levels off after about a half-mile) through a field and a singing bamboo forest to Waimoku Falls. Don't quit at the first falls you see—take a break there if you need one, but then continue on to Waimoku. The total hike is a couple of miles, but I guarantee you won't be sorry you made the trip.

7 Organized Tours

See also Chapter 9, "Maui Sports & Recreation," for information on interisland cruises, horseback tours, bike tours, and other guided sports options.

DRIVING TOURS

Driving around Maui, although time-consuming, can be extremely interesting, especially if you've got someone (or something) to guide your travels.

GUIDED TOURS When most people travel they want to know the favorite attractions of local residents, but they seldom have the opportunity to travel with a local resident. On Maui you can Rent-A-Local (☎ 808/877-4042) who will take you on personalized tours of Hana, Haleakala, and Upcountry. Your local will take you to his or her favorite waterfalls and swimming holes, secluded beaches, snorkel spots, hiking areas, and restaurants. All you have to do is provide the rental car. Renting a local is one of the most entertaining and educational ways to see the island.

Rates for 6- to 8-hour tours are $156 for one person and $195 for two people.

SELF-GUIDED TOURS If your driving is going to take you specifically to Hana, you should stop by **Hana Cassette Guide** (at the Shell Service Station on Route 380; ☎ 808/572-0550 for directions) and pick up one of their audiocassettes. They will provide a tape player if you don't have one in your car, the tape, a flower photo book, and a Hana road map. You can drive at your own pace and along the way the cassette guide will provide all sorts of information about what you'll be seeing. The rental for the full day costs $20. Hana Cassette Guide opens every day at 6:30am.

Another way to see the island is to pick up a copy of Elaine and Tom Clements's *Be Your Own Tour Guide on Maui.* They've put together eight comprehensive, self-guided tours (along with a keyed map) that will take you Upcountry, to the Iao Valley, to and around Lahaina, to Polipoli State Park, along the road to Hana, and along Maui's southeast coast. They tell you where to start your tour, how long the tour will take, and where to stop during the drive. They'll even give you helpful hints along the way. Best of all, they've neatly packaged all this information in pocket-size folders so they're easy to carry around with you. You'll find the *Be Your Own Tour Guide on Maui* packets at the Maui Visitors Bureau and many of the area's hotels. When I last spoke with Elaine Clements, plans were under way to create the tours for various island hotels. The starting points for each tour would be at a specific hotel, with directions to the first stop beginning at that hotel. Check with your hotel to see if they have the driving tours.

HELICOPTER TOURS

Many people believe the best way to see Maui in a short period of time is to take a helicopter tour. The only reason for not doing so is that they're typically rather expensive—about $100 per person. However, if you can afford it, you won't be disappointed—the tour is truly thrilling. Most Maui helicopter-tour operators will take you to Hana, Haleakala, and Molokai in one combination or another. You might be able to book a tour that encompasses all three (that'll probably cost about $220 per person), or one that takes you to both Haleakala and Hana (between $125 and $185 per person). Flight time varies according to the tour you've chosen, but generally last between 45 minutes and 1 hour. The helicopter will touch down in remote areas where you'll see things (such as the spectacular waterfalls of Hana) you'd never be able to see any other way. An hour doesn't seem like much time to see the whole island, but these choppers move fast, and the pilots are exceedingly experienced, so you'll get your money's worth. Many of the tour operators will provide a videotape of your tour, and while you're flying the pilot will comment on the passing scene and you can enjoy recorded music. Some aircraft interiors are soundproof, and a couple of operators offer seating with 180-degree views.

All helicopter-tour companies operate out of Kahului Airport, and you should know that many of them will weigh you when you arrive at the airport so that they can evenly distribute the weight in the helicopter. Some people find the prospect of being weighed while on vacation (without advance warning) stressful, so if it'll ruin your vacation, skip the helicopter tour. Otherwise, consider yourself warned.

Blue Hawaiian (☎ 808/871-8844 or 800/745-BLUE) is family-owned and operated, and you'll be able to fly on one of their new jet helicopters. Blue Hawaiian touches down in several remote locations and features recorded music and narration on its Helicam system. The interiors are soundproof, and wherever you sit, you'll enjoy 180-degree views. Your tour will be videotaped. The first tape is free; additional tapes cost $5.

✪ Sunshine Helicopters (☎ 808/871-0722) also has a superb reputation on Maui. Sunshine offers some less expensive, shorter flights that take you around West Maui. The 20- and 30-minute tours will cost you $79 and $99, respectively, and the West Maui Touchdown (30-minute ride, 20-minute touchdown) costs $119. If you want to take a tour of the entire island (60 to 70 minutes), it will cost $129. There is also a variety of combination tours offered. A video, shot on four different cameras throughout the ride, is free.

There are other helicopter tour companies on the island, but Sunshine and Blue Hawaiian are the only ones with a flawless safety record, so I'd recommend sticking with them.

9

Maui Sports & Recreation

Maui offers a large variety of sports and recreation activities for island visitors. Snorkeling is popular, and for the more adventurous there's scuba diving; hiking and biking are great ways to explore the inland areas; you can take surfing or windsurfing lessons, go hunting, play golf or tennis, and even learn to kayak. No matter what your sports interests are, you'll probably find something you enjoy on Maui. Many people who plan a trip to Maui don't give much thought to physical activity, but after they've spent some days in the sun and done a fair amount of sightseeing, they may be looking for something else to do. That's where this chapter comes in.

A WORD ABOUT ACTIVITIES DESKS   Particularly in Lahaina, you'll be regularly solicited by activities desk personnel to buy heavily discounted tickets to island activities. Be aware, however, that in return you may be asked to listen to several hours of hard-sell promotion for time-share condominiums or other products. Several activities desks are actually "legitimate" and will get you some discounted rates without this hassle. Try the **Tours and Visitor Information** desk in Lahaina's Wharf Cinema Center (☎ 808/667-2112) or **Barefoot's Cashback Tours,** 834 Front St. (☎ 808/661-8889).

In addition to all the independent activities owners listed in this chapter, **Ocean Activities Center,** which offers a range of activities from snorkeling to sportfishing, has offices in many Maui hotels. If you're staying in a hotel with an Ocean Activities Center office, it might be easier for you to book an activity directly through them. If you'd like to participate in something they don't offer, check the listings in this chapter—you'll probably find what you need. For the Ocean Activities main reservations office, call 808/879-4485. Hotel and condominium locations include the Aston Maui Vista (☎ 808/879-1779), Embassy Suites Hotel (☎ 808/667-7116), Kea Lani Hotel (☎ 808/879-8804), Kihei Akahi (☎ 808/879-8998), Mana Kai Maui Resort (☎ 808/879-6704), Maui Hill Resort (☎ 808/879-0180), Maui Lu Resort (☎ 808/879-2977), Maui Marriott (☎ 808/661-3631), and Renaissance Wailea Beach Resort (☎ 808/879-0181). They also have offices at the Lahaina Cannery Mall (☎ 808/661-5309) and Whalers Village (☎ 808/661-4444).

1 Beaches

By Jeanette Foster

Maui has a plethora of sandy beaches—white, black, salt-and-pepper, even red—including some 33 miles of nearly continuous beaches on the south and west shores. Maui's beaches offer a range of activities for all interests, from riding the surf to lazily floating in warm salt water. The beaches listed below are just some of the more attractive beaches on Maui's shoreline:

HONOLUA BAY/MOKULEIA BEACH

These twin bays are located just of Highway 30, just past D. T. Fleming Park (look for the Mokuleia-Honolua Marine Reserve signs). They make up one of the three Marine Life Conservation Districts in Maui County, which means that nothing can be taken (fish, coral, etc.) from the water. Honolua is well known for its world-class surfing in the winter and for excellent snorkeling in the summer. Mokuleia, also part of the protected area, has great bodysurfing (for experts only) in the winter and swimming and snorkeling (for all levels) in the summer. Mokuleia Bay is known as "slaughterhouse beach" by local residents—a slaughterhouse once occupied the cliff above the bay. Few tourists venture down to these beaches in the winter, most preferring to watch the surfing action from the cliffs above. In the summer, the steep access down to the beaches weeds out some beach goers, but the beach is rarely without sunbathers and swimmers on bright sunny days.

D. T. FLEMING BEACH PARK

Want to get away from the crowds? Here's the place to go. This is not always a swimming beach—conditions can be treacherous—but it's a great for surfing and bodysurfing in the winter. Fleming Beach is an exquisite white-sand beach bordered with ironwood trees, with a shaded grassy area for picnicking and a view of Molokai just across the channel. This is a place for quiet contemplation, resting, or just listening to the wind singing through the ironwoods. It's located just past Kapalua on Highway 30 (look for the sign). Parking on the road, rest rooms, showers, picnic tables, and barbecue grills are available.

KAPALUA BEACH

At the entrance to Kapalua, off Lower Honoapilani Road just past the Napili Kai Beach Club, look for a public beach right-of-way sign—this will lead you directly to Kapalua Beach. Formerly known as the Fleming Beach (which now is the name of another nearby beach), this one comes straight out of central casting call for the perfect Hawaiian beach. It's a crescent of white sand bordered by two black rocky points with palm trees providing the shade. Because it's a sheltered bay, swimming and snorkeling are excellent and safe for children. Above the beach is the Kapalua Bay Hotel, so the sand is always packed with hotel guests and local residents. To get a parking space at this popular place, you must get there early in the day; the beachfront parking lot holds only 30 to 40 cars. Facilities include showers, rest rooms, and plenty of shade.

KAANAPALI BEACH

Not surprisingly, one of Maui's best beaches—with granular white sand as far as the eye can see—fronts the elaborate line of hotels and condominiums in Kaanapali. This beach is excellent for summertime swimming. The Kaanapali resort area was built before the public raised a hue and cry over public access, so parking is a problem for nonresort guests. There are two entrances: At the south end, turn off the Honoapilani Highway into the Kaanapali resort and pay for parking there; or, continue on the Honoapilani Highway and turn off at the last Kaanapali exit, at the stop light near the Maui Kaanapali Villas, and park next to the public access beach signs.

Facilities include outdoor rinse-off showers; you can use the rest rooms at the hotel pools. Various beach activity vendors line the beach in front of the hotels, offering nearly every conceivable type of ocean recreation activity and equipment. Because the Kaanapali Beach is so long and because most hotels have swimming pools adjacent, the beach is crowded only in pockets—there's plenty of room to find seclusion. A paved beach path offers a comfortable way to stroll along the beach, people-watching.

The best place to snorkel is around **Black Rock,** which sits in front of the Sheraton Hotel. The water is nearly always clear, calm, and populated with clouds of tropical fish. Black Rock (or *Puu Kekaa*, as the Hawaiians call it) is known as the place where souls leap into the afterlife. According to Hawaiian tradition, when someone is near death, their soul leaves the body and wanders around, making sure that all their earthly obligations have been filled. If all is right, then the soul proceeds to Puu Kekaa to leap from this world into the next.

KAMAOLE III BEACH PARK

Along South Kihei Road, in Kihei, are three county parks: Kamaole I, II, and III. All are popular with local residents and visitors because they are easily accessible and have good parking. On weekends all three are jam-packed with fishermen, picnickers, swimmers, and snorkelers, but the most popular of the three seems to be Kamaole III. It is the biggest of the three beaches, with wide pockets of white sand, and it's the only one with a playground for children; it also has the most parking. Other facilities include rest rooms, showers, picnic tables, and barbecue grills. Swimming is safe here, but parents should watch to make sure that their children don't venture too far out, as the bottom slopes quickly offshore. The winter waves attract bodysurfers. This beach also is a wonderful place to watch the sunset.

ULUA BEACH

This is the most popular beach in Wailea for a variety of reasons: It's a long, wide, crescent-shaped, white-sand beach between two rocky points, and it offers the best snorkeling in Wailea when the ocean is calm. When it's rough, the waves are excellent for bodysurfers. It's located close to the Wailea Ocean Activity Center, where a variety of rental equipment is available. The ocean bottom is shallow and gently slopes down to deeper waters, making swimming generally safe. Facilities include showers and rest rooms. The beach is usually occupied by guests of the nearby Wailea resorts; during the high season (Christmas to March and June to August), the beach is carpeted with beach towels, and the ocean is standing-room-only. To find Ulua Beach, look for the public access sign (Ulua/Mokapu Beaches) on the South Kihei Road in Wailea, near the Stouffer Wailea Beach Resort. A very small parking lot—get there early in the day if you want to get a space—is located nearby.

ONELOA BEACH (BIG BEACH) AT MAKENA

Oneloa means "long sand" in Hawaiian; that's a perfect description of this extraordinary beach, also called "Big Beach" by local residents or "Makena Beach" by visitors. Oneloa is 3,300 feet long and more than 100 feet wide, and it's one of the most

Beaches & Outdoor Activities on Maui

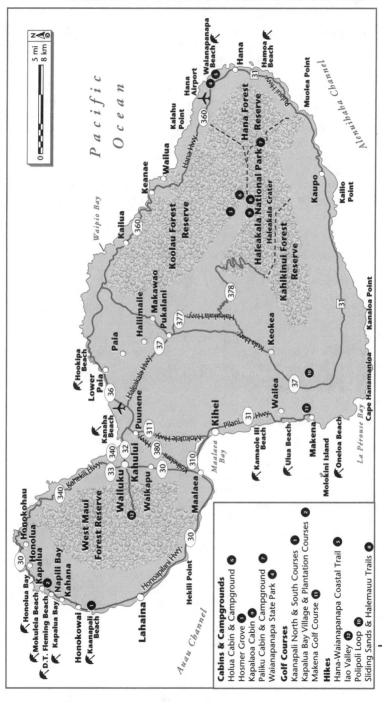

popular undeveloped beaches on Maui. To get there, take the Old Makena Highway to the second dirt road, which leads all the way down to the beach. When the ocean is calm, there is good snorkeling around the north end of the beach at the foot of Puu Olai, a large cinder cone that rises 360 feet above sea level. During a storm—there is no protective reef offshore—the waves roll onto the beach with a dangerous rip current. Occasionally, the surf is appropriate for board and bodysurfing, but only by those experienced. Under the waves the ocean bottom has a quick, sharp drop-off, which, combined with a strong rip current, spells disaster for inexperienced surfers and swimmers. There are no public facilities, but this is a great place for a picnic and the view of Molokini and Kahoolawe.

On the other side of the cinder cone, Puu Olai is a smaller white-sand beach, known locally as "Little Beach." Various visitor publications have labeled this beach as a clothing-optional area, but skinny-dipping is illegal in Hawaii, and occasionally the police conduct "raids" at Little Beach (the charge for nude sunbathing is lewd conduct).

HAMOA BEACH

A couple of miles past Hana, on the way to Kipahulu, is Hamoa Beach (look for the Hamoa Beach turnoff from the Hana Highway). The gorgeous beach is 1,000 feet long, 100 feet wide, and surrounded by 30-foot-high lava cliffs. The left side of the beach is the calmest, offering the best snorkeling in the summer. Hamoa is known as a popular surfing and bodysurfing area. This is an unprotected beach, however, vulnerable to the open—ocean and surf rolls right onto the beach, creating powerful rip currents at times. The upscale Hotel Hana Maui maintains the beach and has numerous facilities for its guests. There is an outdoor shower and rest rooms for nonguests. Entrance is via steps. Parking is limited.

WAIANAPANAPA STATE PARK

Four miles before the town of Hana, off the Hana Highway, is Waianapanapa State Park. The park takes its name from the legend of the Waianapanapa Cave, where Chief Kaakea, a jealous and cruel man, suspected his wife, Popoalaea, of having an affair. Popoalaea left her husband and hid herself in a chamber of the Waianapanapa Cave. She and her attendant ventured out only at night, for food. Nevertheless, a few days later, Kaakea was passing by the area and saw the shadow of the servant. Knowing he had found his wife's hiding place, Kaakea entered the cave and killed her. During certain times of the year, the water in the tide pool turns red as a tribute to Popoalaea, commemorating her death. Scientists claim, however, that the water turns red because of the presence of small, red shrimp.

Waianapanapa State Park's 120 acres have 12 cabins, a caretaker's residence, a beach park, picnic tables, barbecue grills, rest rooms, showers, a parking lot, a shoreline hiking trail, and a black-sand beach (the sand is actually small black pebbles). This is a wonderful area for shoreline hikes—bring insect repellent as the mosquitoes are plentiful—and picnicking. Ocean activities are generally unsafe, though, due to strong waves breaking offshore, which roll into the beach unchecked, and strong rip currents. Because Waianapanapa is crowded on weekends with local residents and their families as well as tourists, weekdays are generally a better bet.

HOOKIPA BEACH PARK

Two miles past Paia, on the Hana Highway, is one of the most famous windsurfing sites in the world. Due to the constant winds and steady supply of waves (especially in the winter), Hookipa attracts the top windsurfers and wave jumpers from around the world. Surfers and fishermen enjoy this small, white-sand beach and surrounding grassy cliff, too. Except when international competitions are being held, weekdays are usually a good time to come and watch the colorful windsurfers swirl in the wind and pirouette over the waves, high into the air. When the waves are absent, snorkelers and divers explore the reef. Facilities include rest rooms, showers, pavilions, picnic tables, barbecue grills, and a parking lot.

KANAHA BEACH PARK

Kanaha means "shattered thing," stemming from an Hawaiian legend about a man who stole the eggs of an Hawaiian *pueo* (owl) and senselessly smashed them against a stone wall in the Kanaha area. Owls from all over the islands flocked to Kanaha and destroyed the man, his family, and everyone living in the area. Today, however, Kanaha is a peaceful place: Shaded lawns slope down to the mile-long, white-sand beach; the only distraction here is the noise from the adjacent Maui airport. On weekends, the park is filled with local families. In the winter, windsurfers from all over the world come here to skim over the water like butterflies. Kanaha Beach is located just before the Kahului Airport—turn left at the sign Kanaha Beach Park, then right on Ahahao Street. Its numerous facilities include rest rooms, showers, picnic tables, barbecue grills, and parking. A couple of warnings, though: The beach park is landscaped with *kiawe* trees, which drop sharp thorns, so don't go barefooted. Also, this is an area rife with theft, so don't leave anything in your car and don't leave your belongings unattended.

2 Water Sports

DEEP-SEA FISHING

If you like deep-sea fishing and want the chance to go after mahimahi, ono, tuna, or marlin, you'll have no problem finding a charter on Maui. Most deep-sea fishing charters carry no more than six people at a time, so you won't get lost in the crowd. There are a couple of ways to arrange for a charter—you can walk the docks at either Lahaina or Maalaea Harbor, or you can book through an activities desk. For those unfamiliar with fishing in Hawaii, many boats tag and release marlin; other fish caught (tuna, mahimahi, or ono) do not belong to the angler catching the fish, but remain with the captain and crew. If these terms are unacceptable—if you want to keep your fish or a portion of it, or you want to take a marlin and have it mounted—you should discuss your desires with the captain in advance.

If you plan to fish out of Maalaea, I recommend **Rhythm & Blues Sportfishing** (☎ 808/879-7098) with Captain Mike Crawford, an experienced fishermen with top-flight fishing gear and a comfortably equipped 36-foot Pacifica sportfishing boat. Or try the activities desk at the harbor, **Maalaea Activities** (☎ 808/242-6982), to book any other fishing boat.

In Lahaina, I recommend **Hinatea Sportfishing,** slip 27, Lahaina Harbor (☎ 808/667-7548). They'll take you out in one of their fleet of deep-sea fishing vessels. They take honors for the most marlin caught and the most marlin tagged and released. Their motto is "No boat rides here; we go catch fish!" You might also check with **West Maui Charters** (☎ 808/669-6193) for boats that offer everything from light to heavy tackle fishing.

Depending on whether you share a boat for half a day or take a full-day private fishing trip, you'll pay anywhere from $80 to $950.

INTERISLAND CRUISES

Club Lanai (☎ 808/871-1144) is one of the most popular interisland cruises (or "adventures") on Maui today. You'll sail over to Lanai, where you'll get to snorkel at a turtle reef, go bicycling, boating, wave skiing, take part in beach sports (such as volleyball), explore marine life in touch tanks, take historical wagon rides, and lounge in hammocks; and you'll visit the beautiful, pristine, white- and dark-sand beaches of Lanai. It's an all-day affair that includes an outdoor buffet and a fully stocked bar and access to a beach reserved specifically for guests of Club Lanai. All-inclusive prices are $79 for adults, $39 for children. The Club Lanai boat departs from Lahaina Harbor (pier 4) at 8am and makes the return trip from Lanai at 3pm.

   Trilogy Excursions (☎ 808/661-4743) offers a cruise to Lanai as well. The Coon family's *Discover Lanai* charter is the only one with access to Lanai's Hulopoe Marine Preserve and Beach Park.

   Maui Classic Charters (☎ 808/879-8188) will also take you to Lanai to explore the turtle reef.

OCEAN KAYAKING

Kayaks were once the fishing vehicle of choice for ancient Hawaiians. Today you too can have a kayak adventure.

South Pacific Kayaks, 2439 S. Kihei Rd. (☎ 808/875-4848) or 505 Front St., Lahaina (☎ 808/661-8400), was Maui's first kayak tour company, and its owners, Michael and Melissa McCoy, have lots of kayak experience (both locally and internationally). They'll provide you with single, double, or triple kayaks equipped with rudder systems for added safety. You'll be able to paddle at your own pace, and South Pacific Kayaks can work with people of virtually any age. You can rent kayaks for the day or the week, or take one of their snorkel/kayak tours ($43 to $130). Tours depart in the morning and last for 2¹/₂ to 5 hours. If you go during whale season, you might get closer to a whale than you ever thought was possible. Kayak rentals are also available.

   You might also try calling **Kelii's Kayak Tours** (☎ 808/874-7652). They're a small, locally owned business, and they'll supply you with a form-fitting, stable, ocean kayak loaded with snorkeling and fishing gear; and they'll take you on one of three tours (Makena, Olowalu, and Kapalua) along Maui's dramatic seacoast. In addition, Kelii's offers a great sunset tour.

   If you're kayaking on your own, you should know that one of the best kayaking spots (when there are no storms) is along the Kihei Coast because there's plenty of easy beach access to calm water. Mornings are best since the wind comes up around 11am, making paddling more difficult.

PARASAILING

Always wanted to parasail? Well, now's your chance, and I guarantee it's an experience you'll never forget. How could anyone forget being suspended hundreds of feet (in some cases up to 900 feet) above the earth? By the time you're on the boat, you'll probably wonder why on earth you signed up to do this in the first place. But after you've been harnessed into the chute and it's too late to say no, you'll forget your fear. These days they launch you right off the boat. In one quick roar of the motorboat's engine you're off and flying, legs dangling, and then suddenly everything becomes quiet, and you feel like you can see into forever. It's over before you want it to be, and when the motorboat cuts its engine, you drift slowly toward the earth and land in the water; or in some cases, they'll just reel you right back onto the boat, and you'll never even have to touch the water. I actually prefer the old way of doing things—on my first parasailing experience, the trip out to the platform (located just off the coast) in a glorified rubber dinghy (it had a motor) was scarier than my actual takeoff; and when I came down I landed right in the water.

There are several reputable parasail companies on Maui. If this sounds like something you want to do, call **Kaanapali Parasail** (☎ 808/669-6555) or **UFO Parasail** (☎ 808/661-7UFO). Rides typically last about 15 minutes. Both companies operate out of Kaanapali and will pick you up right on the beach. The great thing about parasailing is that, relatively speaking, it's quite affordable, and I actually like it better than a helicopter ride because of the absolute sense of serenity you feel when you're in the air.

Note: Parasailing on Maui is permitted only from mid-May through mid-December, due to restrictions placed on the boats during humpback whale season.

SAILING

The blustery winds that funnel through the isthmus between Haleakala and the West Maui Mountains past Maalaea, as well as the constant trade winds off the Lahaina Coast, make sailing from Maui a pleasurable and often exhilarating opportunity. Every type of boat you can dream of—from a three-masted schooner to spacious trimarans, from boats that take on only six passengers to those carrying 146 passengers—is available. There are all sorts of reasons to take one of these sailing trips: Sail for the sheer pleasure of feeling the wind filling the sails to a destination (such as Lanai), or just to see the sunset or enjoy a special dinner.

My favorite (and, in my mind, the best) Hawaii sailing trip is offered by **Trilogy Excursions** (180 Lahainaluna Rd., Lahaina (☎ 808/661-4743). Operated by the Coon family, with their fleet of custom-built, comfortable, multihull sailboats, Trilogy offers day-long trips to Lanai and memories for a lifetime. Your trip begins with continental breakfast as the stable vessel makes its way to Lanai. The crew takes time to provide personalized instruction on how to snorkel in Hulopoe Bay, a Marine Conservation District. After a little snorkeling, they prepare an island-style barbecue lunch, and then offer a van tour of the island. The price of $158.18 for adults and $79.09 for children (which includes breakfast, lunch, and snorkeling equipment) is worth every penny.

Or, you can sail out of Maalaea Harbor to Molokini with **Maui Classic Charters** (☎ 808/879-8188). Sail/snorkel Molokini trips cost about $56 to $66. Maui Classic Charters also offers whale-watches and sunset sails.

For shorter trips, try **Kamehameha Catamaran Sails** (Lahaina Harbor, Slip 67 ☎ 808/661-4522). This 40-foot Hawaiian beach catamaran offers regularly scheduled sailing and snorkeling trips with snacks, soft drinks, free snorkeling equipment, and free use of an underwater camera—just bring your own film. Cost, depending on the length of the trip, runs from $26 to $36.

If the romance of bygone pirating days appeals to you, book a sail on *The Silent Lady* (Maalaea Harbor, Slip 27 ☎ 808/875-1112 or 800/450-2033), a modern-day re-creation of an old pirate ship. A custom-built, luxury schooner, *The Silent Lady* was constructed by owner/captain, Skip Price. Price's dedication to this ship shows in every detail, from walnut and cherry wood inlaid with birch to etched glass cabinet doors below deck. A six-hour sail/snorkel tour costs $54.95 for adults and $39.95 for children 2 to 11 years old. The fare includes continental breakfast, lunch, juices and soft drinks, and all snorkeling equipment.

If you opt for *America II* **Sailing** (Lahaina Harbor, Slip 5 ☎ 808/667-2195), you'll be taking a ride on a veteran of the 1987 America's Cup races (held in

Australia). They offer afternoon, evening, starlight, and moonlight sails as well as snorkeling and whale-watching (in season). Call for rates.

SCUBA DIVING

Diving on Maui means accessing not only the Maui coastline, but also nearby Molokini, Kahoolawe, Lanai, and Molokai. Unforgettable dive opportunities are found at Molokini, a 160-foot-wide, crescent-shaped crater with three tiers of diving: a 35-foot plateau inside the crater basin (used by beginning divers and snorkelers), a wall sloping to 70 feet just beyond the inside plateau, and a sheer wall on the outside and backside of the crater that plunges to 350 feet. This is the most popular dive site in the state due to calm, clear, protected water—it's an underwater park—and an abundance of marine life (from manta rays to clouds of butterfly fish).

The second most popular dive site in the state is known as Cathedrals, off the south coast of Lanai. Just a 45-minute boat ride from Lahaina, this dive site is known the world over for its majestic topography. The Cathedrals earned its name from the way the light shines through a lattice of coral, looking much like the stained-glass windows in a magnificent church. The parishioners here are a multitude of tropical fish. In the choir loft are crustaceans and invertebrates, and occasionally the confessional houses a white-mouth moray eel.

Since most visitors have limited time on their Maui vacation to enjoy these underwater wonders, I would suggest taking a dive class at home, so that you are prepared to dive when you reach the islands. If you don't have an opportunity to prepare before you arrive, most dive operators offer what they call an introductory dive. No experience is necessary, and the cost ranges from $40 to $95; you can learn from this glimpse into the Neptunian world whether diving is for you. Furthermore, many of the hotels in the resort areas offer free first-time lessons. If you're staying in one of those hotels, you should take advantage of the free lesson to decide whether you enjoy the sport. Additional lessons can be expensive.

For personalized diving, I recommend **Ed Robinson's Diving Adventures** (☎ 808/879-3584). This widely published underwater photographer offers specialized charters for small groups. Most of his business is from repeat customers, for good reason. Ed offers two-tank dives for around $85. In Lahaina, call **Lahaina Divers** (☎ 808/667-7496 or 800/998-3483); they've put together a variety of classes and dives for divers of all levels of experience. Lahaina Divers runs open water referral programs and introductory scuba diving experiences daily. Newly certified, or rusty, divers may participate in an afternoon orientation dive. One-, two-, and three-tank dives are available for more experienced certified divers. Lahaina Divers is one of Maui's few Five Star PADI-IDC facilities.

Maui's largest diving retailer, with everything from rentals to scuba-diving instruction to dive-boat charters, is **Maui Dive Shop.** Maui Dive can be found all over the island: in Kihei at Azeka Place II Shopping Center (☎ 808/879-3388), Kamaole Shopping Center (☎ 808/879-1533), and Kihei Town Center (☎ 808/879-1919); in Lahaina at Lahaina Cannery Mall (☎ 808/661-5388) and 626 Front St. (☎ 808/667-0722). Other locations include: Wailea Shopping Village (☎ 808/879-3166), Whalers Shopping Village, Kaanapali (☎ 808/661-5117), Kahana Gateway, Kahana (☎ 808/669-3800), and 444 Hana Hwy., Kahului (☎ 808/871-2111).

SNORKELING

Sunbathing aside, snorkeling is one of the island's most popular activities. You can rent snorkeling equipment from most of the hotels (especially the resort hotels) or from independent agencies. **Snorkel Bob's Inc.** is probably the island's most popular and well-known rental agency. For $15 a week, Snorkel Bob's will provide you with a mask, fins, snorkel, bag, map, fish food (not recommended—feeding fish in the wild can have deleterious effects), "no-fog goop" for your mask, fish ID book, and the extra bonus—"The Legend of Snorkel Bob." Snorkel Bob's is located at 34 Keala Pl., Kihei (☎ 808/879-7449), in the Napili Village Hotel, 5425 Lower Honoapilani Rd., Napili (☎ 808/669-9603), and at 161 Lahainaluna Rd., Lahaina (☎ 808/ 661-4421). **Boss Frog's,** located in Lahaina at 888 Wainee St., #131 (☎ 808/ 661-3333, ext. 2) and Kihei, at 2395 S. Kihei Rd. (☎ 808/875-4477, ext. 2), offers a similar deal. For $15 a week you'll get a mask, snorkel, fins, carry bag, no-fog goop, a snorkel map, a free snorkel sail to Molokini or Coral Gardens, and a free underwater camera per party of two. In all cases, prescription masks will cost more. The **Maui Dive Shop** sells and rents snorkel equipment. It is also represented island-wide. See "Scuba Diving," above, for locations and phone numbers.

GREAT SNORKELING OFF MAUI BEACHES   Before you rent that snorkel- ing gear, you should note that you'll always be able to find a good place to snorkel somewhere on the island, but it might not always be right out your front door. Winter months near Kaanapali, Lahaina, and Olowalu can be very calm, but not far down the coast in Kapalua, the winter months can bring heavy, dangerous surf. In the Kapalua area, summer is the best time to snorkel. The island's south side, near Wailea and Kihei, is ideal virtually year-round, except when there's heavy surf.

For safety reasons, you should always snorkel with someone else. Swim side by side so you'll always be able to see each other. When you're snorkeling, you might have to swim out a little way in order to see much of a particular reef. If you do, always be on the lookout for boats. If the water is not completely calm and you have a ten- dency toward motion sickness, you should pick your face up out of the water every once in a while and focus in on the horizon so you won't get seasick. Sounds rather incredible, I realize, but this actually happens to people sometimes. Always keep the ocean floor in view. If you suddenly lose sight of it, you've gone too far and should turn back—you're not scuba diving. Don't poke your fingers into holes or crevices, and definitely don't swim into caves. Finally, always check the weather and the level of safety of a particular snorkeling site before you head out. Local dive shops should be able to provide you with the information you need. You might also check with your hotel. For more water safety tips see "Health & Insurance" in Chapter 3.

Black Rock, at the Sheraton Maui Resort, just off Kaanapali Beach, is a great place (especially in the winter) for beginners to snorkel. The lava formation is a favorite gathering spot for some colorful Hawaiian fish, and if you arrive on Kaanapali Beach early enough in the morning, you might have the added pleasure of seeing a green sea turtle that likes to spend the morning on the beach near Black Rock. If the surf is at all rough, don't venture out here. Also, try to keep an eye out for cliff divers.

Not only is **Kapalua Beach** one of the best sunbathing and swimming beaches in the world, but it fronts a reef, which makes it an excellent place for beginning snorkelers. All you have to do is swim out to the reef and then go left or right along the coastline looking for tropical beauties. Be careful how far you go to the right, because the water suddenly gets deep. If the surf is low, you can venture out on the north side of the bay.

Honolua Bay, just beyond the Kapalua resort (heading away from Lahaina), is a marine sanctuary. Fish, coral, shells, seaweed, and even the sand are protected, so don't try to remove anything from the area. Winter months here are not good for snorkeling; however, spring, summer, and early fall are excellent times for snorkelers of all experience levels to explore the area around Honolua Bay. The entrance to Honolua Bay is located just beyond Mokuleia Beach. A dirt pathway leads to the water from the parking area.

Between Kapalua and Honolua Bays is **Mokuleia Bay** (also part of the marine sanctuary), a challenge for the more advanced snorkeler. The winter months here, as at Kapalua and Honolua Bays, are not good for snorkeling because the surf is too high. If the weather is good, you can follow one of two paths—head out along the reef or follow the shoreline to the left.

On your way to South or Central Maui, keep an eye out for the small town of **Olowalu.** You'll see a general store and Chez Paul Restaurant. Not far from that small grouping of stores you'll see Olowalu Beach. If you swim out away from shore, you'll come to a reef that is replete with marine life.

Two beaches in Kihei, **Kamaole II** and **Kamaole III,** are both good for the beginner and are best snorkeled before noon. A great spot to view fish is around the rock formation that separates the two beaches. Not far along the coast from Kamaole II and III is **Ulua Beach.** Like the Kamaole beaches, Ulua Beach is separated from a neighboring beach by rock formations where snorkeling is usually good.

Continuing along the coastline in the direction of Makena, **Wailea Beach** is another fine snorkeling spot. Here you'll want to follow the shoreline as you swim.

There is also some snorkeling at **Hana Beach Park,** but if you're not sure of yourself in the ocean, it might be best to avoid snorkeling there because if you go too far out, you could get caught in a strong current. It's easy to lose track of where you are when your face is in the water.

OFF-ISLAND SNORKELING   The best and most well-known off-island snorkeling site near Maui is **Molokini Island,** a small, crescent-shaped islet that rises approximately 130 feet above the ocean's surface and, in some areas, drops below the surface to a depth of 300 feet. Molokini is one of the cinder cones *(pu'u)* in a long chain that begins along the slopes of Haleakala. Molokini and a large hill on the Wailea/Makena coastline (known as Puu Olai) were both produced by one of Haleakala's volcanic eruptions. Ancient Hawaiian mythology describes Molokini and Puu Olai as the head and tail of a mythological lizard that dared to cross the romantic path of the omnipotent Pele. You see, Pele had fallen in love with Lohiau, but Lohiau had eyes for the lizard, and when Pele learned of their marriage, she chopped the lizard in half.

In the 1900s, for some unknown reason, rabbits were introduced to Molokini. They not only survived but thrived for more than 70 years—until the islet vegetation was killed off during a drought. You can't climb around on Molokini—first of all, it has been declared a Marine Life Conservation District and a State Seabird Sanctuary; furthermore, during World War II the U.S. Navy used Molokini for target practice, and there may still be some unexploded bullets and bombs there.

The waters here are usually calm in the morning, but when the trade winds pick up in the afternoon, the water often becomes choppy. For that reason, excursion boats that come to Molokini do so during the morning hours and then return to Maui by early afternoon.

Maui Classic Charters, located in Long's Center in Kihei (☎ 808/879-8188), offers snorkeling and snuba (see "Snuba," in this chapter for more information) cruises on *Four Winds,* their glass-bottom catamaran. They'll take you to Molokini or to various coral gardens just off Maui shores. Barbecue lunch is optional, and there's an on-board water slide. This is a good trip for the whole family. The

Lavengro, a 1926 Biloxi schooner (the oldest on the island) also operated by Maui Classic Charters, also sails to Molokini for snorkeling.

Trilogy Excursions (☎ 808/661-4743 or 800/874-2666) is one of Maui's best charter companies. Tours depart from Maalaea Harbor, and on the way to Molokini, your captain will explain, in detail, the history of the island. While you're exploring the marine life around Molokini, the catamaran's crew will be laying out cheese, crackers, and beverages as a prelunch snack. For lunch you'll get a delicious hot meal (with real flatware—not the plastic variety). Trilogy service is truly first-class.

Pacific Whale Foundation Eco-Adventures (☎ 808/879-8811) offers trips to Molokini with a second snorkeling stop at Turtle Arches (where you'll see giant sea turtles). They also offer a new Wild Dolphin and Snorkeling Adventure that takes you to hidden coves off Lanai for dolphin-watching and snorkeling. All trips are led by experienced and knowledgeable professional marine biologists who get into the water with you for a guided tour of the reefs (many of the other snorkeling companies send you into the water alone while they wait for you on the boat). Pacific Whale Foundation also guarantees that you'll see whales on these snorkeling trips from mid-December until May. Pacific Whale Foundation is an excellent, excellent choice. In addition to getting a great tour, you can be assured that you're helping to protect the environment because all profits from these Eco-Adventures go to benefit marine conservation.

Friendly Charters (☎ 808/871-0985) also makes trips to Molokini on a large catamaran. They depart from Maalaea Harbor (Slip 78) and provide continental breakfast, deli lunch, beverages, snorkeling gear and instruction, as well as free use of underwater cameras.

Gemini Charters (☎ 808/661-2591) sets sail out of Kaanapali and Lahaina for half-day snorkel/sail excursions with hot buffet luncheons.

The *Lahaina Princess* (☎ 808/661-8397), operated by Island Marine Activities, offers trips to Molokini and Olowalu or Molokini and the Five Caves area of Makena.

Prices for most snorkel cruises will run somewhere in the neighborhood of $35 to $60 without a discount, but you can often find discount coupons in magazines such as *Guide to Maui* or *Maui Gold* (which you can pick up at any brochure rack or at the Maui Visitors Bureau).

FISH *(I'A)* TO WATCH FOR   One of Hawaii's most commonly seen reef fish is the **saddle wrasse** (known to Hawaiians as *hinalea lauwili*). It has a purple head and a wide orange stripe around its green body. There are many members of the wrasse family, and though they are not considered good eating fish, early Hawaiians often enjoyed them for dessert. It is also known that these types of fish were frequently offered as a sacrifice to the gods in a plea for fertility. A particular variety, known as the *hinalea'aki lolo,* was thought to cure mental instability if eaten. Literally translated, *'aki lolo* means "to heal brains."

The **raccoon butterfly fish** *(kikakapu kapuhili)* is also frequently seen by Maui snorkelers. There are actually 20 varieties of the butterfly fish, and their predominant coloring is yellow. The raccoon butterfly fish has a black band over the eye, followed by a white band, with several more wide black bands swirling outward and upward toward the fish's back. When viewed at a distance, they do bear a striking resemblance to a raccoon. The **rainbow butterfly** is also common; it can be differentiated by its squarish body, single black stripe through the eye, and teardrop black spot at the center of its back that looks like another eye (to fool predators).

The **convict tang** (or *manini*) gets its name from the evenly spaced black stripes that run the width of its body. You're almost certainly guaranteed to see a school of manini during one of your snorkeling adventures. They typically stay in schools that range from 6 to more than 100 fish. If you see a larger school swimming along a reef, you'll be hooked on this sport for life.

SNUBA

Snuba is a relatively new addition to the water-sports scene. Basically, it combines the freedom and ease of snorkeling with the diving capacity of scuba. The real differences between snuba and scuba are that you won't be carrying your air tanks on your back, and you'll be able to descend to depths of only about 20 to 25 feet. The air tanks will be sitting on a "sea sled," to which your breathing apparatus (and, consequently, you) are attached. As you swim, the sled follows you along. Snuba is a good interim step for people who love snorkeling but are afraid to try scuba diving.

There aren't many snuba operators on Maui because the sport is relatively new, but **Maui Classic Charters** (☎ 808/879-8188) runs snuba expeditions. Children under 12 will not be permitted to participate. If you take one of their charters to Molokini and would rather snuba than snorkel, Maui Classic Charters will provide snuba gear for an extra $50.

SURFING

If you've never surfed before, but you think it looks easy when you watch the locals do it, don't get the idea that you can get out there with them and hang 10. They *do* make it look easy, but actually surfing is difficult and requires practice. No matter what your experience level, you should arrange to take some lessons while you're on Maui. The waves are different here, so it couldn't hurt to get a few pointers.

Try to make an appointment for lessons with **Nancy Emerson** (☎ 808/244-SURF). She's a professional surfer who has been winning competitions since she was just a teenager. She's also been in several movies, including *Joe Versus the Volcano*. In her lessons, Emerson and her highly trained staff place a great deal of emphasis on "water safety and ocean awareness." Soft surfboards, just in case you get hit in the head, are just one of her precautionary measures. Emerson offers 1-, 2-, 5-hour, all-day, or 3- or 5-day classes.

Maui Surfing School (☎ 808/875-0625) guarantees that you'll be standing on your board (in the water, of course) in one lesson, or they'll refund your money. Classes are small and designed especially for "beginners and cowards." Reservations for advanced instruction and adventure (owner Andrea Thomas calls them Surf-aris) can be arranged. Take a 2-hour group lesson, a 90-minute private lesson, or sign up for 3-, 4-, or 5-day sessions.

SWIMMING

Before you go swimming anywhere, be sure to read the ocean safety information in "Health & Insurance," in Chapter 3. If you like freshwater swimming, just about every hotel or condominium complex has at least one swimming pool. The **Grand Wailea,** for example, has a 20,000-foot action pool as well as others. In Kaanapali both the **Hyatt** and the **Westin Hotel** have action pools. The beaches on Maui are almost all excellent for swimming. You need to be aware, however, that the surf is high on one side of the island at one time of the year and not another. In order to swim at the beach by your hotel, you need to be aware of what the surf conditions will be at the time of your visit.

In the winter, surf on the Lahaina side of the island is low. However, just a few miles down the road at Kapalua, the surf will be high and not ideal for swimming. The surf at Kapalua is low in the summer months, but the beaches are generally good for swimming from April to October. Kihei, Wailea, and Makena are generally good year-round, except for short periods of heavy surf and during Kona storms. Beach swimming in Hana is best during the summer months also. Since all the beaches on Maui are public, you shouldn't feel any qualms about going down a dirt road somewhere to get to the beach, or about parking your car at one of the resorts and dragging your family through the hotel to reach a nice beach.

WHALE-WATCHING

Every year humpback whales make the journey from Alaska to Hawaii to mate and give birth. Whale calves may gain up to 100 pounds a day from the nutrients in their mothers' milk, even though the adult whales don't eat at all during their stay in Hawaiian waters. Because of the devastation wreaked on the whale population by the whaling industry (beginning in the early 1800s), whales have been struggling to increase their numbers, but little progress is being made. Today there are all sorts of regulations in place to protect the whales that winter off Maui's shores, and they are strictly enforced. The use of jet skis and motorboats close to shore has been prohibited during the whale season, and the effects have been noticeable. The humpbacks now come closer to shore than ever before, and they are part of the Maui seascape every year between mid-December and mid-May. You really don't need to go on a tour to watch the whales during that period, but if you want to get even closer, you can make a reservation on a whale-watching excursion ship. Try to reserve well in advance because space is limited.

The ✪ **Pacific Whale Foundation** (☎ 808/879-8811 or 800/WHALE-1-1) is an environmental organization that has been at the forefront of whale research since the mid-1970s. If you take one of their tours (all proceeds go to benefit marine life conservation), you'll be guaranteed whale sightings, and you'll get to hear the song of the humpbacks on PWF's hydrophones. These cruises are led by knowledgeable research naturalists who participate in whale studies throughout the Pacific, so you can depend on them for the facts. The cost for whale-watch cruises is $27.50 for adults, $15 for children ages 3 to 12.

Other whale-watching excursions are offered by **Windjammer Cruises** (☎ 808/661-8600), **UFO Whale Express** (☎ 808/661-7836), and **Island Marine Activities, Inc.** (☎ 808/661-8397). Prices vary from one company to the next, but the average is about $30 for adults and $16 for children.

WINDSURFING

Your best bet for windsurfing lessons is **Hawaiian Island Windsurfing** (415 Dairy Rd., Kahului ☎ 808/871-4981). They've been renting boards to Maui windsurfers of all levels for more than 10 years. If you're a beginner, you can sign up for lessons with Hawaiian Island Windsurfing. Instruction is also available for more advanced sailors, which may include (for an extra $5 per lesson) a videotape and instant-replay critique. Classes are small. Three hours of instruction (including equipment) cost about $60 to $75.

The **Maui Windsurf Company** (520 Keolani Place [Airport Rd.], Kahului, HI 96732 ☎ 808/877-4816 or 800/872-0999) also offers semiprivate (maximum four people) lessons to sailors of all experience levels through the Cort Larned Windsurfing School, Maui's "Vela highwind center." The cost for 2½ hours is about $60. Three- and 5-day lesson packages will run you about $165 and $265. Private lessons are also available.

For daily reports on the wind and surf condition, call the Surf and Wind Report (☎ 808/877-3611).

3 Land Sports

BIKING

It's easy to get around Maui by bicycle. You can either rent your own (see Chapter 5, "Getting Around," for information on where to rent bikes) or take a bicycle tour. There are several options.

Chris' Bike Adventures (☎ 808/871-BIKE) offers tours all over Maui, through eucalyptus forests, down Haleakala, and Upcountry to Tedeschi Vineyards. Chris's will even customize tours on Maui, as well as Lanai or Molokai. You'll be picked up in the morning, served breakfast (and lunch later in the day), and you needn't worry about being too slow or too fast—you can bike at your own pace.

Mountain Riders (☎ 808/242-9739) also offers a variety of tours. You can take guided, self-guided, or custom tours. You might choose to bike down the slopes of Haleakala, or perhaps you'd rather try riding from Lahaina to Wailea, stopping to snorkel and sunbathe along the way. All accessories, including helmets, gloves, and windbreakers (for the cold air on the crater), are provided by Mountain Riders.

Maui Downhill (☎ 808/871-2155) specializes in tours that take you down the slopes of Haleakala. It's 38 miles of downhill riding with only 400 yards of pedaling, so even the laziest biker can have a pleasurable experience. Maui Downhill cannot accept beginners—all bikers have *some* experience, whether at the novice or expert level. All bikers must be at least 12 years of age and 5 feet in height.

GOLF

If you've come to Maui to golf, you won't be disappointed. In fact, the number of golf courses on Maui is almost inconceivable. Each of the resort areas (Kapalua, Kaanapali, Wailea, and Makena) has at least two courses of its own, and there are several other courses scattered around the island. The golf courses on Maui are so popular that Maui has been acclaimed "the Gold Coast of golf." Challenging and breathtakingly beautiful courses offer a range of golfing opportunities for everyone, from duffer to professional. Golfing is one of Hawaii's most popular activities with residents and visitors alike, so make your tee time reservations in advance. Greens fees for most of the resort golf courses run about $125, but they change seasonally, so you should ask about prices when planning your trip—if you expect to play a lot of golf, cost could be a big factor, so you might want to time your trip accordingly.

KAPALUA BAY, VILLAGE, AND PLANTATION GOLF COURSES

The **Kapalua Golf Club** has three courses from which to choose. The Bay Course is a par-72, 6,761-yard, Arnold Palmer/Ed Seay design. The course, with its wide fairways is forgiving, but the greens are difficult to read. And, if you lose a ball to the water on holes 4 and 5, you'll be watching it drop off a black-lava peninsula. Even the pros have trouble with number 5, a rocky, par-3, 205-yard hole. Ocean vistas can be enjoyed from virtually every hole on the course. The course has a rating of 73.1 at championship yardage, 69.8 for men, and 69.2 for women. The **Village Course,** a mountain course, was also designed by Palmer and Seay and is a par-71, 6,632-yard course. It has six uphill and nine downhill holes. It's a challenge to players of all levels; in addition to panoramic views of Molokai and Lanai, golfers will be surrounded by eucalyptus trees and Cook pines (planted in the 1920s). The course rating is 70.2 at championship yardage, 68.1 for men, and 68.4 for women. The **Plantation Course,** designed by Bill Coore and Ben Crenshaw (par-73, 6,547 yards), is yet another distinctive Kapalua course. The vegetation is low here, but the valleys are deep and challenging. It's an excellent course for developing your low shots and precise chipping.

The course rating is 74.6 for championship yardage,71.3 for men, and 71.6 for women. Facilities for the three courses include locker rooms, a driving range, and an excellent restaurant. For more information, contact the Golf Club, 300 Kapalua Dr., Lahaina, Maui, HI 96761 ☎ 808/669-8044.

KAANAPALI NORTH AND SOUTH GOLF COURSES

Kaanapali's **North Course,** designed by Robert Trent Jones Sr., has hosted numerous golf events, including the Canada Cup, the Women's Kemper Open, and the Kaanapali Senior Classic. Bing Crosby played in the course's first foursome when it opened in 1962. It's a par-72, 6,305-yard course with a tricky 18th hole (par-4, 435 yards) with a water hazard on the approach to the green. Overall, the course has an abundance of wide bunkers, several long, stretched-out tees, and the largest, most contoured greens on Maui. The championship yardage rating is 72.8, men's 70.0, and women's 71.1. The **South Course,** par-72, 6,250 yards, was designed by Arthur Jack Snyder, and with narrower fairways and smaller greens, it's a challenge to a golfer of any experience level. Just like its sister course, the South Course has a water hazard on its final hole. Options include a driving range, putting course, lunch at the clubhouse, and a 9-hole twilight rate. For information on the Kaanapali courses, contact Royal Kaanapali Golf Courses, Kaanapali Beach Resort, Kaanapali Parkway, Lahaina, Maui, HI 96761 ☎ 808/661-3691.

WAILEA GOLF COURSES

There are now three unique golf courses in the Wailea resort. Opened in the 1970s, the **Blue Course** was Wailea's first. Designed by Arthur Jack Snyder, it's a par-72 course that stretches over 6,700 yards of mountain slopes and is dotted with fragrant plumeria and colorful bougainvillea and hibiscus. One of the Blue Course's predominant features is long, wide fairways, ideal for the golfer who hits long, straight shots. Don't be fooled, however; the Blue Course offers challenges in the form of 4 lakes and 74 bunkers. Championship yardage rating is 71.6, men's is 68.9, and women's is 72.0. The **Gold Course,** a par-72, 7,073-yard course designed by Robert Trent Jones Jr., has a 200-foot elevation difference from top to bottom and gorgeous ocean views. Fairways are narrow, and there are several tricky dogleg holes and some natural hazards (for example, lava-rock walls and native Hawaiian grasses). Ratings for championship, men's, and women's yardage are 73.0, 60.0, and 70.3, respectively. The **Emerald Course,** opened for play in 1995, is another Robert Trent Jones Jr. design. The 6,825-yard, par-72 course has a tropical look, with birds of paradise, bougainvillea, allamanda, gazenia, beach morning glory, plumeria, and many other flowering plants in its landscaping. There's a double green shared by holes 10 and 17 that's bordered by a lake and has an incredible view of the ocean. At press time Emerald Course ratings had not yet been announced. Facilities at the Wailea Golf Club include two clubhouses, a training facility, lockers, pro shops, restaurants, and teaching programs. For more information, contact the Wailea Golf Club, 100 Wailea Golf Club Drive, Wailea, Maui, HI 96753 ☎ 808/332-1614.

MAKENA GOLF COURSES

Wailea's neighbor, **Makena resort,** offers two golf courses; together the courses cover 1,800 acres. Both challenging par-72 courses were designed by Robert Trent Jones Jr. and offer ocean views. The South Course (6,876 yards) has a couple of holes you'll never forget. The view from the par-4 15th hole, which shoots from an elevated tee 183 yards downhill to the Pacific, is magnificent. The 16th hole has a two-tiered green that is blind from the tee 383 yards away (that is, if you make it past the gully off the fairway). Championship, men's, and women's yardage ratings are 70.7, 68.5, and 71.1, respectively. The North Course is more difficult and more spectacular. The 13th hole is located part-way up the mountain with a view that makes most golfers stop and stare. The next hole is even more memorable—a 200-foot drop between tee and green. Facilities include a clubhouse, driving range, two putting greens, a pro shop, lockers, and lessons are available. Course ratings are 70.4 at championship yardage, 68.4 for men, and 70.9 for women. For more information, contact the resort (5415 Makena Alanui, Kihei, HI 96753 ☎ 808/879-3344).

OTHER COURSES

Other island golf courses include **Pukalani Country Club Golf Course,** 360 Pukalani St., Pukalani, HI 96768 (☎ 808/572-1314); **Silversword Golf Course,** 1345 Pilani Hwy., Kihei, HI 96753 (☎ 808/874-0777); and Sandalwood (☎808/242-4653). These courses are not associated with the resorts, so greens fees might be slightly lower. You might not be able to golf on certain days of the week and at certain times, so call ahead for details.

HIKING & CAMPING
HIKING

Maui is a hikers' paradise. There are marked hiking trails all over the island, and you can either hike on your own or take guided tours. If guided tours sound appealing, contact Ken Schmitt with ✪ **Hike Maui,** P.O. Box 330969, Kahului, Maui, HI 96733 (☎ 808/879-5270). He's a longtime Maui resident who specializes in the natural history and geology of the island. His well-informed tour leaders take small groups on a variety of hikes, ranging in difficulty from very leisurely to veritable treks. Prices vary ($75 to $115 per person) according to the tour, but you'll definitely get your money's worth.

If you plan to hike on your own, you can get all sorts of information on Maui hiking trails as well as free hiking maps if you contact Haleakala National Park, P.O. Box 369 Makawao, Maui, HI 96768 (☎ 808/572-9306) and the State Division of Forestry and Wildlife, 52 S. High St., Wailuku, HI 96793 (☎ 808/243-5352). For information on trails, hikes, camping, and permits for state parks, contact: Hawaii State Department of Land and Natural Resources, State Parks Division, P.O. Box 1049, Wailuku, HI 96793 (☎ 808/243-5354).

The Hawaiian Trail and Mountain Club (P.O. Box 2238, Honolulu, HI 96804) offers an information packet on hiking and camping in Hawaii. Send $1.25, plus a legal-size, self-addressed, stamped envelope for information. Another good source is the Hiking/Camping Information Packet from Hawaii Geographic Maps and Books, 49 S. Hotel St., Suite 218, Honolulu, HI 96813 (☎ 808/538-3952); it's available at a cost of $7, which includes postage.

Some of Maui's best hikes are:

Polipoli Loop

One of the most unusual hiking experiences in the state can be found in Polipoli State Park, which is part of the 21,000 acres of the Kula and Kahikinui Forest Reserve on the slope of Haleakala. First of all, at 5,300 to 6,200 feet, where the hiking takes place, it's cold (even in the summer). Second, this former forest of native *koa, ohia,* and *mamane* trees (which was overlogged in the 1800s) was reforested in the 1930s with introduced species: pine, Monterey cypress, ash, sugi, red adler, redwood, and several varieties of eucalyptus. The result is a cool area, with muted sunlight filtered by towering trees. At Polipoli, it's hard to believe that you're in Hawaii.

The Polipoli Loop is an easy, 5-mile hike that takes a little over 5 hours; dress warmly for it. To get there, take the Haleakala Highway (Hwy. 37) to Keokea and turn right onto Highway 337. After less than one-half mile on Highway 337, turn onto Waipoli Road. The road climbs swiftly. After 10 miles, Waipoli Road ends at the Polipoli State Park campgrounds. The well-marked trailhead is next to the parking lot, near a stand of Monterey cypress; the tree-lined trail offers the best view of the island.

Polipoli Loop is really a network of three trails: Haleakala Ridge, Plum Trail, and Redwood Trail. After one-half mile meandering through groves of eucalyptus, blackwood, swamp mahogany, and hybrid cypress, you'll join the Haleakala Ridge Trail. About a mile into the trail, Polipoli Loop joins with the Plum Trail (named for the plums that ripen in June and July); the Plum Trail passes through massive redwoods and by an old Conservation Corps bunkhouse and a run-down cabin. Just after the cabin, the Polipoli Loop continues on the Redwood Trail, which climbs through Mexican pine, tropical ash, Port Orford cedar, and—of course—redwood.

Camping is allowed in the Polipoli State Park with a permit from the **Division of State Parks** (P.O. Box 1049, Wailuku, HI 96793 ☎ 808/243-5354). There is one cabin that is available by reservation.

Sliding Sands & Halemauu Trails, Haleakala National Park

The view into the Haleakala Crater looks like a cross between a barren lunarscape and the backdrop to the 1950s B-movie *The Angry Red Planet.* The view, however, is nothing compared with the experience of hiking into the throat of the dormant volcano. The crater has some 32 miles of marked hiking trails, two camping sites, and three cabins. The terrain ranges from burnt-red cinder cones to ebony-black lava tubes.

The best hikes here are Sliding Sands Trail, which begins on the rim at 9,800 feet and descends into the belly of the beast—to the crater floor at 6,600 feet; and the hike back out, Halemauu Trail. This is a difficult hike and should be done in 2 days. Only the hardiest hikers should consider making the 11.3-mile one-way descent, which takes 9 hours, and the equally as long returning ascent, in 1 day.

The descending and ascending trails are not loops. In fact, the trailheads are miles (and several thousand feet) apart. Arrangements need to be made in advance to provide transportation between the two. The best thing to do is to arrange to stay at least one night in the park (two or three nights would allow more time to actually explore the fascinating interior of the volcano). There are cabins in the National Park, which must be booked at least three months in advance. Contact **Haleakala National Park** (P.O. Box 369, Makawao, HI 96768 ☎ 808/572-9306). Camping permits are available on a first-come, first-served basis at the park headquarters.

A word of warning before you head up the mountain: The weather at nearly 10,000 feet can change suddenly and without warning. Come prepared (no matter how beautiful the weather is at the time) for cold, high winds, rain, and even snow in the winter, by bringing boots, waterproof wear, warm clothes, extra clothing layers, and lots of sunscreen—at 10,000 feet the sun shines very brightly.

Stop at Park Headquarters on your way up to get information regarding camping and hiking. Day hikers must register for the hike down Sliding Sands Trail at the box near the Haleakala Visitor Center. The trailhead to Sliding Sands is well marked, and the trail is an easy to follow switchback over ash and cinders. As you descend, look around—the view of the entire crater is breathtaking. In the afternoon, waves of clouds flow into the Kaupo and Koolau Gaps. Vegetation is spare to nonexistent at the top, but the closer you get to the crater floor the more vegetation you see: bracken ferns, *pili* grass, shrubs, and even flowers appear.

On the crater floor the trail travels through flat, ash-covered flows of basalt and cinder-covered cones, passing by rare silversword plants, volcanic vents, and multi-colored cinder cones.

Leading out, the Halemauu Trail goes over red and black lava, past vegetation like evening primrose, as it begins its ascent up the crater wall. Occasionally, riders on horseback use this trail as an entry and exit from the park. The proper etiquette is to step aside and stand quietly next to the trail and let the horses pass.

Hana-Waianapanapa Coastal Trail

This is an easy 6-mile trail that takes you hiking back in time. Allow 4 hours to walk along this relatively flat trail, which parallels the sea, along lava cliffs and a forest of hala trees. The best time to take the trail is either in the early morning or late evening, when the light on the lava and surf makes for great photos. Midday is the worst time for the hike; not only is it hot (lava intensifies the heat), but there is no shade and no potable water.

There is no formal trailhead; the trail can be joined at any point along the Waianapanapa Campground and traversed in either direction. Along the trail, you'll see remains of an ancient *heiau* (temple), stands of lauhala trees, caves, a blow-hole, and a remarkable plant, *naupaka*, that flourishes along the beach. Upon close inspection, you'll see that the naupaka has half-blossoms only. According to Hawaiian legend, a similar plant living in the mountains has the other half of the blossoms. One ancient explanation for this is that the two plants represent never-to-be-reunited lovers: As the story goes, the two lovers bickered so much that the gods, fed up with their incessant quarreling, banished one lover to the mountain and the other to the sea.

Iao Valley

This is the easiest hike on Maui—you could take your grandmother on this half-hour-long, one-third-mile loop on a paved trail. Iao Valley—with its famous landmark, the Iao Needle (actually a volcanic ridge) rising to 2,250 feet—is a massive green amphitheater ringed by chiseled cliffs and topped by seemingly perpetual clouds. At the back of this amphitheater is the 5,788-foot-high rain-drenched Puu Kukui, the West Maui Mountains' highest point. Iao is a historic valley, where Kamehameha the Great defeated Kalaikupule, chief of Maui, in 1790. The Maui warriors, prepared to fight with spears and clubs, were mowed down by Kamehameha's cannons (supplied by the English). The result was a bloody massacre that was said to have clogged the Iao Stream with bodies.

The easily accessible paved trail wanders through the park and over a footbridge crossing the Iao Stream. This leisurely walk will enable you to enjoy lovely views of the needle and the lush vegetation. Go early in the morning or after 4pm to avoid the hordes of tour buses, which deposit hundreds at the park during the day.

CAMPING

If you plan to camp during your stay on Maui, you should know that camping is permitted in two state parks, two county parks, and two federal parks. For state parks you must obtain a permit from the Division of State Parks (no charge) before you arrive. Contact the **Division of State Parks,** 54 South High St., Wailuku, Maui, HI 96793 (☎ 808/243-5354). You must specify the park where you intend to camp (either **Polipoli** or **Waianapanapa**) and the length of your stay (maximum of five nights). You must also supply identification numbers for all members of your camping party (passport numbers, Social Security numbers, or driver's license numbers).

If you want to camp in **H. A. Baldwin Park** or **Rainbow Park** (both in Paia), you need to contact the **Department of Parks and Recreation,** County of Maui, 1580 Kaahumanu Ave., Wailuku, Maui, HI 96793 (☎ 808/243-7389). Maximum length of stay at any one campground is three nights.

It is not necessary to obtain a permit to camp in **Hosmer Grove** and **Kipahulu Campground.** Both are federal parks on the slopes of Haleakala. The maximum length of stay is three nights. If you want to camp within **Haleakala Wilderness Area,** call or write for details in advance to Haleakala Camping Information, P.O. Box 369, Makawao, HI 96768 (☎ 808/572-9306).

Note: For Haleakala weather information, call 808/572-7749 before heading out.

HORSEBACK RIDING

A great way to see Maui is on horseback. You can cover more ground in a shorter period of time than you could if you were hiking, and well-informed, experienced tour guides will take you to remote locations where you'll be able to swim, picnic, or ride off into the sunset. Several companies on Maui offer a variety of horseback adventures.

Ironwood Ranch, 5095 Napilihau St., Suite 308, Lahaina, Maui, HI 96761 (☎ 808/669-4991), located in the foothills of the West Maui Mountains, not far from Kaanapali and Kapalua, works primarily with small groups of people, all with similar levels of ability, so you won't ever feel like you're being left in the dust. The Introductory Ride ($30 per person) of 1 hour is designed specifically for beginners. Before you start out, your guide will give you some quick pointers on horseback riding, and then you're off to see beautiful views of Molokai and Lanai from the lush tropical greenery of the West Maui Mountains. The West Maui Journey, recommended for all riding levels, costs about $75. The Sunset Ride, also a good choice for those with a wide range of riding abililities, is great for a romantic evening; the cost is $100. If you're an advanced rider, take the Ironwood Odyssey ($125); and if you would like to combine a ride, picnic, and short hike, choose the Picnic in Paradise ride (4¹/₂ hours at a cost of $135). All rides are guided, and the pace is determined by the ability of the least experienced rider. The price includes pick-up and drop-off from Kapalua and Kaanapali resorts, and refreshments are served after the ride.

Adventures on Horseback (Makawao ☎ 808/242-7445 or 808/572-6211) will take groups of no more than six to some of Maui's unspoiled areas. Each of the rides is different, but you're guaranteed to see a different side of Maui than most tourists do, and you'll probably have a chance to swim beneath a waterfall. Morning refreshments and lunch (sandwiches, fruits, vegetables, and beverages) are provided on all excursions. Each ride takes approximately 5 hours, and the rate per person is $140.

Pony Express Tours (P.O. Box 535, Kula, Maui, HI 96790 ☎ 808/667-2200) takes riders on tours through Haleakala Ranch and to Haleakala Crater. You'll "go places only horses can go," and you'll see things you probably would not have seen otherwise. There's a 1-hour ride for those who have driven up Haleakala to see the sunrise and would like to see a little more but want to be back at their hotel in time for lunch. This ride begins at 9am and costs only $35. The longer Paniolo Ride takes 2 hours ($60) and allows riders to explore much more of Haleakala Ranch. If you prefer to ride into the volcano, Pony Express can take you there as well. The cost is $120 per person, and it's a 3¹/₂ to 4-hour, 7¹/₂-mile, round-trip; riders of all experience levels are welcome. Only 10 riders go into the volcano at a time, and throughout the trip, knowledgeable guides explain about the flora, fauna, and Hawaiian mythology and legend. The full-day Kapalaoa Cabin Ride takes adventurous (and hardy) souls right to the crater floor. Along the way, riders will see, among other things, the nene goose and Pele's Paint Pot. Lunch at Kapalaoa cabin, located 6 miles into the crater, is included in the $150 fee.

Makena Stables (Old Makena Rd., Makena, Maui, HI ☎ 808/879-0244) offers a 3- to 4-hour ride during which you'll get to see a 200-year-old lava flow, the Ahihi-Kinau Nature Reserve, and scores of island plants and animals. Only one ride a day is scheduled at Makena Stables, so you can be sure the horses are well rested. Makena Stables also offers a ride to the Tedeschi Vineyards, where participants will be treated to a personalized tour of the winery. The price is $150 per person.

If you're going to be up in Hana, Hana Ranch (Hana Hwy. ☎ 808/248-8211, ext. 3) offers private and group rides daily. You'll ride along the Hana coastline or above Hana town. Call for prices.

All of these companies have a weight limit (somewhere in the neighborhood of 220 to 250 pounds), and all require that you wear long pants (jeans are probably best) and closed-toe shoes. I would suggest that you also take a sweater—mountain temperatures are often significantly lower than beach temperatures. Horseback riding companies also impose age limits for children. Some will not accept children below 16 years of age; others will accept children age 12 and up. Call ahead for information.

HUNTING

Believe it or not, you can hunt on Maui. You must apply for a hunting license ($95 per year for nonresidents) from the **State Division of Forestry and Wildlife,** 1151 Punchbowl, Room 325, Honolulu, HI 96813. As a prerequisite for the license, you must obtain a "Letter of Exemption" or complete an approved hunter education/ safety course beforehand. Contact the **Division of Conservation and Resources Enforcement, Hunter Education Program,** 1151 Punchbowl, Honolulu, HI 96813 (☎ 808/587-0166), for information regarding the education program or exemption qualifications. **Hunting Adventures of Maui,** 645-B Kaupakalua Rd., Makawao (☎ 808/572-8214), specializes in guided hunts for wild pigs, goats, and pheasants. For hunting equipment, **Maui Expedition,** 87 S. Puunene Avenue, Kahului (☎ 808/871-8787) carries everything you need.

Hunting regulations are constantly changing, so if you plan to hunt, I would recommend that when you call the above agencies, you ask for Forestry & Wildlife Title 13, Chapter 122, if you're interested in game-bird hunting; Forestry & Wildlife Title 13, Chapter 123, for big-game hunting.

GAME ANIMALS   None of the game animals you'll find on Maui today are native to the islands—they were all introduced at one time or another. You've got to have a strong will and a strong spirit (not to mention fast feet) to hunt Maui's feral pigs. I've been told that they're hunted using dogs and spears. Feral pigs have contributed to the annihilation of many species of plant life, and they often muddy the waters of Hana's lovely pools. If you plan to hunt feral pigs, make sure you know what you're doing—they're extremely dangerous. In addition to wild pigs, Maui has its share of wild goats. Both wild pigs and goats can be hunted year-round.

There are axis deer (introduced from India) on Maui, as well as on Molokai and Lanai, but you can't hunt them on Maui. Hunting axis deer on Molokai and Lanai is permitted, however. Axis deer are light brown and have beautiful white spots on their backs.

If you're a game-bird hunter, Maui has its share of pheasants (both ring-necked and green), quail, and doves. For a list of birds you can hunt, contact the Department of Parks & Recreation, District Office & Permits (☎ 808/243-7389). The bird season is limited to weekends and holidays beginning with the first Saturday in November and running through the third Sunday in January.

TENNIS

There are tennis facilities all over Maui. As with the golf courses, if you're staying in one of the resorts, you'll have access to any number of tennis courts. Daily and hourly fees vary from place to place, but you can be sure that if you're a resort guest, rates on those courts will be lower.

In addition to the resort facilities, most of which have at least six courts, many other hotels and condominium properties have their own courts (some may not even charge for court time).

Here's a list of the major island resort tennis facilities: **Kapalua Tennis Garden and Village Tennis Center,** Kapalua resort, Maui, HI 96761 ☎ 808/669-5677; **Makena Tennis Club,** 5415 Makena Alanui, Kihei, HI 96753 ☎ 808/879-8777; **Royal Lahaina Tennis Ranch,** 2780 Kekaa Drive, Lahaina, Maui, HI 96761 ☎ 808/661-3611, ext. 2296; **Wailea Tennis Club,** Wailea resort, 131 Wailea Ike Place, ☎ 808/879-1958.

Access to public courts is on a first-come, first-served basis. There are six lighted courts in **Wells Park** (at Wells and Market Streets) in Wailuku; four lighted courts at the **War Memorial Gym** off Kaahumanu Avenue in Kahului; **Maluuluolele Park,** at 520 Front St., also has four lighted courts. **Lahaina Civic Center,** off Honoapilani Highway (near the main post office across from Wahikuli Beach), has five lighted courts; and **Kalama Park,** off South Kihei Road, has four.

SPECTATOR SPORTS

Maui's two most popular spectator sports are outrigger canoe racing and polo. Every weekend from Memorial Day to Labor Day, canoe races are held on Maui. Hundreds of residents, from children to grandparents, participate in the island-wide canoe races held at different harbors and bays every week. For information on the canoe race schedule, check the local papers.

Every weekend from September through November, spirited polo is played on Maui. Spend a pleasant afternoon picnicking on a grassy lawn as the polo players from nearby ranches compete. For information on times and places of polo matches, call 808/244-3530. The grand event of the year is the Michelob Polo Cup and Barbecue, an exhibition match of the highest rated players, which takes places at the Olinda Outdoor Polo Field in Makawao (☎ 808/877-3987).

Other spectator sporting events include:

Basketball In December, top college teams participate in the Maui Invitational Basketball Tournament at the Lahaina Civic Center (☎ 312/755-3577).

Golf Several golf tournaments take place on Maui, including the Asahi Beer Kyosan Golf Tournament at the Wailea Golf Course in February (☎ 808/875-5111), the Kaanapali Classic Senior PGA Golf Tournament in October (☎ 808/661-3271), and the Kapalua International Golf Championship in November (☎ 808/669-0244).

Rodeo Makawao Statewide Rodeo is held on the Fourth of July at the Oskie Rice Arena in Makawao (☎ 808/572-9928).

Running Maui Marathon in March (☎ 808/661-3271), Haleakala Run to the Sun—a 36-mile race up the 10,000-foot volcano in August (☎ 808/871-6441), and the Hana Relay, a 54-mile team relay run from Kahului to Hana (☎ 808/871-6441).

Tennis Kapalua Junior Vet/Senior Championships in May (☎ 808/669-5677), Lahaina Junior Summer Tournament in August (☎ 808/661-8173), Kapalua Open Tennis Championship in September (☎ 808/669-5677), and the Kapalua Betsy Nagelson Pro-Am Tennis Invitational in November (☎ 808/669-5677).

Windsurfing Marui/O'Neil Invitational in April at Hookipa (☎ 808/572-4883) and the Aloha Classic, also at Hookipa, in October and November are spectacular spectator events, even if you know nothing about windsurfing (☎ 808/579-9765).

Appendix

A Hawaiian Vocabulary

The first thing you're likely to notice about the Hawaiian language is that it seems to use the same letters over and over again in the same word. That's because the Hawaiian alphabet consists of only seven consonants (H, K, L, M, N, P, and W) as well as the five vowels. You'll be confronted by scores of repeating vowels and consonants, and virtually all street names will look the same to you in the beginning. Pronunciation is actually a lot easier than it seems. Just pronounce every letter and you'll be on the right track. If you see two vowels side by side, like o'o or a'a, pronounce them both, like this: "oh-oh" or "ah-ah." Don't worry if you're not pronouncing something correctly at first—it takes a while. Listen to the way the locals say it. You'll get the hang of it!

WORDS

English	Hawaiian	Pronunciation
rough lava	**a'a**	ah-ah
sharp gravel	**a'a' pu'upu'u**	*ah*-ah-poo-oo-poo-oo
yes	**ae**	*ah*-ee
Why?	**aha**	*ah*-ha
friends	**aikane**	eye-*kah*-nay
road	**ala**	*al*-lah
welcome, farewell, love	**aloha**	ah-*low*-hah
no	**aole**	ah-*oh*-lay
pineapple	**halakahiki**	hah-lah-kah-*hee*-kee
school	**halau**	*hah*-lau
house	**hale**	*hah*-lay
work	**hana**	*hah*-nah
Caucasian	**haole**	*how*-lay
half	**hapa**	*hah*-pah
happiness	**haouli**	how-*oh*-lee
ancient temple	**heiau**	hey-*ee*-au
to walk	**hele**	*hey*-lay
to run	**holo**	*ho*-low
to kiss	**honi**	*ho*-nee
angry	**huhu**	*hoo*-hoo
to dance	**hula**	*hoo*-lah

underground luau oven	**imu**	*ee*-moo
priest	**kahuna**	kah-*hoo*-nah
sea	**kai**	kye
old-timer	**kama'aina**	kah-mah-*eye*-nah
man	**kane**	*kah*-nay
keep out	**kapu**	*kah*-poo
food	**kaukau**	kow-*kow*
child	**keiki**	kay-*kee*
porch	**lanai**	lah-*nye*
garland/necklace	**lei**	lay
feast	**luau**	*loo*-ow
thank you	**mahalow**	mah-*hah*-low
seaward	**makai**	mah-*kye*
toward the mountains	**mauka**	*mau*-kah
chant	**mele**	*may*-lay
coconut	**niu**	*nee*-oo
delicious	**ono**	*oh*-no
Hawaiian cowboy	**paniolo**	pah-nee-*oh*-low
finished	**pau**	pow
hors d'oeuvre	**pupu**	*poo*-poo
woman	**wahine**	wah-*hee*-nay
Hurry, quickly	**Wikiwiki**	wee-kee-wee-kee

PHRASES

English	Hawaiian	Pronunciation
Bottoms up!	**Okole maluna**	oh-*ko*-lay mah-*loo*-nah
Good evening	**Aloha ahiahi**	ah-*low*-ha ah-hee-*ah*-hee
Good morning	**Aloha kakahiaka**	ah-*low*-ha kah-kah-hee-*ah*-kah
Come and eat	**Hele mai ai**	hey-lay-*my*-eye
Many thanks	**Mahalo nui loa**	mah-*hah*-low noo-ee *low*-ah
What is your name?	**Owai kau inoa?**	*oh*-why *kah*-oo ee-no-ah

B Glossary of Island Foods

Bento   Japanese box lunch.

Chicken luau   Young taro or spinach leaves cooked with chicken and coconut milk.

Crackseed   A popular Chinese confection, akin to dried, candied fruit.

Guava   A slightly sour fruit that grows on mountainside trees. On Maui you will see roadside guava trees as you drive up to Hana. In the Hawaiian Islands guava is used most frequently in the making of jellies and juices.

Halakahiki   You're not likely to encounter anyone using this Hawaiian word to refer to pineapple, but since you'll be visiting the pineapple capital of the world on your trip to Maui, I thought you should know it.

Haupia   Coconut pudding that is a traditional luau dish.

Laulau   Directly translated, laulau means "wrapping" or "wrapped." As a food item, laulau is individual servings of pork, beef, or salted fish with bananas, sweet potatoes, and taro tops wrapped in a ti or banana leaf and baked in the imu (ground oven) or steamed. The term *laulau* might be used to refer to any sort of netting or wrapping.

Lilikoi Passion fruit. There are several varieties, including the purple water lemon or the purple granadilla; however, the variety that is grown commercially in the islands for the purpose of manufacturing juice (guava/passion fruit juice is very popular) is yellow and has a more pleasant taste than the purple variety.

Macadamia nuts These flavorful nuts are grown primarily on the Big Island and are in abundance on all of the islands. Dry-roasted macadamia nuts are tasty; however, you should also try them raw (you'll need a good hammer to get them open). Macadamia nut honey, made from the flower of the macadamia nut tree, has a very light flavor.

Malasadas Square, deep-fried Portuguese doughnuts, served hot and coated with sugar.

Manapuas A relative of Chinese dim sum, manapuas are steamed dumplings filled with beef, pork, or bean paste.

Maui onions Every restaurant on Maui serves these onions, which are sweeter than most varieties. They are grown Upcountry in Kula and are sometimes referred to as Kula onions.

Niu Coconut.

Papayas At breakfast you'll discover that papayas are the grapefruit of the Hawaiian Islands. Most papayas are grown on the Big Island.

Pipikaula Beef jerky.

Poi Often referred to as "the Hawaiian staff of life," poi is made from cooked, mashed taro root. It's pounded until smooth and then thinned with water. There are many varieties of taro, and therefore many different kinds of poi.

Portuguese bean soup A wonderful combination of *linguica* (Portuguese sausage), beans, kale, potatoes, and various other vegetables in a beef/tomato broth.

Portuguese sweet bread A staple of the Portuguese diet, this soft, sweet bread is made with eggs and has a consistency similar to Jewish challah bread (only slightly lighter).

Saimin A very popular island dish, saimin is a soup of noodles in a clear broth with shrimp, pork, chicken, fish, and vegetables.

Sashimi Raw fish. You'll find sashimi offered on just about every Maui restaurant menu. It's a Japanese delicacy. Ahi is the fish most often used in the preparation of sashimi.

FISH

Ahi Yellowfin tuna. This fish is often used for sashimi, but it is equally delicious cut into steaks and broiled or pan-seared.

Mahimahi Dolphin fish (not actual dolphin), mahimahi is probably one of Hawaii's best-known fish.

Ono A delicious, long, thin, mackerel-like fish. Incidentally, the Hawaiian word *ono* means "delicious."

Opakapaka Though most people will tell you that opakapaka is pink snapper, I've seen it referred to as blue snapper in many dictionaries.

Ulua You won't often find this fish on the menu, but if you do, why not give it a try? It's a sort of crevalle, jack, or pompano gamefish.

Index

FROMMER'S COMPLETE TRAVEL GUIDES
(Comprehensive guides to destinations around the world, with selections in all price ranges—from deluxe to budget)

FROMMER'S FRUGAL TRAVELER'S GUIDES

(The grown-up guides to budget travel, offering dream vacations at down-to-earth prices)

Australia from $45 a Day
Berlin from $50 a Day
California from $60 a Day
Caribbean from $60 a Day
Costa Rica & Belize from $35 a Day
Eastern Europe from $30 a Day
England from $50 a Day
Europe from $50 a Day
Florida from $50 a Day
Greece from $45 a Day
Hawaii from $60 a Day

India from $40 a Day
Ireland from $45 a Day
Italy from $50 a Day
Israel from $45 a Day
London from $60 a Day
Mexico from $35 a Day
New York from $70 a Day
New Zealand from $45 a Day
Paris from $65 a Day
Washington, D.C. from $50 a Day

FROMMER'S PORTABLE GUIDES

(Pocket-size guides for travelers who want everything in a nutshell)

Charleston & Savannah
Las Vegas

New Orleans
San Francisco

FROMMER'S FAMILY GUIDES

(The complete guides for successful family vacations)

California with Kids
Los Angeles with Kids
New England with Kids

New York City with Kids
San Francisco with Kids
Washington, D.C. with Kids

FROMMER'S AMERICA ON WHEELS

(Everything you need for a successful road trip, including full-color road maps and ratings for every hotel)

California & Nevada
Florida
Mid-Atlantic
Midwest & the Great Lakes
New England & New York

Northwest & Great Plains
South Central & Texas
Southeast
Southwest

FROMMER'S WALKING TOURS

(Memorable neighborhood strolls through the world's great cities)

Berlin
Chicago
England's Favorite Cities
London
Montréal & Québec City
New York

Paris
San Francisco
Spain's Favorite Cities
Tokyo
Venice
Washington, D.C.

SPECIAL-INTEREST TITLES

Arthur Frommer's Branson!

Arthur Frommer's New World of Travel

The Civil War Trust's Official Guide to the
Civil War Discovery Trail

Frommer's America's 100 Best-Loved State
Parks

Frommer's Caribbean Hideaways

Frommer's Complete Hostel Vacation Guide
to England, Scotland & Wales

Frommer's Food Lover's Companion to
France

Frommer's Food Lover's Companion to Italy

Frommer's National Park Guide

Outside Magazine's Adventure Guide to
New England

Outside Magazine's Adventure Guide to
Northern California

Places Rated Almanac

Retirement Places Rated

USA Sports Traveler's and TV Viewer's
Golf Tournament Guide

USA Sports Minor League Baseball Book

USA Today Golf Atlas

Wonderful Weekends from NYC

FROMMER'S IRREVERENT GUIDES

(Wickedly honest guides for sophisticated travelers)

Amsterdam	Miami	Santa Fe
Chicago	New Orleans	U.S. Virgin Islands
London	Paris	Walt Disney World
Manhattan	San Francisco	Washington, D.C.

BAEDEKER

(With four-color photographs and a free pull-out map)

Amsterdam	Greece	San Francisco
Athens	Greek Islands	St. Petersburg
Austria	Hawaii	Scandinavia
Bali	Hong Kong	Scotland
Belgium	Israel	Singapore
Budapest	Italy	South Africa
California	Lisbon	Spain
Canada	London	Switzerland
Caribbean	Mexico	Venice
Copenhagen	New York	Vienna
Crete	Paris	Tokyo
Florence	Prague	Tuscany
Florida	Provence	
Germany	Rome	

FROMMER'S BY NIGHT GUIDES

(The series for those who know that life begins after dark)

Amsterdam	Los Angeles	New York
Chicago	Miami	Paris
Las Vegas	New Orleans	San Francisco
London		

FROMMER'S BEST BEACH VACATIONS
(The top places to sun, stroll, shop, stay, play, party, and swim, with ratings for each beach)

California
Carolinas & Georgia
Florida
Hawaii

Mid-Atlantic (from New York to Washington, D.C.)
New England

FROMMER'S BED & BREAKFAST GUIDES
(Selective guides with four-color photos and full descriptions of the best inns in each region)

California
Caribbean
Great American Cities
Hawaii

Mid-Atlantic
New England
Pacific Northwest

Rockies
Southeast
Southwest

FROMMER'S DRIVING TOURS
(Four-color photos and detailed maps outlining spectacular scenic driving routes)

Australia
Austria
Britain
Florida
France

Germany
Ireland
Italy
Scandinavia

Scotland
Spain
Switzerland
U.S.A.

FROMMER'S BORN TO SHOP
(The ultimate guides for travelers who love to shop)

France
Great Britain

Hong Kong
London

Mexico
New York

TRAVEL & LEISURE GUIDES
(Sophisticated pocket-size guides for discriminating travelers)

Amsterdam
Boston
Hong Kong

London
New York
Paris

San Francisco
Washington, D.C.

UNOFFICIAL GUIDES
(Get the unbiased truth from these candid, value-conscious guides)

Atlanta
Branson, Missouri
Chicago
Cruises
Disneyland

Euro Disneyland
The Great Smoky & Blue
    Ridge Mountains
Las Vegas
Miami & the Keys

Skiing in the West
Walt Disney World
Washington, D.C.